Quicken 2006 for Starters
THE MISSING MANUAL

Quicken 2006 for Starters
THE MISSING MANUAL

Exactly what you need to get started

Bonnie Biafore

POGUE PRESS™
O'REILLY®

Beijing • Cambridge • Farnham • Köln • Paris • Sebastopol • Taipei • Tokyo

Quicken 2006 for Starters: THE MISSING MANUAL

by Bonnie Biafore

Published by O'Reilly Media, Inc., 1005 Gravenstein Highway North, Sebastopol, CA 95472.

O'Reilly books may be purchased for educational, business, or sales promotional use. Online editions are also available for most titles (*safari.oreilly.com*). For more information, contact our corporate/institutional sales department: (800) 998-9938 or *corporate@oreilly.com*.

Printing History:
November 2005:   First Edition.

RepKover. This book uses RepKover™, a durable and flexible lay-flat binding.

ISBN: 0-596-10127-9
[M]

TABLE OF CONTENTS

THE MISSING CREDITS

About the Author

 **Bonnie Biafore** writes about personal finance, investing, and project management, although she dreams of writing a best-selling crime novel and selling the movie rights for oodles of money. As an engineer, she's steadfastly attentive to detail but redeems herself by using her sick sense of humor to transform these drool-inducing subjects into entertaining reading. Her *NAIC Stock Selection Handbook* won major awards from the Society of Technical Communication and APEX Awards for Publication Excellence (but the raves she receives from beginning investors mean much more to her).

Bonnie is also the author of O'Reilly's *Online Investing Hacks* and *QuickBooks 2006: The Missing Manual.* She writes a monthly column called "WebWatch" for *Better Investing* magazine and is a regular contributor to *www.womenswallstreet.com*. As a consultant, she manages projects for clients and wins accolades for her ability to herd cats.

When not chained to her computer, she hikes in the mountains with her dog, cooks gourmet meals, and practices saying no to additional work assignments. You can learn more at Bonnie's Web site, *www.bonniebiafore.com* or email her at *bonnie.biafore@gmail.com*.

About the Creative Team

Nan Barber (editor) is associate editor for the Missing Manual series. She works in O'Reilly's Cambridge office and enjoys at least reading about people who have their finances organized. Email: *nanbarber@mac.com*.

Michele Filshie (editor) is O'Reilly's assistant editor for the Missing Manual series and editor of four Personal Trainers (another O'Reilly series). Before turning to the world of computer-related books, Michele spent many happy years at Black Sparrow Press. Email: *mfilshie@oreilly.com*.

James Barnett (copy editor) has copy edited over a thousand articles for O'Reilly's Web sites. A freelance technical editor, painter, and printmaker, he wrote a couple of books a while back, but likes the editing side better. Web: *www.elreyart.com*.

Sohaila Abdulali (copy editor) is a freelance writer and editor. She has published a novel, several children's books, and numerous short stories and articles. She is currently finishing an ethnography of an aboriginal Indian woman. Web: *www.sohailaink.com*.

Babette Bloch (technical reviewer) has used computers since the late 80s. She now teaches Quicken in an adult education program, consults with Quicken users, and leads a Quicken SIG for the Golden Gate Computer Society. Email: *babette.bloch@ggcs.org*.

Jeff Boevingloh (technical reviewer) is an information technology consultant who resides in the Denver area. He has been a dedicated Quicken user since 1994.

Bruce Downs (technical reviewer) is a CPA and Certified QuickBooks Pro Advisor specializing in new and small business accounting and QuickBooks consulting. He routinely conducts classes and seminars for professional groups and individuals seeking guidance in personal finance. Email: *bhdowns@bellsouth.net*. Web: *www.brucedownscpa.com*.

Louis Hopfer (technical reviewer) is an attorney and high school teacher in Sonoma County. He's a native of Manhattan but since 1982 has lived in Sebastopol, CA with his wife and two cats. Email: *biglouis552003@yahoo.com*.

Rose Cassano (cover illustration) has worked as an independent designer and illustrator for 20 years. Assignments have ranged from the nonprofit sector to corporate clientele. She lives in beautiful Southern Oregon, grateful for the miracles of modern technology that make working there a reality. Email: *cassano@highstream.net*. Web: *www.rosecassano.com*.

Acknowledgements

Writing a book is hard work but the folks at O'Reilly make the hours and sweat tolerable. Thanks to Sarah Milstein for convincing me to write this book, for handling all the details so dependably, and, most importantly, for laughing at my jokes. My eternal gratitude goes to Nan Barber for reining in my rambling words and to everyone else at O'Reilly for doing their usual amazing job.

I also want to thank the technical reviewers, Babette Bloch, Jeff Boevingloh, Bruce Downs, and Louis Hopfer, for reviewing the manuscript and providing so many great tips for wrangling Quicken into submission.

Of course, no set of my acknowledgements is complete without thanks to my husband, Pete Speer, for putting up with me while I work to meet book deadlines. I am not fun to be around when I'm writing a book, but he always handles it with aplomb. Just ask him. And finally, my special thanks go to our dog, Emma, who graciously negotiated one walk a day for the duration of the manuscript.

The Missing Manual Series

Missing Manuals are witty, superbly written guides to computer products that don't come with printed manuals (which is just about all of them). Each book features a handcrafted index; cross-references to specific page numbers (not just "see Chapter 14"); and RepKover, a detached-spine binding that lets the book lie perfectly flat without the assistance of weights or cinder blocks.

Recent and upcoming titles include:

Access 2003 for Starters: The Missing Manual by Kate J. Chase and Scott Palmer

AppleScript: The Missing Manual by Adam Goldstein

AppleWorks 6: The Missing Manual by Jim Elferdink and David Reynolds

Creating Web Sites: The Missing Manual by Matthew MacDonald

Dreamweaver 8: The Missing Manual by David Sawyer McFarland

Windows 2000 Pro: The Missing Manual by Sharon Crawford

Windows XP Power Hound by Preston Gralla

Windows XP for Starters: The Missing Manual by David Pogue

Windows XP Home Edition: The Missing Manual, Second Edition by David Pogue

Windows XP Pro: The Missing Manual, Second Edition by David Pogue, Craig Zacker, and Linda Zacker

INTRODUCTION

- ▶ **Personal Finance and Quicken**
- ▶ **What's New in Quicken 2006**
- ▶ **About This Book**
- ▶ **About the Outline**
- ▶ **The Very Basics**
- ▶ **About MissingManuals.com**

LIKE THOUSANDS OF OTHER PEOPLE, you hope Quicken can help you control your mountains of financial information—credit cards, tax deductions, loans, retirement plans, and assets. You want a program that gives you an overview of your financial health, while sparing you the time and tedium of balancing your checkbook and tracking every investment by hand. As you'll discover in this book, Quicken can do all that and more. Its hundreds of features share one common purpose: to help you manage your personal finances. If you have trouble remembering to transfer extra cash into higher-interest-rate savings, for example, Quicken can remind you. If budgets are your downfall, Quicken can take your financial goals and help you build a budget to achieve them.

Quicken isn't hard to learn. Using the program as an electronic checkbook isn't much different from recording checks and deposits in a paper register. Features and techniques that you're familiar with from other programs work just as well in Quicken, including windows, dialog boxes, drop-down menus, and keyboard shortcuts. Best of all, once you enter a bit of financial information into Quicken—like a check, deposit, credit card transaction, or loan payment—you never have to type it again. Quicken can use that information over and over to calculate things like budget averages, debt balances, or even your net worth. Every minute you spend learning the program is time well spent.

Your Quicken ambitions may be no bigger than balancing your checkbook. Yet somehow, the program gets you thinking about aspects of your personal finances that you were content to completely ignore in the past. As you learn to do more with Quicken, you'll expand your knowledge and ideas about money. Then again, sometimes Quicken seems to raise more questions than it answers: Return of capital from stock—what's that? What does "net worth" mean anyway—and why do you need to know it? Luckily, the book you're holding picks up where Quicken's help resources leave off.

This book begins by telling you how to set up Quicken to fit *your* needs. It explains the program's basic features and answers questions you're likely to have (but Quicken Help doesn't answer). If speed is your thing, this book shows you

the fastest ways to perform financial tasks—like keyboard shortcut̠
vides comprehensive discussions and step-by-step tutorials for peopָ
a bit of handholding. Along the way, you'll discover a few features anɗ
most Quicken owners never knew existed.

Personal Finance and Quicken

Quicken is more than an electronic checkbook—it's a personal finance management program. Sure, the register you use to record transactions electronically
looks like your paper register. But by harnessing the power of your PC and the
Internet, Quicken opens up new horizons for performing financial tasks more
quickly and easily.

What Quicken Does

Perhaps the first benefit you'll come to know and love is that you no longer have
to worry about arithmetic. Quicken automatically updates your account balances when you record transactions, calculates the remaining funds when you
divvy up a paycheck, matches downloaded transactions to recorded ones, and
tells you when you've successfully reconciled your account.

Because Quicken can categorize every transaction, collecting your tax-related
information and building a budget are no longer frantic treasure hunts through
shoeboxes of paper. Instead, a few quick clicks produce the information you
need—ready to print out or feed into another of Quicken's features. You can also
export tax-related data to programs like Turbo Tax. You can then import your
tax return results into Quicken to plan next year's tax strategy.

Quicken doesn't just track what you've done with your money in the past. The
program's planning features help you decide what to do with your money in the
future. From simple reminders to pay credit card bills on time and avoid late fees
to portfolio reports that show you whether your investments are working as well as
they could be, Quicken is bursting with tools to improve your financial situation.

What Quicken Doesn't Do

Quicken *isn't* a true bookkeeping or accounting program. Although the Quicken Premier Home & Business edition offers business features like invoices, accounts receivable, and payroll, it *doesn't* offer ledgers, true double-entry accounting, a chart of accounts, inventory control, or certain financial reports that accountants and the IRS need. For example, because Quicken doesn't include equity accounts, you can't generate a balance sheet like the ones your accountant is used to. (However, Quicken's "Income and Expense by Category" report can pass as a profit-and-loss report or income statement.)

If you have a small business and you *don't* track inventory or generate standard financial reports, you can get by with Quicken Premier Home & Business. However, if you work with a bookkeeper or accountant, you've no doubt heard pleas to switch to QuickBooks, Intuit's small-business accounting program—and it's generally a good idea to listen. Yes, QuickBooks costs a bit more and dumps you unceremoniously into the Scylla and Charybdis of debits and credits. But if you pay your accountant for advice and she's willing to help you get started with QuickBooks, the transition won't be painful. (And you may find features in QuickBooks that can help you become even more productive.)

 Note: If you decide to use QuickBooks for your business, you'll still need Quicken for your personal finances, since QuickBooks doesn't track investments.

Quicken and Accounting

Although Quicken isn't an accounting program, it does perform *some* accounting tasks. If your financial horizon is no further than your next paycheck, some of Quicken's features may seem like mystical arts. Yet, in a cruel twist, Quicken's accounting features are equally mysterious to those who *are* familiar with accounting. Here's a quick overview of how Quicken accounts for your money.

Accounts versus categories

Assets are things you own, like checking accounts, certificates of deposit, brokerage accounts, a house, and your car. Quicken includes several types of accounts for your assets: checking, savings, house, vehicle, and a generic asset account for assets that don't fall under any of the other account types (like the Faberge egg your Aunt Katrinka left you in her will). Furniture and clothing are assets as well, although most folks don't bother tracking them in Quicken.

Liabilities are what you owe to others, like credit cards, mortgages, and other types of loans. Quicken includes liability accounts to cover every type of debt you carry.

In business accounting, income accounts track money that an organization receives, whether from selling services, selling products, or obtaining research grants. Expense accounts track money the organization spends, like employee salaries, office rent, and accountants' fees. Quicken, by contrast, doesn't have income and expense accounts. Instead, you create income and expense *categories*. When you record a check, charge, or deposit—in fact, any kind of transaction—you assign the money to one category or another.

Following the money

Business accounting uses *double-entry accounting*, in which every transaction represents a debit in one account and a credit to another account. Although accountants, bookkeepers, and other financial geeks can spot debit entries and credit entries from a mile away, the rest of us don't need that kind of detail.

Quicken takes a more intuitive approach that only partially mimics double-entry accounting. For example, in Quicken, credit cards act like negative cash, which is an appropriate way to think about it. Whether you spend cash or credit card debt, you're nibbling away at your bottom line. When you pay your credit card bill, Quicken deducts cash from your checking account and adds it to the credit card account, thereby decreasing the balance owed.

Equity

In business accounting, anything worth tracking goes into a separate account, even the difference between the value of your assets and liabilities. An *equity* account is the holding place for that difference. In business, the financial report called a *balance sheet* gets it name because the total for all of the asset accounts equals the total of all of the liability accounts and equity accounts.

Quicken doesn't have equity accounts, but it can still calculate your *net worth*, which is your total assets minus your total liabilities. In other words, it's the value of everything you own *after* paying off all your debts. Net worth is as important in personal finances as equity is in business. Increasing the value of what you own while decreasing the amount you owe increases your net worth—a goal that helps you achieve all those other goals in life. (Quicken displays your net worth in the Quicken Home window to remind you of your progress.)

Choosing the Right Quicken Edition

Unlike QuickBooks, its small business accounting cousin, Quicken comes in only three editions. Deciding which one suits you is relatively easy. Here's an overview of what each edition does:

▶ **Quicken Deluxe** ($49.95) handles all the basic personal finance tasks, from tracking cash to budgeting, paying bills, and tracking your investments. If you plan to use the program to track your spending, gather your tax data, track investments, and do a little planning, Deluxe is all you need.

 Note: You may run into an edition called Quicken Basic, if you buy a computer with some preinstalled programs, like Microsoft Works. Quicken Basic is a stripped-down edition that can get you started.

▶ **Quicken Premier** ($69.95) is for people who are more serious about their investing. This edition does everything that Quicken Deluxe does, but throws in additional investment portfolio tools. It also offers to help find tax deductions you may have missed.

▶ The only reason you'd spring for **Quicken Premier Home & Business** ($79.95) is if you run a small business and want to track both your personal and business finances with the program. This edition contains everything that the standard Quicken Premier offers, but adds payroll, accounts receivable, invoicing, and mileage tracking.

Tip: If you track inventory, handle payroll for more than a few employees, or need financial reports formatted to the typical accounting standard, consider forking over the extra cash to purchase Intuit's QuickBooks product. Intuit offers Simple Start to first-time QuickBooks users for $99.95 (only $20 more than Quicken Premier Home & Business). QuickBooks Pro, the most inexpensive edition, costs $199.95 ($99.95 for upgrades from previous versions).

What's New in Quicken 2006

Most of the time, new versions come with enhancements, timesaving features, and more online tools to make your work easier and faster. You don't *have* to upgrade every year, but Intuit drops support for versions older than three years. With a rebate for existing customers, upgrading doesn't cost all that much for the benefits you receive.

Some changes take some getting used to. Not that long ago, Intuit changed the way budgeting worked and completely overhauled the investment register. For some changes, it simply takes some time to learn how to make the most of the new techniques, as was the case with budgeting. Other changes are more like Coke Classic. Customers provided copious feedback and Intuit responded by resurrecting or reworking the features it removed.

Quicken 2006's changes fall more in the evolutionary than revolutionary camp, but a few additions might make you sit up and take notice:

▶ **Storing electronic statements and other images.** With Quicken 2006, you can link electronic statements from your real-world accounts to the corresponding accounts in your Quicken data file. For example, you can download an electronic checking account statement and store it with your checking account in Quicken. If a question arises about a transaction, you can remain resolutely seated in your computer chair instead of bouncing back and forth between your desk and filing cabinet.

You can also store electronic files with transactions; link images of canceled checks to your check transactions; store downloaded or scanned receipts with purchase transactions for proof of purchase; and store with transactions the receipts, warranties, and other material that you tend to forage for. When you need information, Quicken has it all.

- **Saving reports as PDF files.** For people tracking only personal finances, this feature is helpful from time to time—to send financial information to your accountant or financial advisor at tax time or when updating your financial plan. This feature is handy more often for those using Quicken Premier Home & Business for electronically transmitting invoices, business forms, and reports to customers and business associates.

- **Entering investment transactions in the investment register.** Intuit eliminated this option at one point, only to bring it back by popular demand. In Quicken 2006, you can once again enter and edit investment transactions via the register (or a dialog box if you prefer).

About This Book

Despite the many improvements in Quicken over the years, one feature has grown consistently worse: Intuit documentation. For a topic as complicated as personal finance, all you get with Quicken is an electronic copy of *Getting Started with Quicken*, which is little more than a guide to tasks Quicken performs, with a few step-by-step instructions.

Even if you don't mind reading instructions in one window as you work in another, you'll quickly discover that Quicken Help is hardly worth the screen space it consumes. The help topics often cover the basic material you already know, but fail to answer the burning questions that made you launch Help in the first place. In addition, Quicken Help rarely tells you *why* you might want to use any feature. And underlining key points, jotting hard-earned insights in the margins, and reading about Quicken while sitting by the pool are out of the question.

Quicken 2006 for Starters: The Missing Manual is the book that *should* have come with Quicken 2006. Although each version of Quicken introduces new features

Importing Data into Quicken

Why can't I import data into Quicken?

One of the biggest changes in recent years (starting with Quicken 2005) is the format that Intuit uses to communicate with financial institutions. The new format, called *OFX* (Open Financial Exchange), makes it much easier to activate accounts for online financial services through Quicken and to download transactions from financial institutions into Quicken accounts.

Unfortunately, OFX eliminates the ability to *import* transactions to checking, savings, credit card, 401(k), and brokerage accounts. You can still import transactions into asset, liability, and cash accounts. Importing data is transferring data from one place to another using specially formatted files (similar to importing a comma-delimited file into Microsoft Excel).

Because Quicken 2006 can't use the old QIF (Quicken Interchange Format) format, you can no longer import data from other programs (helpful if you want to convert from programs other than Microsoft Money) from Quicken data files (sometimes helpful with data corruption issues), or from financial institutions that opted not to support Quicken's new OFX format.

To make matters worse, Intuit also dropped support for online financial services that use the old format, rendering Quicken versions prior to 2005 useless for downloading transactions or paying bills online. So some customers who upgrade Quicken also have to switch banks if they want to continue downloading transactions.

If you're just getting started with Quicken, all this controversy may seem like a tempest in a teapot. But many Quicken fans consider these draconian measures on Intuit's part. Unfortunately, if you want to use online financial services, you must either use the new version of Quicken or choose a different program.

and enhancements, you'll still find this book useful if you're tracking your finances in an earlier version of Quicken. (Of course, the older your version of the program, the more dissimilarities you'll run across.)

Note: This book covers the Windows version of Quicken. The program's development for the Mac was completely separate—and different—from the ground up. Accordingly, Quicken differs significantly on the two platforms.

In this book's pages, you'll find step-by-step instructions for using the most popular and useful Quicken features, including those you may not have quite understood, let alone mastered: budgeting (Chapter 8), recording investment transactions (page 45), archiving Quicken data files (page 86), and so on. Along the way, the book helps you evaluate Quicken's features and decide which ones would be most useful in your situation.

Quicken 2006 for Starters: The Missing Manual is designed to accommodate readers at every technical level. The primary discussions are written for beginner or intermediate Quicken users. But if you're a first-time Quicken user, special boxes with the title "Up To Speed" provide the introductory information you need to understand the topic at hand. On the other hand, advanced users should watch for similar shaded boxes called "Power Users' Clinic." These sidebars offer more technical tips, tricks, and shortcuts for the experienced Quicken fan.

About the Outline

Quicken 2006 for Starters: The Missing Manual is divided into three sections, each containing several chapters:

- ▶ Chapters 1, 2, and 3 cover everything you must do to set up Quicken based on your own needs. These chapters explain how to create a Quicken data file, create accounts and categories, configure preferences, and protect your financial information.

- ▶ Chapters 4, 5, 6, and 7 follow your money from the moment you earn it to when you report your financial activities to the IRS. These chapters describe how to make deposits, pay for expenses, track the things you own and how much you owe, perform financial tasks online, reconcile your accounts, and care for your Quicken data file.

- Chapter 8, 9, and 10 elucidate some of the features that help you increase your financial success. These chapters explain how to create and use budgets, track investments, and generate Quicken reports to prepare your tax returns or evaluate the state of your financial fitness.

At the end of the book, two appendices provide a quick review of the most helpful keyboard shortcuts and a reference to help resources for Quicken.

 Tip: This book includes four bonus appendices that you can download in PDF format for printing or reading on your PC. They include a guide to installing and upgrading Quicken (Appendix C), importing and exporting Quicken data (Appendix D), maintaining your Quicken data file (Appendix E), and a bunch of cool techniques and under-appreciated features like Quicken email and the Pin Vault (Appendix F). Go to *www.missing-manuals.com/cds* and click this book's link, then click the link for each appendix to download it to your PC.

The Very Basics

To use this book, and indeed to use Quicken, you need to know a few basics. This book assumes that you're familiar with a few terms and concepts:

- **Clicking.** This book gives you three kinds of instructions that require you to use your computer's mouse or track pad. To *click* means to point the arrow pointer at something on the screen and then—without moving the pointer at all—press and release the left button on the mouse (or laptop track pad). To *double-click*, of course, means to click twice in rapid succession, again without moving the pointer at all.

  When you're told to *Shift-click* something, you click while pressing the Shift key. Related procedures, like *Ctrl-click*, work the same way—just click while pressing the corresponding key.

  To *right-click*, you do the exact same thing, but pressing the *right* mouse button instead. Usually, clicking with the left button selects an onscreen element or presses a button onscreen. A right-click usually reveals a *shortcut menu*, which lists some common tasks specific to whatever you're right-clicking on.

▸ **Dragging.** To *drag* means to move the pointer while holding down the (left) button the entire time. To *right-drag*, of course, means to do the same thing but holding down the right mouse button.

▸ **Menus.** The *menus* are the words at the top of your screen: File, Edit, and so on. Click one to make a list of commands appear, as though they're written on a window shade you've just pulled down.

Some people click to open a menu and then release the mouse button; after reading the menu command choices, they click the command they want. Other people like to press the mouse button continuously as they click the menu title and drag down the list to the desired command; only then do they release the mouse button. Either method works, so choose the one you prefer.

▸ **Keyboard shortcuts.** Nothing is faster than keeping your fingers on your keyboard, entering data, choosing names, triggering commands—without losing time by grabbing the mouse and then selecting a command or list entry. That's why many experienced Quicken fans prefer to trigger commands by pressing combinations of keys on the keyboard. When you read an instruction like "Press Ctrl+J to open the Scheduled Transactions List window," start by pressing the Ctrl key; while it's down, type the letter J, and then release both keys.

About → These → Arrows

Throughout this book, and throughout the Missing Manual series, you'll find sentences like this one: "Choose Edit → Preferences → Quicken Program." That's shorthand for a much longer instruction that directs you to navigate three nested menus in sequence, like this: "Choose Edit. On the Edit menu, point to the Preferences menu entry. On the submenu that appears, choose Quicken Program." Figure I-1 shows the menus this sequence opens.

Similarly, this arrow shorthand also simplifies the instructions for opening nested folders, like My Documents → Quicken Data → Backup.

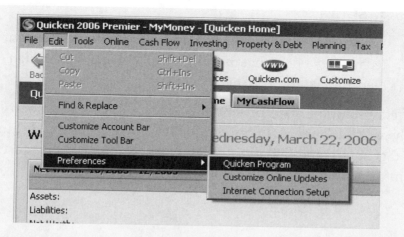

Figure I-1. Instead of filling pages with long and hard-to-follow instructions for navigating through nested menus and folders, the arrow notations are concise, but just as informative. For example, choosing "Edit → Preferences → Quicken Program" takes you to the menu shown here.

About MissingManuals.com

At *www.missingmanuals.com*, you'll find news, articles, and updates to the books in this series. The Web site also offers corrections and updates to this book (to see them, click the book's title, and then click Errata). In fact, you're invited and encouraged to submit such corrections and updates yourself. In an effort to keep the book as up to date and accurate as possible, each time we print more copies of this book, we'll make any confirmed corrections you've suggested. We'll also note such changes on the Web site, so that you can mark important corrections into your own copy of the book, if you like.

In the meantime, we'd love to hear your suggestions for new books in the Missing Manual line. There's a place for that on the Web site, too, as well as a place to sign up for free email notification of new titles in the series.

Safari® Enabled

 When you see a Safari® Enabled icon on the cover of your favorite technology book, that means it's available online through the O'Reilly Network Safari Bookshelf.

Safari offers a solution that's better than e-books: it's a virtual library that lets you easily search thousands of top tech books, cut and paste code samples, download chapters, and find quick answers when you need the most accurate, current information. Try it for free at *http://safari.oreilly.com*.

CHAPTER 1:
SETTING UP YOUR
QUICKEN ENVIRONMENT

▶ Launching Quicken

▶ Setting Up Your Quicken Data File

▶ Opening a Quicken File

▶ The Quicken Guided Setup

▶ A Quick Guide to Quicken Preferences

After you install Quicken (see Appendix C for instructions), you have just a few more steps before you experience the joys of electronic personal finance. Quicken stores all your information and settings in a *data file*, which is like an electronic version of the filing cabinet that contains your financial papers. (Actually, behind the scenes, it's a small *set* of files, as the box on page 17 explains.)

Despite the awkward name, a data file is a good thing, because it lets you back up your Quicken data, move it to another computer, keep different family members' info in separate files, and so on. The first time you launch Quicken, the program asks you to help set up your data file.

If you've used a previous version of Quicken, your setup process is shorter, but even existing data files require a quick conversion to work with the new version of Quicken. If it's your first time using Quicken, the program asks you a few questions, creates a new data file, and then launches the Quicken Guided Setup to help you tailor the file to your needs.

In addition to setting up your data file, it's a good idea to take a look at Quicken's *preferences*. Preferences (called Options in some other programs) are the settings that control how Quicken looks and acts. You'll return to the preferences dialog box throughout this book, but there are some you want to set right away—like which currency you're using and which screen you want to see when you start up each day.

Launching Quicken

To start using Quicken, you launch it like most any program. Here are some popular methods:

▶ **Quick Launch toolbar.** Clicking the Quicken icon in this toolbar launches Quicken, making it the fastest way to get going.

 Tip: The Quick Launch toolbar is to the right of the Start button. If you don't see Quicken's icon there—or *any* icons there—see the box on page 18.

What Is a Quicken Data File?

Despite Intuit's insistence on the singular term data *file*, Quicken actually stores your data in five separate files, similar to your word processing or spreadsheet files. (Technical types call this kind of file collection a *data set*, but don't worry, there's no quiz later.) Quicken's data file is the electronic equivalent of the filing cabinet, drawers, and paper folders you use to store your checking account and credit card statements.

The granddaddy of the group is the one with the .qdf file extension. It contains your account information and transactions. In the folder with the .qdf file, you'll also find files with the same filename but different file extensions:

.qel, .qph, .qsd, and .qtx. Quicken updates these other files behind the scenes, and there's no need to worry about what they do. In fact, you could even delete these additional files, only to find that the program recreates them the next time you open the .qdf file.

▶ **Desktop shortcut.** Double-click the Quicken 2006 desktop shortcut that Quicken added to your computer during installation.

▶ **Programs menu.** Without a desktop icon, you can launch Quicken from the Windows Start menu. Click Start, and then choose Programs → Quicken → Quicken 2006.

Setting Up Your Quicken Data File

The first time you launch Quicken, the "Get Started with Quicken 2006" window pops up with two options: If you're a Quicken neophyte, the program helps you

Quick Launching Quicken

Windows' Quick Launch toolbar (no relation to Quicken) gives you a fast way to launch programs you use most often, helping keep your desktop from being overrun with shortcut icons. Unlike the Start menu, you won't see installed programs automatically appear in the Quick Launch toolbar—you have to add them yourself.

The Quick Launch toolbar appears in the taskbar at the bottom of your screen, as shown here. If you don't see this toolbar, it just means you need to turn it on. To reveal it, right-click an empty area on the taskbar, and then choose Toolbars → Quick Launch from the menu that pops up. A checkmark appears on the menu next to Quick Launch, indicating you've turned it on.

To install Quicken's icon on the Quick Launch toolbar, you simply right-drag it there from somewhere else.

If you have a Quicken desktop shortcut (like the one the setup program offered to create during installation), right-drag its icon onto the Quick Launch toolbar and then choose Copy Here to create a shortcut on the toolbar. (If you're trying to clean up your desktop, choose Move Here to move the shortcut to the Quick Launch toolbar.) You can also use the right-drag technique to copy or move a shortcut from the Start menu or in Windows Explorer.

build your data file from scratch; if you've used Quicken in the past, you can get started by using an existing Quicken data file. The setup program guides you through the conversion process.

In the "Get Started with Quicken 2006" window, choose one of the following options:

- **I am new to Quicken.** Choose this option if you want to create and set up a brand new Quicken data file using Quicken Guided Setup. Read on for detailed instructions on creating a brand new data file.

- **I am already a Quicken user.** Choose this option to get started without all the handholding; for instance, if you already have a Quicken data file and have installed Quicken on a spiffy new laptop. For your options and instructions, skip to page 20.

 Tip. If you're converting a data file from an earlier version of Quicken, you should back up your data and take a few other preliminary steps. See the box on page 23 for instructions.

I Am New to Quicken

When you choose the "I am new to Quicken" option and click Next, the process of setting up a brand new data file begins. The first screen asks, "What do you want to call your data file?" You get two options: Let Quicken name and save your data file, or tell Quicken what you want to name the file and where you want to store it.

- **I will use the default file name and location.** If you choose this option, Quicken creates a folder called Quicken in your My Documents folder and puts your data file in there, with the catchy name *QDATA*. (It stands for "Quicken data"—get it?)

 Tip. Unless you like to hunt around your hard drive for obscurely named files, choose the second option (as described next). But if you've already let Quicken name and save a *QDATA* file and need help finding it, see the box on page 25.

- **I want to choose a different file name and location.** With this option, you can assign your Quicken data file a meaningful name, like *MyMoney* or *Fred's Finances*, and store it in any folder you like. Personalized filenames are essential when you create more than one data file; for instance, when you also track your parents' finances, or manage money for your geeky child who's grown rich from her patents.

With this option, clicking Next displays the Create Quicken File dialog box. As demonstrated in Figure 1-1, navigate to the folder you want and, in the File name box, type the name for your data file. Click OK to create the file.

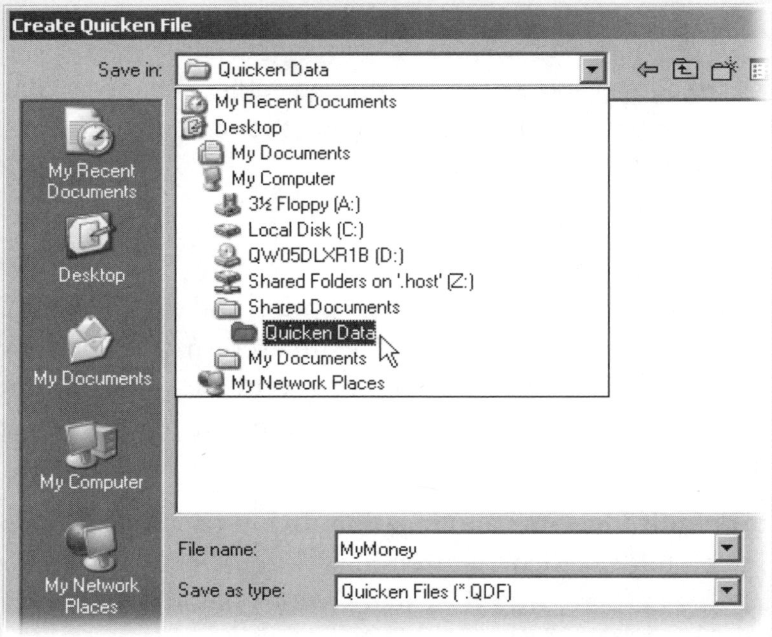

Figure 1-1. This is the Create Quicken File dialog box. In this example, you're saving the file MyMoney in the Quicken Data folder *within* the Shared Documents folder.

After Quicken creates your data file, it launches the Quicken Guided Setup to help you set up the file—creating accounts, categories, and other features for tracking your finances. To get started, see page 23.

I Am Already a Quicken User

If you have an existing data file from a previous version, first make sure you've backed up your existing data (and perhaps printed out parts of it). With your

Before (and After) You Convert

Quicken does a great job converting data files created in previous versions of the program. All you have to do is select the existing data file during Guided Setup—or just open it in Quicken 2006. To make the transition even smoother, though, here are some preparatory steps you can take *before* converting your data:

Print lists from your current data file. Converting a data file to Quicken 2006 might drop some of the customizations you've made, or even some transactions. In case you have to recreate some of these items later, a hard copy to refer to is a big help. So print, for example, your Account List (page 54), Scheduled Transaction List (page 162), Online Payees (page 245), Category List (page 75), and the information in your PIN Vault (Online Appendix F).

(To print a list, open the appropriate window—press Ctrl+A to open the Account List window, for example—and click Print in the window menu bar.)

Back up your data file. Although Quicken automatically backs up your data file before converting it, untrusting types can create their own data file backups to a CD or Zip disk prior to opening the data file in Quicken 2006 for extra insurance (see page 86).

Then, *after* you convert your data file, compare the account balances before and after conversion to look for discrepancies. If the balances are different, open the register for that account and look for transactions with values equal to that of the discrepancy.

backup and printouts in place, choose the "I am already a Quicken user" option, and then click Next. The Select Your Data File screen offers three options:

▶ **Open a file located on this computer.** If you have an existing Quicken data file on your hard disk, choose this option and click Next. In the Open Quicken File dialog box, navigate to the folder that contains your data file, select the filename, and click OK to open the file.

Tip: If you're lucky (or unlucky) enough to have a home network, the Open Quicken File dialog box can access a Quicken data file in any shared folder on your network.

▶ **Restore a Quicken data file I've backed up to CD or disk.** This option works only with files backed up with Quicken's Backup command, as described in Chapter 3. When you choose this option and click Next, the Restore Quicken File dialog box appears. To restore the backup file, navigate to the folder or CD that contains the backup file, select the filename, and click OK. Once the data file is snuggled comfortably in the folder, you can choose File → Open to work with it.

▶ **Start over and create a new data file.** If you've mangled or lost the only copy of your data file in a horrible disk-cleaning accident, take a deep breath, make a mental note to back up your data in the future, and then choose this option to tell Quicken to create a brand new file.

When you click Next and the Create Quicken File dialog box appears, navigate to the folder you use for Quicken data. In the File name box, type a name for the new file and click OK. Quicken creates the data file and launches the Quicken Guided Setup.

Note: You can bypass the "Get Started with Quicken 2006" screen by opening an existing data file directly (by double-clicking it, for example). To convert your data file from there, see the box on the next page.

Opening a Quicken File

Once you've opened a data file, Quicken accommodatingly opens that file the next time you launch the program. If you have only one Quicken data file—and most people do—you may never have to choose File → Open again.

Even with a handful of data files, you need go no further than the File menu to open them, as demonstrated in Figure 1-2.

Converting Quicken Data Files

The first time you open a data file that was created with a previous version of Quicken, the program opens the Convert Your Data dialog box. To convert the file to the new version, just click OK. Quicken saves a copy of your existing data file in *C:\Documents and Settings\<your username>\My Documents\Quicken\Q05Files* (or ...\Q01Files if you're converting from the 2001 version) and converts your data file to the Quicken 2006 format.

When the conversion is complete, Quicken launches the Quicken Guided Setup (see below). If the file is fine as is, click Exit Setup and you're ready to manage your money. If you have some changes to make, such as adding an account or changing your profile, you can use the Quicken Guided Setup or click Exit Setup and choose commands from the Quicken menu bar (as described in Chapter 2).

From now on, you'll be working in the all-new, improved Quicken 2006 copy of your data file. Your previous data file remains on your hard drive right where you left it, until you delete it. Should you decide to go back to using the previous version of Quicken, you can always open this pre-conversion data file in the previous version.

The Quicken Guided Setup

There's no escaping the Quicken Guided Setup—Quicken opens it as soon as you create a data file (or convert one from a previous version). If you know your way around Quicken, you can do everything that the Guided Setup does using menu commands. The first time around, though, the Guided Setup's step-by-step procedure can't be beat. It clearly lays out all your options, lets you make your own financial choices, and then gives you an error-free data file that's tailor-made for you.

For example, the setup tool helps you create *accounts*, which are the electronic cousins of the accounts you have at financial institutions—checking accounts, savings accounts, credit cards, Individual Retirement Accounts (IRAs), and so

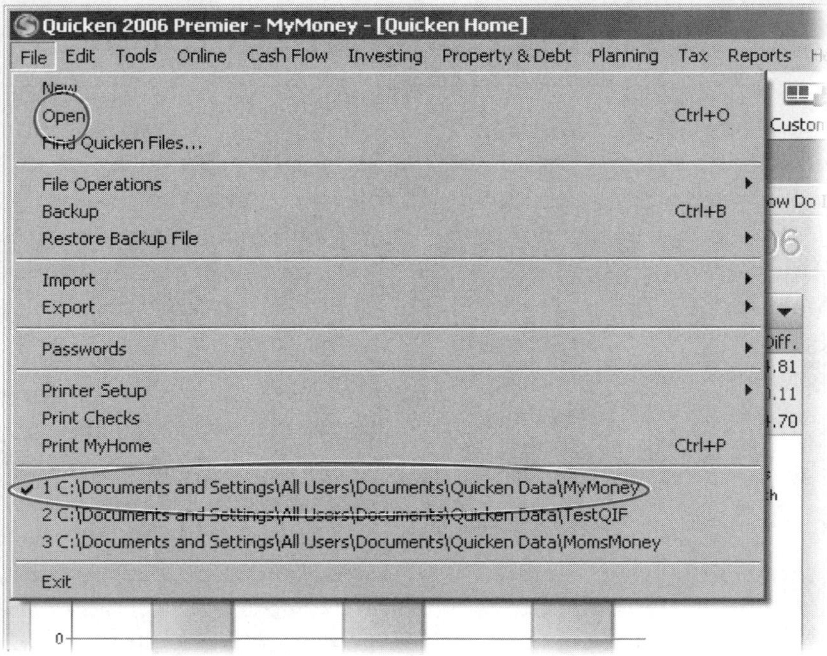

Figure 1-2. This is the File menu. To find and open a Quicken data file, choose Open (circled), or press Ctrl+O. The bottom of this menu lists recently opened data files and adds a checkmark to the one that's currently open (in this case, MyMoney). Click a file name to open that file.

on. It can also create *categories* that help organize your budget and track the money you spend. For instance, if you tell the Guided Setup that you own a house, it adds a category for mortgage interest.

From the Quicken Guided Setup Welcome screen, shown in Figure 1-3, you can navigate the setup process in two different ways. Clicking Next Step to proceed to the next setup task is the easiest way to work through the Guided Setup. If this isn't your first time through the tool, you can also click a category on the left side of the window to jump to the task you want.

Who Moved My Data File?

For Quicken 2005 and later, Quicken stores data in *C:\Documents and settings\<your username>\My Documents\Quicken*—unless you choose a different folder during installation or move your data file afterward. The advantage of this small change is that a backup (using a program like Windows Backup, not Quicken's Backup command) that backs up your My Documents folder grabs your Quicken data without any extra work.

Finding your data files is rarely an issue if you start off on the right foot by creating a folder specifically for your Quicken data. If you move a data file to another folder, Quicken isn't smart enough to find it. As long as you know where the file is, choose File → Open, navigate to the folder, and double-click the data filename.

If you've no idea where you placed your data files, you can search for files ending in a .qdf file extension. Here's one way: In the Windows Explorer icon bar, click Search. (If you don't see the Search icon, choose View → Toolbars → Standard Buttons.) In the Search Companion pane, click "All files and folders." In the "All or part of a file name" box, type *.qdf. In the "Look in" drop-down menu, choose a likely location, like My Documents or Local Hard Drives → C:.

By the way, if you already have some Quicken experience under your belt, don't feel embarrassed if you can't find your data file: Prior to Quicken 2005, Quicken tucked your data files in the same folder as the Quicken software itself (*C:\Program Files\Quicken*). Resist the temptation to store it there for old times' sake, however. If you use a backup program, it's likely to skip the Program Files folder, since most people don't keep their files and documents there. (See Appendix E for more information on moving and copying your data file.)

Note: If you want to use the Guided Setup but Quicken *hasn't* displayed it, simply choose Tools → Quicken Guided Setup.

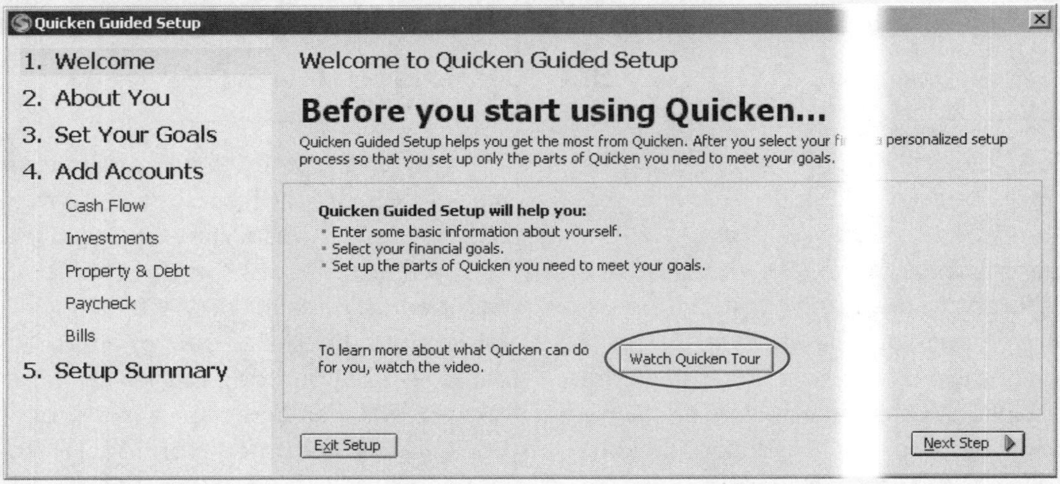

Figure 1-3. In the list to the Welcome Screen's left, the slightly darker gray bar shows which setup step you're currently working on (in this case, it's the Welcome Setup). If you're in the mood for some educational entertainment, click Watch Quicken Tour (circled) for a brief audiovisual presentation.

The Welcome screen lists all the things you'll be doing in the setup. As noted below, the rest of the chapters in this book provide detailed instructions for setting up your data file on your own.

▶ **Create cash flow accounts.** Cash flow accounts cover checking accounts, savings accounts, credit cards, and plain old cash. Chapter 2 explains how to create them from scratch.

▶ **Create investment accounts.** Whether your investment accounts are retirement or taxable, brokerage or mutual funds, Chapter 9 explains how to create them from scratch.

▶ **Create asset and liability accounts.** If you want to track how much you own and owe, Chapter 5 explains how to create accounts for assets and loans.

- ▶ **Set up paychecks.** Chapter 4 explains how to use Quicken's Paycheck Setup tool to automate the entry of paychecks, regardless of how many deductions your company makes.

- ▶ **Set up bills you pay regularly.** If you pay the same bills time after time—even if the amount changes from payment to payment—you can automate your bill entry by following the steps described in Chapter 4.

If this process sounds like a lot of work, you're right! But you can break up the setup process into smaller chunks, as discussed in the box on page 28. Before you dive in, you'll need to have some information handy and think about how you want to use Quicken, as described next.

What You Need for Setup

To set up Quicken to handle your financial needs going forward, you have to gather some information about your present position. At minimum, you need the account balance from the most recent statement for each bank account. With the most recent ending balance, you can begin to manage accounts in Quicken. However, a more useful (though time-consuming) approach is to go back to the beginning of the current year. By starting with the ending balance from the previous year and bringing all your transactions up to date, you can take advantage of Quicken to prepare this year's tax returns and analyze your yearly finances.

If you're up to the task of entering a few months of transactions, collect all of your account statements through the last month of the *previous* year. You can use the account balance from the last statement of the previous year and enter all the transactions from the following statements to bring your Quicken accounts up to date.

 Tip: If you plan to use online services (which you can read about in Chapter 6), don't worry about entering transactions. Your first download may import all the transactions you need. See "Downloading Transactions" on page 50 for more detail.

Budgeting Your Time

The number of steps that the Guided Setup offers is daunting, but fear not. The tool is considerate about the human need for breaks and doesn't care whether you perform every step straight through. Attack the Guided Setup using any of the following strategies:

Marathon setup. You *can* blast through setup in one long session if you really want to. Sure, it's exhausting, but you won't have to perform any additional setup—at least until you open a new account or want to make changes.

Multiple sessions. Divide the setup among several sessions until you've finished them all. For example, you can start by setting up your checking and savings accounts in one session, do all your credit cards another night, then set aside a weekend for setting up your investments and loans.

As needed. This is the most pragmatic approach. You can use the Guided Setup to create the very basics: your checking account, savings account, and perhaps a cash account for the money you spend straight from your wallet. After only a few minutes, you're ready to put Quicken to work. Click Exit Setup to close the Quicken Guided Setup. As financial tasks come up, you can open the Guided Setup (choose Tools → Quicken Guided Setup) to complete more of the setup; for instance, to add an investment account, your new car loan, or your paycheck.

Tell Quicken about Yourself

Quicken starts by asking for a little personal information. Don't worry—it's only to determine some of the appropriate accounts and categories to track your finances. On the left side of the Quicken Guided Setup window, click About You, and then provide your age (be honest), whether you're married, and whether you own a home. Click Next Step when you're finished.

Set Your Goals

Quicken is a personal finance program with many powerful features, but telepathy isn't one of them. Nor can Quicken take the place of a personal financial advisor. Before you dive into setting up the accounts in your data file, you need to know what you want to track with Quicken—and more importantly, how diligent you're likely to be at tracking financial details.

The Set Your Goals screen isn't about defining your financial goals; it's about your goals for using Quicken to manage your finances. Each checkbox corresponds to a feature that Quicken offers. Turn on a checkbox to see what setup you need to perform, as illustrated in Figure 1-4. For example, turning on the "Manage my checkbook and bills" checkbox adds an icon to Cash Flow (the category for checking accounts) and Bills.

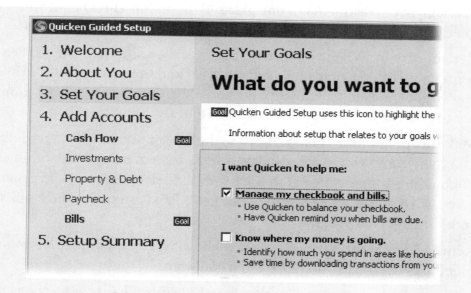

Figure 1-4. In this example, "Manage my checkbook and bills" is the chosen task, so Quicken tells you that you need to set up a Cash Flow account and a Bills account.

As you can see on the Set Your Goals screen (Figure 1-4), Quicken Guided Setup comes equipped to tailor your data file for a number of common financial concerns. Start by choosing the goal that is closest to your current situation, although you can (and probably will) adjust your goals (and your data file) later.

- **Manage my checkbook and bills.** Turn on this checkbox if you want the Guided Setup to help you create your checking account and set up the bills you pay.

- **Know where your money is going.** If you whip out a calculator at lunch to divvy up the bill to figure out each person's cost to the penny, you'll appreciate the tracking that Quicken can perform. Turn on this checkbox if you want the Guided Setup to help you create categories to track your income and expenses.

- **Save more money.** When you turn on this checkbox, Quicken Guided Setup helps you set up a budget to rein in your spending.

- **Track all my investments in one place.** Turn on this checkbox if you want Quicken Guided Setup to help you create investment accounts.

- **Get out of debt.** When you turn on this checkbox, Quicken Guided Setup helps you create accounts for what you own and the money you owe. Once you've got Quicken set up, you can choose Planning → Debt Reduction Planner to learn how to get out of debt more quickly.

- **Make tax preparation easier.** If you're the type of person who jams dollar bills and change into your pocket and notices a problem only when nothing comes out but lint, you might want to track only tax-related income and expenditures. Turn on this checkbox to set up tax-related categories and a link to Intuit's TurboTax program.

- **Retire when I want.** Turn on this checkbox if you want to prepare an investment plan that helps you retire when you want.

- **Know my net worth.** Turn on this checkbox to make sure you create all the accounts you need to stay on top of how much you're worth.

 Tip: Although it's good to start with a clear idea of what you're going to do in Quicken, you don't have to get the level of detail *perfect* the first time. As you'll learn in Chapter 2, you can add, delete, or change categories any time you want.

Add Accounts

In the Quicken Guided Setup, the Add Accounts step is where the real work gets done. Between creating accounts, setting up your paycheck, and setting up the bills you pay, this step hits almost every area of your financial life. In fact, completing this step in one session might be more than you can handle. The good news is that you can stop any time you want and come back to do a bit more (see the box on page 28) after you've downed a grande latte or two.

Moreover, you can start *using* any accounts you have created before you complete the setup. Simply click Finish Later to close the Quicken Guided Setup window and perform the financial tasks you want. For example, if you want to enter some checks you've written, see "Recording Checks" on page 103. When you're ready to continue, choose Tools → Quicken Guided Setup and you'll be back where you left off.

Setting up cash flow accounts

If you click Cash Flow underneath Add Accounts, you'll see the "Add cash flow accounts" screen. The types of accounts you add on this screen all relate to spending and saving money—checking, savings, credit cards, and, of course, cash. To the right of the type of account you want to start with, click the Add Account button, as shown in Figure 1-5.

Note: The Quicken Credit Card account has *two* Add buttons (Figure 1-5). If you already use a Quicken credit card, click Add Account to create an account in your data file. Click Apply Now only if you want to succumb to Intuit's marketing ploy and apply for its credit card.

After you click the Add Account button, a Quicken Account Setup dialog box appears, which is the very same dialog box you see if you create an account without the Guided Setup's help. You can see what it looks like in Figure 1-6.

The setup tool starts by selecting the option to specify the financial institution that holds the account. In the text box, type the name of the bank. For example,

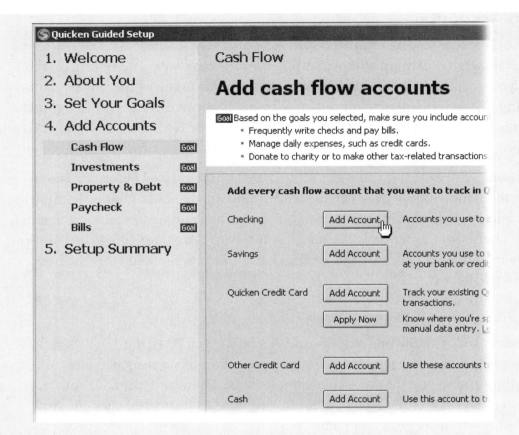

Figure 1-5. All cash flow accounts have something to do with spending and saving money, but Quicken provides different types of cash accounts, since they each work a bit differently. You can read the full descriptions of each on page 56.

the name of the bank where your checking account is, or the bank that issued your Visa card. As you type, Quicken automatically selects the closest matching name from its list of participating financial institutions. For example, by the time you've typed *citi*, Quicken displays Citibank. (On the other hand, if your savings are stuffed in your mattress, you can choose the "This account is not held at a financial institution" option.)

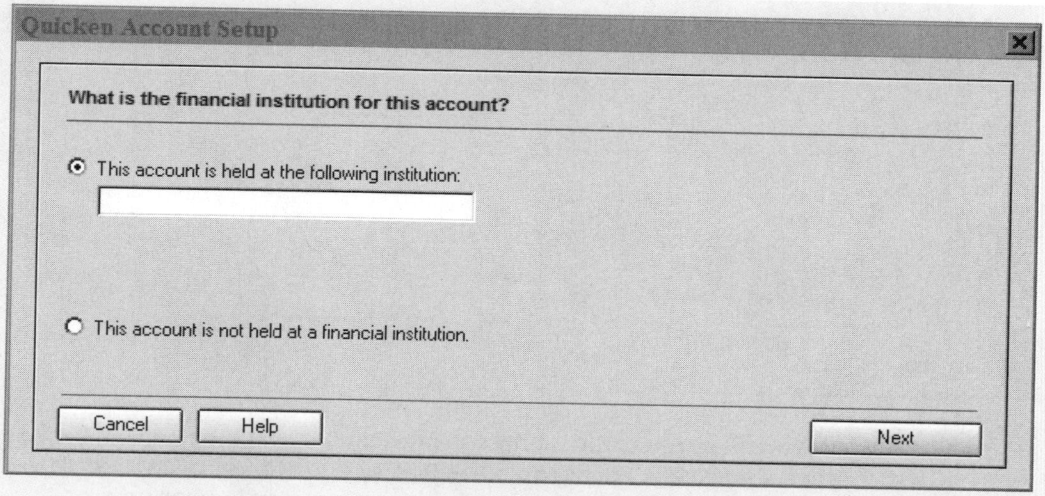

Quicken Account Setup ☒

What is the financial institution for this account?

⊙ This account is held at the following institution:

○ This account is not held at a financial institution.

| Cancel | Help | | Next |

Figure 1-6. The first thing you specify when you create an account is the financial institution where it resides.

Once you've selected your bank, click Next. Then continue to choose options and answer questions, clicking Next to move to the next bit of information required. If you need help, the entire process is described in detail on pages 62–68 in Chapter 2. When you click Done, Quicken creates the account and adds it to the list at the bottom of the screen, as illustrated in Figure 1-7.

Tip: If you don't have balance information handy, or can't decide about some account details right now, you can edit these items at any time. See page 68.

Setting up investment accounts

Underneath the Add Accounts step, click Investments to add brokerage, retirement, and mutual fund accounts to your data file. The "Add investment accounts" screen contains buttons for adding brokerage accounts, IRA or Keogh accounts, 401(k) or 403(b) accounts, and single mutual fund accounts.

Spending & Savings Accounts		
Account	Financial Institution	Ending Balance
Spending		
InterestChecking	Citibank	1,000.00 Edit Delete
Jeff's Cash		26.50 Edit Delete
Marsha's Cash		52.00 Edit Delete
Savings		
CitiSavings	Citibank	512.97 Edit Delete
ING Savings	ING DIRECT	12,103.45 Edit Delete

Credit Card Accounts					
Account	Financial Institution	Credit Limit	Available	Balance	
Bank One Credit Card	Bank One	3,000.00	2,840.98	-159.02	Edit Delete

Exit Setup   Finish Later   Watch Quicken Tour   ◀ Previous Step   Next Step ▶

Figure 1-7. Mistakes are easy to correct in the list of accounts at the bottom of the screen. On the right side of the account row, click Edit to open the Account Details dialog box. Click Delete to remove an account. To change an ever-increasing credit limit, in the Credit Limit column, click the hyperlink showing your current credit limit and, in the dialog box that appears, type the new limit.

In a process similar to adding cash flow accounts, you click an Add Account button to open the Quicken Account Setup dialog box. The first screen looks like the one in Figure 1-6, but after that, you'll see screens with specific investment account options. No request for an ending balance is a pleasant surprise, but you're not off the hook. As you'll discover in Chapter 9, you specify the ending balance for an investment account later when you add securities. You'll find the entire setup process described on pages 308–314.

When you're done, click Done. The Quicken Account Setup dialog box closes and, in Quicken Guided Setup, your new account appears in the list of investment accounts at the bottom of the "Add investment accounts" screen.

Setting up accounts for what you own and what you owe

Also on the Add Accounts setup screen, click Property & Debt to add accounts for your assets and loans. The next screen contains buttons for adding asset accounts for houses, cars, and other items of value (jewelry, Beanie Babies, or the odd Renoir), just like the one in Figure 5-3 (page 187). You can set up these accounts to track their value over time, as you buy more Beanie Babies or make improvements on your home, for example. Quicken uses this information to calculate your net worth.

The fourth option on this screen is a bit different from the other three. It's designed to track not how much you own but how much you *owe*. While assets add to your net worth, liabilities are in the *minus* column.

Asset and liability accounts work together with your cash flow accounts, so when you write a check for a loan payment, Quicken lets you immediately see a reduction in the amount you owe and an increase in the equity you own. For example, most people write checks from their checking accounts to pay off their loans. If you track your loans in Quicken, one transaction deducts the money from your checking account *and* shows that your loan balance goes down as well. If you use Quicken to calculate your net worth, you'll often find you have *both* an asset and a liability account for the same piece of property or the same vehicle. (However, you can own an asset without a loan or borrow money without having a corresponding asset, as in the case of a student loan for college.)

If you start by adding a house or car, the Guided Setup creates an account for the asset. But that's not all. If you borrowed money to buy the asset, the setup can keep going and take you right through the process of setting up the corresponding liability account and even setting up your regularly scheduled loan payment. If setting up the asset account was enough work for the day, in the Quicken Account Setup dialog box, click Cancel. When you're ready to continue setting up asset and liability accounts, the complete instructions are on page 183.

When you're done setting up accounts for the time being, in the list of steps on the left, click Paycheck.

Setting up your paycheck

Setting up your paycheck in the Guided Setup doesn't actually create any additional accounts. It does, however, set up a scheduled transaction with as much detail about your paycheck deductions as you can bear to specify. Underneath the Add Accounts step, click Paycheck to launch the Paycheck Setup tool, described in detail in Chapter 4 on pages 168–172. If your most recent pay stub isn't clutched in your hand at the moment, you can also click Next Step to move on to setting up the bills you pay.

Setting up bills to pay

If you pay bills—and who doesn't—click Bills under the Add Accounts category. Quicken offers an incredibly handy feature, called a *scheduled transaction* that reminds you to pay your recurring bills. The "Add bills" screen offers a Quicken Bill Pay button. Click it if you've signed up to part with your money electronically using this service. Quicken not only remembers that the bill is due, but pays it for you, based on the instructions you give here. (Full details on setting up Online Bill Pay are in Chapter 6.)

If you simply want Quicken to give you a friendly reminder to write paper checks, or you use a different online bill paying service, click Add Bills Manually. Figure 1-8 shows how easy it is to schedule your bills, but for further instruction, see pages 162–168 in Chapter 4.

Click OK when you're done adding bills. The Set Up Bills dialog box closes and you can click Setup Summary in the step list on the left to survey how much of the setup you've completed.

Finishing Up the Guided Setup

When you're done setting up Quicken (or getting antsy to do something else), click Exit Setup to close the Guided Setup tool. On the other hand, if you've dutifully clicked Next Step on each Guided Setup screen, you reach Setup Summary nirvana. As shown in Figure 1-9, the final screen shows every account you've created, the paychecks you've set up, and the bills you've created for regular payment. Click Done and vigorously congratulate yourself.

Set Up Bills

Enter Your Recurring Bill Information

Edit your recurring bills so Quicken can remind you when they are coming due. If the amount varies each time, enter zero and Quicken will prompt you for the correct amount before entering it into your account register.

Payee	Account	Category	Amount	Frequency	Next Date
Exciting Electric	InterestChecking	Utilities:Gas & Electric	125.00	Monthly	3/14/2006
Divine Dumpster	InterestChecking	Utilities:Garbage & Re...	60.00	Quarterly	3/7/2006
Talk It Up	InterestChecking	Utilities:Telephone	29.95	Monthly	3/28/2006
Citibank	InterestChecking	Bank Charge	9.95	Monthly	3/2/2006
ASPCA	InterestChecking	Charity	15.00	Monthly	3/23/2006
Hartford	InterestChecking				5/15/2006
Cingular	InterestChecking			ly	4/15/2006
Bank One	InterestChecking			ly	3/1/2006

Drop-down menu items:
Fuel
Insurance
Loan
Registration
Service
Bank Charge   Expense
Business   Expense
Depreciation
Cash   Expense
Charity   Expense

[New]   [Delete]

Figure 1-8. For most recurring bills, you can type in all the particulars: the payee, the account you use to pay the bill, the category, the amount, how often you pay the bill, and when it's due next. Except for the amount, each field includes a drop-down menu of likely choices, including the list of categories in your data file. You'll learn much more about categories in Chapter 2.

A Quick Guide to Quicken Preferences

Quicken doesn't give you as much control over its behavior as some other programs. You won't find anything like the vast array of options in Microsoft Word, for example. Some of Quicken's preferences make tiny changes barely worth noticing, while others—like Backup—just might save your sanity. This section describes the preferences you're most likely to change and why.

To open the Quicken Preferences dialog box, choose Edit → Preferences and then choose Quicken Program. These preferences determine Quicken's basic

Setup Summary

Review your data

Review each section to make sure you have the accounts, bills, and paychecks you want.

To add additional items, click the appropriate Add button in the lower-left corner of each section. When you have finished adding accounts, bills, and paychecks, click Done to go to Quicken.

Property & Debt Accounts

Account	Ending Balance		
Property (Assets)			
02 Forerunner	22,500.00	Edit	Delete
63 Mustang	-5,000.00	Edit	Delete
Flex Spending MM	325.00	Edit	Delete
House	343,950.00	Edit	Delete
Debt (Liabilities)			
02 Forerunner Loan	-19,628.42	Edit	Delete
Adjustable rate Loan	-127,572.83	Edit	Delete
House Loan	-122,908.66	Edit	Delete

[Add Account]

Set Up Paycheck

Name	Amount	Frequency	Year To Date Amount		
Medical Miracle	2,000.00	Every two weeks	6,000.00	Edit	Delete
O'Reilly	2,000.00	Every two weeks	6,000.00	Edit	Delete

[Add Paycheck]

Bills and Scheduled Transactions

Date	Status	Name/Payee	Amount	Web	Action		
Bills							
3/1/2006	Overdue!	Bank One	-467.41		Enter	Edit	Skip
3/2/2006	Overdue!	Citibank	-9.95		Enter	Edit	Skip

[◀ Previous Step] [Done]

Figure 1-9. The Setup Summary screen lets you bask in the glory of your achievement (or to put it more prosaically, "Review your data"). You'll have to scroll down to see all the accounts, paychecks, and bill payments you've set up.

behavior and appearance, so you might find yourself drawn back from time to time to make adjustments as your experience grows and your needs change.

Note: When you choose Edit → Preferences, you'll see two other menu choices: Customize Online Updates and Internet Connection Setup. Both of these categories let you control how Quicken handles your online transactions. See Chapter 6 for the details.

Startup

The Startup preference tells Quicken what to display when you first launch the program. Out of the box, the program displays Quicken Home, a financial shopping mall for all your Quicken tasks. To choose a different view, or even a single account, choose Startup. In the "On startup open to" drop-down menu, choose the Quicken Center or account you'd rather see. For example, if you use Quicken as a checkbook, choose your checking account or Cash Flow Center to see checking, saving, and credit card accounts and options.

Note: Before you turn off Quicken Home, note that you can customize it to show only what you want to see. Learn how in Online Appendix F.

Setup

The Setup category is home to settings that control Quicken's basic appearance, keyboard shortcuts, and sounds, shown in Figure 1-10. Since your preferences for keyboard shortcuts and your noise tolerance are individual matters, this panel can have a big impact on your Quicken experience.

Turn on Quicken sounds

If your PC or laptop has speakers, you can't help but notice the odd noises that erupt as you use Quicken. If you prefer to listen to Brandenburg concertos on your stereo without Quicken's percussion section, turn off the "Turn on Quicken sounds" checkbox, as illustrated in Figure 1-10.

Account Bar display

You can display the handy Account Bar, shown in Figure 1-11, on the left or right side of the Quicken window. If you almost always work in the same account

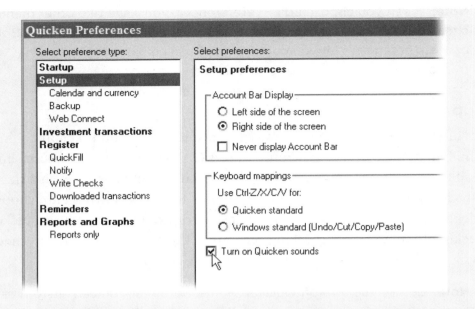

Figure 1-10. If you can't stand the beeps, burps, and ka-chings of Quicken sounds, join the crowd and turn off the "Turn on Quicken sounds" checkbox (indicated by cursor).

(or can't afford to give up any screen real estate), hide the Account Bar by turning on the "Never display Account Bar" checkbox.

Tip: When the Account Bar isn't showing, you can always open an account from the Quicken menu bar. For example, to open an investing account, choose Investing → Investing Accounts and then, on the submenu, choose the account name.

Keyboard mappings

If you're a speed demon with Windows programs, you've probably burned Ctrl+Z, Ctrl+X, Ctrl+C, and Ctrl+V into your muscle memory. But undo, cut, copy, and paste don't come up much in Quicken activities, so the program automatically chooses the "Quicken standard" setting to assign different meanings to

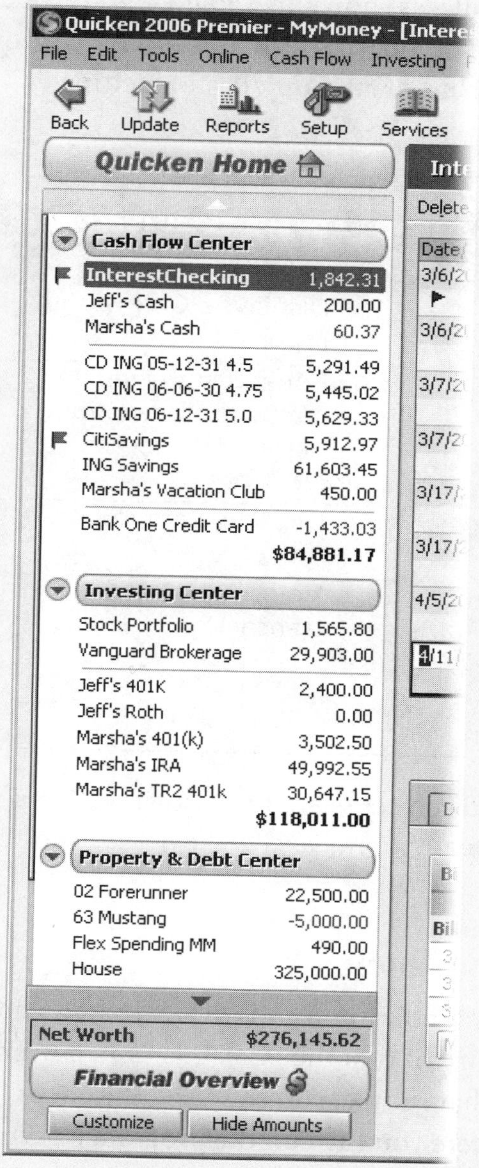

Figure 1-11. This is the Account Bar. Many consider it the fastest way to get to any account. It lists all of your accounts in one convenient panel and a quick click of any account opens its register.

these keyboard shortcuts, as shown in Table 1-1. If the idea of two different meanings for the same keyboard shortcut is more than you can bear, choose the "Windows standard (Undo/Cut/Copy/Paste)" setting.

Table 1-1. Quicken and Windows Keyboard Mappings

Keyboard shortcut	WINDOWS COMMAND	WHAT IT DOES IN QUICKEN	QUICKEN COMMAND
Ctrl+Z	Undo	Displays a QuickZoom report	Double-click a report entry
Ctrl+X	Cut	For active transaction, jumps to transaction in transfer account	Right-click transfer and, on shortcut menu, choose "Go to matching transfer"
Ctrl+C	Copy	Displays Category List	Tools → Category List
Ctrl+V	Paste	Voids active transaction	Right-click transaction and, on shortcut menu, choose "Void transaction(s)"

Tip: Keyboard shortcuts are the fastest way to perform their corresponding tasks. To learn more Quicken keyboard shortcuts, see Appendix C.

Calendar and Currency

If your year begins in January and ends in December, and you deal with only U.S. dollars, you can skip right past the "Calendar and currency" preferences. But if your life is just not that simple, you can tell Quicken to follow your fiscal year. This panel is also where you turn on the program's currency exchange feature.

▶ **Working calendar.** Quicken sets the "Calendar year" option automatically. If you want to work with a fiscal year (for example, to track a home-based business), choose the "Fiscal year" option and choose the month in which your fiscal year begins.

Note: If you track your personal finances and a small business, it's wise to create separate data files for your home and business finances. That way, you can set your personal data file to use a calendar year and the business data file to use the company's fiscal year.

▶ **Multicurrency support.** If your income is in Euros rather than U.S. dollars or you travel the world spending money in dozens of local currencies, turn on the "Multicurrency support" checkbox. Quicken sets the currency for all your current transactions to the currency you've chosen in Windows' Regional and Language Options control panel (see the box on page 44).

Backup

If you use your computer for more than managing your money, you probably run backup software, like Windows Backup, to protect *all* of your data. One backup procedure can capture letters to your mom, your Quicken data file, and pictures of your dog.

So why should you care about Quicken's backup preferences? For one thing, your Quicken data file may change more often than your other information. Unless you're disciplined about running a regular backup procedure, Quicken's backups provide extra insurance for your finances. Likewise, if you often mutter "I should really back up my data today" but rarely follow through, Quicken's backup reminders could be the nudge you need.

Tip: Another reason you might fall to your knees in gratitude for Quicken backup copies is when you've forgotten the new password you recently set. As long as at least *one* of the Quicken backup copies doesn't have the new password assigned, you can open *that* data file, recreate the missing transactions, and you're set. Oh yeah, and assign a new password that you'll be able to *remember*.

Quicken's backup preferences control how often the program's automatic backup (page 92) runs and how many backup copies it keeps. The following are some guidelines for setting these preferences.

Dollars and Dinero

The Regional and Language Options in Windows XP control the language the operating system uses, as well as number formats, currency, times, and dates. Currency is the only setting here that affects your work in Quicken. In fact, you *must* set your local currency in Windows XP for it to appear correctly in Quicken. Begin the process by choosing Start → Settings → Control Panel → "Regional and Language Options," which opens the "Regional and Language Options" dialog box.

In the Regional Options tab, next to the box that shows your home language (and country), click Customize. When the Customize Regional Options dialog box opens, click the Currency tab. You can set your preferred currency symbol, formatting for positive and negative numbers, decimal-point style, and whether you use a period or comma to separate thousands

and millions. Click OK to close all of the dialog boxes when you're done.

Quicken uses these control panel settings to display monetary amounts. However, you can assign a different currency to any transaction by typing the amount spent or received *in the foreign currency*. First, turn on Quicken's multicurrency support, as described on page 43. Then, before you record the transaction, Choose Tools → Currency List. In the Currency List window, choose the foreign currency and click Use. Quicken converts the value you typed to the currency of the account. To learn how to work with multiple currencies, press F1 to open Quicken Help. Click the Index tab and in the keyword text box, type *multiple currencies* to display the "Using multiple currencies in Quicken" help topic.

▶ **Remind after running Quicken _ times.** When you type a number in this box, Quicken reminds you to back up your data file after you've launched Quicken that number of times. If you tend to slog through marathon Quicken sessions entering dozens of transactions, set the reminder to *1*.

If only one or two transactions dribble in each time you run Quicken, set this preference to 3 or higher. You still won't spend much time recreating lost transactions, but you'll have backups that span a longer timeframe.

▶ **Maximum number of copies.** Quicken automatically saves several copies of the backups it creates on your hard disk, so you can retrieve lost data from several sessions past. Quicken sets this preference to 5—the middle ground between safety and disk space conservation. To recover older files (and if you've got disk space to spare), choose a higher number (up to 9). To use less disk space, choose a number as low as 1. See page 95 to learn where Quicken stores these backups and how it cycles through the copies.

▶ **Warn before overwriting old files.** Quicken turns on this checkbox automatically to make sure you don't accidentally overwrite backup files that you want to keep. This preference applies to the backups you tell Quicken to make (not the ones it makes automatically each week). Turn it off if you're satisfied that your Quicken and Windows backup routines are keeping your data safe and want Quicken to stop asking.

Investment Transactions

Investment transaction preferences are a new addition to Quicken. These settings give you more control over how your investment register looks onscreen.

▶ **List display.** Choose One Line or Two Line in the drop-down menu to specify whether Quicken shows one or two lines in the investment register. If you prefer to conserve screen space, choose One Line. With this setting, Quicken shows each transaction on one line—except the currently selected one, which expands to two lines for better visibility.

▶ **Sort choice.** In this drop-down menu, you can choose Ascending Date or Descending Date to show your investment transactions from earliest to most recent or vice versa. If you add new transactions frequently, stick with Ascending Date, which the program chooses automatically. That way, your new transactions appear at the bottom of the list as you add them.

- **Show hidden transactions.** Quicken leaves this checkbox turned off initially, but you can turn it on if you want to see placeholder transactions or balance adjustments. If you notice an error and can't seem to find its source, turning on this checkbox to show all transactions can help you find the problem.

Register

Unlike your paper check register, you can change how the Quicken register looks and behaves. Because entering transactions in registers is such a big part of using Quicken, it pays to set up the Register preferences to your liking. Most of these options are a matter of taste, but a few are worth special mention because they have a direct effect on your working speed.

- **Remove memorized payees not used in last _ months.** The memorized payees feature alone is almost worth Quicken's purchase price (see "Managing Memorized Payees" in Chapter 4). As soon as you type a memorized payee name in a transaction, Quicken fills in the amount, category, and memo for you. Unfortunately, as you buy stuff from more companies, the Memorized Payee list can bloat bigger than the aunt who super-sizes all her meals, ultimately slowing down your data entry. The more names in the Memorized Payee list, the more characters you have to type before Quicken finds the matching payee, *and* the more names you must slog through in the payee drop-down menu.

  To tell Quicken to remove companies you haven't purchased from in the last year from your Memorized Payee List, turn on this checkbox and type *12* in the box, as shown in Figure 1-12.

- **Maximize my register view.** Turning on this checkbox (or pressing F11 when a register is visible) hides the Account Bar and fills the Quicken main window with the register. As a result, the register fields get larger, so you can see more payee name and memo information.

Quicken Preferences

Select preference type:

- **Startup**
- **Setup**
  - Calendar and currency
  - Backup
  - Web Connect
- **Investment transactions**
- **Register**
  - QuickFill
  - Notify
  - Write Checks
  - Downloaded transactions
- **Reminders**
- **Reports and Graphs**
  - Reports only

Select preferences:

Register preferences

Register fields
- ☑ Show Date in first column
- ☐ Show Memo before Category

Data entry
- ☐ Automatically enter split data
- ☑ Use automatic categorization
- ☐ Automatically place decimal point

Register appearance
- ☑ Show transaction toolbar
  - ☑ Show attachment button
  - ☑ Show rate payee button
- ☑ Gray reconciled transactions
- ☐ Maximize my register view
- ☑ Show rate payee link

[Fonts...]
[Colors...]

- ☑ Remove memorized payees not used in last [12] months
- ☐ Keep register filters after Quicken closes

Figure 1-12. For a leaner list, choose a lower number of months than the 12 months shown here. To keep payees around longer, choose a higher number.

Note: Maximizing the register view makes the fields larger, but the *typeface* remains the same size. Unfortunately for baby boomers, there isn't a way to change the font size in Quicken. But there are quite a few things you can do in Windows to make text easier to read onscreen: Choose Start → Control Panel → Display tab or Start → Control Panel → Accessibility Options. Consult *Windows XP for Starters: The Missing Manual* by David Pogue for more information on accessibility.

▶ **Use automatic categorization.** Quicken turns this preference on initially, with good reason. It tells the program to fill in the transaction category automatically if the payee you type matches a company in the Quicken database, which is, of course, likely to be the correct category. Otherwise, you'd have to remember to choose a category manually every time.

QuickFill

QuickFill (page 102) is Quicken's attempt to speed up your data entry. Most of the time, it works surprisingly well. If you approve of Quicken's fill-in assistance, you can bypass this panel altogether. But if transactions seem to take on a life of their own during data entry, turn off this checkbox to rein in QuickFill's assistance:

▶ **Automatically memorize new payees.** Quicken comes with this checkbox turned on, which tells the program to save new payees you use in transactions to the Memorized Payee List. Although this setting ensures that the next transaction for a payee fills in automatically, it can lead to overpopulation, too. And then there are the vendors you'd rather not memorize—like the diner that gave you food poisoning. To decide which payees to add to the Memorized Payee List, turn off this checkbox.

As if you need more justification to turn off this checkbox, consider that Quicken stops memorizing new payees automatically once your Memorized Payee List hits 2,000 entries. The automatic memorization gunks up the list with payees you don't want and then may not memorize payees you *do* want.

 Tip: If you turn off automatic memorization, you can memorize a payee as you add a transaction by pressing Ctrl+M.

Notify

The Notify preferences tell Quicken when to warn or remind you about potential problems as you work. Here are the settings and when you may want to turn them on or off:

▶ **When entering out-of-date transactions.** This notification warns you when you type a date that is more than twelve months away from today's date. It's a godsend those first few weeks (or months) or every year, before you get used to typing the new year in dates.

- **Before changing existing transactions.** This option warns you when you try to save an existing transaction that you've changed. If you know your way around Quicken and often change existing transactions (say, to add memos to downloaded transactions), turn *off* this checkbox to eliminate the frequent interruptions.

- **When entering uncategorized transactions.** Almost every transaction should have a category. This notification simply reminds you to do the right thing and supply one. Don't turn it off.

- **To run a reconcile report after reconcile.** You can turn off this checkbox without a trace of guilt. Reconcile reports tell you mostly what you already know: which transactions have cleared, which haven't, and whether there's a discrepancy between your and your bank's records. If you've had to do some fancy footwork to reconcile your checking account one month, you can document that with a reconciliation report by choosing Reports → Cash Flow → Reconciliation.

- **Warn if a check number is reused.** About the only time you'll use the same check number is when you're renumbering checks that you entered out of order. Keep this checkbox turned on to receive well-deserved warnings when you type a check number you've already written.

Write Checks

The Write Checks preferences control the appearance of checks you write through the Write Checks window and subsequently print. If you write your paper checks by hand, skip this section altogether. This section describes the few preferences you might want to change and why.

- **Allow entry of extra message on check.** If the company you're paying wants you to include your account or member number, you can type that information in the Write Checks window. If you turn on this checkbox, Quicken prints the message on the check.

- **Change date of checks to date when printed.** Quicken initially turns off this checkbox, which means that the date on the check is the date that you type in the Write Checks window, regardless of when you print the check. If your budget is tight and you consider post-dating checks a critical cash management technique, this setting is ideal. On the contrary, if you're a stickler for accuracy, turn this option off so checks always show the exact date you print them.

Downloaded Transactions

When you download transactions from your bank or credit card carrier into Quicken, you're at the mercy of somebody's (or more likely, some machine's) bizarre naming schemes. Your first instinct is to pounce on the keyboard and rename the transactions to something that will actually help you remember what you did or bought. Quicken's ready to help: It automatically creates *renaming rules* by "watching" you edit the transactions. The next time you download, the program then substitutes your preferred payee names for you.

For example, perhaps you stopped at 40 different Texaco gas stations on a cross-country vacation, and each downloaded charge shows "Texaco" followed a bunch of cryptic numbers. If all you care about is that you spent that money on gas, you simply replace "Texaco 140562789" with "Gas." Quicken sets its "Downloaded transactions" preferences to create renaming rules automatically when you change a payee name, and tells you it's doing so.

Here's what the "Downloaded transactions" preferences do:

- **Apply renaming rules to downloaded transactions.** Quicken automatically turns on this checkbox, which applies existing renaming rules to transactions as you download them. As in the above example, when you download a Texaco fill-up, Quicken changes the payee name to "Gas."

- **Automatically create rules when manually renaming.** Quicken comes with renaming rules turned on. Turning *off* this checkbox blocks Quicken from creating rules based on your edits, so that when you edit a transaction, you're only editing that *one* transaction.

- **Don't display a message when renaming.** This checkbox is initially turned off, so you'll see a message any time Quicken renames a payee. Turn this checkbox off to tell Quicken to rename payees without notifying you.

 Note: Technically, renaming rules create *aliases* for the seemingly infinite number of payee names that come with downloaded transactions. In software as in real life, an alias is simply a substitute name.

Reminders

The one preference in this category tells Quicken which calendar notes you want to see. For example, you can change the "Show calendar notes for" preference to "Next 14 days" to see your notes to yourself about what's coming up in the next two weeks. Or, if you're at the other end of the dependability spectrum, change it to "Last week" to see tasks you've missed.

Reports and Graphs

Quicken wouldn't be much good if it couldn't produce a list of your tax-deductible expenses or a pie chart showing your investment diversification. In this category of preferences, you can specify the data range for reports and graphs you generate and what to do when you customize a report. Here are the options and why you may want to adjust them:

- **Default date range.** In the Default date range drop-down menu, choose the period that you use most often in reports; for example, "Year to date" or "Current month."

- **Default comparison date range.** For reports that compare two time periods, choose the period for the comparison date range. For example, if you set the Default date range to Current Year, set this preference to Last Year to compare the two years.

- **Customizing reports and graphs.** If you frequently customize reports, you can choose options to either create new reports and graphs from the customized report or save the customizations to the current report or graph.

Customize report/graph before creating. If you tweak every report you produce, turn on this checkbox to open the Customize dialog box immediately when you choose a report from the Reports menu. (See Chapter 10 for the full story on Quicken's reports and graphs.)

Reports Only

These preferences control the appearance of reports, not graphs, and are mostly innocuous. You may want to tinker with the following settings:

▶ **Use color in report.** If you prefer to see reports in black and white, turn off this checkbox. However, keeping it turned on shows any shortfalls or investment losses in red to catch your attention.

▶ **Remind me to save reports.** If you've customized every report to meet your needs, you probably don't need a reminder to save reports and can turn this checkbox off.

▶ **Decimal places for prices and shares.** Quicken sets this preference to 3. If you reinvest dividends, you're likely to own infinitesimally small fractions of shares. The best setting for this preference is the number of decimal places for the most exacting of your financial institutions. For example, if your Vanguard IRA reports prices and shares to six decimal places, type 6 in the box.

CHAPTER 2: ACCOUNTS AND CATEGORIES

- ▶ How Accounts and Categories Work
- ▶ Types of Accounts
- ▶ Creating Cash Flow Accounts
- ▶ Editing Account Information
- ▶ Hiding Closed Accounts
- ▶ Categories
- ▶ Customizing Categories

Quicken abounds with tools to help you plan, track, and analyze your finances. If you use the Quicken Guided Setup as described in Chapter 1, it creates an assortment of accounts and categories for you. That arrangement's a mere starting point, though.

This chapter defines Quicken's various account types and shows you how to set up new accounts, as well as manage existing ones. You'll also learn how to organize your finances by category, so you can see where your money's coming from and what you're spending it on.

Armed with this knowledge, you can make changes to your data file as your financial needs change over time. For example, whenever you switch banks, succumb to a fabulous credit card offer, or take out a home equity loan to get your mobile dog-grooming business going, you'll need a new account. Or say you get married and need new accounts and categories to track your husband's salary, taxes, and all those salon facials.

Tip: Sometimes, the arrival of a new business or person in your life means you need to create an additional data file as well. See the box on page 55.

How Accounts and Categories Work

As you learned in the previous chapter, an *account* in Quicken corresponds to an account you have at a financial institution, like a checking account at a bank, a savings account at a credit union, a Roth IRA at a brokerage, and so on. Quicken also lets you give each transaction a *category*, which identifies it as belonging to an area of your financial life. Categories like Groceries, Auto Insurance, and Poker Winnings help you see where your money is going (or coming from). Every time you record a deposit, check, or credit card charge, you can assign it a category.

To get a handle on the difference between accounts and categories, consider how a married couple uses Quicken:

▶ Marsha uses one Quicken data file to manage both her and her husband Jeff's finances.

Data Files

In the first chapter, you learned that data files are where Quicken stores all the information about your finances: bank, investment, and other accounts and all the transactions in them. If you take on managing someone else's money with Quicken, the first decision is whether you need another Quicken data file. And the answer is, "It depends."

Separate tax returns are often a big hint that you should create a separate data file for Party Number Two. For example, suppose you manage your parents' money or keep the books for a local nonprofit organization. Their money isn't your money, and you prepare separate tax returns. Gunking up your Quicken data file with someone else's income and tax deductions is just asking for trouble. The safe route is to create another data file.

Separate tax returns but joint accounts are one exception that may make a single data file the right answer. For example, suppose an unmarried couple files separate tax returns, but pools their money as if they've been married for years. They have a mixture of joint and individual accounts, from joint checking and taxable investment accounts to their individual 401(k)s and IRAs. Despite the glaring absence of a marriage certificate, these folks look a lot like spouses, which makes one data file the easiest approach. (As you'll learn in this chapter, Quicken provides categories for each spouse for tracking tax-related deductions and other spousal spending.)

Although it's easy to transfer funds between accounts in the same data file, you can't transfer funds from an account in one data file to an account in a *different* data file. For example, if you transfer money between your personal and business checking accounts and use two separate data files, you must create a check transaction in one checking account to remove the funds. Then, in the other checking account, you create a deposit. (If you use Quicken Home & Business edition, you can create one data file for your personal records and a second for your business.)

▶ She and Jeff have a checking account at Citibank, which she manages with a checking account in Quicken.

Figure 2-1 demonstrates how checks that Marsha writes in Quicken change the checking account balance and track how the couple spends money.

Types of Accounts

As complicated as personal finances can be in the 21st century, Quicken has an account type for every situation. When you create an account in Quicken, you must choose from the dozen types that the program offers. Quicken further divides each account type into different types of financial activities, as the Account Bar in Figure 2-2 illustrates. This section describes the types of accounts you can create in Quicken and what you use them for.

Cash Flow Accounts

Cash flow accounts deal with the money that flows into and out of your life—checks, paycheck deposits, credit card charges, or the wadded-up bills you hand to the toll taker on the turnpike. Each type of cash flow account offers slightly different features, based on how you use it. For example, Checking and Savings account registers include a Num field for entering a check number. Credit Card and Cash account registers omit this field, because transactions aren't typically numbered.

Here's Quicken's selection of cash flow accounts.

- **Checking.** Use this type of account to track your real-world checking accounts.

- **Savings.** This type of account works for real-world accounts that pay interest on your deposits, including passbook savings accounts, money market accounts, and certificates of deposit. You can also use Savings to track other stockpiles of money that don't pay interest or aren't at a bank.

- **Credit Card.** This account type represents real-world accounts that extend a line of credit to you, including credit cards, charge cards, and other lines of credit. Use this type of account when you can withdraw money (charge) and make payments. (By contrast, the Liability account type discussed on page 61 is designed for loans that you pay back through regularly scheduled payments of principal and interest.)

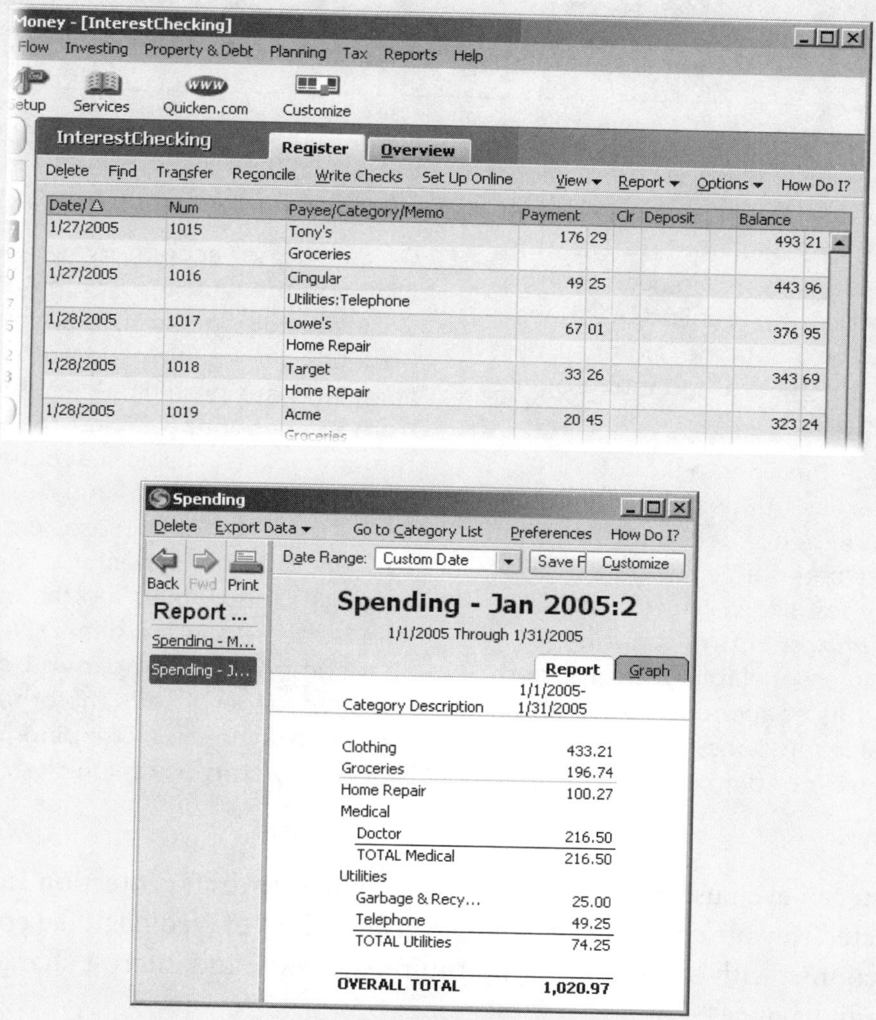

Figure 2-1. Top: As you can see in the checking account register, the checks that Marsha writes reduce the balance in the Quicken checking account. The assigned categories appear below the Payee's name.

Bottom: Marsha can generate a report (see Chapter 10) that uses the categories they assigned to their checks to see how they spent their money.

Accounting Versus Quicken

Bookkeepers, certified public accountants, and other financial professionals may face confusion because Quicken's definition of an account differs from the one they use in the accounting field. Accounting is called that because every flavor of income, expense, asset, and liability gets tossed into a bucket called an account.

In bookkeeping and accounting, expenses like utilities and advertising reside in expense accounts. Income accounts categorize revenue into different types, like services and products. Other aspects of a business appear in asset, liability, equity, and other types of accounts. Accounts at financial institutions, likewise, have their corresponding accounts in book keeping and accounting practice. All the accounts for a business appear in what's known as the *chart of accounts*.

Quicken is not accounting software, although the Quicken Home & Small Business edition can help some small-business owners manage both personal and business finances. If you're used to accounting-style accounts, remember that Quicken accounts are usually accounts at financial institutions. Instead, Quicken uses categories to track different types of income and expenses. You won't find the concept of a *ledger*—as in the general ledger that comprises a company's books—in Quicken, either. That's the other omission that rattles bookkeeping folks when they start using Quicken.

You can even use the Credit Card type for an overdraft protection feature connected to your checking account. Overdraft lines of credit act like credit card accounts, with credit limits, minimum payments, and interest charged on the credit balances.

▸ **Cash.** Use a cash account if you want to track how you spend your money to the penny (or dollar), or to track travel advances you receive. If you write a check to "cash" or withdraw money at the ATM, for example, you can create those transactions as transfers to your cash account. You can then spend the cash any way you like, but the transaction serves as a record of how much cash you're spending. (You can see some creative ways of using this type of system on page 127.)

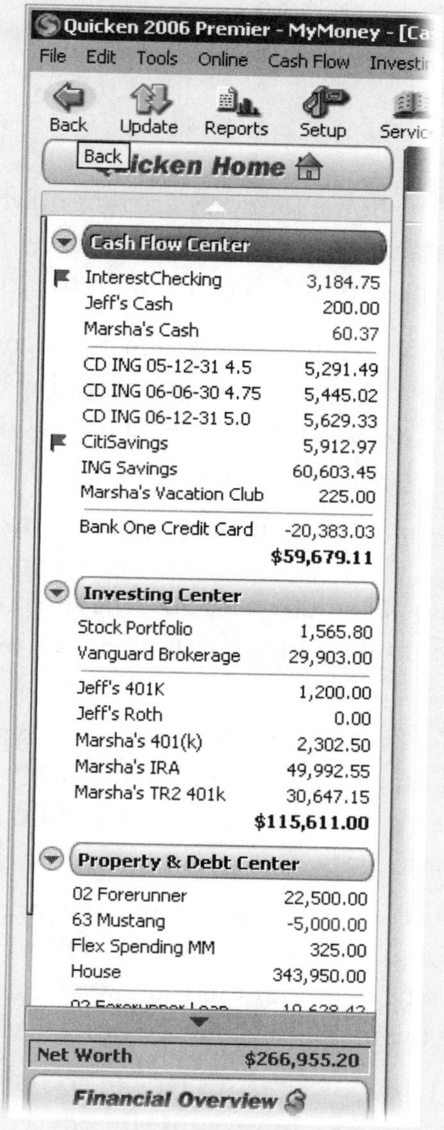

Figure 2-2. In addition to the financial centers—Cash Flow, Investing, and Property & Debt—every account in Quicken breaks down into things you own (assets) or money you owe (liabilities). Assets include money in checking, savings, and investments, as well as more tangible items like your house, car, and first-edition books. Liabilities, which include credit cards and loans of any ilk, show up with negative balances.

Note: You can create up to 512 accounts of each type. If you have that many credit cards, though, even Quicken can't help you get your spending under control.

Investing Accounts

The Investing Center is the home for every account in which you hold securities, whether it's a tax-advantaged 401(k) for your retirement or a taxable brokerage account earmarked for the trip to Tahiti you want for your 20th anniversary.

Creating investing accounts is similar—though not identical—to creating cash flow accounts. To learn the details of creating investing accounts, see "Creating an Investment Account" in Chapter 9. Here's a list of Quicken's investing accounts and when you should use them:

▶ **Brokerage.** Unless your investment account falls into one of the special tax-advantaged categories, this is the investing account type you'll use most of the time. The Brokerage type handles accounts that hold one or more securities, be they stocks, bonds, mutual funds, annuities, real estate investment trusts—you name it.

▶ **IRA, SEP, Keogh.** Use this type of account for any type of individual retirement account (IRA). In addition to traditional IRAs, this type includes Roth, Simplified Employee Pension (SEP), Simple, and Education IRAs. Keogh plans also fall in this category.

▶ **401(k)/403(b).** In the real world, 401(k) and 403(b) accounts are employee-sponsored retirement plans named after the section of the tax code that created them. Use this type of account to track your employer-sponsored accounts (including the matching contributions that your company makes).

▶ **Single Mutual Fund.** In Quicken, this type of account comes with conditions that render it mostly useless. However, if you buy a mutual fund directly from the mutual fund company, don't have a cash balance in the account, and hold only one fund in the account, this type is very simple to use.

Property & Debt Accounts

The Property & Debt category contains accounts for tangible things you own and any money you've borrowed. Asset and liability accounts in Quicken include more fields for information than other type of accounts. If you wish to track your assets and liabilities in Quicken, learn how to create property and debt accounts in the section "Setting Up Asset and Liability Accounts" on page 183.

Meanwhile, here are the account types you can choose from:

▶ **House.** This special type of asset account comes with features unique to property ownership. For example, you can track your original purchase price and value adjustments for improvements you make. When you create a House account, Quicken can help you create the corresponding liability account for your mortgage.

▶ **Vehicle.** This special type of asset account includes balance adjustments for reducing the value of a vehicle due to depreciation. Quicken can help you create the corresponding liability account.

▶ **Asset.** Before you add an asset account for other things you own, consider not only whether the items have value, but also whether you can sell them. For example, your wardrobe may have cost a fortune, but you won't make much selling it. On the contrary, if you own the white sequined costume Elvis wore in Las Vegas, the selling price on eBay could cover that Miami retirement timeshare you've been eyeing. For the Elvis outfit, you may want to create an asset account. (As for your other clothing, you can take digital pictures for insurance purposes and store them on your PC rather than making your wardrobe an asset in Quicken.)

 Note: Loans you make to others are *assets* for you, and liabilities for the people to whom you lent the money.

▶ **Liability.** This account type tracks how much you owe on a loan. For example, when you create an asset account for the $20,000 car you just purchased, Quicken can help set a corresponding liability account for the car loan to track how much you've paid and how much you still owe.

Creating Cash Flow Accounts

The steps for creating any type of banking account aren't difficult. Once you've gone through the steps the first time, you'll get a feel for it and be able to create new accounts much more quickly. This section walks you through the process, start to finish.

To create an account, you must first get to the Quicken Account Setup dialog box, which you can do in any of the following ways:

▶ **The Account Bar.** If you keep the Account Bar visible (as most people do), right-click it and choose "Add new account" from the shortcut menu.

▶ **The Quicken menu bar.** Perhaps the fastest access to the Quicken Account Setup dialog box is from the Quicken window's menu bar. For example, to create a cash flow account, choose Cash Flow → Cash Flow Accounts → Add Account. The Investing and Property & Debt menus have similar entries.

▶ **The Account List.** In the middle of the Account List menu bar, choose Add Account. For the keyboard maven, opening the Account List window requires no more than pressing Ctrl+A. You can also open the Account List window by choosing Tools → Account List.

▶ **Cash Flow Center.** If you launch Quicken displaying the Cash Flow Center, simply click Add Account to create any type of cash flow account in Quicken.

▶ **The File menu.** The fastest (and perhaps least obvious) way to the Account Setup dialog box is choosing File → New. In the "Creating new file" dialog box that opens, choose the New Quicken Account option and click OK

 Tip: If you can't get enough of the Quicken Guided Setup, which you first saw as you were setting up your Quicken environment (page 23), you can instead use that tool to create new accounts.

Creating a Banking Account: Step by Step

Despite a few major differences between types of accounts in the Cash Flow category, you'll find the steps for creating these accounts refreshingly similar. Savings

Where Did My Window Go?

If you click anywhere in the Quicken main window while the Account List window is open, the Account List window disappears. Don't panic. Tucked away at the bottom of the Quicken main window are buttons for each window that Quicken has minimized, as shown here. To restore any of these windows, simply click its button.

For some windows, like the Account List, Category List, and Scheduled Transaction List, reissuing the command to open the window simply restores the window to view. Using their corresponding keyboard short-cuts (Ctrl+A, Ctrl+C, and Ctrl+J)

restores the windows and may be faster than clicking the buttons at the bottom of the program's main window.

For reports, be sure to click the report button at the bottom of the Quicken main window. If you choose Reports and then choose the report name you want, Quicken creates a *second* report window instead of restoring the first one to view.

accounts pay interest, whereas credit card accounts charge interest and limit how much you can spend. Yet, in the Quicken Account Setup dialog box, the fields you must fill in are almost identical.

Here are the steps for creating a checking, savings, credit card, or cash account:

1. **Choose Cash Flow → Cash Flow Accounts → Add Account.**

   The Quicken Account Setup dialog box opens and asks the first of several questions you must answer to create an account: "What is the financial institution for this account?" For banking accounts, online or not, leave "This account is held at the following institution" selected (see the box on page 65).

Choosing the Financial Institution

Do I have to specify a financial institution?

In days of yore (before the Internet, that is), adding the name of a account's financial institution didn't do much. Even now, if an account is a financial institution orphan, like an account you create for the money you hide in your mattress, you should choose the "This account is not held at a financial institution" option.

If you plan to use online services, though, the financial institution is a necessity. Quicken can't download your transactions if it doesn't know which bank to get them from. On the other hand, choosing a financial institution doesn't mean you *must* use its online services, but you can take a few seconds to set it up now in preparation for the future.

2. **For banking accounts, in the text box, begin to type the name of the financial institution.**

   As Figure 2-3 illustrates, Quicken attempts to fill in the name for you.

3. **With the name of the institution in place, click Next.**

   If the financial institution you specified offers online services, you can set those up now, later, or never, as you can see in Figure 2-4. Click Next to either complete or bypass the online setup. Either way, the next screen is "Choose the type of account to add."

    Tip: Chapter 6 explains in detail how to set up accounts for online services.

Quicken Account Setup
What is the financial institution for this account?
This account is held at the following institution:
Fidelity & Trust Bank
Fidelity & Trust Bank
Fidelity Bank
Fidelity Bank - Birmingham, MI
Fidelity Bank & Trust - Baton Rouge,LA
Fidelity Bank- Wichita

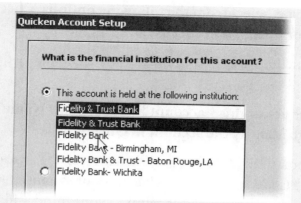

Figure 2-3. Quicken displays the names of all the financial institutions that match the letters you've typed so far. For example, typing *Fid* displays the banks shown here. If you see the one you want, click it. If your bank isn't in Quicken's database, you'll have to type the entire name.

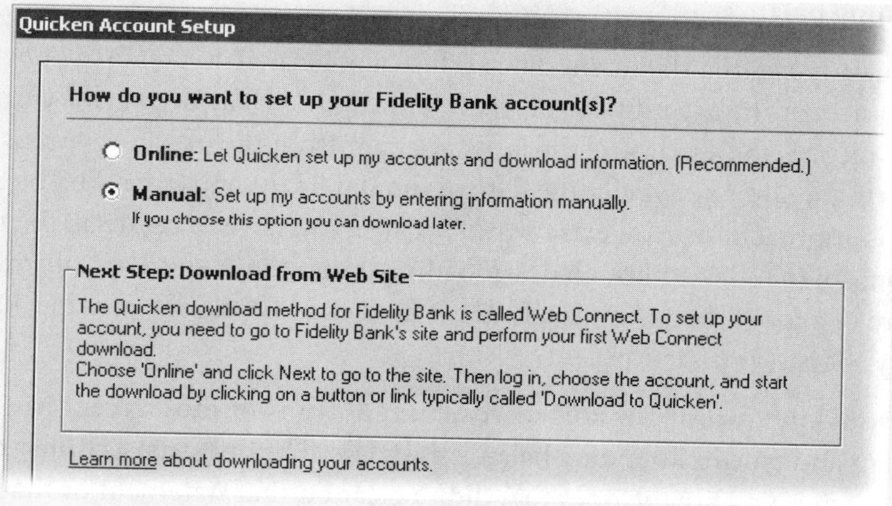

Quicken Account Setup
How do you want to set up your Fidelity Bank account(s)?
Online: Let Quicken set up my accounts and download information. (Recommended.)
Manual: Set up my accounts by entering information manually.
If you choose this option you can download later.
Next Step: Download from Web Site
The Quicken download method for Fidelity Bank is called Web Connect. To set up your account, you need to go to Fidelity Bank's site and perform your first Web Connect download.
Choose 'Online' and click Next to go to the site. Then log in, choose the account, and start the download by clicking on a button or link typically called 'Download to Quicken'.
Learn more about downloading your accounts.

Figure 2-4. Quicken automatically selects the Online option, which initiates online setup and downloading when you click Next (not shown). The text on the screen describes the type of online services your institution offers and describes the basic setup steps. If you've no intention of using online services or simply want to set them up later, choose the Manual option.

4. **For account type, select from the following options: Checking, Savings, Credit Card, or Cash. Then click Next.**

   Each option includes a brief and mostly self-explanatory description of the account type.

5. **In the "Tell us about this _ account" screen, in the Name this account box, type a name to identify the account in Quicken.**

   Quicken automatically fills in a generic name for the type of account you're creating—like *Checking* for a checking account. Change Quicken's entry to a name that clearly identifies the account in your mind—like *ING Savings* or *Marsha's Vacation Club*, for instance. (For more account-naming advice, see the box on page 67.)

   Click Next when you're done.

6. **In the final screen, type the ending date from your bank statement and its ending balance.**

   Quicken uses the statement date and ending balance to create the opening balance for the account. If you want your Quicken file to provide complete tax records for a year, use the last statement from the previous year as your starting point and type in the date of the statement and its ending balance. This approach requires extra work, because you have to create all the transactions up to today, although downloading transactions electronically may take care of a lot of that grunt work. Most financial institutions provide 30 to 60 days of past transactions.

   If you don't care about tax records, hunt down your most recent bank statement and type in its ending balance and date. The only transactions you have to catch up on are the ones that didn't clear on that statement or that you made after its ending date.

What's in an Account Name?

The name you give an account can do much more than identify its financial institution or describe its purpose. Since Quicken lists accounts of each type in alphabetical order, you can get incredible mileage from an organized account naming system. For example, if you name your certificate of deposit (CD) accounts haphazardly, they'll be scattered among your passbook savings accounts, money market accounts, and other savings accounts. But if you have a naming scheme, perhaps beginning each money market account with "MM" and each CD with "CD," accounts of similar types all appear together in lists and menus, as shown here.

But why stop there? For CDs and similar products, you may want to keep an eye on when they mature, so you can research rates and options *before* it's time to reinvest. Quicken account names can include up to 40 alphanumeric characters, so you've got plenty of space to include the financial institution, the maturity date, and the interest rate, such as *CD ING 05-12-31 4.5*. If

you want your CDs to show up in chronological order of maturity, include the year first, then the month, and finally, the day.

In the case of credit cards, it's a good idea to include only the last four digits of your card number, rather than the full number. (You often see this security measure on credit card receipts, for example.) Those last four digits provide enough information for you to identify the account (*Visa 9214*, say), without the risk of your entire account number falling into the wrong hands. It's bad enough if thieves abscond with your computer. You don't want them to gain access to your bank accounts as well.

Note: If the account is brand new, use today's date and *0* (zero) for the ending balance.

7. **Click Done to create the account.**

   Creating an account doesn't fill in every field for an account. For example, you may want to specify the interest rate for a savings or interest checking account. Or you can further organize your records by typing in a contact name and phone number. The next section explains how to add and edit all of this information.

   Figure 2-5 shows a few of the places that your new account appears in Quicken.

Editing Account Information

Once you've created an account, you can edit its details any time you want. You may have set your accounts up perfectly the first time, but the Account Details dialog box is worth a visit, if only to see the many *other* account characteristics you can document. Look at Figure 2-6, for example. In addition to the name and other information you entered when you set up the account, you've got space for comments and a nifty Alerts feature, so you can have Quicken warn you when your balances reach certain levels.

Note: Just about the only thing you can't change about an account is its type. Quicken doesn't let you change a savings account into a checking account, for instance.

To edit the details of an account, use either of the following methods:

▶ In the Account Bar, right-click the name of the account and choose Edit Account from the shortcut menu.

▶ In the Account List window, select an account, and then click Edit in the menu bar.

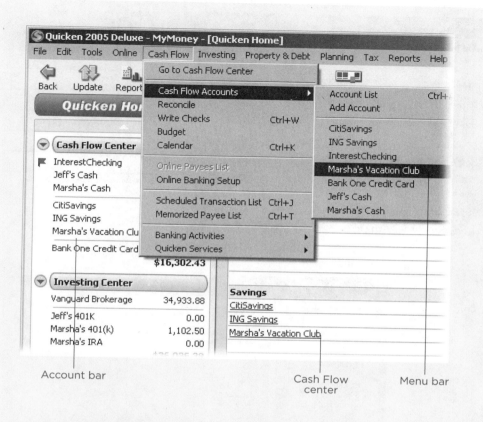

Figure 2-5. When Quicken creates the new account, you can open its register from several places. Here are just a few: the Account bar, the Menu bar, and the appropriate Quicken Center, such as the Cash Flow center.

Note: Investing, asset, and liability accounts have a few fields that are totally different from the ones you see for banking accounts. See Chapter 5 (asset and liability accounts) and Chapter 9 (investing accounts) to learn about them.

Hiding Closed Accounts

Over time, you'll probably close some accounts: CDs mature, you switch banks, or you finally smarten up and move your credit card balance to one with a

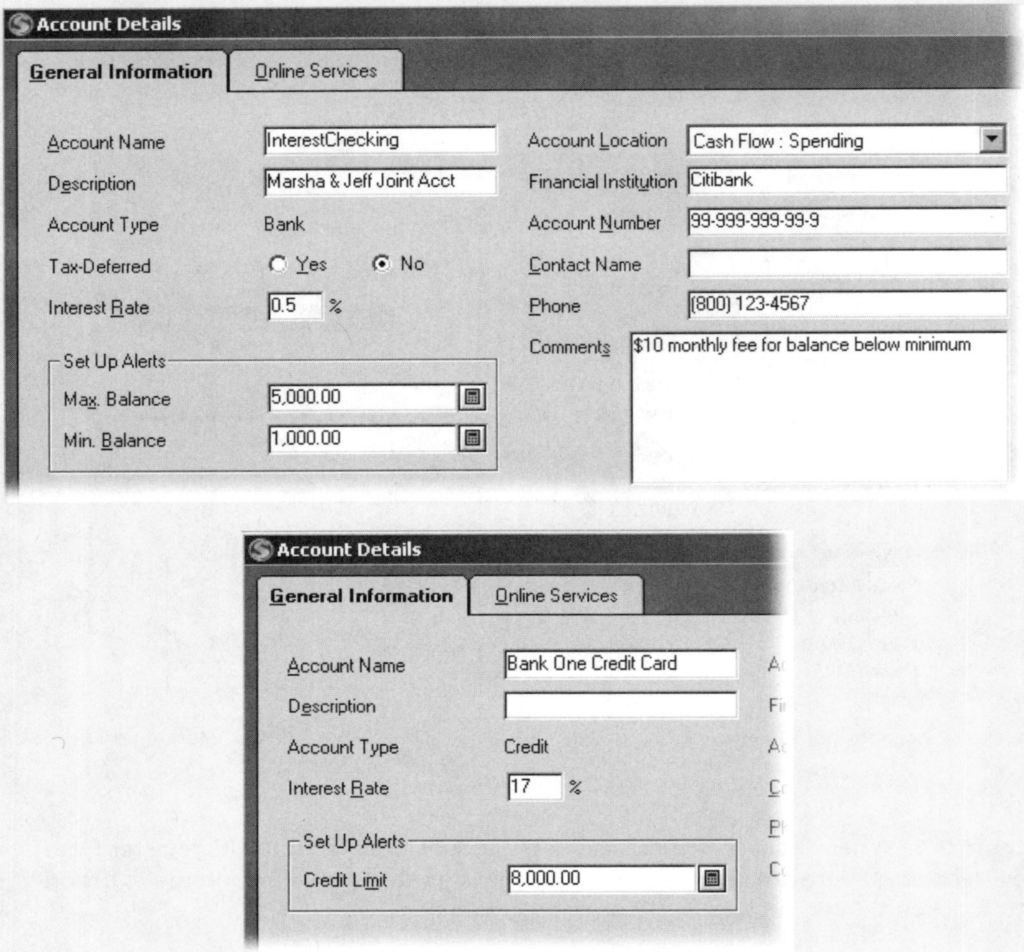

Figure 2-6. Top: For cash flow accounts, you can add a description, the account number, the interest rate, and a contact phone number. The Comments box is perfect for noting fees or rules.
Bottom: The fields that change from account type to account type are usually in the Set Up Alerts area. For example, the credit card account has an alert for the credit limit on the card, while the checking account in the top figure has alerts for both minimum and maximum account values.

single-digit interest rate. In Quicken, you don't delete accounts that you're no longer using, even if they have a zero balance. Deleting an account deletes *all of*

Staying on Top of Tasks with Alerts

As you'll learn throughout this book, Quicken offers *alerts* that notify you of tasks you should perform or situations you may want to respond to. For example, the minimum-balance alert is particularly useful for checking accounts that charge exorbitant fees if your balance drops too low. Conversely, most banks wouldn't dream of telling you that you've deposited too much. But *you* can use the alert for the maximum balance field to see when it's time to move some money into an account with a higher interest rate.

You'll probably see some alerts whenever you launch Quicken. Alerts also appear in the Cash Flow Center, or if you customize Quicken Home to display them. Get in the habit of reviewing the list of alerts, because Quicken *doesn't* always display a message box with an obvious warning as soon as something triggers the alert. Occasionally, the program pops up a message box, but not often enough to ensure that you'll see it in time.

the transactions in the account, including transfers to and from other accounts— potentially mangling those accounts!

Fortunately, there's a way of getting those old accounts off your Account Bar and Account List (and out of your hair). All you have to do is *hide* your closed or inactive accounts. Hidden accounts—and, more importantly, their transactions—remain in your data file, but you won't see them in account lists.

You hide accounts using the Manage Accounts tab of the Account List window. Here's how:

1. **In the Account Bar, right-click any account and, from the shortcut menu, choose "Delete/hide accounts in Quicken."**

    If you press Ctrl+A to open the Account List window, you'll see the View Accounts tab, which shows your unhidden accounts, their balances, and a few other bits of account information. Click the Manage Accounts tab.

2. **To hide an account, in the "Hide in Quicken" column, turn on the account's checkbox.**

    Figure 2-7 shows an account being hidden.

3. **Click Close when you're done.**

Categories

When you first create a new Quicken data file, the program automatically sets up a boatload of categories for you. Quicken chooses these categories based on the answers you give during setup, including your marital status and whether you own a home. For commonly used categories, Quicken also specifies the tax form and line item to which the category applies, saving you a lot of heartburn when it comes time to generate tax reports.

Categories are the foundation of Quicken's tracking and budgeting features. You can use them to budget how much you spend on different items, see how your income and expenses are allocated, or generate reports to make it easier to fill out that tax return.

In Quicken, categories come in three basic types. *Income* categories are for the money that comes into your personal coffers, like salary, part-time income, and winnings from the gals' bunko game. *Expense* categories represent the money you spend, including unavoidable expenses like Groceries and discretionary expenses like Hobbies. As you create or edit categories as described in this section, you can assign them to either Income or Expense. However, the Category List includes one additional type of category—*Transfers and Payments*. This type of category works a little differently: Quicken automatically creates categories representing each of your accounts. Then, when you transfer money from checking to savings or make a mortgage payment, you use these categories to show which accounts the money is going into and out of.

Before you start modifying Quicken's categories en masse, read this section to gain an understanding of how they work as you think about how you need to categorize your own information. (For more advice, see the box on page 78.)

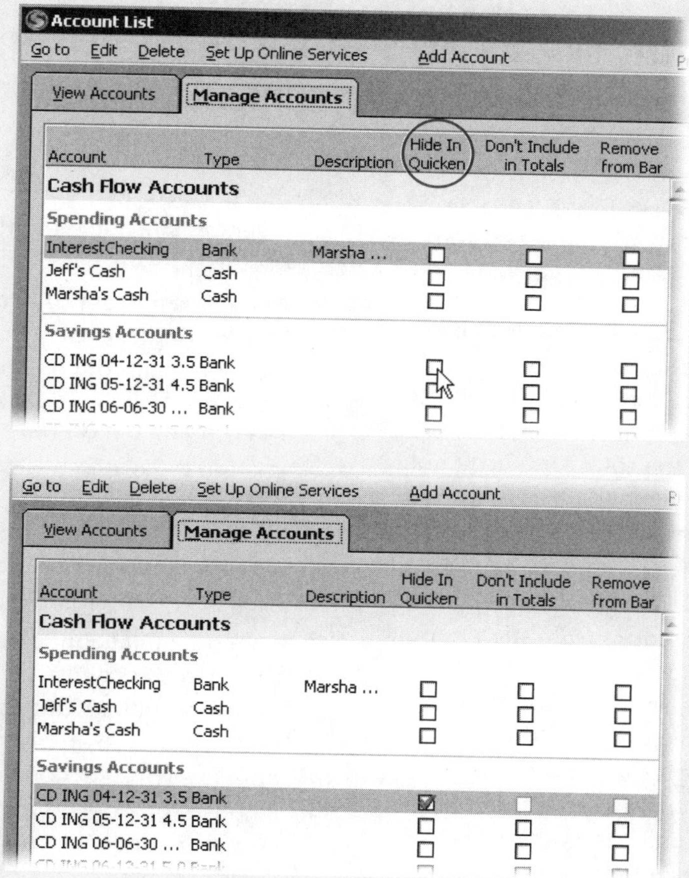

Figure 2-7. Top: Accounts start out with their Hide checkboxes turned off, so that they automatically show up in all lists and reports.
Bottom: When you turn on the "Hide in Quicken" checkbox, the program turns off and dims the "Don't Include in Totals" and "Remove from Bar" checkboxes.

▶ **Category.** If you want to track how much you earn or spend on some aspect of life, tax-related or not, you need a category to put it in. Likewise, you need a category if you want to establish a budget of how much you'd like to spend in a particular area, such as Supplies or Entertainment.

Other Ways to Manage Accounts

The Manage Accounts tab isn't just for hiding accounts. It offers helpful features that even experienced Quicken fans don't know about. Here's what you can do:

* **Remove an account's balances in Account Bar totals.** Turn on an account's "Don't Include in Totals" checkbox if you want to remove its balance from the total for a group of accounts. For instance, you might do this to omit the balances for your medical savings accounts and petty cash from your net worth.

* **Remove an account from the Account Bar.** Quicken automatically displays all your accounts in the Account Bar. As the number of accounts grows, finding an account takes more time and scrolling. If you have some accounts that you use daily and others that you open only a few times a year, you can remove those more stable accounts from the Account Bar. The accounts you remove from the bar are still visible in the Account List window and on the Quicken menu bar (for instance, when

you choose Cash Flow → Cash Flow Accounts). Although the accounts don't appear in the Account Bar, their balances still appear in the total for the group.

* **Change the order of accounts.** Quicken initially lists accounts in alphabetical order. If you want to see your most frequently used accounts at the top of each section, you can change the order in which accounts appear in the Account List and Account Bar. Click the name of the account you want to move and then click Move Up or Move Down.

* **Change an account's group.** Quicken associates accounts with one of the Quicken Centers, but you can change that, too. For example, suppose you open a savings account earmarked for a house remodeling project. You can switch that account to the Property & Debt group by selecting the account, clicking Change Group, and then in the Change Group dialog box, clicking the Asset option.

▶ **Subcategory.** As its name implies, a subcategory is a category within a category. By lumping several subcategories underneath one top-level category, you can generate reports that summarize your income and expenses. For example,

Quicken automatically includes a Tax category, with subcategories for federal, state, local, and other types of taxes you pay. Or, you can create a category called Fun and then create subcategories, like Dining Out, Recreation, Vacation, and Horses. The resulting tree structure (which you can see at top in Figure 2-8) makes it easy to spot the categories you want.

Note: Although Quicken lets you create multiple subcategory levels, you usually won't need more than one. If you find you're creating subcategories within subcategories, take a look at your overall category structure. You may be making your life too complicated.

▶ **Category Group.** Out of the box, Quicken includes three *Category Groups*: Discretionary, Income, and Mandatory Expenses. These are high-level categories that encompass a group of individual categories. You can work with Quicken for years without a glimmer of a reason to use Category Groups. However, power users find all sorts of uses for them. For example, if you want to determine how much money you need to cover expenses should you lose your job, you can create a budget for all the categories in the Mandatory Expenses group.

The Category List Window

The list of categories that Quicken starts with meets *most* needs for *most* people, but chances are good you'll want to make at least a few changes. Choose Tools → Category List to open the Category List window, which is where you make those changes (Figure 2-8, top).

The Category List window gives you plenty of tools to help organize the categories you're working with:

▶ **Show.** In the Show drop-down menu, choose a type of category to display just those categories (and filter out the others). For instance, choose "Tax-related categories" to check whether you've assigned your tax categories to tax line items correctly (see page 367).

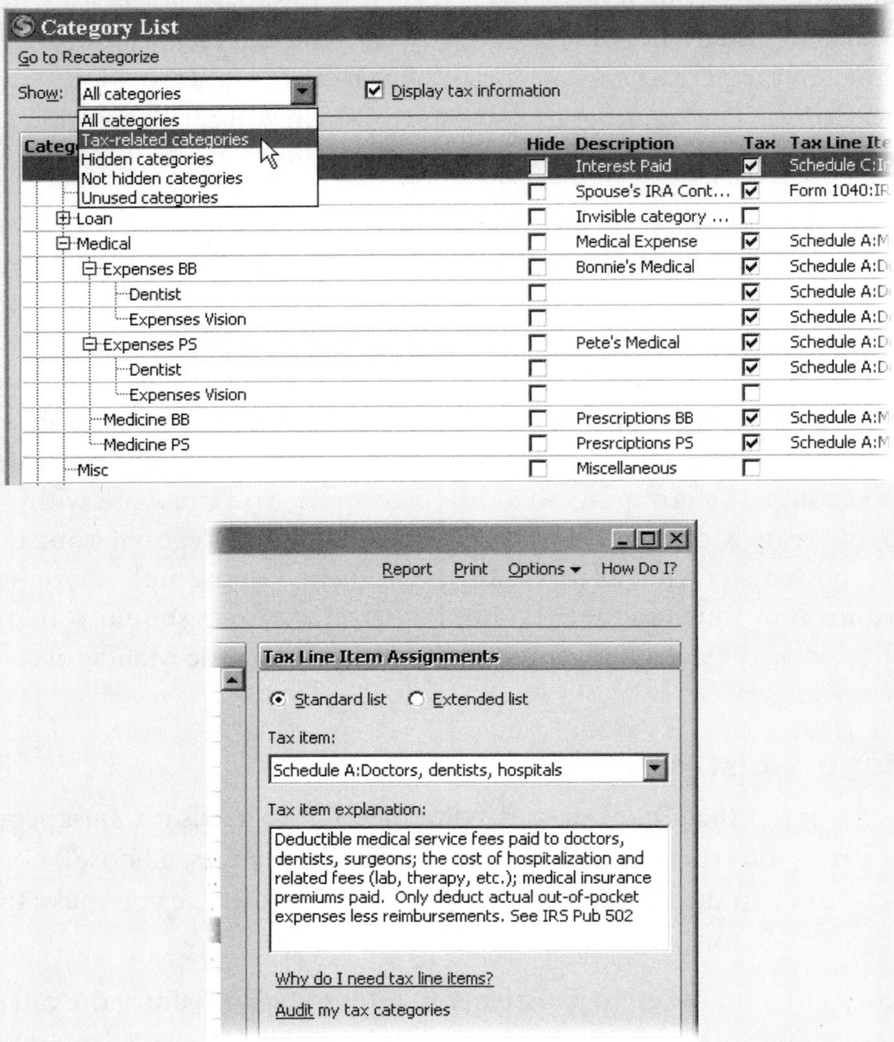

Figure 2-8. Top: Turning on the "Tax information" checkbox displays tax settings for categories. Quicken shows all categories automatically, but you can filter the list for tax categories by choosing Tax-related categories in the Show drop-down list. Bottom: When you select a category in the Categories List, the Tax Line Item Assignments pane on the right side of the window lets you choose the tax item for the category. Quicken displays an explanation of the tax item you select..

- **Display tax information.** Turn on this checkbox to see the Tax Line Item to which categories are assigned. The Tax Line Item Assignments pane appears on the right side of the window, making it easy to choose or correct the tax line item assignment for the selected category.

- **Go to Recategorize.** In the window menu bar, choosing Go To Recategorize opens a dialog box in which you can reassign transactions to a different category (see page 139).

- **Options.** From the Options menu, you can choose what you want to see in the window. For example, you can show or hide category descriptions, category groups, or the type (income, expense, and sub). To assign a category group, choose Options → "Assign category group".

- **Category tasks.** Along the bottom of the Category List window, you'll find buttons for working with categories, like New, Add from List, Edit, Delete, and Merge. You'll learn about these in the remainder of this chapter.

Customizing Categories

Now that you understand category characteristics, you can make changes to the categories that Quicken set up for you. Initially, you'll probably spot several categories that you don't need (like Rent if you're a homeowner). You can hide or delete categories you don't want, or consolidate several of Quicken's categories under one main category.

You don't have to get your categories perfect before you start doing your finances in Quicken. If you enter a credit card charge and can't find the category you want, you can add a new category to the Category List then and there. You can even recategorize transactions if you decide to revamp the categories you use.

Removing Categories

You can remove categories from the Category List by hiding or deleting. For example, if personal hygiene isn't a priority, you can (if you must) delete the Personal Care category. If you own a home but worry about your spouse kicking you out, you may want to hide the Rent category only temporarily.

Categories and Budgeting

How do I use Quicken categories to prevent overspending and analyze income?

Quicken offers lots of ways to *track* your spending—but it can't *control* your spending for you. There's no magic button in Quicken that stops you from pulling out your credit card to buy a cobalt blue Kitchen Aid mixer at Nordstrom.

But tracking is the first step to understanding your financial situation, and ultimately, to controlling it. To track income and spending, you assign categories to the transactions you create—the paycheck you deposit, the mortgage payment you make, or the checks you write. For example, if you work full-time during the day and earn freelance income as a superhero at night, you can create two income categories: Salary and Skeeter Boy Donations. To reserve your tax expense categories for the taxes you pay, you can create an Income category for Tax Refund.

To build a budget in Quicken, you specify the maximum amount you want to spend for a category. When you generate a report that shows your budgeted amounts compared to your actual spending, you can see where you've done well and where spending has gone horribly awry. (Chapter 8 discusses creating and working with budgets.)

▶ **Hiding a category.** In the Category List window, turn on the Hide checkbox for the category you want to hide. To show it again, turn *off* the same checkbox.

Tip: If you don't see the category you want in the Category List window, check for hidden categories with the Show drop-down menu by choosing either "All categories" or "Hidden categories."

▶ **Deleting a category.** In the Category List window, click the name of the category you want to delete and then, at the bottom of the window, click Delete. If there are transactions assigned to the category, Quicken asks you to recategorize them, as shown in Figure 2-9. If you don't recategorize transactions, they become uncategorized and won't show up in reports (for taxes or actual spending, for example).

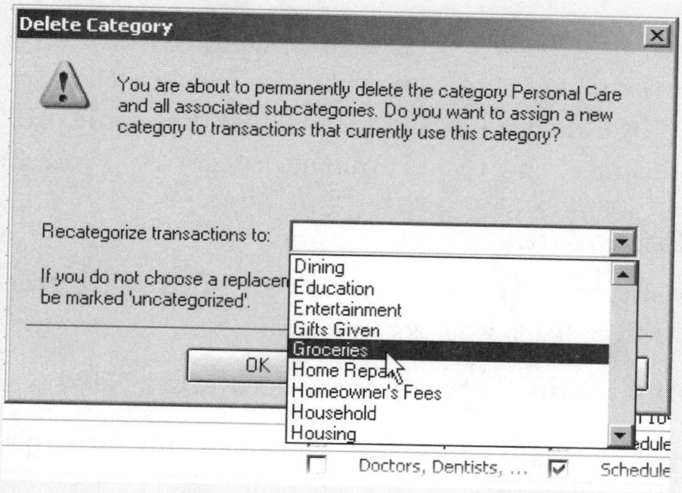

Figure 2-9. In the "Recategorize transactions to" drop-down menu, choose the existing category to which you want to reassign transactions and then click OK. For every transaction that referred to the old category, Quicken switches the category to the one you selected.

Note: If you delete a category that hasn't been used, Quicken displays a dialog box asking you to confirm that you want to delete the category. Although deleting a category is permanent, go ahead and click Yes. It's easy enough to recreate a category later.

Adding Quicken Categories

Keep in mind that the list of categories you see depends on the answers you gave during setup. If you have children, buy a house, or get married (not necessarily in that order), you don't have to create categories from scratch. Quicken includes predefined categories for those situations. Here's how you add them to your Category List.

1. **At the bottom of the Category List window, click "Add from List."**

   Quicken opens the Add Categories dialog box.

2. **In the Available Categories drop-down menu, choose the category you want.**

   The categories include life events, like Married, as well as special cases like Rentals & Royalties, for types of income that only some people have. Figure 2-10 demonstrates how to add available categories to your Category List.

Creating Categories

If you want a category that Quicken hasn't provided, you can create categories from scratch with only a few clicks and keystrokes. Here's how:

1. **At the bottom of the Category List window, click New.**

   The Set Up Category dialog box appears with only the Expense option selected.

2. **In the Name box, type a name for the new category.**

   Use names that completely identify the purpose of the category—even if you're creating a subcategory. A subcategory name like "Fees" makes sense when you can see the parent category, but could be obscure in a report or transaction.

 Tip: If a category name is descriptive, you can skip the Description box. However, the Description box is helpful as a reminder of what a category represents.

3. **If you want to assign the category to a category group, in the Group drop-down menu, choose a group.**

   For example, most people would choose Discretionary for a category that tracks the money you spend on cappuccino. If you can't function without fancy coffee, choose Mandatory Expenses instead.

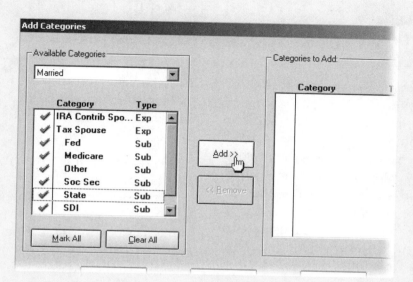

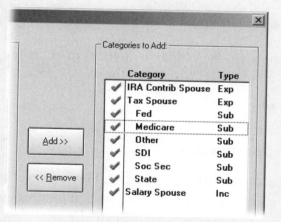

Figure 2-10. Top: When you choose an Available Category, Quicken displays the categories in the list box. You can select individual categories by clicking them, or select all categories by clicking Mark All. Click Add.
Bottom: When you click Add, Quicken adds the categories to the "Categories to Add" list. These categories still aren't in your Category List. Click OK to add them (not shown).

Tracking Reimbursements

If your company or volunteer association reimburses you for expenses, consider creating a category to track your reimbursements, to help make sure you receive all the money you're due. Here's how: Create an income category called, say, Business Reimbursements. (You could just as easily use an Expense category, but Income categories are usually fewer in number and thus easier to spot.)

Every time you spend money on reimbursable expenses (like parking), assign the transactions to Business Reimbursements. Then, when you run an Itemized Categories report (page 361), the value for Business Reimbursements shows up as a *negative* number—your cue that you're still waiting for your reimbursement.

You can review the money you've spent in the Itemized Categories report to prepare your expense report. Then, when you receive your check for reimbursed expenses, assign the deposit to the Business Reimbursements category as well. You'll know you've been reimbursed for all your expenses when the total for this category is zero. (Create a customized report to show only this one category to make it easy to see what you should report.

4. **Choose the type of category.**

   You have three options to choose from. For top-level categories, select either the Income or Expense option—the two broadest categories of all. To create a subcategory, select the "Subcategory of" option, depicted in Figure 2-11.

5. **If the category corresponds to income or deductions on your tax return, turn on the "Tax-related" checkbox. In the "Tax line item" drop-down menu, choose the entry that corresponds to the tax form *and* line on that form.**

   When you choose a tax line item, Quicken displays a description of that item, but it doesn't guarantee that your choice is correct. You can use last year's income tax return to check your line item assignments, or to be sure, ask the IRS or your accountant.

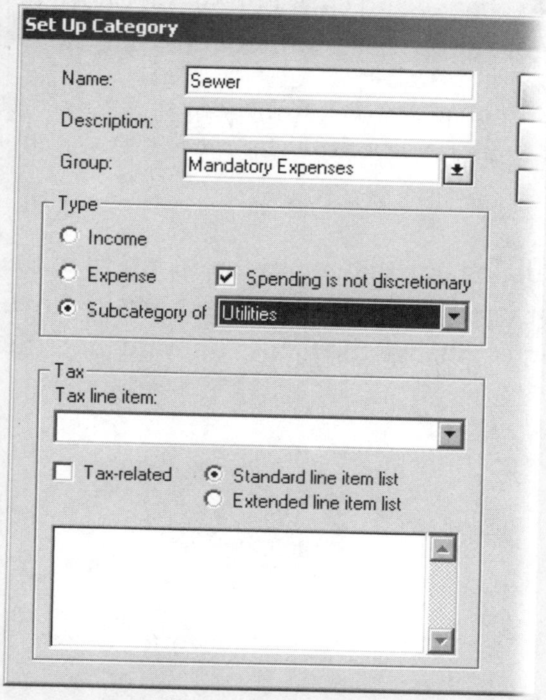

Figure 2-11. This is the Set Up Category dialog box. In the "Subcategory of" drop-down menu, choose the category that you want as the parent. When you choose a category, Quicken sets the Group field to match that of the parent, and also changes the "Spending is not discretionary" checkbox, based on the parent category's Group.

6. **Click OK.**

Quicken adds the category to the Category List window.

Modifying Categories

You can modify any aspect of an existing category. For example, you can rename it to something more meaningful, switch it into a subcategory, assign a tax line item for expenses you joyfully realized qualify for tax deductions, and so on. To change characteristics of a category, in the Category List window, right-click the category you want to change and click Edit on the shortcut menu. The changes you make to a category apply to all transactions that use the category.

 Note: If your mouse needs more exercise, you can also click a category and then, at the bottom of the Category List window, click Edit.

The Edit Category dialog box that appears is identical to the Create Category dialog box—except for its title and the fact that the fields are filled in with the category's current settings. Change the fields you want, and then click OK to save your changes.

CHAPTER 3:
BACKING UP YOUR
FINANCIAL INFORMATION

▶ Backing Up Data Files

▶ Restoring Quicken Backups

Once you start using Quicken, paper and pencil rapidly start to look like an unthinkable hassle. You can now balance your checkbook, prepare your taxes, plan for a comfortable retirement, and have enough time left over to go spend some money—and dutifully enter those transactions into Quicken, as well.

The pleasure of doing your finances in Quicken evaporate instantly, though, if you lose your data to a hard-disk crash or other computer disaster. Good backups, as this chapter outlines, get you back to work quickly.

Backing Up Data Files

Quicken provides several backup methods, all of which work well for backing up your data files. But like millions of others, you may already back up *all* the information on your PC. If you're already using, say, Windows Backup, then Quicken backups may seem as useful as an icemaker in Siberia. After all, your Quicken data is getting backed up on a regular basis with all your other files.

Quicken backups can give you an extra layer of *flexibility* as well as protection. Suppose you're about to experiment with a Quicken feature, like downloading transactions or archiving your data; there's no sense backing up everything on your computer. You can back up only your Quicken data by running a Quicken *manual backup*, which immediately creates a backup data file. Then, if the experiment goes horribly wrong, you can restore your Quicken backup and try a different approach. A Quicken backup is also a good idea if you've spent several hours getting your accounts, categories, and preferences just the way you want them, and your next scheduled Windows backup won't kick in until 3:00 tomorrow morning. Just run a manual backup (and sleep like a baby).

Quicken offers a second type of backup, the *online backup*. In the Quicken Backup dialog box, select the Online option if you want Intuit to handle backing up your data file. This service sends your files via the Internet to Intuit's data center, as described in the box on page 94.

FREQUENTLY ASKED QUESTION

How Often to Back Up

How often should I back up my data?

Good question. The closest thing to a right answer is "When you wouldn't want to recreate the data you'd lose." If you hammer out more transactions a day than Stephen King writes best-selling pages, a daily backup is an excellent choice. And if you've successfully completed a particularly gnarly Quicken task, a mid-day backup isn't out of the question.

On the other hand, if you pay a few bills each month and use your PC as a sticky-note holder the rest of the time, a monthly backup may be all you need. Of course, that monthly backup may mean you back up your Quicken file every time you use the program.

If you aren't sure which data you need to back up and how often you should back it up, check out *Windows XP Pro: The Missing Manual* to learn about using Windows XP to back up your data.

Manual Backups

If you just spent several hours creating transactions in Quicken, setting Quicken preferences, activating your bank accounts for online services, and customizing Quicken investment reports, you're sure to want to save your work right away. Here's what you do to run a backup immediately:

1. **Open the Quicken Backup dialog box by choosing File → Backup or by pressing Ctrl+B.**

   The Quicken Backup dialog box opens, showing your current backup settings (Figure 3-1). The "Select the Quicken file to back up" section displays the name and full path of the data file that's open, which is the very file you're about to back up. If you want to back up a Quicken data file other than the one you're working on, click Browse and select that file instead. (Although Quicken shows only the .qdf file, it backs up all of the files that make up your data file.)

   The program also automatically turns on the "Add date to file name" checkbox—with good reason. This setting makes it easy to identify your latest backup by appending an eight-digit date to the filename. For example, if you back up your *MyMoney.qdf* file on July 21, 2005, the backup filename prefix becomes *MyMoney_20050721*. If you turn this checkbox off, you create a backup that uses the data file's name as the prefix and each manual backup you perform simply overwrites the previous one.

    Tip: Adding the date to your backup names means that every backup creates a completely new set of files instead of overwriting the previous backup. If you back up to Zip disks, keep a good supply on hand, since dated backups fill up disks quickly.

2. **In the "Where do you want to save your backup file?" section, click Browse and navigate to the folder or removable media you use for backups.**

   If you want to make a backup of your Quicken data file before you try an unfamiliar procedure, the BACKUP subfolder that Quicken chooses is fine.

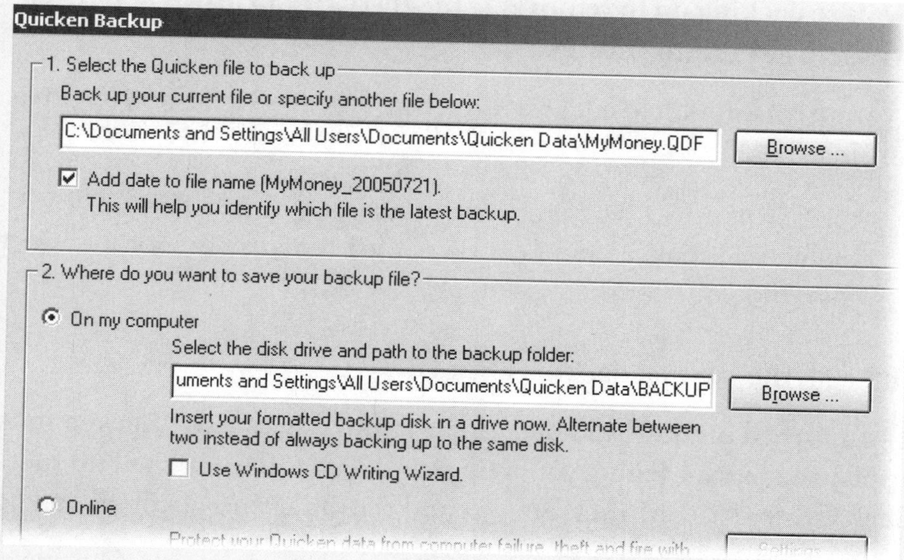

Figure 3-1. The first time you back up your data file, Quicken automatically sets the backup location to a subfolder, named BACKUP, within the folder that contains the data file. If you use third-party software like Windows Backup to save all your data, this location is fine. Otherwise, the safest choice is to switch the backup to a CD or other removable media. Quicken uses this location for every subsequent backup of that file.

But saving a backup file to the same hard drive that contains your data file won't help if your hard disk crashes. To protect your data from human error *and* hardware failure, back up your file to a different hard drive, or to removable media, like a CD or DVD.

For the ultimate in backup protection, rotate your backups among several copies of removable media and store one of your backups offsite. For example, take a backup CD to your office or give it to a trustworthy neighbor. If your house burns down, melting your computer *and* your removable media, you'll still be able to retrieve your electronic financial records.

3. **If you're backing up to removable media (CD, Zip disk, DVD, diskette, and so on), insert it into your PC.**

   If you're backing up to a CD, see the box on page 91 for further advice on burning CDs.

    Tip: Use floppy disks for backup media only as a last resort. In addition to holding miniscule amounts of data, they tend to deteriorate over time, rendering your backups useless.

4. **To begin the manual backup, click OK.**

   If you turned on the "Add date to file name" checkbox, Quicken most likely displays a message telling you that your data has been backed up successfully. Click OK to close the message box and the Quicken Backup dialog box.

   If you've already created a backup file with the same name, Quicken asks if you want to overwrite that file. Click Yes only if you are *absolutely* sure you don't need the previous backup.

   To retain your previous backups, click Cancel. Open the Quicken Backup dialog box again and either turn on the "Add date to file name" checkbox or choose a different folder for your backup.

Backup Reminders

If you have trouble remembering important tasks like backing up your data or picking up your kids at school, Quicken backup reminders help ensure that at least *one* of your to-dos is done. You can set a preference (page 44) that tells Quicken to remind you to back up your data file. After you've opened the file the number of times you set in the preference, Quicken reminds you with the message shown in Figure 3-2. If you mangle your data or it becomes corrupt in some way, you can restore one of these backups; see "Restoring Quicken Backups" on page 95.

Back Up Directly to CD

When you're choosing a location to save your Quicken backup file, you may notice a Use Windows CD Writing Wizard checkbox. Quicken leaves this checkbox turned off initially, since it apparently assumes you're going to use a third-party program like Roxio Easy CD Creator. If you back up data frequently, you can leave a CD in the drive and continue writing backups to it. (You must first format the CD and set up your CD drive to work like another hard drive on your computer, also using the third-party software.)

If your computer runs Windows XP, it comes with the Windows CD Writing Wizard for burning files to CD. To backup directly to a CD, turn the Use Windows CD Writing Wizard checkbox on. Quicken hands responsibility for backing up to the Windows CD Writing wizard. Getting through the wizard steps successfully is *your* responsibility. Here's what to do:

1. In the "Select the disk drive and path to the backup folder" box, click Browse and select your CD drive. When you click OK, Quicken displays a message telling you that your data file has been copied to XP's temporary CD Burning folder.

2. Just above your System tray (way down in the lower-right corner of your screen), you see a balloon telling you that you have files waiting to be written to a CD. Click the balloon to open the ephemeral "Files Ready to Be Written to the CD" folder in Windows Explorer.

3. Be sure to insert a CD into your drive, and then click "Write these files to CD," as shown here. Continue to follow the wizard's instructions.

4. When your CD holder pops open, click Finish. Your backup is complete.

Remove the CD from the drive, label it with the backup name and date, and store it somewhere safe.

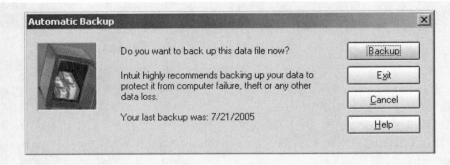

Figure 3-2. This is the Automatic Backup dialog box that pops up on your screen when you set your preferences to remind you. To follow through on the reminder, click Backup, which opens the Quicken Backup dialog box. If you decide to continue working in Quicken, click Cancel. On the other hand, if you didn't make many changes to the file, click Exit to close Quicken without backing up the file.

Automatic Backups

It's a horror story that happens in home offices every day. You try to open your data file and Quicken begins to cough and wheeze (in its own computerized way). You grow nervous as you try to remember the last time you backed up your Quicken data—but what if that's *never*? Don't panic: Quicken actually performs some backups for you behind the scenes, and you may be able to restore one of those files.

Quicken's *automatic backup* feature creates a copy of your data file about once a week. (It kicks in when you close the program by choosing File → Exit, opening another data file, closing the Quicken window, and so on.) These copies are separate from backups you create manually or via a Quicken reminder. For example, if your data file is named MyMoney and you peek in the folder that you use for Quicken backups, you see other files like the ones in Figure 3-3. Because automatic backups are copies, you don't have to choose File → Restore Backup File to open them. Simply choose File → Open and select the name of the automatic backup file you want to open.

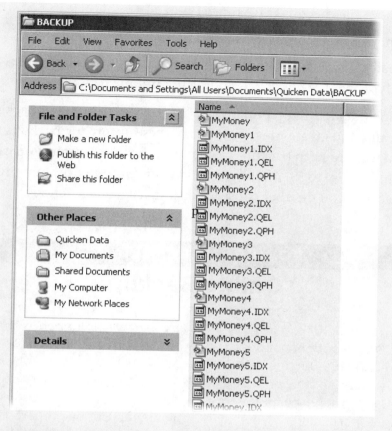

Figure 3-3. Automatic backup files append a single digit to the prefix of your Quicken data file, such as MyMoney1 and MyMoney2 in the figure. Because each Quicken data file includes several files with different extensions, you see several files with each filename prefix.

Out of the box, Quicken creates five automatic backup files in your backup folder, for example, MyMoney1 through MyMoney5. Here's what Quicken does when it creates an automatic backup (using the MyMoney data file as an example):

▶ Quicken renames MyMoney1 files to MyMoney2 (including the .qdf, .idx, .qel, and .qph file extensions.)

▶ MyMoney2 files become MyMoney3 files.

- MyMoney3 files become MyMoney4 files.
- MyMoney4 files become MyMoney5 files.
- And finally, Quicken creates a copy of the current MyMoney files and names them MyMoney1. The cycle is complete until the next week.

Quicken includes a backup preference, "Maximum number of backup copies," that you can set to create more or fewer of these automatic backups (see page 45). If you want to keep backups that go back further in time, you can choose a higher number (up to 9). Alternatively, if your computer backup procedures are impeccable and you'd rather conserve disk space, you can choose a number as low as 1.

POWER USERS' CLINIC

Online Backup

The Quicken Backup dialog box includes an Online option. As usual, the "Learn more" link is your clue that Intuit charges extra for this service. But the Online Backup service has a couple of advantages, particularly if you have a shaky grasp of your computer's operation. The service can automatically select, encrypt, and send your files to Intuit's data center, where IT professionals use elaborate technology to protect your data from human error, computer problems, fire, theft, and so on. The basic Online Backup service backs up Quicken data files up to 50 megabytes, and runs $34.95 a year.

If you're willing to part with more money, you can sign up for higher levels of backup service. For example, the Full System Backup service backs up any data on your computer up to 10 gigabytes. But be prepared to part with $24.95 a month for that. Regardless of your budget, any kind of online backup isn't a viable option if you only have a slow dial-up Internet connection.

If the price seems high just to save a few minutes backing up data to a CD, in the Quicken Backup dialog box, simply keep that "On my computer" option selected.

Restoring Quicken Backups

Here's the reason you've been so carefully getting your Quicken backup routine in place. After you've survived a hard drive crash, power outage, or natural disaster, you have to take one of those backup files and turn it into a working data file before you can start using Quicken again.

If you're restoring a backup file after a hard disk crash, you'll have to reinstall Windows and Quicken 2006 before you can complete these steps. Once your PC is up and running and you've launched Quicken, proceed as follows:

1. **If you backed up your data to removable media, put the disk containing your backup in the appropriate drive.**

    If you instead backed up your data to another hard drive on your computer or on a home network, you must connect to it. For example, if the backup file is on a laptop, connect it to your desktop PC and turn on file sharing.

     Tip: For more information about sharing files on different computers, see *Windows XP for Starters: The Missing Manual* by David Pogue.

2. **Choose File → Restore Backup File.**

    Quicken displays a submenu, which lists the backup copies that you've made. If the backup that you want to restore is listed on the menu, click its name.

    To restore any other files, click Browse at the bottom of the submenu. In the Restore Quicken File dialog box, navigate to the folder or media that contains the backup you want to restore.

3. **Select the filename and click OK.**

    When you see the message that says your data has been restored successfully, you're ready to open the data file.

4. **Open the data file and look it over. Reenter any transactions that the backup doesn't contain.**

   For example, look for a gap between the last check number in Quicken and the number on your next paper check and reenter any checks that don't appear in Quicken. Alternatively, you can wait until you receive your next bank statement and add missing transactions as you reconcile your account.

5. **Back up your recovered data file onto removable media or a different computer** *now*.

   See page 88 for instructions on performing a manual backup.

In the process of finding and recovering your data file, you've had a chance to see how well (or poorly) your backup system worked. Anything that will make your life easier next time—buying more blank CDs, setting more frequent backup reminders, or signing up for Quicken's online backup service—do it *now* before you forget.

TROUBLESHOOTING MOMENT

It's the Quiet Ones...

Hard disk crashes used to be dramatic events accompanied by impressive grinding noises. Hard disks today are smaller, have closer tolerances, and run nice and quietly—perhaps *too* quietly. Even a massive hard drive crash can sneak up on you before you have time to back up.

If you hear *any* odd sounds emanating from your computer—little chirps or squeaks, for instance—stop what you're doing and quickly back up your key files and any that you've been working on recently. Keep a blank CD or a USB thumb drive near your computer for such occasions.

If your computer won't reboot due to a disk crash, a data recovery company can sometimes collect some of your data, but the price is often in the thousands of dollars.

CHAPTER 4:
BANKING, CREDIT CARDS, AND CASH

- ▶ Transaction Basics
- ▶ Quicken's Quicker with QuickFill
- ▶ Recording Checks
- ▶ Recording Deposits
- ▶ Paying with a Credit Card
- ▶ Paying with Cash
- ▶ Splitting Transactions
- ▶ Transferring Money Between Accounts
- ▶ Editing Transactions
- ▶ Voiding Transactions
- ▶ Searching for Transactions

- ▶ The Transaction Edit Menu
- ▶ Managing Memorized Payees
- ▶ Scheduling Transactions
- ▶ Automating Your Paycheck in Quicken

4

As you run errands, you probably write a few checks, swipe your credit card, and hand over some coins and bills. When you get home, you can record all your transactions to keep your Quicken account balances in sync with your wallet and the accounts at your financial institutions. You can create Quicken transactions as easily as handwritten ones—easier, in fact, since the program automatically completes entries for you, lets you schedule transactions to happen automatically, or downloads them from your bank.

You can take even more work off your plate by automating transactions in Quicken. With scheduled transactions, you don't have to remember when bills or deposits are due—Quicken reminds you and fills in all the fields for you. Although automation requires a bit of setup, the time you save down the road makes it all worthwhile.

This chapter describes how to record your daily cash flow transactions and how Quicken features can make short work of them. You'll also learn how to handle other common transaction tasks, like transferring money between accounts, voiding transactions, or finding transactions you recorded a while back.

Transaction Basics

You'll learn best how transactions work when you enter some yourself, as you'll learn in this section. Later, when you take advantage of automatic features like scheduled transactions, you'll understand exactly what Quicken's doing. You record Quicken transactions in a *register* that looks much like the paper type. Each account you create in Quicken has its own register.

Getting to the Register

The Account Bar is the fastest way to open up a register—simply click the account name. If the Cash Flow Center is visible, you can click an account name there as well. From the Quicken menu bar, choose Cash Flow → Cash Flow Accounts, and then choose the account. Figure 4-1 shows one way to open an acount register and some of the helpful features you'll find when you do.

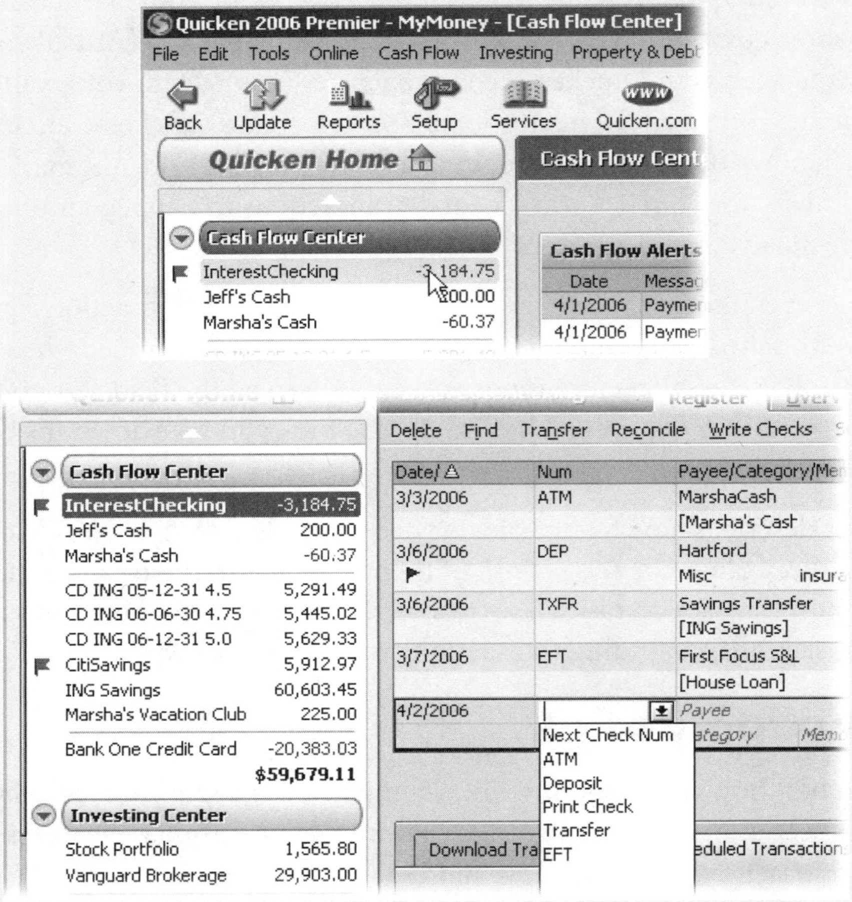

Figure 4-1. Top: On the Account Bar, open a register by clicking the name of the account.
Bottom: A Quicken register (right box) looks like a paper register, but every field has timesaving shortcuts. For example, in the Num field, you can choose Next Check Number to fill in a check number one higher than the last check number you used.

Navigating a Transaction

Here are some keystrokes that will move you through the fields of a transaction faster than grain through a goose:

- **Move to a new transaction.** In the register, press Ctrl+N or Ctrl+End to jump to the first blank row in the register. You're ready to record a new transaction.

- **Move to the next field.** If you're creating a transaction directly in the register, pressing Tab is the fastest way to move to the next field and display its Quick-Fill options. You can skip fields by pressing Tab several times in succession or by clicking the next field you want to enter.

- **Record a transaction.** As soon as all the fields you want have values, click or press Enter to record the transaction. Keyboard shortcut mavens can press Alt+T to record a transaction at any time.

UP TO SPEED

To Tab or to Enter

With Quicken's factory settings, you press Tab to move between fields and press Enter to record the transaction. This method's advantage is that you can press Enter as soon as the transaction fields are filled in—which can be almost immediately if QuickFill features and memorized payees do their jobs.

You can change this behavior, though, so that you press Enter to move through every field and then press it one more time to record the transaction. This way, you don't have to jockey between Tab on the left side of the keyboard and Enter on the right.

The downside to this approach is that the Enter key no longer provides a shortcut to accepting the QuickFill entries in one fell swoop. You must either press Enter through every field, or click the Enter button in the second row (or press Alt+T) to complete the transaction.

If you want to switch to using the Enter key to move through fields, choose Edit → Preferences → Quicken Program. In the Select preference type list, click QuickFill. Turn on the "Use enter key to move between fields" checkbox.

Quicken's Quicker with QuickFill

Before you learn how to record a transaction from A to Z, you can bask in the knowledge that you rarely have to do it. Quicken works hard to do as much of your transaction data entry as it can, and, most of the time, it does an outstanding job. Every time you create a transaction, Quicken remembers what you did and fills in your next transaction for the same payee. In no time, you can add transactions by typing just the date and a few letters of the payee's name. Quicken takes care of the rest.

The first time you record a transaction for a payee, Quicken memorizes almost everything about it to the Memorized Payee List (page 48): the payee, amount, categories, and memo text. For new transactions, you still have to fill in the date, and, for check transactions, the check number.

Then, when you record a new transaction and choose a payee, the QuickFill feature automatically fills in all the other transaction fields for you, as demonstrated in Figure 4-2.

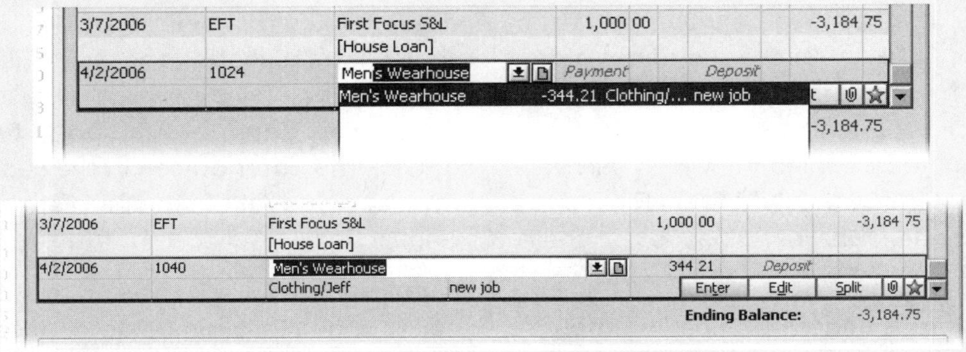

Figure 4-2. Top: As you type letters in the Payee field, QuickFill displays matching payee names from the Memorized Payee List.
Bottom: When you choose a payee and move to another field, QuickFill fills in the other fields with values for the memorized payee. You can modify field values, for instance to enter a different amount, before recording the transaction.

Recording Checks

Quicken provides three ways to record checks. Fortunately, your choice is easy because it depends on how you produce your check:

▶ **Register.** The register is the easiest and fastest way to record checks that you've written by hand. See page 100 for several ways to open an account register.

▶ **Write Checks window.** If you plan to print your checks in Quicken, the Write Checks window's Print button makes it easy to queue up checks for printing (see "Recording Printed Checks" on page 110). Open the Write Checks window by choosing Cash Flow → Write Checks or by pressing Ctrl+W.

▶ **Online Center window.** You can generate electronic payments directly in the register, but the Online Center window's Payments tab (page 234) is the easiest way to create and send electronic payments.

Recording a Check in the Register

With a combination of keyboard shortcuts, clicks, and the occasional typed character, you can make short work of recording checks in the register. Remember to press Tab (or Enter, as explained in the box on page 101) to move to the next field. Here are the steps:

1. **To create a new transaction in the register, press Ctrl+N.**

    If you've been scrolling through past transactions, pressing Ctrl+N takes you to the end of the register and places the pointer in a blank transaction. You can also jump to a new transaction at the end of the register by pressing Ctrl+End.

2. **In the Date field, enter the date you want for the check.**

    Quicken automatically fills in today's date and if you want a date that's only a few days away, press – to move back one day at a time, or + to advance one day at a time.

For other dates, Quicken assumes the current year so you can type just the month, a slash (/), and the day (*12/4*, for example). If you're overwriting the entire date, you don't have to type any slashes in a date. As you type numbers, Quicken automatically moves to the month and then year. For example, to change the date to November 15, 2006, you can type *111506*. Appendix C includes additional keyboard shortcuts for selecting dates.

Note: Although slower, the Quicken calendar is the most foolproof method for entering a date. In a Date field, click the Calendar icon. To switch months, click the right or left arrows. When the month you want is visible, click the day.

3. **In the Num field, type *N* (for Next Check Num) to automatically fill in the next check number in sequence, as demonstrated in Figure 4-3.**

   When you choose Next Check Num in the Num field drop-down menu, Quicken fills in a check number that's one higher than the previous one. If the next check number that Quicken fills in doesn't match the one on your next paper check, don't panic (or look for another box of paper checks). Simply double-click the check number and type the number that's on the paper check.

   If you're recording checks that you plan to print on preprinted checks, choose Print.

Tip: If details like missing check numbers drive you mad, you can check for them by scanning the check numbers in the register as you go. Or choose Reports → Banking → Missing Checks to produce a report of check numbers that don't appear in your Quicken data file. The report lists all your transactions, but you'll see entries like *** **Missing Check 2452** ***.

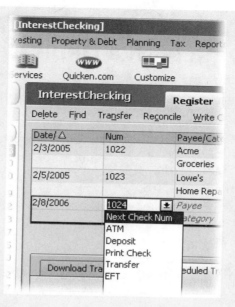

Figure 4-3. In the Num field drop-down menu, type the first letter of a transaction type to choose that type. For example, type N to fill in the next check number in sequence.

The Num field indicates the type of transaction, and you need to type no more than the first letter of the type of transaction. Type *A* to specify an ATM withdrawal or *D* for a Deposit. You can also create Transfers (type *T*), Electronic fund transfers (type *E*), or specify a check to Print (type *P*). If your account is set up for online banking, type *S* to Send an online payment.

4. **In the Payee field, start typing the payee's name.**

If this transaction is the first for a payee, you must type the entire name. Otherwise, as you type letters, Quicken scans the names in your Memorized Payee List and the QuickFill feature displays a drop-down menu of the names that match the letters you've typed so far. As soon as the program selects the one you want, press Tab to move to the Payment field.

Debit cards got their start in paranoid metropolises where no one trusts personal checks. But today, folks swipe their debit cards to pay for everything from coffee to surgery. To record a payment you make with a debit card, in the Num field, choose EFT (for electronic funds transfer). Fill in the rest of the fields as you would for a paper check you write.

To flag your debit card transactions, you can type something in the Memo field, like *DC* (for debit card).

Tip: If the name highlighted in the list is close to the correct entry in the Payee list, press the up or down arrow keys to move up or down in the list. Pressing + or – also moves you up and down in the list.

5. **In the Payment field, change the amount for the check if the value isn't what you want. Click or press Enter when you're done.**

   QuickFill automatically fills in the last values you used for that payee and selects the payment value so you can type a different amount. You can enter numbers from the keyboard or the numeric keys on the keypad. If the amount is the same each time, you can move to the next field or click Enter to record the check. If the transaction's a check, Quicken advances to the Category field when you press Tab.

   You don't have to precede the value with $, but Quicken does require a decimal point to separate dollars and cents (or corresponding denominations in other currencies). The maximum amount for a transaction in Quicken is $9,999,999.99. (Apparently, Intuit is optimistic about its customers' financial success.)

Tip: A new feature in Quicken 2006 can add the decimal point automatically: Choose Edit → Preferences → Quicken Program and, in the Select preference type list, choose Register. Turn on the "Automatically place decimal point" checkbox. In transaction value fields, you can type all the digits for dollars and cents without hunting for the decimal point key.

6. **If the Category field doesn't show the correct category, begin typing the category you want.**

   You can click this field and *choose* a category, but you rarely have to. Quick-Fill automatically fills in the last category you used for the payee you've chosen. Quicken even has a database of commonly used payees and the most likely categories for them. The first time you type one of these payees (Safeway, for example), Quicken fills in the category as well (Groceries).

   If QuickFill doesn't take care of picking the category, type a few letters until Quicken chooses the right category—or at least gets close. You can press the up or down arrow keys (or + or – keys) to move up or down in the list.

7. **To add a reminder about what the check's for, type a brief description in the Memo field.**

   For many transactions, you can skip the Memo field entirely. The date of the check and the payee usually tell the whole story, like a check to Cingular on June 20 for the June telephone bill.

   On the other hand, the Memo field can contain up to 63 characters, so you can record important details about purchases or payments. For example, you can store the brand, model, and serial number of major purchases in the Memo field. You can also use Quicken's Find feature to search for Memo text when you're trying to find a check. For example, search for "Panasonic" if you need to locate the check you wrote for that widescreen TV.

Changing Your View

Out of the box, Quicken uses two lines of the register to show each transaction. The date, check number, payee, and amount show up on the first line, whereas the longer entries for category and memo appear on the second line. If you'd rather see more transactions (and rarely refer to the Memo field anyway), you can make the register show just one line per transaction, as shown here.

To switch to one line for each transaction, in the Register menu bar, choose View → One-line display to place a checkmark in front of the option. To switch back to a roomier view or to see memos again, choose View → One-line display once more.

The standard sort order for transactions—first by date and then by amount—isn't all that helpful. Sorting by cleared status (choose View → Sort by cleared status) keeps you focused on transactions that aren't yet reconciled. This sort order displays reconciled transactions first, followed by

cleared transactions, and finally uncleared. For example, if you see an older check that isn't cleared, you can follow up to see if the payee received your payment.

You can temporarily switch to other sort orders for troubleshooting. For example, to look for missing or duplicate check numbers, sort by check number. Or, to spot missing monthly payments, sort by payee. Besides the View menu, you can change the field Quicken sorts by simply by clicking a column heading above the register.

Adding More Information to Transactions

Quicken 2006 boasts powerful new features that let you add gobs more information than would fit in the 63-character Memo field.

To see these new possibilities, select a transaction in the register. Then click the paper clip button (to the right of the Enter, Edit, and Split buttons) to display a drop-down menu of commands for annotating transactions.

Choosing either "Add follow-up flag" or "Add note" opens the Notes and Flags dialog box, shown in Figure 4-21 (with the insertion point in the Notes box). Type a lengthy note about the transaction or the reminder to follow up. Turn on the "Flag this transaction" checkbox to display a follow-up flag underneath the transaction's date in the register.

The other commands on this menu, "Attach check," "Attach receipt/bill," and "Attach other image" all open the Transaction Attachments window to the appropriate tab. If you attach an image to a transaction, Quicken indicates it by an icon (a piece of paper with a paper clip) in the Date field.

* On the "Check image" tab, click the "Click here" link to attach an electronic check image to its corresponding check transaction in Quicken. Now that banks rarely return paper checks, this way is great to organize your canceled checks. When you click "Click here," Quicken opens the Select Attachment File dialog box, which lets you choose any file on your computer.

* If you want to store the image of a bill or receipt with its corresponding payment transaction, on the "Receipt/ Bill image" tab, click the "Click here" link to find the image file you want. You'll find receipts much faster than scrounging through your filing cabinet.

* You can attach other images to transactions, like a digital picture of the television that the check purchased. On the "Other attachment" tab, click the "Click here" link.

Tip: On the right side of a transaction, you will see a button with a blue star. If you want to rate the payee for the transaction, either to laud their customer service or warn other customers away, click this button to launch a browser window that takes you to the Zipingo.com Web site. You'll also find customer reviews on that site that may help with your own buying decisions.

8. **If you use Tab to move between fields, press Enter to record the check.**

   If you use Enter to move between fields, press the Enter key one more time or (in the transaction row) click Enter to record the check (see the box on page 101).

Quicken calculates the new balance to reflect the check you wrote and—if sounds are turned on—makes a cash register sound to indicate success. (If all this racket scares the cat off the windowsill in the next room, see the box on page 111 to turn the sounds off.)

Note: When you create transactions, Quicken skips over the Clr field, which shows the status of a transaction as uncleared, cleared, or reconciled. Reconciling (Chapter 7) and downloading transactions (Chapter 6) changes the Clr value automatically. The rest of the time, you're better off leaving this field alone.

Recording Printed Checks

You can print checks right from the register by choosing Printed Check in the Num field, but if you're printing a lot of checks at once, you can have the Write Checks dialog box automatically put them in the printer queue. When you choose Cash Flow → Write Checks (or, if you're keyboard shortcut savvy, press Ctrl+W), the Write Checks dialog box appears. Not surprisingly, it looks like a paper check, as you can see in Figure 4-4. You can fill in check fields and then click Record Check to add the check to the list of payments waiting to print. When you've recorded all the checks, clicking Print sends them to a printer, which hopefully you've already loaded with preprinted checks. (Full printing instructions begin on page 114.)

Using the Write Checks dialog box not only tells Quicken what to print on each check, it also enters the transaction in the Quicken register for you. If you can't see the register, drag the Write Checks dialog box off to the side or minimize it.

Choose the checking account

You create a check in the top half of the Write Checks dialog box much as you would write a check by hand. The one important difference is that the Write Check dialog box doesn't belong to a specific account, so the first choice you must make is in the "Write checks from" drop-down menu.

If you have only one checking account, Quicken automatically selects that account. However, if you write checks from a checking account most of the time and a money market account every once in a while, choose the correct account for the checks you're about to write.

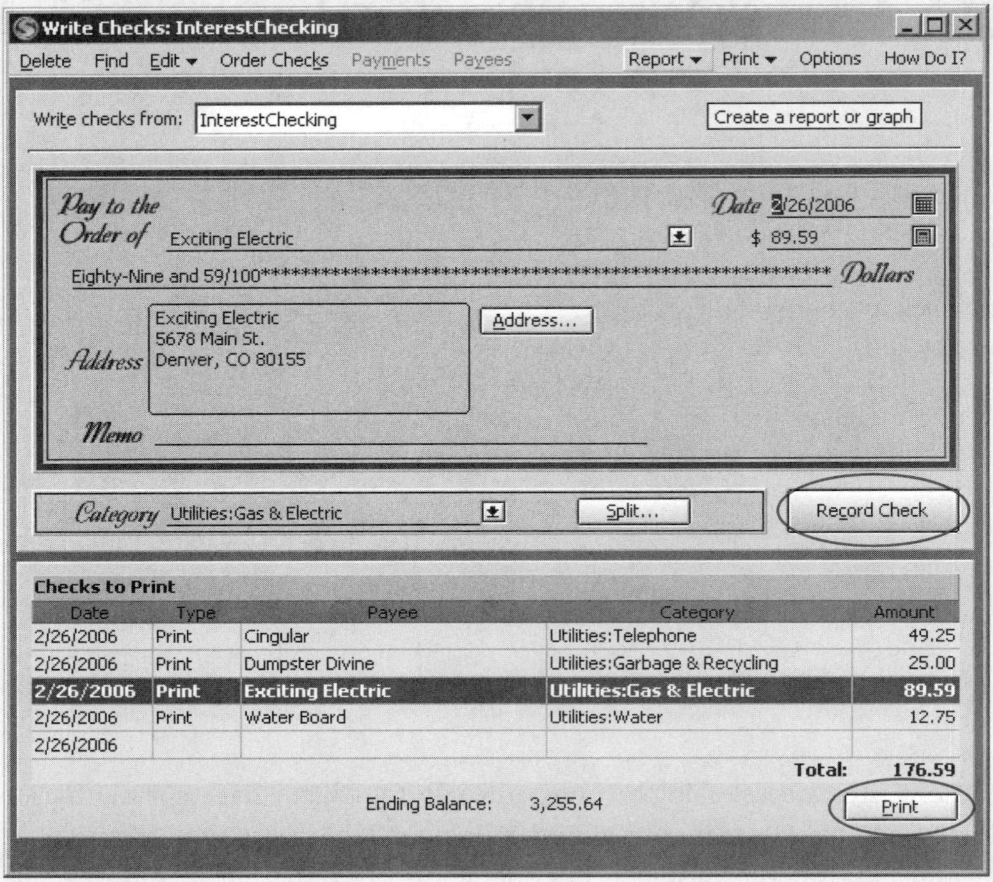

Figure 4-4. When you click Record Check, Quicken adds the check to the list of checks waiting to print at the bottom of the dialog box. Once all your checks are ready to go, click Print to send them to the printer loaded with preprinted check forms.

Filling in check fields

As in the register, you can press Tab to move from field to field (page 101), entering the date, payee, and amount. QuickFill and other data entry shortcuts also work exactly as in the register.

The one field you *don't* see in the Write Checks dialog box is the check number. Printed check forms are prenumbered, since banks can't process stop payments properly without preprinted numbers. Unprinted checks appear in the Quicken check register with the word "Print" in the Num field. Later, when you send the checks to print, you provide the first preprinted check number, and *then* Quicken adds check numbers to the transactions.

QuickFill usually takes care of filling in the category. If the Category field is still blank after you've chosen the payee, move to the Category field and start typing the name of the category. When Quicken chooses the category you want, click Record Check.

 Note: You can split a check between multiple categories. Say you're buying a T-shirt from your favorite nonprofit organization and making a tax-deductible donation at the same time, but paying with only one check. At the bottom of the drop-down category list, click Split, and follow the instructions on page 107. (If the category drop-down menu isn't visible, look to the lower right of the window, below the transaction. There's a Split button there, too.)

Mailing addresses

If you use window envelopes to mail your checks, the first time you write a check to a payee, be sure to click Address and enter the mailing address for that payee. Quicken opens the Edit Address Book Record dialog box, in which you can provide the mailing address and other contact information. When you print checks, Quicken prints the address on the check to show through the window on the envelope.

Reviewing the checks to print

At the bottom of the Write Checks dialog box, Quicken lists the checks you've queued up to print. *Before* you send these checks to the printer and chew through several preprinted check forms, review your checks for accuracy.

If you find a mistake in the Checks to Print list, select the check with the error. Quicken displays the check in the top half of the dialog box. Correct your mistake and click Record Check to record the revised transaction.

 Note: If you created a check by mistake but haven't yet printed it, you can choose Delete in the Write Checks menu bar to completely remove that check. However, once you've printed a check, you must void it *in the register* as described on page 142.

When you're working in the register, it's easy to avoid bouncing checks. Quicken updates the account balance as you add transactions, as shown in Figure 4-1. In the Write Checks dialog box, you have to look a little harder: There are two crucial numbers at the bottom of the window. Below the Amount column, Quicken displays the total amount for all the checks you've queued up to print, shown in Figure 4-4. In the bottom right corner, you find the Current Balance, which is the balance in the account as of today. If the Total for the checks you're printing is greater than the Current Balance, you must deposit or transfer money into the account to cover your checks.

Printing Checks

If you write dozens of checks each month, printing to preprinted computer checks saves both time and your writing hand. You must perform some setup the first time around, but from then on, you simply load preprinted checks into your printer and press a few keys.

Setting up Quicken to print checks

The first step to a successful check printing experience is telling Quicken what type of preprinted checks you use and whether you want to save paper by printing partial pages of checks. The program remembers these settings, so you need to go through this process only once. After you've specified your check printing settings, Quicken fills them in automatically in the Print dialog box. (You can always edit these options before you print).

Purchasing Preprinted Checks

Do I have to order checks from Intuit?

Intuit sells preprinted checks that work with Quicken, but you can purchase checks from your bank or a business form company like Clarke (*www.clarkeamerican.com*) or Deluxe (*www.deluxe.com*) just as easily. Banking regulations require the company to preprint your bank account number, bank routing number, and the check number. Quicken prints the payment information like date, payee, address, and amount.

Although you don't have to buy from Intuit, their preprinted checks have a few advantages. Intuit reminds you when you're running low on checks. You can order from within Quicken by choosing Cash Flow → Quicken Services → Order Checks and Supplies.

Intuit checks work perfectly with Quicken. And the price is about the same as from other sources.

To order Intuit checks, choose Cash Flow → Quicken Services → Order Checks & Supplies. If the Write Checks dialog box is open, in the menu bar, you can click Order Checks. In your Web browser, navigate to *www.intuitmarket.com/qknsupplies.*

If you order your checks from anywhere else, be sure to tell the vendor that you use Quicken. The checks you purchase must have fields positioned to match the locations where Quicken prints data.

Here's how you set up Quicken to print checks:

1. **Choose File → Printer Setup → For Printing Checks.**

   The Check Printer Setup dialog box appears, shown in Figure 4-5, which provides all the settings you need to match Quicken's printer options with the preprinted checks you've purchased.

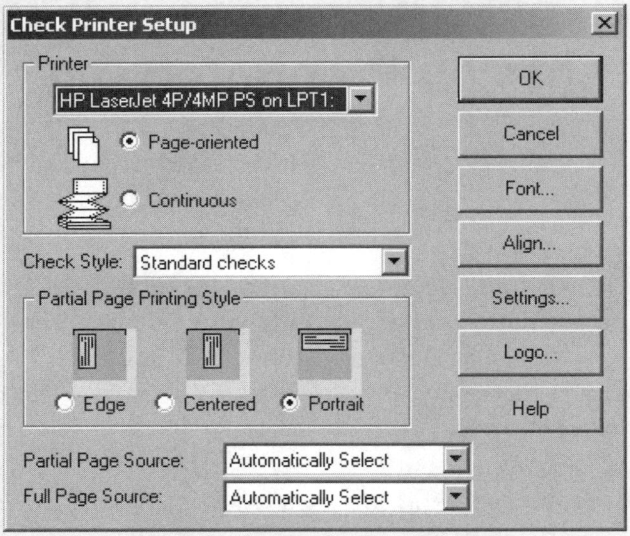

Check Printer Setup

Printer
HP LaserJet 4P/4MP PS on LPT1:

- ⦿ Page-oriented
- ○ Continuous

OK
Cancel
Font...
Align...
Settings...
Logo...
Help

Check Style: Standard checks

Partial Page Printing Style

- ○ Edge
- ○ Centered
- ⦿ Portrait

Partial Page Source: Automatically Select
Full Page Source: Automatically Select

Figure 4-5. Once you've purchased preprinted checks or ordered a new type of pre-printed check, open the Check Printer Setup dialog box to set up Quicken to work with your checks.

2. **In the Printer box, choose the printer you want to use to print checks.**

The Printer drop-down menu contains all the printers that Quicken finds connected to your PC. For example, if you use a laser printer or inkjet printer, Quicken automatically selects the Page-oriented option to feed one sheet at a time to the printer. If you use a printer that feeds paper from a roll, the program chooses the Continuous option.

Tip: If you print checks on continuous feed paper, the alignment of the paper in the printer is critical. You can save time and a lot of wasted checks by aligning the paper *before* you print batches of checks, as described in the box on page 118.

3. **In the Check Style drop-down menu, choose the style of checks you purchased.**

   Quicken chooses Standard Checks, which are plain checks without a voucher or extra stub. Standard Checks are popular because they use the smallest amount of paper. Your Quicken data file contains the record of your check.

   Voucher Checks are forms that contain a check and a detachable voucher that contains complete check information including category and class. Pick this check style if you want a record beyond the electronic one in your Quicken data file. Furthermore, because voucher checks come one to a page, you don't have to bother with feeding partial pages of checks as described in step 4. Wallet Checks print complete check information on a stub on the form's left side.

4. **For page-oriented printers loaded with either Standard or Wallet Checks, choose the option for how you want to feed partial pages of checks into the printer.**

   Quicken chooses the Portrait option automatically, which means feeding the *top* edge of a check into the printer first. If you want to feed the left edge of a check into the printer, choose the Edge option to align the checks to the left edge of the feeder (or choose Centered to center a partial page of checks in the feeder). Because option names aren't all that helpful for visualizing the check orientation, the window includes a graphic example of how to feed the check, which you can see in Figure 4-5.

 Tip: For printers with multiple feed mechanisms or trays, you can choose which feeder to use in the Partial Page Source and Full Page Source drop-down menus. For example, you can feed full pages of checks through the regular feed tray. But when you print partial pages, you can specify Manual Feed to use the sheet that you insert into the manual feed slot.

5. **Click OK to save the settings for check printing.**

   The next section tells you how to print your checks.

Aligning Checks

The slightest gap between what Quicken prints and the corresponding field on a preprinted check can make printed checks hard to read. Unfortunately, printers and preprinted forms sometimes need a little nudge before they play well together. Before you print a big batch of checks, it's a good idea to check the alignment of your preprinted check forms with a test page.

If you're using a page-oriented printer, in the Check Printer Setup dialog box, click Align. In the Align Checks dialog box, click Full Page of Checks. In the File Alignment dialog box (shown here), type distances to adjust where Quicken prints vertically and horizontally. The numbers in Vertical and Horizontal boxes represent hundredths of an inch. So, to realign printing 1/10 of an inch down and to the right on the checks, for instance, type *10* in both boxes. Click Print Sample to test the alignment. Lather, rinse, and repeat until Quicken prints values in the right spot on the preprinted form.

Aligning forms in continuous feed printers varies depending on how badly the alignment is off. The first step is the same: In the Check Printer Setup dialog box, click Align. With the Continuous option set, the dialog box that opens includes a Coarse button and a Fine button. If your checks are off by more than one line of text, click Coarse. After the sample form prints, you see instructions on the screen for adjusting the coarse alignment. Once the vertical alignment is close, click Fine to display the same Fine Alignment dialog box that you see for page-oriented printers (shown here).

Printing to preprinted checks

With check printing settings in place and a list of checks waiting to print, you're finally ready to watch Quicken print your checks in one fell swoop. Here's what you do:

1. **Load your printer with preprinted checks.**

   Getting preprinted checks loaded into continuous feed printers is easy: Line up the holes in the paper with the pins in the printer and make sure that the preprinted side of the check faces up. You may have to experiment a bit if you've never loaded preprinted forms into your printer's tray. The manual that comes with your printer should include instructions for loading paper.

2. **To print the checks-in-waiting, in the Write Checks dialog box, click Print.**

   If the Write Checks dialog box isn't open, press Ctrl+P or choose File → Print Checks. Quicken opens the Select Checks to Print dialog box. As you can see in Figure 4-6, the dialog box title also shows the name of the checking account you're using.

    Note: If you want to write checks from a different account, click Cancel and recreate the checks with the correct account.

3. **In the First Check Number box, type the check number on the first pre-printed check you're using.**

   Quicken uses this number to fill in the Num fields on this batch of checks.

4. **Choose an option to specify the checks you want to print.**

   Quicken automatically selects the All Checks option, which prints all the checks in the queue regardless of their dates. If you tend to queue checks long before you want to pay them, select the Checks Dated Through option and specify the check date.

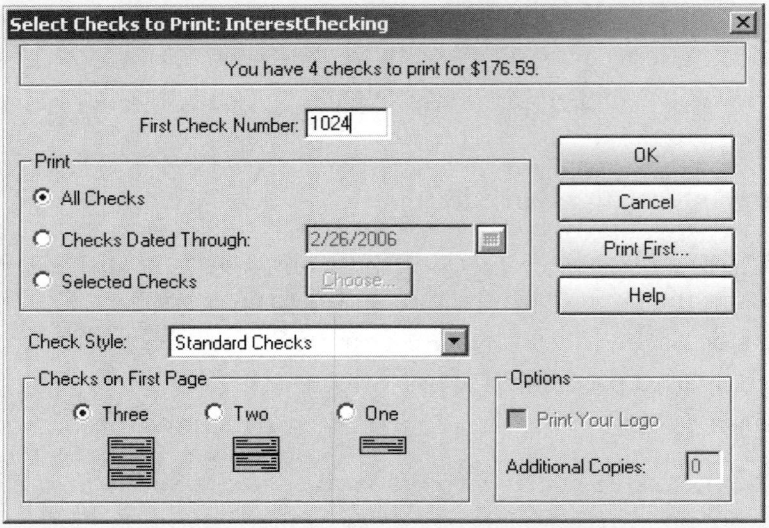

Figure 4-6. If necessary, in the First Check Number box, type the number on the first preprinted check loaded in your printer. Make sure you check all the settings before you click OK, because that's the signal for Quicken to send the checks to the printer.

The Selected Checks option lets you choose individual checks to print, for instance to hold off printing a credit card payment until your next paycheck has cleared.

5. **Make sure the Check Style matches the checks you've loaded in your printer.**

   Quicken uses the Check Style that you set in the Check Printer Setup dialog box (page 116). If you've changed check styles, choose the new style here.

6. **For page-oriented printers, choose the option for the number of checks on the first page.**

   Quicken automatically selects Three, which represents a full page of checks. If the first page has only one or two checks, choose the corresponding option.

Note: If you use the Voucher Checks style, you can use the Additional Copies box. You can type a number in this box if you want Quicken to print extra copies of the voucher. Those copies come in handy if someone you've paid claims that your check was incorrect. You can review the information on your voucher copy to resolve the problem.

7. **Click OK or Print First.**

   To print all the checks, click OK. To print only the first partial page of checks, click Print First. After Quicken prints the checks on a partial page, it updates the number in the First Check number box and changes the Checks on First Page option to Three. Now, you can click OK to print the remaining full pages of checks.

   Quicken sends the checks to the printer and displays a dialog box, asking whether the checks printed correctly. Before you click OK, inspect the checks that come off the printer. If something didn't work right, try again as described in Figure 4-7.

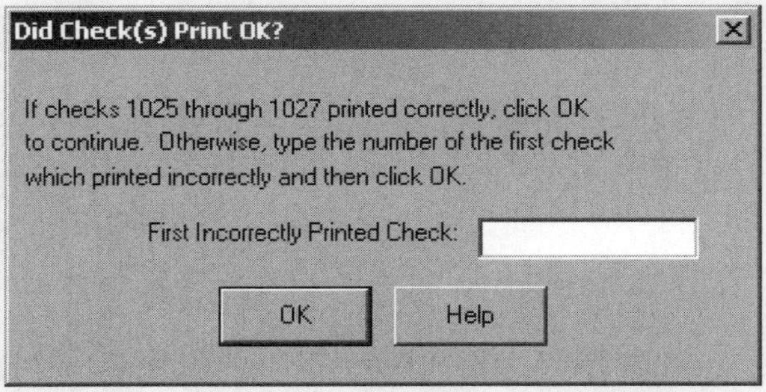

Figure 4-7. If you run into trouble printing your checks—a paper jam, a misalignment, or no toner, for example—in the First Incorrectly Printed Check box, type the number of the first check that didn't print correctly, and then click OK to try again.

8. **If your checks printed correctly, click OK and you're done.**

   Quicken adds the check numbers for the printed checks to the transactions in the checking account register. Now, all you have to do is sign the checks, stuff them in envelopes, and get them in the mail.

Recording Deposits

Recording a deposit into an account is *almost* identical to recording a check. Figure 4-8 shows an example of a deposit being entered. Follow the steps starting on page 103, but with the following adjustments:

In the Num field, choose Deposit (or type D) instead of entering a check number. When you choose Deposit, Quicken changes the order in which you tab through fields to match the task at hand. The program automatically jumps to the Deposit field instead of the Payment field for deposit transactions, to stop you from accidentally recording the deposit as a payment.

Here are the fields and the order in which Quicken moves through them:

▶ Date

▶ Payee

▶ Deposit

▶ Category

▶ Memo

In the Deposit field, type how much money you're depositing.

Like checks, deposits can belong to categories, but there are some special considerations, as described in the box on page 124.

Paying with a Credit Card

Credit cards have become many people's favorite way to pay. Some folks like the convenience of swiping a card out at the gas pump and avoiding the junk food

The Quicken Calculator

If your deposit includes more than one item, turn your attention to the Quicken Calculator icon in the Deposit field. This feature isn't a data entry shortcut or a replacement for your business calculator. You'll use it most often to add up several checks you're depositing for the same category, because it automatically fills in the Deposit field with the result when you're done.

The Quicken calculator does the same simple calculations that the Windows calculator or the calculator keys on your computer do: addition, subtraction, multiplication, division, and percentages. In fact, when the pointer's in a transaction's Payment or Deposit field, you can start pressing the calculator keys on your keyboard and Quicken automatically launches its calculator for you. As you press number keys, the digits appear in the field. And if you press +, -, *, or /, the Quicken calculator keypad appears immediately below the field and shows the results of your keystrokes.

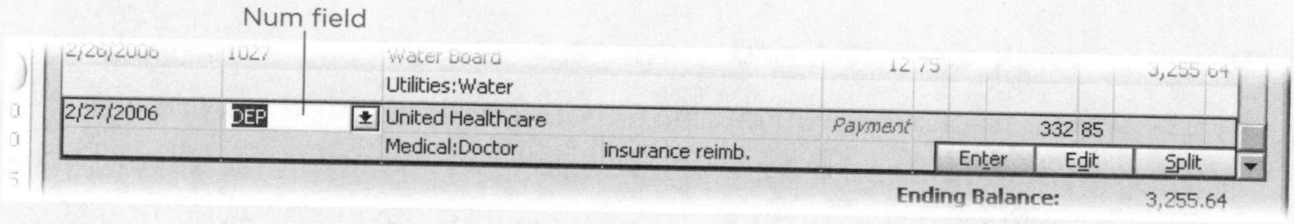

Figure 4-8. To deposit money in an account, in the Num field, choose Deposit. The Deposit field is where you specify how much money you're depositing.

inside the station. Others like the airline miles or cash back they receive. And of course, some people seem to enjoy paying obscenely high interest rates on the balances they carry on their cards. In Quicken, there are two ways you can track your credit card charges: Create a cash flow account to record each credit card charge, or record just the payments to the credit card company in your Quicken

Assigning a Category for a Deposit

The category that you assign to a deposit depends on the type of deposit. For example, when you deposit your paycheck or a monetary gift from your Dad, you might choose a category like Salary or Gift Received, respectively.

For *some* deposits, you might choose a category that you typically use for expenses. For example, suppose you go to the doctor and assign Medical:Doctor as the category for the check you wrote to pay for the office visit. When your health insurance plan reimburses you for the doctor's charges, you can assign the deposit to Medical:Doctor as well. This action reduces the total amount you've spent in the Medical:Doctor category, which is just what you want at tax time when you need to know your out-of-pocket medical expenses for your tax deduction.

check register. As you'll see in this section, though, tracking each credit card charge individually offers so many advantages, it's almost a no-brainer.

How to Track Credit Card Charges

The best way to track what you charge to your credit card is to record individual charges every few days and assign each charge to a category in Quicken. Then, when your credit card statement arrives, you can reconcile the account (see Chapter 7) and record the check you write to pay your credit card bill (see page 103). This approach has two huge advantages:

▶ **Complete spending records.** If you pay for a lot of what you buy with your credit card, you can assign every charge to one or more categories and know exactly how you spend your money. With doctors, dentists, and just about everyone else accepting credit cards for payment, you'll also have complete records of your tax deductions.

- **Spending red flags.** If you feel as if credit card charges somehow don't use *real* money, tracking individual charges as you make them keeps the cash you owe in plain sight. Swiping your card at the store is still incredibly easy, but the alarming increase in your credit card balance may diminish your yearning for that five-way massage chair. (For more tips on keeping charges under control, see the box on page 128.)

In Quicken, recording credit card charges is just as easy as recording checks. If you set up your credit card for online downloads, you don't have to record charges, although manual recording using your charge slips as references is a great way to catch erroneous or fraudulent charges on your credit card statement. For example, after entering your charges manually, you can download the charges from your credit card company (page 233) and compare them. If you see extra charges that don't match the ones you entered, either you forgot to record a charge or someone's buying stuff with your card. If you check your charges every few days, you can report the activity to your credit card company before the thieves have too much fun at your expense.

 Note: Don't even think about bypassing individual credit card transactions by recording only the check you write to pay your credit card bill. You'll have a much harder time trying to split your check transaction across lots of categories than creating many individual transactions. Moreover, if you have a problem with a charge, you'll have a really hard time finding the original charge among all those splits.

Recording Credit Card Transactions

Recording credit card transactions is mostly the same as recording checks and deposits in other accounts. The basic steps are described on pages 103–110. You specify the date, payee, amount, category, and optionally a memo. A credit card register, though, has a Ref (for *reference*) field instead of the Num field. Quicken includes this field on the off chance that you want to type the terribly long identification strings that you see on your credit card statement. Just press Tab to move past the Ref field and choose the payee.

Credit card transactions come in a few flavors. Figure 4-9 and the list that follows show how you handle each one:

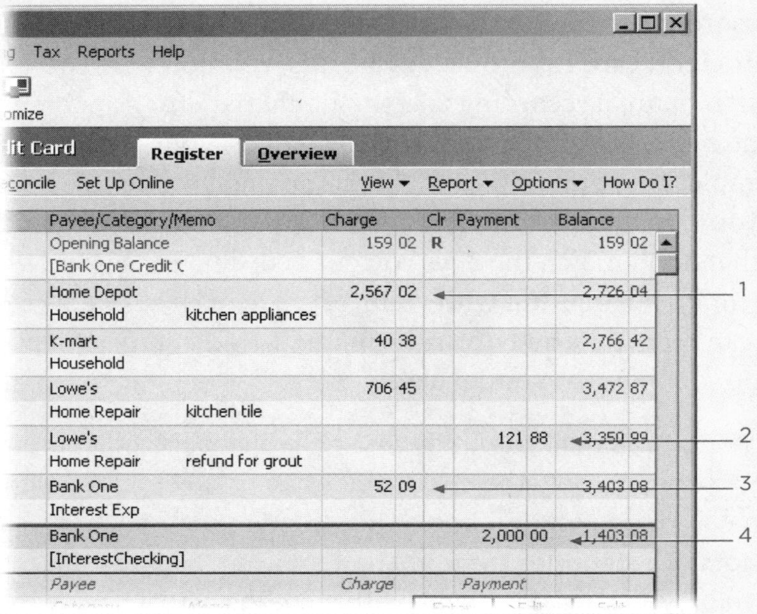

Figure 4-9. In a credit card register, amounts for charges go in the Charge field (1). Payment amounts, whether for credits or payments, go in the Payment field (2). Finance charges are like other charges but go to a category, like Interest Exp (3). Payment transactions (4) appear in the account register when you write a check for a payment (transferring the money to the credit card account in Quicken).

▶ **Charges.** Create credit card charges in the register. The merchant who accepted your credit card is the payee. Type the amount in the Charge column.

- **Payments.** Typically, you'll create a credit card payment by recording a check in your checking account. In the check transaction, when you assign the Xref Acct (the account to which you're transferring funds, as described on page 137) to your credit card account, Quicken automatically records the payment in your checking account register and deposits the payment amount in your credit card register.

- **Other credits.** If you return the Vespa scooter you bought because you don't like bugs in your teeth, the Vespa dealer might post a credit to your credit card account. To enter a credit, fill in all the fields as you would for a charge, except for the amount field. Type the amount in the *Payment* field instead of the Charge field.

- **Finance charges and fees.** If you don't pay your balance each month, the credit card company charges you interest—and usually lots of it. For a finance charge transaction, type the name of the credit card company in the Payee field, and then choose a category like Interest Exp.

- **Credit card rebates.** If you use a credit card that pays some sort of rebate, the technique for recording the rebate depends on the rebate and your preference. For example, if the credit card company sends you a check, you can record the deposit as you would any other. One way to categorize the rebate is to use an income category, perhaps one dedicated to rebates.

  If the card pays a rebate on specific types of purchases, you can record the deposit against the corresponding category. For example, if you receive a rebate for auto fuel, you can use the Auto:Fuel category for your deposit, which reduces your total fuel expenses.

Paying with Cash

You can withdraw money from an ATM, spend it, and, within hours, have not the foggiest idea how you spent it. Unfortunately, Quicken doesn't improve your memory for petty cash expenditures in the least, so your memory's the deciding factor in how you track what you buy with cash. This section outlines two of the most popular methods.

Putting the Brakes on Charging

If you've charged ahead once too often, Quicken alerts can raise a red flag before you get into trouble. A credit card account in Quicken includes a Credit Limit field, which you can set so that Quicken displays an alert when you've exceeded your limit. With credit cards, you don't want to *exceed* your credit limit, because that could result in an embarrassing turndown when you try to use your card, for instance to pay for dinner on a first date.

Instead of filling in the Credit Limit field with the *actual* credit limit on your card, use a value a few thousand below your limit. Better yet, fill in the Credit Limit field with the limit you set to ensure that you can afford to pay the balance off each month.

The fastest way to change the credit limit on a credit card account is in the Account Bar. Right-click the credit card account and, on the shortcut menu, click Edit account to open the Account Details dialog box. In the Credit Limit text box, type the value at which you want Quicken to alert you, and then click OK.

The only downside to this alert feature is that Quicken's subtle with its warnings. You can see alerts that you've triggered if you open the Cash Flow Center or if you include alerts in Quicken Home (see the box on page 71 for more detail.)

Cash Tracking for Photographic Memories

If you remember every dime you've spent since the first grade *and* you want to track your cash expenditures, here's the rigorous way to track cash:

1. **Create a cash flow account for the cash in your wallet.**

   For a refresher on creating accounts, see page 62 in Chapter 2.

2. **When you withdraw money from the ATM, the drive-through window, or even inside at a teller window, record that withdrawal in Quicken as a transfer to your cash account.**

   The transfer reduces the balance in your checking or savings account and increases the amount of money in the cash account.

3. **Every few days, create transactions in the cash account to reflect what you've purchased—cappuccinos, video rentals, or that tasteful tattoo.**

   If the balance in the Quicken cash account matches the money in your wallet, you're all set.

 Tip: You can even reconcile your cash account in Quicken to the cash you have in your wallet (see page 265). (If you actually do that, though, you may need counseling for obsessive financial tracking.)

No matter how close your habits resemble Felix Unger's, you *will* forget how you spent cash every now and then. Don't panic. Just assign the money to a category like Cash. Likewise, you probably don't care about change spent on a newspaper or chewing gum. When you compare your cash on hand to your Quicken cash account balance, create one catch-all transaction assigned to the Cash category to square things up.

When Your Memory Is Like a Sieve

If remembering how you spent your cash is a lost cause or you use cash very rarely, you can take a much simpler approach in Quicken. You can treat your wallet like a "payee" instead of creating a separate cash flow account.

When you withdraw spending money, create a transaction using ATM in the Payee field. Name the payee something like Cash or Mad Money. Assign the transaction to a catch-all category (Quicken automatically creates one called Cash).

At the end of the year, run an Itemized Categories report (Chapter 10) to see how much cash you spent. If your unaccounted spending amounts to the gross national product of a small nation, you might consider saving all your receipts or capturing cash spending in a notebook or PDA, and then recording transactions for cash spending in Quicken.

Splitting Transactions

Most of the time, a check or a credit card charge applies only to one category. Life is simple: You create the transaction, pick the category, and Quicken tracks how you spent that money. But more often than you might think, a transaction applies to *more than one* category. For example, you deposit a mélange of checks—a birthday present from your favorite aunt, a health insurance reimbursement, and the $20 prize you won in a pie-eating contest. The popularity of monumentally huge supermarkets also means that one check may cover groceries, auto supplies, running shoes, and a photo of your baby. Quicken handles these multipurpose payments with *splits*—transactions that you split among several categories.

Another fine use of a split transaction is when you want to deposit only *part* of a check amount in the bank and take the rest in cash. Simply record the check deposit into the bank account as one part of the transaction and a transfer to your Quicken cash account as another.

Adding Multiple Categories to a Transaction

To split a transaction, begin creating the transaction as you normally would, by typing the payee name and the amount.

Then follow these steps to split a payment among several categories:

1. **In the register, select the transaction you want to split, and then click the Split button (Figure 4-10, top) or press Ctrl+S.**

   The Split Transaction dialog box opens with the insertion point in the first row in the Category column.

   You can also open the Split Transaction dialog box from the Category field. Click the down arrow and then, at the bottom of the Category drop-down menu, click the Split button or press Ctrl+S.

	3/7/2006	EFT	First Focus S&L			1,000	00			-3,184	75	
			[House Loan]									
	3/1/2006	1028	Target			393.12 🔲		Deposit				
			Category	Memo		Enter		Edit		Split		

Ending Balance: -3,?84.75

Download Transactions   Scheduled Transactions (10 Due)

Split Transaction

Enter multiple categories to itemize this transaction; use the Memo field to record more details.

	Category	Memo	Amount
1.	Groceries		226 33
2.	Auto:Service	oil	24 95
3.	Clothing		109 62
4.			32 22
5.	**Cash** — Expense		Next Edit
6.	**Charity** — Expense		
7.	**Charity-Non Cash** — Expense		
8.	**Clothing** — Expense		
9.	**Computer** — Expense		
10.	**Dining** — Expense		
11.	**Education** — Expense		
12.	**Entertainment** — Expense		
13.	Show Hidden		
14.			

Figure 4-10. Top: Click Split (indicated by cursor) to open the Split Transaction dialog box. You can also click Split at the bottom of the Category drop-down menu. Bottom: You don't have to enter the amount for the last split, because Quicken calculates how much of the payment's still unassigned after each split (in this case, it's 32.22).

2. **In the Category field, choose the category you want.**

The Category fields in the Split Transaction dialog box work the same way as the Category field in a transaction. You can type the first few letters of a category name and let Quicken fill in the category. Or, you can scroll through the Category drop-down menu to choose the one you want.

> **Note:** If you want to add a memo about the split, in the Memo field, type the text *before* moving to the Amount field.

3. **Press Tab to move to the Amount field, and then type the amount that belongs in this category.**

   Press Tab once more to move to the next row. Quicken automatically subtracts the amount for the category from the total transaction amount and fills in the Amount field in the new row with the unassigned amount (Figure 4-10, bottom). If the amount for the category doesn't match the remaining unassigned amount, double-click the Amount field and type the new value.

4. **Repeat steps 2 and 3 for each additional category.**

   For the last category, the remaining unassigned amount should match the amount intended for that category, if you did your math right.

5. **To save the splits, click OK.**

   Back in the register in the Category field, you see "--Split--," but you're not quite done.

6. **Click Enter to record the transaction.**

   Now you're done.

Editing Splits

You can tell that a transaction has splits when you see "--Split--" in the Category field. Quicken also displays two new buttons (Figure 4-11), which you can use to view or edit the splits:

- ▶ **Green checkmark.** Click this button to open the Split Transaction dialog box. You can view and edit the splits.

- ▶ **Red X.** Click this button to clear all categories and split values. If you confirm that you want to remove the splits, Quicken removes all categories and split values.

Using Split Transactions to Total Deposits

If you're faced with a pile of checks to deposit, don't reach for your calculator—you can use the Split Transaction dialog box to figure out the total of your deposit. The Quicken calculator is fine if you're adding up several checks for the same category. But to create a deposit transaction that assigns each check to a different category, splits are the way to go.

To coax Quicken into playing calculator, don't fill in a value in the transaction's Deposit field. Instead, click the

Split button to open the Split Transaction dialog box. The Transaction Total at the bottom of the dialog box is initially 0.00, but it shows the total of all your checks as you enter them in the split rows. When you've accounted for all your checks, click OK to save the splits. In the register, Quicken fills in the transaction's Amount field with the total that it calculated.

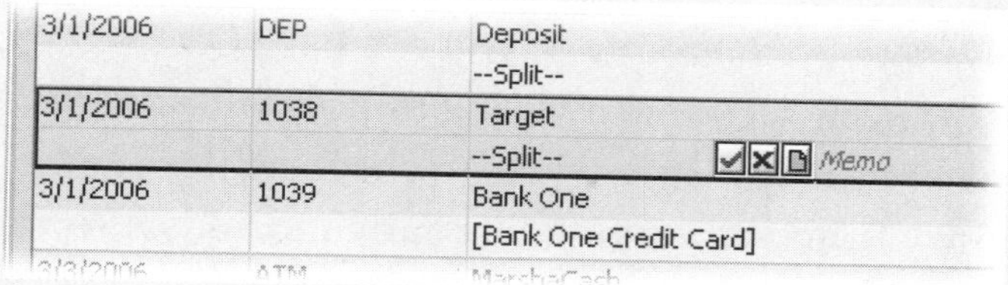

Figure 4-11. To view or edit the splits on a transaction, click the button with the checkmark. If you want to clear all the splits, click the button with the X. When the message box appears asking if you want to clear all split lines, click Yes only if you want to clear all categories and amounts.

Handling Remaining Amounts

Every once in a while, you'll end up with a Remainder value, which is the difference between the total that Quicken calculates from all your splits and the total amount for the transaction, which you entered in the register in the Payment or

Deposit field. For example, suppose you create a deposit transaction and enter *500* in the Deposit field. In the Split Transaction dialog box, you then enter each check you have to deposit and they total only $490. Quicken calculates the Remainder value of 10.00.

With a Remainder value, you have two choices:

▶ **Adjust the transaction total.** If the values of all your splits are correct and the transaction total is the number that's wrong, click Adjust. This move keeps your splits as they are and changes the value for the transaction, as you can see in Figure 4-12.

▶ **Correct the split values.** If you're missing a category or split values are incorrect, make the changes until the Remainder value is 0.00. Then click OK to save the splits.

Transferring Money Between Accounts

Chances are you transfer money between accounts all the time. For example, you keep your cash in a savings account where it earns interest and transfer it to your checking account only when it's time to pay the plumber. (What are those pipes made out of, anyway—*gold*?) Anyway, you can have Quicken record the movement of money between accounts by using *transfer transactions*. When you tell Quicken to transfer money from savings to checking, for example, the program removes the money from your savings account and adds it to your checking account. The clever thing about Quicken transfers is that the category you assign isn't a category like Groceries but the account to which you're transferring money. This section shows you how the whole process works.

Recording a Transfer Between Accounts

Recording a transfer between accounts is much like recording a check, with a few minor differences. You can use Quicken's Transfer dialog box, which provides some handholding to help you get the transfer the right way 'round, but the quickest way to record a transfer is directly in the account register. Here are the steps:

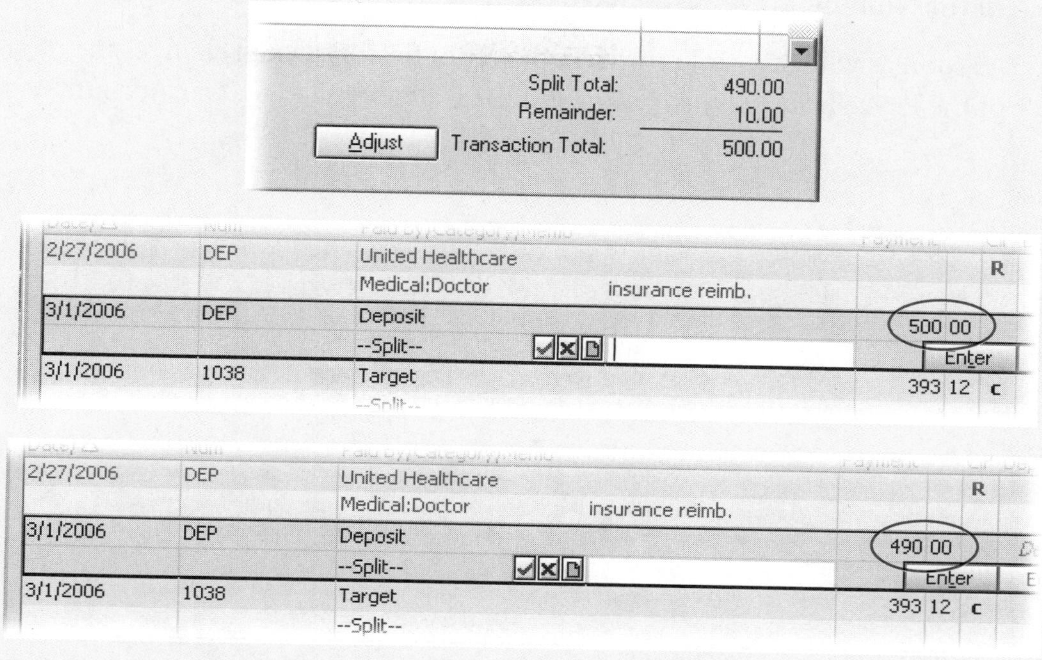

	Split Total:	490.00
	Remainder:	10.00
Adjust	Transaction Total:	500.00

2/27/2006	DEP	United Healthcare			R
		Medical:Doctor	insurance reimb.		
3/1/2006	DEP	Deposit		500 00	
		--Split-- ☑☒🗋 |		Enter	
3/1/2006	1038	Target		393 12	c
		--Split--			

2/27/2006	DEP	United Healthcare			R
		Medical:Doctor	insurance reimb.		
3/1/2006	DEP	Deposit		490 00	D
		--Split-- ☑☒🗋		Enter	E
3/1/2006	1038	Target		393 12	c
		--Split--			

Figure 4-12. Top: This is the transaction with its original total. To keep the split amounts and adjust the transaction total, click Adjust.
Middle: Quicken removes the Remainder value from the transaction total.
Bottom: This is the transaction after adjusting its total.

1. **Open the register for the account *from which* you're transferring money.**

   For example, if you're transferring money from your checking account to savings, open the register for your checking account. When you open a register, Quicken automatically positions the insertion point in a blank transaction.

2. **In the Date field, choose the date for the transfer.**

   If your financial institution has rules about when transfers occur, you can keep your account balances more accurate by using the date when the money will actually move between accounts.

3. **In the Num field, type T to make the transaction a Transfer (Figure 4-13).**

As soon as you choose Transfer in the Num field, Quicken changes the name of the Payee field to Description and the Category field to Xfer Account.

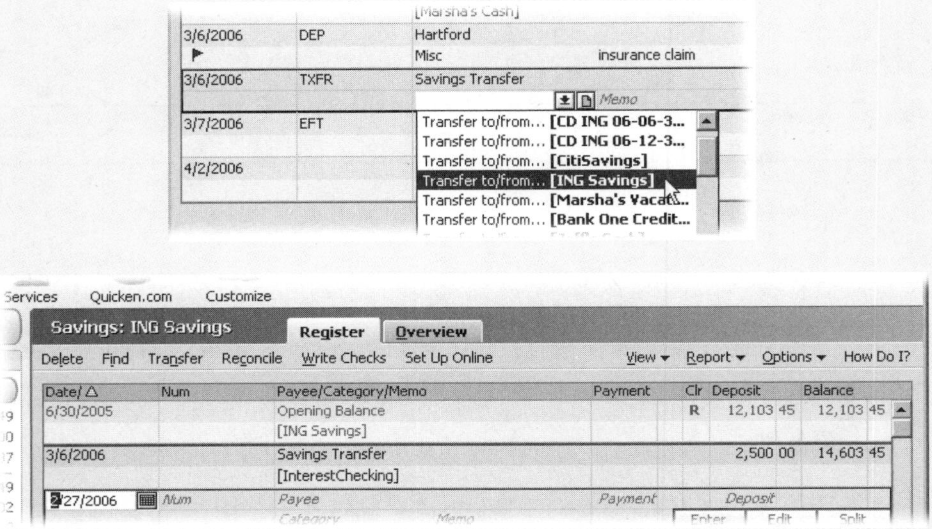

Figure 4-13. Top: When you choose Transfer in the Num field, Quicken automatically displays accounts in the Category field.
Bottom: After you record a transfer in the account from which you remove money, you can view the other half of the transfer in the register for the account that receives the money.

4. **In the Description field, type a name for the transfer you're making.**

Because Quicken memorizes payees, you can use this description to recall the values for this transfer the next time you move money between accounts. For example, when you type *Savings Transfer* in the description field, Quicken automatically chooses your savings account and the amount of the transfer.

5. **In the Payment field, type the amount you're transferring out of the account.**

   Most people think of transfers as moving money *out of* one account and into another, typing the transfer amount in the Payment field, as in this example. But it's perfectly fine to do it the other way: You'd create the transaction in the register for the account that's receiving the money and type the transfer amount in the *Deposit* field. The result is the same either way. (For example, the transfer into savings shown at the bottom of Figure 4-13 shows the amount in the Deposit field.)

6. **In the Xfer Account field, choose the account that receives the money for the transfer.**

   As soon as you press Tab or click to move into the Xfer Account field, Quicken displays a drop-down menu of accounts, as you can see in Figure 4-13. Although Quicken shows you the account names within brackets, you can quickly choose an account by typing the first character or two of the name.

7. **Press the Enter key or click Enter to save the transfer.**

   That's it! Quicken knows your money has switched to another account.

Seeing the Other Side of a Transfer

For transfers, Quicken actually creates a *second* transaction in the account at the other end of the transfer. In the register, right-click a transfer transaction and, on the shortcut menu that appears, choose "Go to matching transaction." If you use Quicken's standard keyboard mapping (page 40), you can press Ctrl+X to jump to the other end of the transfer.

Transfers Masquerading as Checks

Sometimes, checks that you write act like transfers in Quicken. For example, consider the check you write to pay your credit card bill. In the real world, the credit card company cashes your check and credits your account with the payment. In Quicken, the check transfers money out of your checking account to reduce the balance on your credit card account. Similarly, the check you deposit into your money market account transfers money from your Quicken checking account to your Quicken money market account.

When you record a check in Quicken, you can transform the check transaction into a transfer simply by choosing the appropriate *account* in the Category field. You have to scroll to the very bottom of the drop-down menu to find them, but, because Quicken encases accounts in square brackets, you can type [(an open bracket) to jump to the first account on the Category drop-down menu.

Editing Transactions

If you notice a mistake in a transaction (the wrong amount, the wrong payee, or a check you wrote for dog food assigned to the Interest Exp category), you can simply go back to the transaction and change those details, as described in this section.

You can edit freely as long as you haven't yet reconciled the transaction. Quicken doesn't stop you from editing a reconciled transaction, but you must do so with the utmost care or your next account reconciliation will be fraught with problems. See the box on page 139 for more information.

Editing a Field in a Transaction

Editing a transaction in the account register is simple. Click the transaction field that contains the mistake, correct the information, and then click Enter.

If you click another transaction without first clicking Enter, Quicken displays a message box that asks you if you want to save the changes to the transaction. Click Yes to save the changes. Click No to discard them. If you were distracted by a phone call and can't remember which transaction you were working on, you can click Cancel until you remember what you were doing.

 Tip: If you want to replace many occurrences of a value in transactions, try using the Find/Replace command, described on page 149.

WORKAROUND WORKSHOP
Editing After Reconciling

Once you've reconciled a transaction, which is indicated by an "R" in the Clr field, you shouldn't change its amount unless you're looking for a mindbender of a problem to solve. Changing the amount of a reconciled transaction means that the numbers for your next reconciliation for the account won't balance.

Because Quicken doesn't tell you which transaction you edited after reconciliation, correcting the error usually requires digging out last month's statement and reviewing discrepancies carefully. To use Quicken's reconciliation report to find errors, choose Reports → Banking → Reconciliation. (See "A Quick Guide to Quicken Reports" on page 359 for more detail.)

However, if you find that you assigned the wrong category to a transaction, you can click the Category field of a reconciled transaction, ever so carefully change *only* the category (below), and then click Enter to save the change.

Recategorizing Transactions

The day may come when you realize that your Category List isn't quite what you need. For example, you start with Medical:Doctor and Medical:Medicine, but at tax time you see that you can declare deductions for doctor visits, medicines, dentistry, eyeglasses, and more. You dive in and create several new categories only to be disappointed by reports for tax-deductible expenses that don't look any different. Quicken isn't a mind reader. You have to reassign your *existing* transactions to the *new* categories. Fortunately, the Recategorize command does just what you want. Here's how you put it to work:

1. **If a category that you intend to use doesn't exist, create it before choosing the Recategorize command.**

   The Recategorize command doesn't include an option to add a category. You must create all the new categories (as described on page 80) to which you want to reassign transactions *before* you open the Recategorize dialog box.

2. **Choose Edit → Find & Replace → Recategorize.**

   Quicken opens the Recategorize dialog box with the insertion point in the Search Category box.

3. **If you want to look for specific types of transactions, in the Recategorize menu bar, click Find, and then choose the type of transaction.**

   Quicken automatically chooses Transactions, which searches all transactions in all accounts. To limit the search to payees you use frequently, try choosing Memorized Payee. You can also limit the search to scheduled transactions, for instance to find all instances of a scheduled transaction that you miscategorized when you set it up last year.

4. **In the Search Category drop-down menu, choose the category you want to change.**

   Choose a category even if you're planning to change only some of the transactions in that category. As you can see in Figure 4-14, you can select individual transactions to recategorize.

    Note: In the lower left corner of the dialog box, Quicken automatically turns on the Show Matches in Split checkbox, which is the best way to ensure that you recategorize everything you want. If you split transactions among several categories, this setting finds every use of a category.

5. **Click Find All.**

   Quicken displays all the transactions assigned to the category you chose and activates the Replace With box.

6. **In the Replace With drop-down menu, choose the new category.**

   For example, to break your medical expenses into doctor's and dentist's expenses, in the Replace With drop-down menu, choose Medical:Dentist.

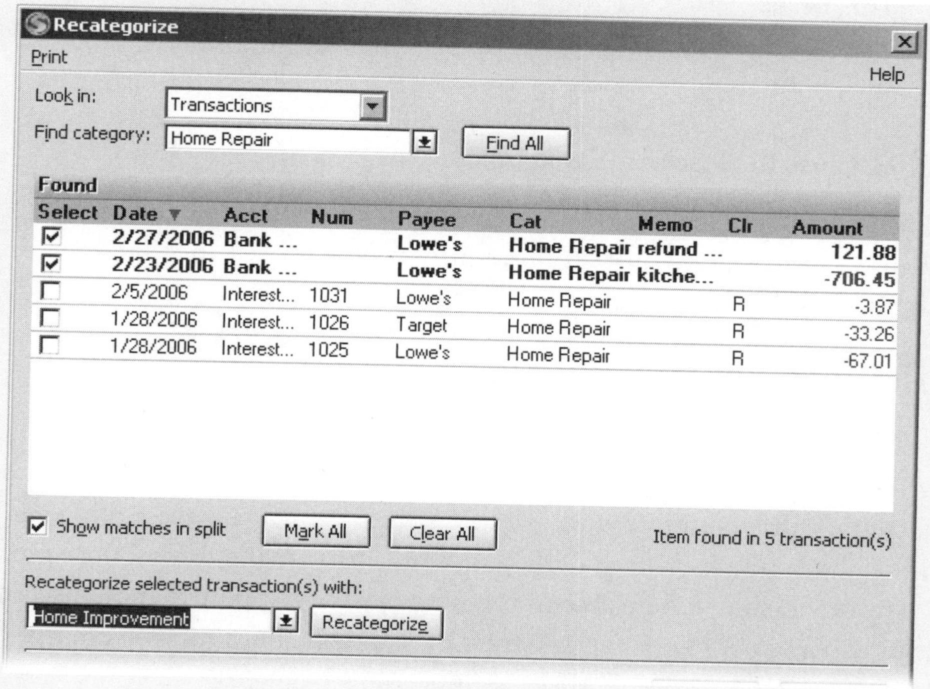

Figure 4-14. The Recategorize command can find transactions assigned to one category and reassign the transactions you choose to a different category. In this example, the two checked Home Repair transactions will be recategorized as Home Improvement.

7. **To select a transaction to recategorize, click the first column in the row for the transaction.**

   Quicken adds green checkmarks to transactions that you select. To reassign all transactions in the list, click Mark All. Click a green checkmark to unselect a transaction.

8. **Click Recategorize.**

   A confirmation box appears, asking if you're sure that you want to make the replacement. Click OK to continue. Click Cancel if you have a change of heart. When you click OK, Quicken immediately changes the transactions listed in the dialog box, so you can review the results before continuing.

Tip: Unless your category names are very terse, you may not notice the change. Position your pointer over a category to make Quicken reveal its full name.

9. **Click Close to close the dialog box.**

   The Recategorize dialog box remains open after you replace a category. If you want to recategorize more transactions, repeat steps 3 through 8. If you're done, click Close.

Voiding Transactions

Occasionally, you may want to cancel a transaction but keep a record of it in Quicken. For instance, if you write a check to the Princess Telephone Historical Society and think better of your donation, you can tear up the paper check and void the check transaction in Quicken. You'll still see the transaction and the check number, so you'll be able to remember what happened and know that you didn't drop a paper check on the street by accident. But Quicken changes the amount to zero so it doesn't affect your account balance.

The quickest way to void a transaction is to right-click the transaction in the register and then, on the shortcut menu that appears, choose "Void transaction(s)". When you void a transaction, Quicken makes the following changes to the transaction:

▶ Adds the word "Void" to the beginning of the Payee field.

▶ Changes the status of the transaction to cleared, indicated by a checkmark in the Clr field.

▶ Changes the field containing the transaction amount to zero. Quicken also zeroes out any categories and splits.

If you use the Quicken Standard keyboard mapping, you can also void a transaction by selecting it and then pressing Ctrl+V.

Tip: You can get rid of a transaction completely in case you need to remove a duplicate deposit that makes your account balance look much better than it really is. In the register, right-click the transaction and then, on the shortcut menu, choose Delete. You can also press Ctrl+D.

Searching for Transactions

Before you know it, your Quicken registers will be teeming with transactions. You can scroll through the register or press the Page Up and Page Down keys to sift through the register as if you're thumbing through the dog-eared pages of a paper register. But Quicken has easier ways to find a specific transaction, like the check you wrote that piqued the IRS's interest. The program includes several features that help you track down transactions that you want to look at or edit—including a one-click method that's new to Quicken 2006.

Finding Recent Transactions with One Click

A new, if tiny, icon appears to the right of the Payee and Category drop-down arrows in all transactions in Quicken 2006. Clicking these buttons lets you review recent transactions for payees and categories across *all* your accounts, as shown in Figure 4-15. For instance, you can check to see whether you paid the electric bill or find out how much your husband has spent on lawn maintenance this summer.

When you click the little piece of paper next to the Payee arrow, Quicken opens a box showing the last several transactions for the payee in any account. Review those transactions to make sure you've paid a bill, to see how much you've spent during a certain time period, or to look for trends in spending. To see previous transactions for a category in any account, click the icon next to the Category drop-down arrow.

In the pop-up transaction list, you see a time period immediately below the payee or category name. To change the period, click the down arrow to the right of the date range and choose from the drop-down menu. You can set the range

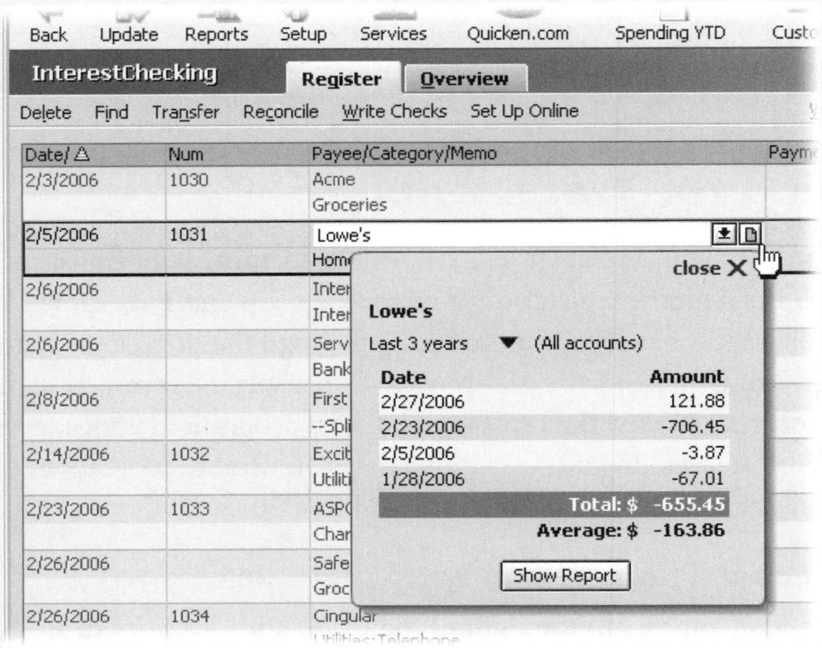

Figure 4-15. Clicking the icon next to the Payee drop-down arrow pops up a list of the last several transactions for the payee. Clicking the icon next to the Category drop-down arrow (not shown) shows recent transactions for the selected category.

from as short as the last 30 days to the last 3 years. To see more detail about these transactions, click Show Report, and Quicken generates a report showing the transactions for the payee or category for the last 12 months.

Finding All Transactions

To search for payments and deposits regardless of which account they're in, use the text box and the Find All button in the upper right corner of Quicken's main window (Figure 4-16). Although the tip text in the text box initially says "Find Payment or Deposit," you can type text or values in the box to search every field of payment, deposit, and transfer transactions. You can type a portion of the text or value you want to find. Quicken searches for transactions in all the accounts listed in the Cash Flow Center that contain the search text anywhere in a field. Click Find All to open the Search Results window, which lists all the matching transactions that Quicken locates.

If you want to change a value in one or more transactions, first select the transactions you want to edit by turning on their checkboxes. Then, click Edit Transaction(s) to open the Find and Replace dialog box (see the next section for instructions).

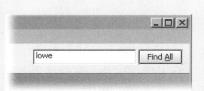

lowe
Find All
Search Results
Print Zoom
Help Close
Found
Select Date Acct Num Payee Cat Memo Clr Amount
2/27/2006 Bank O... Lowe's Home Repair refund f... 121.88
2/23/2006 Bank On... Lowe's Home Repair kitchen tile -706.45
2/5/2006 Interest... 1031 Lowe's Home Repair R -3.87
1/28/2006 Interest... 1025 Lowe's Home Repair R -67.01
Show matches in split
Item found in 4 transaction(s)
Edit Transaction(s)
Close

Figure 4-16. Top: In the Find All text box, type all or a portion of the text you want to find, and click Find All to search all cash flow accounts. This all-encompassing search feature is new in Quicken 2006.
Bottom: Quicken opens the Search Results dialog box, which lists all matching transactions. You can select and edit the transactions in the list. In this example, the first line item is selected.

Finding Transactions

If you're sure the transaction you're looking for is in the open register, you can limit your search to that register by using Find instead of Find All. The Find and Find Next commands work together to locate transactions in the active account that contain the *value* you specify in the transaction *field* that you choose. Quicken's Find feature isn't sophisticated, but you'll quickly learn how to find the transactions you're looking for. Here's what you do:

1. **Press Ctrl+F to open the Quicken Find dialog box.**

    In the register menu bar, you can also choose Find. Or, in the Quicken main window, choose Edit → Find & Replace → Find.

    > **Tip:** If you right-click a field in a transaction and, on the shortcut menu, choose Find, Quicken uses the value in the field to fill in the Search field and Find field in the Quicken Find dialog box. For example, if you right-click the Category field for a transaction that's assigned to Home Repair, Quicken sets the Search field to Category/Class and the Find field to Home Repair.

2. **In the Search drop-down menu, choose the field you want to search.**

    Quicken fills in all the boxes of the Quicken Find dialog box with your last search criteria and positions the insertion point in the Find box, as shown in Figure 4-17.

    If you want to search for a value in *all* transaction fields instead of just one, choose All Fields. This choice is incredibly helpful if you know that the transaction you want includes a word, like "market," but you can't remember in which field it appears.

3. **If you want to broaden or narrow the search, in the "Match if" drop-down menu, choose how precisely the results must match the value in the Find box.**

    Quicken automatically chooses Contains, which is the most relaxed match. Contains says that the value you're looking for appears *somewhere* in the

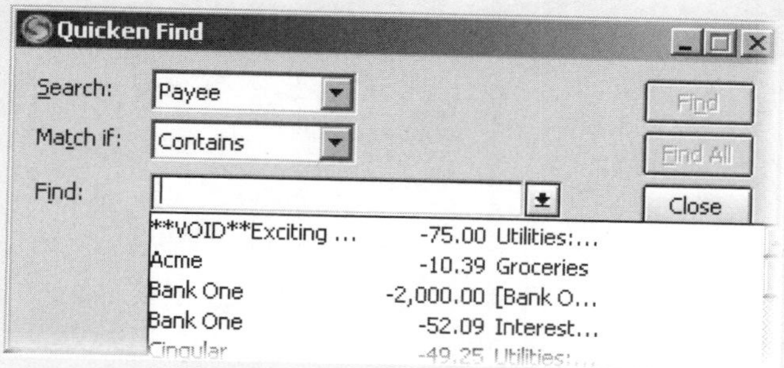

Figure 4-17. Quicken fills in the search criteria with the last criteria you used (in this case, Payee), making it easy to choose a different payee name or value. Once you've selected or modified your search criteria, the Find button becomes available. Click it to launch your search.

result. For example, if you type "Bank" in the Find box, the Contains criterion can find Citibank, Bank One, and First National Bank of Saskatchewan.

At the other end of the spectrum, choosing Exact tells Quicken to return only transactions that exactly match the value in the Find box. For example, if you're looking for the amount 100.50, Exact finds only amounts equal to 100.50, not one like 1100.50.

Starts With and Ends With are ideal for looking for text at the very beginning or very end of an entry. For numbers, you can also choose Greater, Greater or Equal, Less, and Less or Equal, which work just like they did in your elementary school math classes. (To see how to use wildcards to determine a match, see the box on page 148.)

4. **In the Find box, type the value you're looking for, or choose it from the drop-down menu.**

   If you choose the transaction field in the Search drop-down menu first, Quicken automatically fills the Find drop-down menu with appropriate choices. For example, if you choose Payee in the Search box, the Find drop-down menu includes your payee names. Choosing Category in the Search box fills the Find Drop-down menu with the entries in your Quicken Category List.

Using Wildcards to Find Transactions

The "Match if" options may not be sufficient if you're looking for a surgical search. You can use wildcards in the Find box to tune the value you're looking for. Here are the wildcards and what they do:

* **?** acts as a wildcard for a single character. For example, h?tch finds hatch, hitch, and hutch.

* **..** (two periods) represent any number of characters at the beginning, middle, or end of the field. For example, First..Bank finds First National Bank and First Union Bank.

* **~** (tilde) excludes matching values from the results. By typing a tilde followed by text, Quicken finds all the transactions that do not match your search criteria. For example, searching for ~Bud's Ferrari Repair returns all transactions except those for Bud's fine automotive service work.

5. **If you want to search into the future, turn off the Search Backwards checkbox.**

   Quicken automatically turns on the Search Backwards checkbox, because you're usually looking for transactions in the past. Searching forward comes in handy if you want to search between a specific date and today. For example, suppose you want to find all the money you've spent on gas since you started your new job. To move to the first transaction for that time frame, press Ctrl+G, and then type your hire date. Then, in the Quicken Find dialog box, turn off the Search Backwards checkbox and search for the Auto:Fuel category.

   Tip: You don't have to turn off the Search Backwards checkbox to search in the future. When the search in the past is unsuccessful, Quicken asks if you want to search from the end of the register, which actually means the entire register, past and future.

6. Tell Quicken to start searching.

To look for the first transaction that matches your criteria, click Find. If you want to see all the transactions that match in all of your accounts, click Find All. Quicken opens the Search Results window with the matching transactions it found as illustrated in Figure 4-18.

Select	Date ▼	Acct	Num	Payee	Cat	Memo	Clr	Amount
☐	2/27/2006	Bank On...		Lowe's	Home Repair	refund fo...		121.88
☐	2/23/2006	Bank On...		Lowe's	Home Repair	kitchen tile		-706.45
☐	2/5/2006	Interest...	1031	Lowe's	Home Repair		R	-3.87
☐	1/28/2006	Interest...	1026	Target	Home Repair		R	-33.26
☐	1/28/2006	Interest...	1025	Lowe's	Home Repair		R	-67.01

Figure 4-18. The Search Results window displays either the one matching transaction or all matches. If Quicken found many matches, you can sort the results. For instance, if you want to see transactions from most recent to oldest, in the Search Results dialog box, click the Date heading.

7. If you clicked Find and want to find the next matching transaction, click Find again.

Click Find as many times as it takes to find the transaction you want. If you click Find All, you can scan the results for the transaction.

When you perform a search, Quicken remembers your search criteria for the remainder of your Quicken session. The Find Next command repeats your last search. To issue Find Next, right-click a transaction and, on the shortcut menu, choose Find Next. For fast access, press Shift+Ctrl+F.

Finding and Replacing Values

Find/Replace finds every occurrence of one value in all your accounts and replaces it with another. Suppose an unfortunate typo has created several transactions with a payee Aunt Large, when it should be Aunt Marge. Find/Replace can correct this gaffe in a jiffy.

 Tip: Although Find/Replace can replace transactions that you've categorized incorrectly, the Recategorize feature (page 139) provides a more streamlined process for that task.

Here's how you use Find/Replace:

1. **Choose Find & Replace → Find/Replace.**

   As you can see in Figure 4-19, Quicken opens the Find and Replace dialog box, which looks like an amalgamation of the Quicken Find dialog box on top with the Search Results window hanging off the bottom.

2. **At the top of the Find and Replace dialog box, fill in the Search, Match if, and Find boxes to specify your search criteria.**

   Page 146 explains how to set these criteria.

    Note: Quicken automatically turns on the "Show Matches in split" checkbox in the lower-left corner of the dialog box. This setting searches for matches in every category of split transactions, which is important if you're searching for text in Memo fields or categories.

3. **Click Find All.**

   At the bottom of the Find and Replace dialog box, Quicken displays all matching transactions.

4. **In the Replace box, choose the field that you want to replace.**

   Although you can search for transactions based on a matching value in all transaction fields, you can replace in only one field at a time. If you chose All Fields in the Search drop-down menu to find the value "Aunt Large" in every transaction field, you'll have to repeat the replace operation, each time choosing a different transaction field. For example, you'll repeat it in the Payee field first and then in the Memo field.

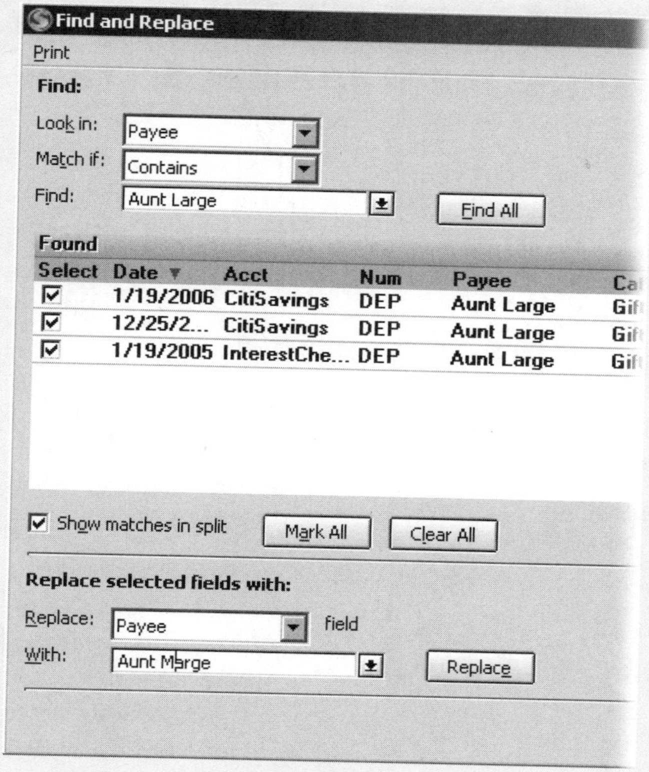

Figure 4-19. At the top of the Find and Replace dialog box, fill in the search criteria to find the transactions you want to change, and then click Find All. Use the Replace box and the With box to specify the changes you want to make, and then click Replace.

5. **In the With box, type the replacement value.**

For example, if you searched the Payee field for "Aunt Large," typing *Aunt Marge* in the With box replaces all occurrences of *Aunt Large* with *Aunt Marge*.

6. **To select all matching transactions, click Mark All.**

Quicken adds green checkmarks to transactions that you select. You can click a checkmark to unselect a transaction or click an empty row to add a checkmark.

Categorizing Uncategorized Transactions

Even with a helping hand from Quick-Fill, the most meticulous trackers can slip up and create a transaction without assigning a category. Once in a while, it's a good idea to look for uncategorized transactions and fill in the appropriate categories, for instance, before you run tax deduction reports (page 366).

The Find command gives you an easy way to find and recategorize all transactions that don't have assigned categories.

1. Press Ctrl+F to open the Find dialog box.

2. In the Search box, choose Category/Class.

3. In the Find box, type a space, and then click Find All.

4. In the Search Results window, select all the transactions that apply to one category and click Edit Transaction(s).

5. In the Find and Replace dialog box, in the Replace drop-down menu, choose Category/Class.

6. In the With drop-down menu, choose the new category to assign.

7. Click Replace to assign the category to the selected transactions.

The transactions remain in the Search Results dialog box, but the category column displays the newly assigned category. The Search Results dialog box remains open, so you can select another batch of transactions to assign to a different category. Click Done to close the Search Results dialog box.

Note: The Replace button remains grayed out until you select at least one transaction to change.

7. **Click Replace.**

A confirmation box appears asking if you're sure that you want to make the replacement. Click OK to continue. Click Cancel if you've decided not to replace the values. When you click OK, you immediately see the changes in the transactions listed in the dialog box.

8. **Click Close to close the dialog box.**

The Find and Replace dialog box remains open after a replace operation. If you want to perform another find and replace, repeat steps 2 through 7. If you're done, click Close.

The Transaction Edit Menu

You can do just about any transaction-related task you want from the Edit shortcut menu, shown in Figure 4-20. To pop it up, right-click a transaction or click its Edit button. Some of these commands you use all the time, like New, which takes you to a blank transaction as if you pressed Ctrl+N. Other commands don't see nearly as much action, but you can get to them just as easily from this same shortcut menu.

Most of the commands on the transaction Edit menu are covered throughout this chapter, as the choices on this menu vary depending on which transaction

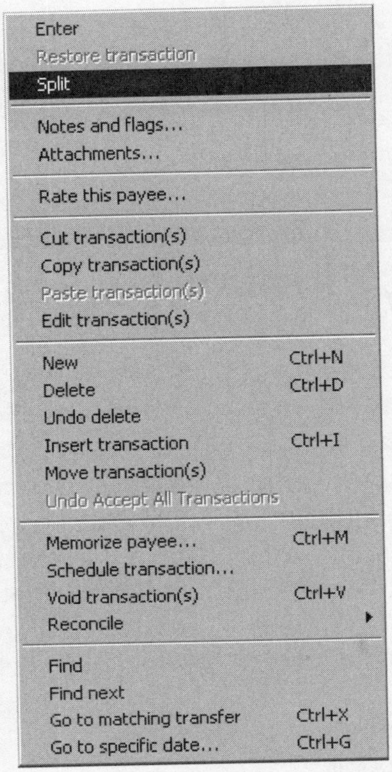

Enter
Restore transaction
Split

Notes and flags...
Attachments...

Rate this payee...

Cut transaction(s)
Copy transaction(s)
Paste transaction(s)
Edit transaction(s)

New   Ctrl+N
Delete   Ctrl+D
Undo delete
Insert transaction   Ctrl+I
Move transaction(s)
Undo Accept All Transactions

Memorize payee...   Ctrl+M
Schedule transaction...
Void transaction(s)   Ctrl+V
Reconcile   ▶

Find
Find next
Go to matching transfer   Ctrl+X
Go to specific date...   Ctrl+G

Figure 4-20. This is the transaction Edit menu. You can display it by either right-clicking a transaction in the register or by clicking the Edit button in a selected transaction.

field you right-click. Think of this section as a cheat sheet. The following list explains what each command does and where you can find out more about it.

▶ **Enter.** Records the active transaction. Does the same thing as clicking the Enter button in the transaction row or pressing Enter.

▶ **Restore transaction.** If you edit a transaction and want to undo the changes you've made, choose this command. It undoes any changes you've made *as long as* you haven't yet clicked Enter.

- **Split.** Choose this command (or press Ctrl+S) to open the Split Transaction dialog box for the current transaction (page 130).

- **Notes and Flags.** New to Quicken 2006, this feature attaches notes and reminders to transactions, as shown in Figure 4-21. For example, when you record a payment for a magazine renewal, you can add a note that indicates when it'll be time to renew so you can ignore premature requests. Or you may add a note to check that your credit card company reversed the late charges it levied.

  The advantage to using a note instead of text in the Memo field is that you can add a visual cue that a note exists by turning on the "Flag this transaction" checkbox. In the register, a flag appears below the transaction's Date field. If you turn on the "Alert for follow-up on" checkbox and choose a date, Quicken adds an alert to the list in the Quicken Center panel (Online Appendix F).

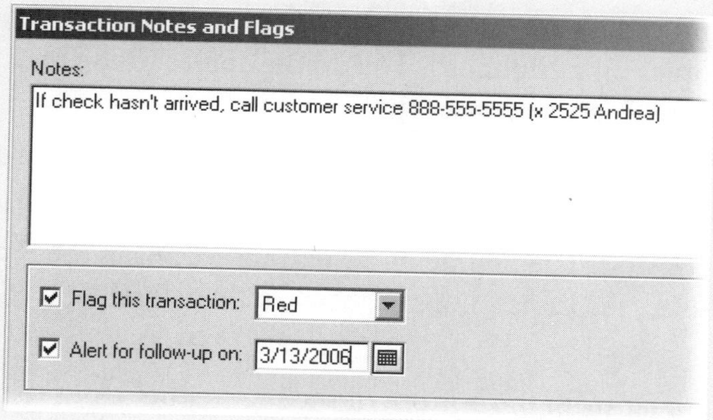

Figure 4-21. Use Notes and Flags to add a note about a transaction or a reminder to follow up. If you turn on the "Flag this transaction" checkbox, Quicken adds a flag below the transaction date. The "Alert for follow-up on" checkbox creates an alert for the note on the date you specify.

- **Attachments.** In Quicken 2006, you can attach electronic images of checks, receipts, bills, or even digital pictures to your transactions. Choose this command to open the Transaction Attachments window (see the box on page 109).

- **Rate this payee.** In Quicken 2006, you can click this command to open a browser window to Zipingo.com (page 110). On this Web site, you can rate businesses you've used and view ratings from other customers.

- **Cut transaction(s).** This command removes the transaction or transactions that you've selected and places them on a clipboard, in exactly the same way that pressing Ctrl+X in Windows adds what you cut to the Windows clipboard. If you want to remove several transactions from a register, use this command. (Delete only deletes the current transaction.)

> **Note:** If you want to move one or more transactions from one account to another, choose "Move transaction(s)", as described on page 157.

- **Copy transaction(s).** If you want to copy one or more transactions, for instance to quickly duplicate several transactions you forgot to add last month, this command is the one to choose. Quicken leaves the originals in the register but places copies on a clipboard. To add the copies to the register, follow this command with "Paste transaction(s)".

- **Paste transaction(s).** To copy the transactions on the clipboard to the register, choose this command.

- **Edit transaction(s).** To edit one or more transactions in the Find and Replace dialog box, select the transactions, right-click them, and then choose this command.

- **New.** If you're far from the bottom of the register but can't remember any keyboard shortcuts, choosing this command places the insertion point in a fresh blank transaction at the bottom of the register. It's just like pressing Ctrl+N.

- **Delete.** This command removes all traces of a transaction from your Quicken data file. This command is perfect if you created a duplicate of an existing transaction. If you want to eliminate a transaction but keep a record of it, choose "Void transaction(s)" instead (see page 158).

- **Undo delete.** With the Delete command right below the New command, inadvertently deleting a transaction is almost inevitable. You can recover the deleted transaction by choosing "Undo delete" *immediately*. (That is, before you issue any other command.)

▶ **Insert transaction.** If you select an existing transaction, "Insert transaction" adds a blank transaction immediately below it, with the same date, as shown in Figure 4-22. Note the difference from the New command, which places you at the bottom of the register and automatically selects today's date. With "Insert transaction," you can easily go back and fill in a transaction that you missed.

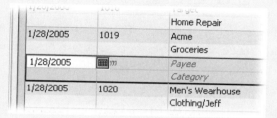

Figure 4-22. "Insert transaction" adds a blank transaction immediately below the selected transaction and sets the new transaction's date to match.

▶ **Move transaction(s).** If you put a transaction (or several) in the wrong account (deposited money in the wrong savings account, say), simply select the misplaced transactions and then choose "Move transaction(s)." In the dialog box that appears, in the "Move to account" drop-down menu, choose the correct account, and then click OK.

▶ **Undo Accept All Transactions.** If you download transactions and choose Accept All, you can choose this command to return the transactions to their original downloaded state, as described on page 233.

▶ **Memorize payee.** Quicken comes with the "Automatically memorize new payees" feature turned on, so that Quicken automatically memorizes every new payee you enter. If you turn this checkbox off (in QuickFill preferences), you can handpick the payees to add to the Memorized Payee List (page 159). For instance, if the current transaction is for a payee you'll do business with again, choose "Memorize payee" to add the payee to the Memorized Payee List.

- **Schedule transaction.** If you want to schedule the selected transaction to repeat in the future or recur on a set schedule, choose this command. See "Scheduling Transactions" on page 162 for detailed instructions.

- **Void transaction(s).** If you want to eliminate a transaction but keep a record of it, choose this command (see "Voiding Transactions" on page 142).

- **Reconcile.** If a transaction's status isn't correct—Unreconciled, Cleared, or Reconciled—choose this command, and then choose a different status from the submenu. (For full details on reconciling accounts, see Chapter 7.)

Warning: Be careful when you change the status of a transaction outside of the Quicken reconciliation process. When you change an item's status, you can get accounts that don't reconcile properly.

- **Find.** Choose this command (or press Ctrl+F) to open the Find dialog box, described in detail on page 146.

- **Find next.** To find the next occurrence of the current search criteria, choose this command.

- **Go to matching transfer.** If the selected transaction is a transfer, choosing this command jumps to the transaction at the *other* end of a transfer. For example, if the selected transaction is a transfer from checking to savings, choosing "Go to matching transfer" opens the register for the savings account and selects the corresponding deposit.

- **Go to specific date.** This command delivers you to the first transaction on any date you specify. Choose this command and, in the Go To Date dialog box, select the date you want. When you click OK, Quicken jumps to the first transaction that occurred on that date and highlights it. This command comes in handy for things like reviewing your end-of-the-year tax activity.

Tip: Keyboard mavens can also press Ctrl+G to open the Go To Date dialog box.

Managing Memorized Payees

Without any help from you, Quicken's QuickFill feature usually does a fine job filling in transaction information for you, almost as if the program had ESP. As explained on page 102, though, there's no magic involved, just a list of values stored in Quicken's electronic brain—the Memorized Payee List. All the software does is find matches based on your first few keystrokes, one of the things software does really well, and really fast.

Of course, even Quicken's ESP isn't perfect. Sometimes the information it memorizes is incorrect, or outdated, or just not what you want—like when Quicken memorizes "RBROS7537-2XX-CANL" instead of "Rocha Brothers Market (Canal St)." With a little human input, you can make QuickFill even better. You can perform some electronic brain surgery, so to speak, to improve Quicken's psychic abilities. All you have to do is open up the Memorized Payee List and edit away. This section shows you how.

GEM IN THE ROUGH

Where Quicken Keeps It

When you're trying to edit the information Quicken uses to auto-fill transaction fields, remember that Quicken grabs payee information from several places: the Memorized Payee List, the Address Book, and the list of Online Payees. If you don't find a payee in the Memorized Payee List, check the other lists as well.

Quicken's Address Book is where it stores the addresses it prints on checks. To open the Address Book to add or edit payees and their addresses, choose Tools → Address Book. (See "Printing Checks" on page 114 for more detail.)

You may also have an Online Payees list, if you use Quicken for online bill payment. Choose Online → Online Payee List to see the companies you pay electronically. You create online payees and specify a payee's address in the Set Up Online Payees dialog box (page 245).

Removing Payees from the Memorized Payee List

One downside to this automatic memorization is that Quicken can be overly enthusiastic about memorizing payees. Before you know it, the program has memorized every Tom, Dick, and Harry—and Sally, Teresa, Bubba, and so on. If your Memorized Payee List has bloated to a startling degree, you've got three strategies:

▶ Limit how long Quicken remembers memorized payees.

▶ Tell Quicken to remember payees on a case-by-case basis (instead of automatically memorizing *every* payee).

▶ Delete memorized payees.

Limiting the length of Quicken's memory

The easiest way to keep your Memorized Payee List under control is with a Quicken Register preference (page 46). Choose Edit → Preferences → Quicken Program, and then click Register. By turning on the "Remove memorized payees not used in last" checkbox and typing a number (in months), you tell Quicken to continually review your Memorized Payee List and toss out any payees that you haven't used in that time frame.

If you have companies that you pay once a year, like your insurance company or the septic tank cleaner, type, say, *14* in the months box. By giving yourself a few extra months, Quicken won't remove memorized payees before you've had a chance to reuse them.

Turning off automatic memorization

Another way to keep your Memorized Payee List down to size is to prevent Quicken from memorizing one-hit wonders and other unimportant payees in the first place. In this scheme, you tell Quicken to *not* memorize payees at all, and then add individual payees to the list yourself. This method is more work for you, but it gives you the most control over the Memorized Payee List.

In the Quicken Preferences dialog box, in the "Select preference type" list, click QuickFill. Turn off the "Automatically memorize new payees" checkbox. Then, to memorize a payee you do want, select a transaction that uses that payee and press Ctrl+M.

Deleting memorized payees

If your Memorized Payee List is already cluttered with names you never want to see again, you can excise these entries from the list. Open the Memorized Payee List by pressing Ctrl+T or choosing Tools → Memorized Payee List. (Deleting memorized payees doesn't remove them from previously recorded transactions.)

To delete memorized payees, select one or more payees and, in the Memorized Payee List menu bar, choose Delete (Figure 4-23). Quicken displays a confirmation box asking if you're sure you want to delete the payees. Click OK to delete. Click Cancel to spare them.

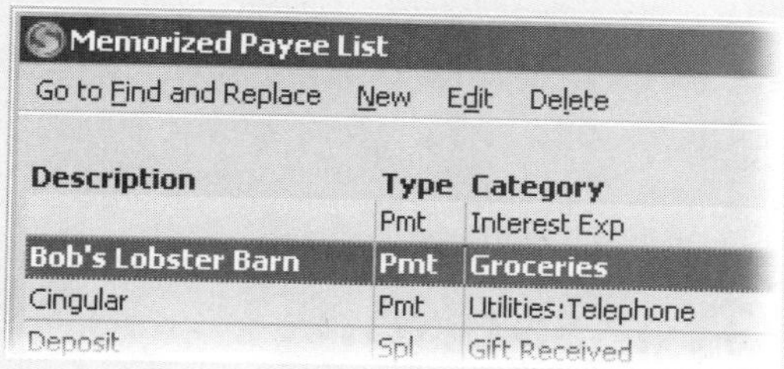

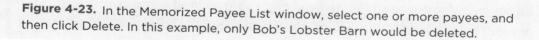

Figure 4-23. In the Memorized Payee List window, select one or more payees, and then click Delete. In this example, only Bob's Lobster Barn would be deleted.

You don't have to delete only one memorized payee at a time. You can click one entry and then Shift+click another entry several rows down to also select all the memorized payees in between. For more individualized selections, Ctrl+click each memorized payee you want to trash. When you click Delete, the program deletes all the selected payees.

Locking a Memorized Payee

When Quicken memorizes payees, it stores them in an *unlocked* state, which means that Quicken can overwrite the values for the memorized payee when you create a new transaction. For example, if your electric bill is different every month, the amount of the *previous* month's payment always appears in the Payment field.

If you want to keep a memorized payee the same, regardless of what you do with it in a new transaction, you can *lock* the entry so that the Memorized Payee List remembers the same value no matter what. For example, suppose you have a memorized payee for your cable TV bill. Every month, you pay $36.95 for the privilege of surfing through 150 channels of reruns, so you lock the entry at that amount. One month the bill is only $20 because you received a credit for a week's service outage, so you edit the amount for that transaction. But when you create the payment next month, the regular amount of $36.95 pops up again.

In the Memorized Payee List window, the fastest way to lock an entry is to click in its row in the Lock column. You'll know that an entry is locked by the gold padlock in the Lock column. To unlock an entry, click its padlock icon.

 Tip: If you want to lock several entries at once, select all the entries and then click the button with the picture of the padlock on it.

Scheduling Transactions

Often, bills are due at the same time every month, and some are even the same *amount* every month. For example, your electric bill is due the 19th of the month, but the amount varies each time. Your mortgage may be due on the 5th, and it's the same amount every month. Scheduled transactions are perfect for payments like these. You set up scheduled transactions with the same information you provide for a check you record in the register, and you also tell Quicken when and how often you make this payment.

Not only can the program create future transactions for you, but Quicken also doesn't forget that they're due. When it's time to make a payment or deposit, Quicken reminds you of the task. If the amount is the same each time, you can tell Quicken to create the transaction automatically. With one additional step to set up scheduled transactions as repeating online payments (see Chapter 6), you can turn off your computer, drop the cat off at a neighbor's, and take a month's sabbatical to study reef winkles in Tahiti, confident that your mortgage is paid on time. (After you send the instructions for repeating online payments to your financial institution, it sets up all your future payments automatically and processes them without further action on your part. See "Setting Up a Repeating Online Payment" on page 250 to learn more.)

You can schedule a transaction to happen just once to make sure that you don't forget to pay it (perhaps for the down payment on the Ferrari that's on sale until March 31), but scheduled transactions are even better for transactions that occur again and again. They work equally well for checks, transfers, and deposits you make on a periodic basis, from the garbage bill to a disability benefit. In fact, unless you have a scheduled transaction for *every* transaction you make regularly, you're cheating yourself out of Quicken's most timesaving—and potentially *money* saving—feature.

The Scheduled Transaction List is a one-stop shop for working with scheduled transactions. Whether you want to set up, edit, delete, or record scheduled transactions, press Ctrl+J or choose Tools → Scheduled Transaction List to open the window shown in Figure 4-24. In the Cash Flow Center, you can open the Create Scheduled Transaction dialog box directly by clicking Add a Transaction.

Setting Up a Scheduled Transaction

The Create Scheduled Transaction dialog box may seem daunting at first, but the top half is nothing more than the same fields you fill in when you record a check in an account register. The bottom half of the dialog box is where you set up the schedule. To open the Create Scheduled Transaction dialog box, in the Scheduled Transaction List menu bar, choose Create New → Scheduled Transaction. This section explains how to use each section to its fullest.

Enter Skip Create New ▼ Edit Delete   Options ▼ Print How Do I?

	Monthly Bills & Deposits		**All Types**							

☑ Show graph   ☑ Show calendar

Name/Payee	Amount	Date	Show in List	#Left	Method	Frequency	Web	Action		
Medical Miracle	1,115.38	2/17/2006	3 days before		Payche...	Every 2 weeks		Enter	Edit	Skip
O'Reilly	1,072.76	2/17/2006	3 days before		Payche...	Every 2 weeks		Enter	Edit	Skip
Citibank	-9.95	3/2/2006	3 days before		Payment	Monthly		Enter	Edit	Skip
Transfer	-500.00	3/2/2006	3 days before	10	Transfer	Monthly		Enter	Edit	Skip
Divine Dumpster	-60.00	3/7/2006	3 days before		Payment	Quarterly		Enter	Edit	Skip
Exciting Electric	-125.00	3/14/2006	3 days before		Payment	Monthly		Enter	Edit	Skip
ASPCA	-15.00	3/23/2006	3 days before		Payment	Monthly		Enter	Edit	Skip
Talk It Up	-29.95	3/28/2006	3 days before		Payment	Monthly		Enter	Edit	Skip
First Focus S&L	-920.10	4/1/2006	3 days before	177	Payment	Monthly		Enter	Edit	Skip
Hartford	-521.49	5/15/2006	3 days before		Payment	Yearly		Enter	Edit	Skip

Figure 4-24. In the Scheduled Transaction List window, you can set up new scheduled transactions, edit or delete existing scheduled transactions, or record (by clicking Enter) scheduled transactions. Though you can't see it in this figure, overdue transactions appear in red.

Note: The other command on the Create New menu is Paycheck, which you can choose to set up and schedule your paychecks (see page 168).

Transaction values

The top half of the Create Scheduled Transaction dialog box, shown in Figure 4-25, has the same fields as an account register, plus a few more bells and whistles. Unlike transactions you create in an account register, QuickFill doesn't work in this dialog box. You must choose values from drop-down menus or type the values you want.

Here's how you use the boxes and options Quicken offers:

▶ **Account to use.** Choose the account to which you make a payment or receive a deposit. This account is the one whose register you would open to record the transaction.

▶ **Transaction method.** These are equivalent to the selections in the Num field in an account register. For example, Payment is equivalent to Next Check Num; the only difference being Quicken won't know the next check number until it's time to make the payment. Deposit and Transfer are available, and the Printer Check method from the register is named Printed Check for a scheduled transaction.

▶ **Repeat this online payment automatically even if I don't go online.** For accounts that are set up to process online payments, you can turn on this checkbox (Figure 4-25) to create a repeating online payment—the ultimate in transaction convenience. When you turn on this checkbox, Quicken sends the instructions for the repeating online payment to your bank. A month before the payment is due, your bank queues up a payment according to the schedule you set. The next time you launch Quicken and go online, the program downloads the transaction for the next installment of your repeating online payment into your account register.

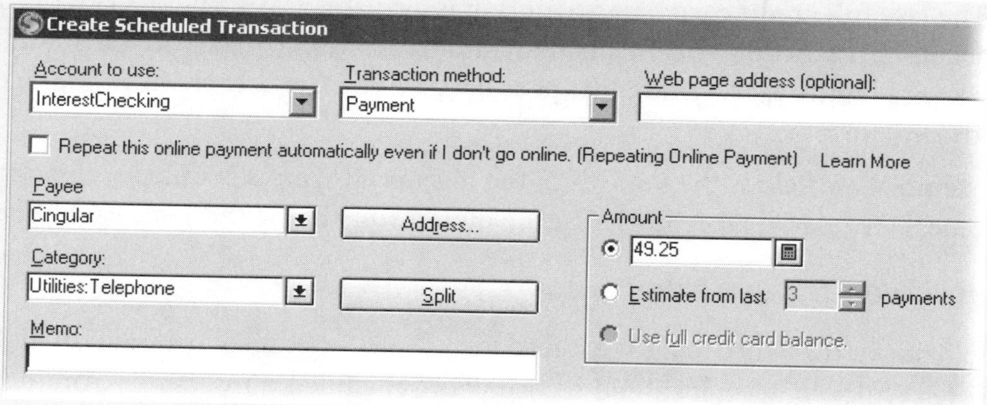

Figure 4-25. Although most of the boxes emulate their register counterparts, you can turn on the "Repeat this online payment automatically even if I don't go online" checkbox to set up a fully automated payment that requires no further effort on your part. The Amount section includes an option that sets up a credit card payment whose Amount equals the balance on your credit card.

- **Payee.** This familiar field works the same as in a register transaction.

- **Address.** Clicking Address opens the Edit Address Book Record, just as clicking Address in the Write Checks window does.

- **Category.** Choose from this drop-down menu of all categories.

- **Split.** Because the Category drop-down menu in this dialog box doesn't include the Split button (page 130), you click *this* button to split a scheduled transaction among categories.

- **Amount.** The Amount section includes three options. Quicken automatically selects the first, which is simply a text box for entering the amount for the transaction.

  The **Estimate from last _ payments** option calculates a rolling average from past payments. That is, it adds up the last three amounts and divides by three. If you're whittling down a big credit card balance, you might choose this option to set up a regular payment based on your recent payment amounts.

  The **Use full credit card balance** option is available if you choose a credit card account. It schedules payments that automatically pay the entire outstanding balance on the card. (And quite possibly give you the best credit rating in the known universe.)

- **Memo.** This field is the same as in the register. If your scheduled transaction repeats regularly, remember that the memo will also be the same each time.

Scheduled transaction frequency

The fields in the Scheduling section of the Create Scheduled Transaction dialog box tell Quicken *when* it should record your scheduled transactions. Among its advantages, setting up a schedule for transactions lets you:

- Record transactions ahead of time.

- Set reminders based on how often you use Quicken.

- Be sure to record transactions.

The bottom half of the Create Scheduled Transaction dialog box looks awfully busy, but it boils down to three ways to control your transaction schedule.

- **Start on.** In the "Start on" box, choose the date for the future transaction (or the first of many recurring transactions). Quicken chooses **Remind Me**, which displays a reminder when it's time to actually record the transaction. If the amounts are the same each month, you can choose **Automatically Enter** and let Quicken add the transactions without any effort on your part.

  The number of days in advance depends on how addicted you are to Quicken. If you launch Quicken every day without fail, you can set the number of days somewhere between 1 and 3. If you use Quicken off and on, you should set the number of days box to a higher number, so you're more likely to see the reminder before it's too late.

- **Frequency.** Choose **Only Once** for a one-time transaction or choose one of the time frames, like **Weekly** or **Yearly**. There's also an **Estimated Tax** choice for setting up estimated tax payments on the 15th of January, April, June, and September. You can specify the day of the month or choose a specific weekday. For example, if your investment club meets on the second Tuesday of each month, you can schedule your contribution to match.

- **Ending on.** If you choose the **No end date** option, the scheduled transaction keeps going like the Energizer bunny—until you delete the scheduled transaction. If you choose the **On** option, you can specify the ending date. The **After** option is the most popular. For example, you can use it to set up a transfer to pay off a home equity line of credit over, say, two years: Simply choose After and type *24* in the **times** box.

Paying and Skipping Scheduled Transactions

You can wait until Quicken reminds you to pay a scheduled transaction, or even pay a scheduled transaction *before* its scheduled time. This second option is especially handy if you're leaving for an extended vacation and don't want your car repossessed before you return. To manually record a scheduled transaction regardless of when it's due, in the Scheduled Transaction List window (press Ctrl+J), click the Enter button in the transaction row.

On the other hand, if you take a temporary assignment in Katmandu and put your cable service, ISP, and garbage pickup on hold, you want to skip some of your scheduled payments. To skip one transaction of the schedule, in the Scheduled Transaction List window, click Skip in the transaction's row.

Automating Your Paycheck in Quicken

Paychecks seem to grow more complicated every year, what with pre-tax medical and retirement deductions, taxes, and after-tax deductions (like your voluntary contribution to your company's executive legal defense fund). Whether you're content to let your employer summarize your payroll on a W-2 each year or you want to track your paycheck to the penny, the Set Up Paycheck tool can simplify your record keeping. This section explains how to set up paychecks and add them to your account register.

 Note: If you already have a paycheck set up, choosing Cash Flow → Banking → Set Up Paycheck opens the Manage Paychecks dialog box, in which you can add, edit, or delete paychecks (see page 176).

Basic Paycheck Fields

The first time you choose Cash Flow → Banking Activities → Set Up Paycheck, Quicken displays the Paycheck Setup wizard. On the first screen, you can first read about all the great things that you can do with a paycheck in Quicken, or you can click Next to get started. Then follow these steps:

1. **Choose Cash Flow → Banking Activities → Set Up Paycheck.**

    Another way to open the Paycheck Setup wizard is via the Scheduled Transaction list window. In that window's menu bar, choose Create New → Paycheck.

2. **When you click Next, the screen shows options for your and your spouse's paychecks.**

    Choose the option for the person whose paycheck you're creating.

3. **In the Company Name text box, type the name of the employer.**

   You don't need the full legal name of the company. What you type in the Company Name box is what you'll see when you create a paycheck transaction, so you can make it short—but recognizable. Click Next to continue.

4. **Choose the option for the level of detail you want to track.**

   Quicken automatically selects the "I want to track all earnings, taxes, and deductions" option. If you want to use Quicken to help minimize the taxes you pay or keep track of company benefits, you want to choose this option. For example, you'll know how much money is available in your flexible spending account.

   For folks who just want to know how much money goes into the checking account to pay bills, the "I want to track net deposits only" option may be a better choice. You don't get the benefits of tracking all paycheck deductions, but setup is much simpler.

5. **Click Next to begin the paycheck setup in earnest.**

   The Set Up Paycheck dialog box that appears depends on which level of detail you chose. The "I want to track net deposits only" option opens a compact dialog box with a few boxes for the net deposit and scheduling frequency. If you see a Set Up Paycheck dialog box that runs from the top of your screen to the bottom, you know you're about to track full detail. See the next section for steps to complete paycheck setup.

Setting Up Paycheck Details

If you choose the "I want to track net deposits only" option, the Set Up Paycheck dialog box includes a place to enter the value of your net paycheck and fields to specify when and how often you get paid. This option is easy to set up, but it doesn't give you the sort of information you need if you want Quicken to help with tax-related tasks—one of the main benefits of electronic personal finance.

If you choose the "I want to track all earnings, taxes, and deductions" option, the Set Up Paycheck dialog box includes sections, boxes, and buttons for specifying every last item on your pay stub. Although Figure 4-26 shows only a portion of this behemoth, running through all the options is quite simple. To add a paycheck item, you click one of the "Add" buttons and choose the type of earning, tax, or deduction. For each, a small dialog box opens with a few text boxes, most of which Quicken fills in for you. After you've added all items on your pay stub, click Done.

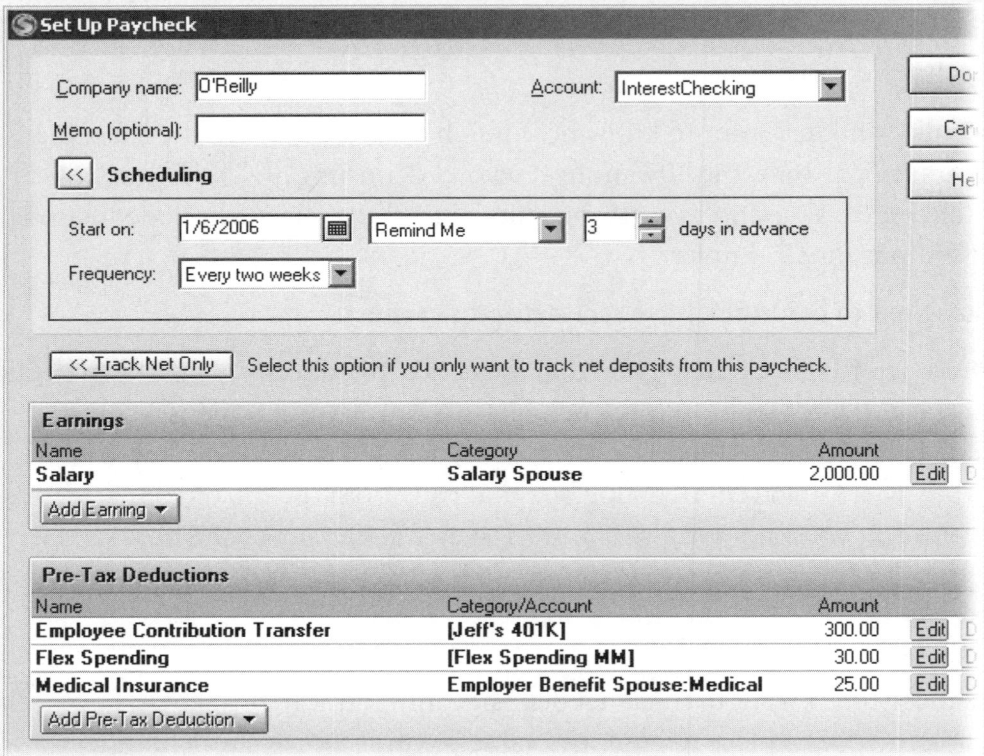

Figure 4-26. After you set up the frequency of your paycheck, you can click an Add button to include another tax, deduction, or type of earning in your paycheck. To change a value, click the value and type the new number. To change the name or category for an existing entry, click its Edit button.

As soon as you click Done to save a new paycheck, Quicken opens the Enter Year-to-Date Information dialog box and asks if you want to enter the year-to-date amounts for the paycheck. The program automatically selects the "I want to enter the year-to-date information" option, which is the only logical choice if you want complete tax records for the year. This option opens the Paycheck Year-to-Date Amounts dialog box. Grab your most recent pay stub and use its year-to-date amounts to fill in the values for each paycheck item.

Account and scheduling

The first section in the Set Up Paycheck dialog box identifies the account to which you deposit your check and tells Quicken when and how often you're paid. Here are the boxes you fill in:

- **Account.** In the drop-down menu, choose the account to which you deposit your paycheck (whether you hand-deliver it to the bank, mail it, or use your employer's auto-deposit).

- **Start on.** Choose the next date that you'll receive a paycheck. If you're setting up Quicken to fill in your data from the beginning of the year, you can choose the first payday of the current year.

- **Remind Me.** Quicken automatically chooses Remind Me, which reminds you to enter your paycheck transaction several days in advance. When the program reminds you to add your paycheck transaction, you have a chance to make any adjustments to match your pay stub. If you receive one of those rare paychecks whose values never vary, you can choose Automatically Enter, which tells Quicken to add the paycheck transaction without asking for permission.

- **Days in advance.** Choose how many days in advance you want to record your paycheck. Quicken sets this box to 3, mainly because employers often hand out pay stubs a few days before the pay date. If you like to plan your cash flow in advance, you can choose a higher number to add your paycheck transaction to the register earlier. (Although the transaction shows up in the register earlier, the transaction date is still based on your Start on date. On the other hand, if you tend to spend the money you can see, you can set this value to 1 to hide your income as long as possible.)

▶ **Frequency.** Quicken can handle almost any paycheck schedule, unless your employer pays you as soon as there's enough cash to cover payroll. Choose from Weekly, Every two weeks, Twice a month, Every four weeks, Monthly, and so on.

Adding and editing paycheck items

Quicken makes adding and editing earnings, tax, and other deductions as easy as possible, a real boon when your paycheck seems to have more entries than the local phone book. Paycheck items are grouped into four categories, shown in Figure 4-27.

When you choose a paycheck item on one of the drop-down menus, a small dialog box opens for setting up that item. Quicken fills in most of the boxes for you, as the Add 401(k) Deduction dialog box in Figure 4-28 illustrates. Quicken fills in the Name box with a generic name, which you can change to be more descriptive. For example, the Quicken name for a 401(k) deduction is *Employee Contribution Transfer*, but you can rename it *401k Spouse* if you like. The program often fills in the Category box with one of its built-in Categories. For most items, you have to provide only the amount and click OK to save it.

Tip: The Pre-Tax Deduction for 401(k), 403(b), or 457 retirement programs has an additional text box labeled Employer Match. If your employer is generous enough to match some of your contributions, type the dollar value of the match.

Entering a Paycheck Transaction

As you can see from the scheduling options in the Set Up Paycheck dialog box, Quicken sets up your paycheck as a scheduled transaction (page 162). In addition to receiving a reminder to enter your paycheck, a scheduled paycheck transaction takes only a couple of clicks to complete.

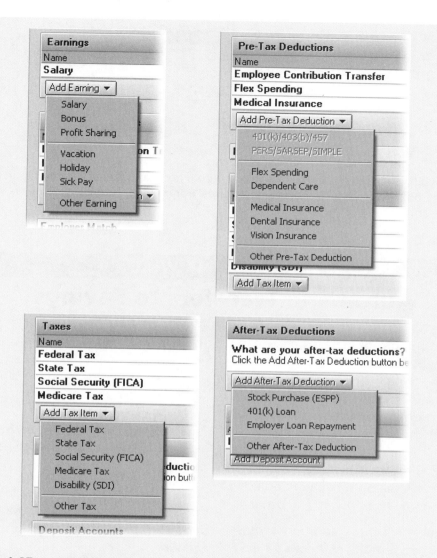

Figure 4-27. To add a paycheck item, click one of the Add buttons, like Add Earning. On the drop-down menu, choose the type of paycheck item you want. The paycheck items are grouped into Earnings (your gross pay), Pre-Tax Deductions (calculated before taxes are taken out), Taxes, and finally After-Tax Deductions (calculated after taxes are deducted).

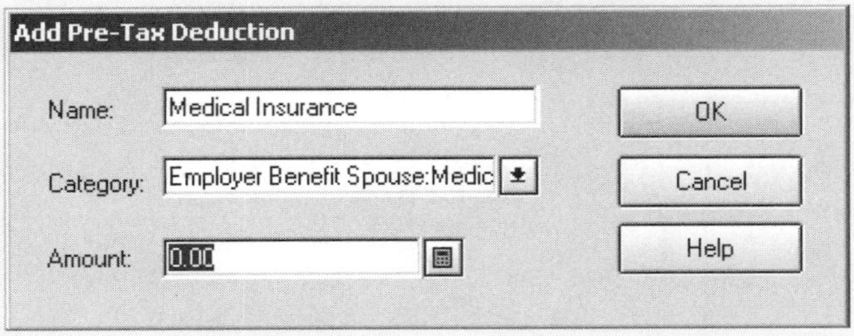
Add Pre-Tax Deduction
Name:
Medical Insurance
Category:
Employer Benefit Spouse:Medic
Amount:
0.00
OK
Cancel
Help

Figure 4-28. Quicken fills in the Name box with a generic name and often fills in the Category box with one of its built-in categories. For most items, you have to provide only the amount.

WORD TO THE WISE

Automatic Transfers to Savings

"Out of sight, out of mind" is an adage that still applies when it comes to saving money. One of the least painful ways to save money is to have money deducted from your paycheck and deposited to your savings account. After all, you're less likely to spend money you forgot you have. The Set Up Paycheck dialog box can handle this deduction as easily as any other.

After you set up these additional transfers with your employer, here's what you do in Quicken:

1. Click Add Deposit Account.
2. In the Add Deposit Account dialog box, in the Account drop-down menu, choose your savings account, like Marsha's Vacation Club.
3. In the Amount box, type how much you transfer to savings with each paycheck.
4. Click OK.

Quicken automatically deducts this transfer amount from the amount deposited to your primary deposit account.

If Quicken Home includes Bills and Scheduled Transactions, you can enter a scheduled paycheck transaction by clicking Quicken Home and then clicking your paycheck's Enter button, as demonstrated in Figure 4-29. The "Edit

Current Paycheck and Enter into Register" dialog box opens. If your pay stub shows different values, make those changes first, and then click Enter to record the paycheck.

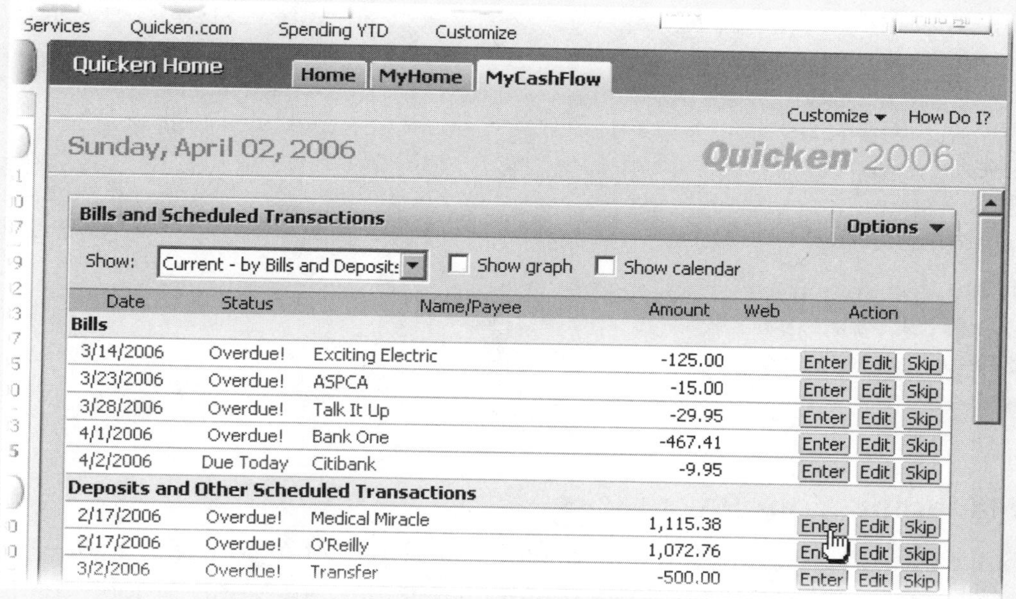

Figure 4-29. To enter a scheduled transaction, click its Enter button. You'll get a chance to make any last-minute changes to values before you click Enter to add the paycheck to your account register.

Tip: Although the values in the dialog box don't *look* like text boxes, you can click a value to make it editable.

You can also easily enter a paycheck if you press Ctrl+J to open the Scheduled Transaction List window, and then click the Enter button for the paycheck you want to enter.

When Paycheck Values Vary

If the amounts on your paycheck are never the same, for instance if you're paid by the hour and work different hours each week, the Set Up Paycheck dialog box may not seem all that useful. Why set up a paycheck if you have to edit the numbers each time?

Filling in the Set Up Paycheck dialog box *without* values still saves you quite a bit of effort. When Quicken creates a paycheck transaction, it creates a transaction with a category split for every paycheck item, but leaves the value blank. When you select the transaction and click Split, the Split Transactions dialog box that appears lists each category from your pay stub with no values. You can skip choosing split categories and proceed directly to entering the numbers for your current paycheck.

Managing Your Paychecks

Since life is rarely simple, the meticulous paycheck setup you've just gone through won't last forever. Even minor changes in your family or job situation can alter the numbers on your paycheck. At least in Quicken the necessary adjustments are easy to make. When you have one or more paychecks set up, choosing Cash Flow → Banking Activities → Set Up Paycheck opens the Manage Paychecks dialog box. Here's what you can do:

▶ **New.** To create a new paycheck, for example to add the paycheck for the second job you've taken on, click New. Quicken opens the Paycheck Setup dialog box. See page 168 for the step-by-step details.

▶ **Edit.** Select one of the paychecks in the list and then click this button to open the Edit Future Paychecks dialog box. This dialog box is the same as the Set Up Paycheck dialog box, except that it makes changes only to paychecks you record in the future.

▶ **Delete.** If you quit a job and no longer receive a scheduled paycheck, select the paycheck in the list, and then click Delete.

FREQUENTLY ASKED QUESTION

Consistently Inconsistent Paychecks

The amounts on my pay stub are supposed to be the same every time, but sometimes they're rounded up or down by a penny! Grr! Does this mean I can't do automatic paychecks in Quicken?

You can stop growling. For many people, paycheck values change slightly between the first and second paycheck of the month. For example, the deduction for Social Security (known as FICA) may be 133.18 on the first paycheck of the month and 133.17 for the second paycheck.

To automate your paychecks in this situation, set up one paycheck with the values for the first paycheck of the month and schedule it to occur monthly on the first payday of the month. Set up a second paycheck with the values for the second paycheck also scheduled to occur monthly, but on the *second* payday of the month.

CHAPTER 5:
PROPERTY AND DEBT

▶ **Understanding Property & Debt in Quicken**

▶ **Setting Up Asset and Liability Accounts**

▶ **Setting Up a Loan**

▶ **Making a Loan Payment**

▶ **Editing a Loan**

▶ **Refinancing a Loan**

As you learned when you set up your Quicken accounts in Chapter 2, you use asset accounts to track the value of your *property* (the things you own) and liability accounts to track your *debt* (the money you owe). Quicken has many advantages when you're managing these accounts. For one, if you set up a loan in Quicken to pay off a liability, the program reminds you when it's time to make a payment. In addition, if you track both your liabilities and assets, Quicken can calculate your net worth (the value of your assets minus the balance of your liabilities), which is a telling indicator of your financial health.

Although borrowing can get awfully complicated with adjustable-rate mortgages, interest-only loans, refinancing, and so on, Quicken can handle just about anything you throw at it. Most people have a hard time understanding the underlying accounting. Once you know how to follow the money, you can easily set Quicken up to track it. This chapter explains both.

Understanding Property & Debt in Quicken

Assets, liabilities, and loans form the foundation for tracking what you own and owe, and Quicken groups them in the Property & Debt Center. To make the most of Quicken's property and debt features, you need to understand the following concepts.

▶ **Assets** are things that you own that have value, like your house, car, appliances, and the baseball signed by Mickey Mantle. If you want Quicken to help you figure out how much you're really worth, track the value of your assets in Quicken. (By the way, your *physical* assets don't count, unless, of course, you earn your living as a supermodel.)

Quicken uses asset accounts to track the value of what you own. These accounts (along with liability accounts) have registers just as checking accounts do. As you can see in Figure 5-1, you can record transactions to reflect changes in the value of your assets, for instance due to depreciation, improvements you make, increases in the cash value of whole life insurance, or market changes.

There's no need to create asset accounts for every last item you own. Quicken has specialized asset accounts for houses and cars since those are the most valuable things most people own. However, if you have other items of value that you'd like Quicken to include in your net worth (like jewelry, artwork, a stamp collection, and so on), create asset accounts for them as well.

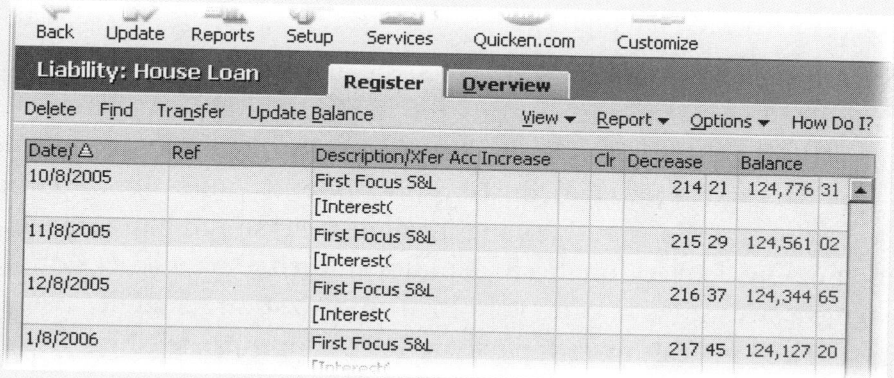

Back
Update
Reports
Setup
Services
Quicken.com
Customize
Liability: House Loan
Register
Overview
Delete
Find
Transfer
Update Balance
View
Report
Options
How Do I?
Date/
Ref
Description/Xfer Acc
Increase
Clr
Decrease
Balance
10/8/2005
First Focus S&L
[Interest(
214 21
124,776 31
11/8/2005
First Focus S&L
[Interest(
215 29
124,561 02
12/8/2005
First Focus S&L
[Interest(
216 37
124,344 65
1/8/2006
First Focus S&L
217 45
124,127 20

Figure 5-1. The register for an asset or liability account contains transactions that increase or decrease the balance in the account. In this example, interest payments are decreasing the House Loan balance.

Tip: You can also create a single asset account that includes an estimate of the value of the rest of your personal property (furniture, clothes, tools, Beanie Babies, and so on).

- **Liabilities.** Liabilities represent money you owe, whether for an asset, like a house or car, or something less tangible but no less important, like your college education.

  In Quicken, you create liability accounts for the money you borrow. For example, if you borrow money from Capital One to buy your car, from Bank One to purchase your home, and from Fifth Third Bank to pay for your child's college education, you'll have a liability account for each debt, whether or not it's secured by an asset that you own.

▶ **Loans.** When you borrow money, the loan is your legal commitment to pay the money back according to the terms of the loan contract. If you've purchased a house, you already know the mountains of paperwork (and writer's cramp) involved. Part of the paperwork is the loan document, which describes the amount being borrowed—the *principal*—the interest rate, the length of the loan, the number of payments, and how much principal and interest you fork over with each payment.

Most loans *amortize* your payoff, which means that the total for each payment is the same, but is made up of a different amount of principal and interest. Early in the loan's life, your payments are mostly interest and very little principal—which is great for tax deductions. By the end, you're almost entirely paying off principal. Constantly changing allocations sound like a tracking nightmare, but Quicken automatically handles amortized payments without breaking a sweat. It calculates your loan amortization schedule, assigns the principal and interest in each payment to the appropriate categories or accounts, and even handles escrow payments.

▶ **Equity and net worth.** The *equity* you hold in an asset is the value of that asset minus the balance that you owe on it. For example, if your house is worth $200,000 and the balance on your mortgage is $125,000, you have $75,000 in equity in your home.

Net worth is the big picture of equity—the value of all your assets minus the balance of all the money you owe. Net worth is a key measure of your financial health. For example, you might own houses, cars, boats, and other toys that are worth $4,000,000. But if you borrowed $3,950,000 to buy them, you're still a financial pauper with a net worth of only $50,000. On the other hand, a couple who have a house, car, and retirement fund with a combined value of $850,000, and a mortgage balance of only $25,000 are well on their way to millionaire status with a net worth of $825,000.

By linking loans in Quicken the asset accounts of the items they help purchase, you can see how much equity you have in each asset as well as your overall net worth.

Setting Up Asset and Liability Accounts

You need asset and liability accounts in Quicken to track what you own and owe. The program helps you create all the accounts you need. If you buy an asset with borrowed money, like a house mortgage or a car loan, you can create the asset account in Quicken and the program asks if you want to set up a liability account and loan.

Types of Accounts

Quicken includes three types of accounts for your assets and one for liabilities. Here are the types and what you use them for:

▶ A **House** account can represent any type of real estate (house, condo, or water-front property in the Bahamas), whether you have a mortgage or own it free and clear. When you create a house account, you specify the original purchase price and the current value. As time passes, you can also adjust the balance for the account to reflect the house's increase in market value or improvements you make, like the commercial-quality kitchen and the eight-person hot tub.

▶ A **Vehicle** account works much like a house account. When you create a vehicle account, you specify the make, model, year, original purchase price, and an estimate of the current value. Quicken asks you if you want to set up a loan for the vehicle. As time passes, you can adjust the balance for the account (although for vehicles, adjustments are usually a *decrease* in value).

▶ An **Asset** account is the one to use for miscellaneous possessions—from the tchotchkes that clutter your house to your signed Ansel Adams photographs. Quicken doesn't ask you about associated loans when you create a generic asset account, but if you borrowed money to purchase the asset, you can always link that loan to the Asset account.

▶ **Liability.** A liability account represents money you borrow, whether you take out a mortgage on a house, a bank loan on a car, or a personal loan from Aunt Marge to buy a cello.

When Loans Are Assets

Most of the time, the loans you create in Quicken represent liabilities—the money you owe to a financial institution or an individual. But loans are two-way agreements. On one side, someone is borrowing money (a liability), but the other party is lending money. To the lender, a loan is an asset.

This dual definition doesn't bother Quicken at all. In fact, when you create a new loan, as described on page 190, the first thing the program asks is whether you are borrowing or lending money. If you're borrowing, it creates a liability account to go with the loan. If you're lending, it creates an asset account.

Creating an Asset Account

If you borrow money to buy an asset, you can create the asset account in Quicken and, in the process, set up the loan and corresponding liability account. Occasionally, you want to create an asset account *without* a loan, for instance, to include the value of your wine cellar in your net worth (assuming you didn't borrow money to buy the bottles).

There are three basic ways to create an asset account:

▶ Using the Property and Debt Center, as described in this section.

▶ Relaunching the Quicken Guided Setup that you used when you first started using Quicken, and repeating the procedure for adding accounts (page 62).

▶ Working directly in the Account List window: Press Ctrl+A to open the Account List window and then, in the Account List menu bar, choose Add Account. Because the Account List window includes every type of account you can create in Quicken, you must answer more questions than you do when you create an asset account from the Property & Debt Center.

Note: You can approach the process the other way round by creating a loan and having Quicken create the liability and asset accounts that go with it. The only downside to this approach is that the program doesn't give you the option to specify the *type* of asset account that you want to create. It creates a regular asset account.

Here are the steps for creating an asset account, using a vehicle account as an example:

1. **In the Account bar, click Property & Debt.**

    Quicken displays the Property & Debt Center, which includes an Add Account button.

2. **In the Property & Debt Center, in the Property & Debt Accounts area, click Add Account.**

    The program opens the Quicken Account Setup dialog box, which shows the four types of property and debt accounts, illustrated in Figure 5-2.

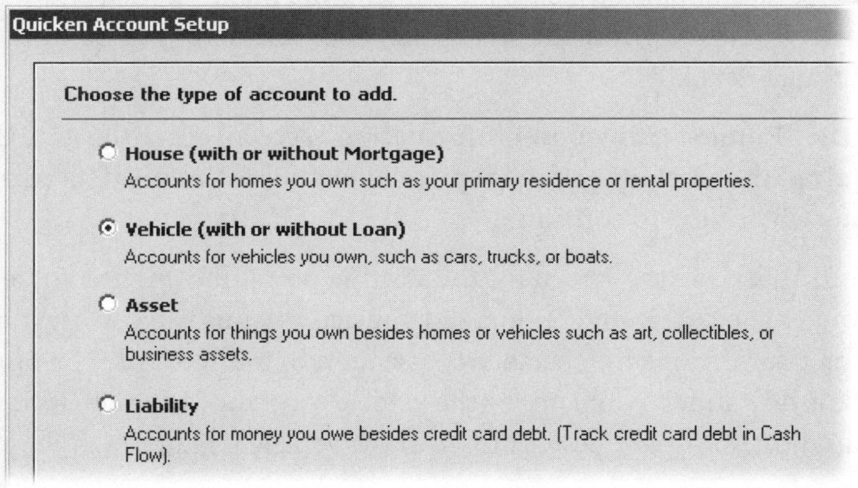

Quicken Account Setup

Choose the type of account to add.

○ **House (with or without Mortgage)**
Accounts for homes you own such as your primary residence or rental properties.

● **Vehicle (with or without Loan)**
Accounts for vehicles you own, such as cars, trucks, or boats.

○ **Asset**
Accounts for things you own besides homes or vehicles such as art, collectibles, or business assets.

○ **Liability**
Accounts for money you owe besides credit card debt. (Track credit card debt in Cash Flow).

Figure 5-2. If you aren't sure which type of account you need, read the descriptions of each type before you choose an option.

3. **In the Quicken Account Setup dialog box, choose the type of account you want.**

    If you're creating an account for a house or a vehicle, your choice is pretty simple. Choose either the House or Vehicle option. For all other valuable belongings, choose the Asset option. Click Next to begin telling the program about your asset.

4. **In the "Tell us about this (house, vehicle, asset) account" screen, in the "Name this account" text box, type a descriptive name for the account. Click Next to continue.**

    Quicken fills in the "Name this account" text box with a generic name (something like House for a house account, Car for a vehicle account, and Asset for an asset account. You'll want to change the name so it uniquely identifies the asset, for instance, *Aspen Vacation House, 02 Forerunner*, or *Wine Cellar*.

    For Vehicle asset accounts, the "Tell us about this vehicle account" screen includes additional text boxes for filling in the make, model, and year of the vehicle. But if you name the vehicle asset account well, you don't need that additional detail.

5. **On the "Enter starting point information" screen, enter the date that you acquired the asset, its purchase price, and your estimate of its current value. Click Next to continue.**

    Figure 5-3 shows the screen for the starting point information for a vehicle account. The date in the "When did you acquire this vehicle?" text box sets the date for the opening balance transaction in the account. The purchase price is how much you paid for the vehicle. And the "Estimate its current value" box is for your best estimate of the vehicle's value.

    For plain Asset accounts, you don't have to provide a purchase price. All you do is choose a starting date for tracking the asset's value and specify your estimate of the value on that date.

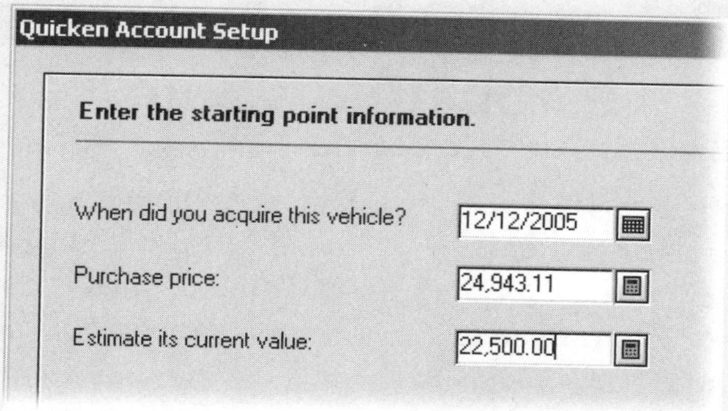

Figure 5-3. To create a house or vehicle account, you specify the date on which you purchased the asset, how much you paid for it, and how much it's worth now.

Tip: See the box on page 188 for advice on estimating vehicle and other asset values.

6. **If you plan to transfer money in and out of the account, click the Tax button to assign tax form line items for these transfers.**

The Tax Schedule Information dialog box opens with drop-down menus of the tax form and tax line to use for money that flows in or out of the account. Quicken almost always has the tax line items set up correctly, so you can click Done to create the Asset account.

Tip: To change tax information later, open the Account Details dialog box as described on page 68. At the bottom of the dialog box, click Tax Schedule Info and choose the tax line items for Transfers In and Transfers Out.

7. **In the "Is there a loan on this vehicle?" screen (titled "Is there a mortgage on this property?" for house accounts), choose the option that matches your loan situation.**

You may think there are only two choices: yes or no. But in Quicken, you have three choices, shown in Figure 5-4. The most common situation is that

Estimating Value

If you're creating a house asset account, the purchase price and your estimate of its current value may be identical if you think your purchase price was fair. For hard bargainers who don't buy *anything* unless it's a good deal, the estimated value may be higher than the purchase price.

Vehicles are a different story. If you buy a new car, its value drops by 10 to 15 percent as soon as you drive it off the lot—that first tenth of a mile turns your new car into a used car. Used car dealers make their money by purchasing used cars for less and selling them

for more. In fact, if you were to buy a used car from a dealer and try to sell it back the very next day, the price may drop by a few thousand dollars!

Other types of assets are even harder to estimate, because value is in the eye of the beholder. In fact, you may have to pay to have the magenta bathroom fixtures you paid extra for hauled away. If you're having trouble coming up with a value, try searching for similar items on the Internet (eBay.com, perhaps), before you shell out for a professional appraisal.

you have a loan or mortgage, but haven't created the liability account in Quicken. In this case, choose "Yes, create a liability account for me" option.

For a loan or mortgage that already exists in your data file, choose the "There is a loan and I'm already tracking it in Quicken" option and, in the Account drop-down menu, choose the liability account.

If you bought the asset with cash or have already paid off the loan on the asset, choose the "This vehicle is paid for, so I don't need a liability account" option. For a house account, this option is "This property is paid for, so I don't need a liability account."

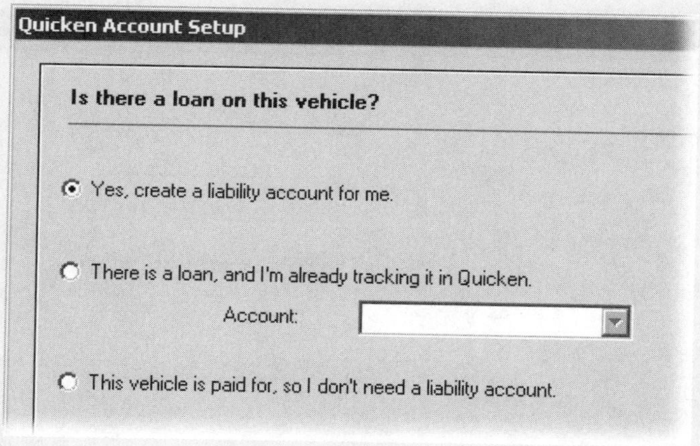

Figure 5-4. Choose the option that fits your loan situation: a loan that you want to create in Quicken, a loan that already exists in Quicken, or an asset for which you don't owe any money.

8. **Click Done.**

   If you don't owe any money on the house or vehicle, or you already have a loan set up in Quicken, you really are done. Quicken creates the asset account and, if the loan exists, links the asset and the loan.

   If you told Quicken to create a liability account, clicking Done creates the asset account, creates a liability account, closes the Quicken Account Setup dialog box, and opens the Edit Loan dialog box, so you can set up the loan or mortgage, as Figure 5-5 illustrates.

You're done! You'll learn how to fill in the Edit Loan dialog box in the next section.

Creating a Liability Account

Lenders who don't require you to pay back what you borrow are rarer than lips on a chicken, so you're not likely to create a liability account *without* a loan that describes how you're going to pay the liability back. You can most easily set up both a liability account and the loan it represents by creating a loan in Quicken and telling the program to create a new liability account, as described next. (You

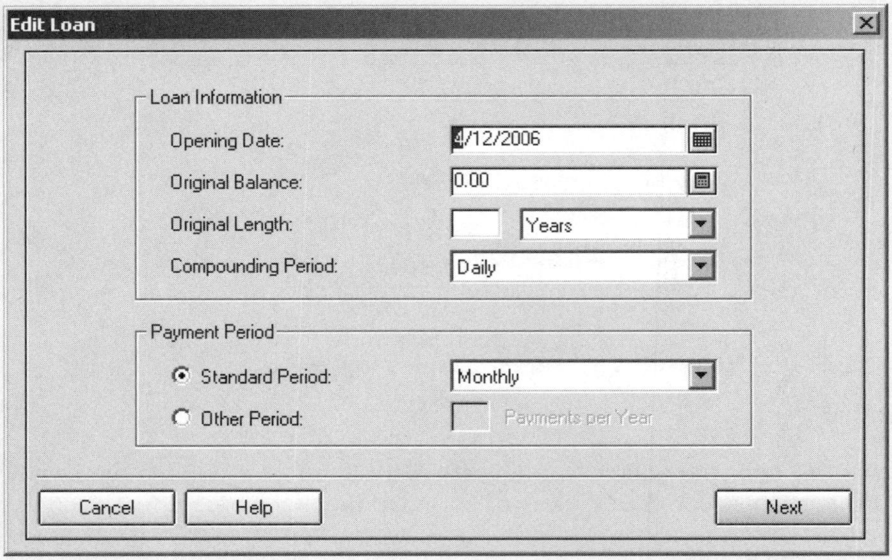

Figure 5-5. If you create an asset account in Quicken for something you bought with borrowed money, the Quicken Account Setup dialog box sends you to the Edit Loan dialog box to create the loan and liability account. Your loan documents contain the information you need to fill in the text boxes.

can also create a liability account first, create a loan, and then link the loan to the liability account, but it's a little more work.)

> **Tip:** If you take out a home equity loan on your house, you can create either a liability account or credit card account for the loan. If you create a liability account, link it to the corresponding House account to track the equity. If you use a credit card account, add transactions to withdraw money from your line of credit—or deposit money when you pay some of the line of credit back.

Setting Up a Loan

Quicken makes it so easy to track a loan and make loan payments that it's well worth the time spent in setup. Before you begin, gather your loan documents as close as the cards in a killer poker hand, because the program wants to know every detail of your loan, as you'll soon see.

Creating a Loan

As with so many tasks in Quicken, you can create a loan in more than one way. The method you choose determines which dialog boxes you'll see, but Quicken gathers the same information about your loan one way or another. Here are the two primary ways to create a loan:

▶ **The Loan Setup wizard.** This wizard can handle loans for borrowing money, loans for lending money, loans that don't pay for things you buy, and the various characteristics of each loan. You can launch the Loan Setup wizard by pressing Ctrl+H to open the View Loans window, and, in the window's menu bar, choosing New.

The one thing the Loan Setup wizard *doesn't* do is give you the opportunity to specify the *type* of asset you create to go along with the loan. If you want to set up a loan for a house or car, create a house or vehicle asset account and, when Quicken opens the Edit Loan dialog box, you can use that account to set up your loan.

Tip: For another way to launch the Loan Setup wizard, in the Account bar, click Property & Debt. In the Property & Debt Center, click Add Loan.

▶ **Creating an asset account.** If you create a house or vehicle account in Quicken, the program can tack on creating a liability account (and loan), as described on page 189. Because the program already knows that you're borrowing money, it creates the liability account and opens the Edit Loan dialog box to dive into the loan details.

Quicken needs quite a bit of information about your loan to correctly calculate the amortization schedule (the allocation of each payment to principal and interest). It takes a lot of steps to create a loan, but each step is easy and the process takes surprisingly few minutes. The list that follows explains how you use the Loan Setup wizard to create a loan.

1. **Press Ctrl+H to open the View Loans window, and then, in its menu bar, choose New.**

   The Loan Setup wizard launches and displays the Easy Step tab. The screen tells you that you'll need about 10 minutes to set up a loan, which is a lot less time than it takes to get a loan from a financial institution. You can click Next to begin stepping through one question at a time, but it's much less painful to click the Summary tab and answer several questions per screen, as Figure 5-6 illustrates.

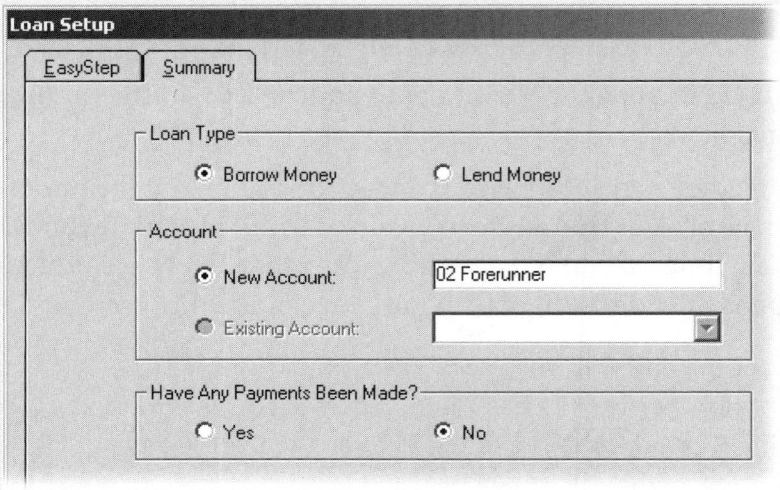

Loan Setup

EasyStep | Summary

Loan Type
(•) Borrow Money   ( ) Lend Money

Account
(•) New Account: 02 Forerunner
( ) Existing Account: [▼]

Have Any Payments Been Made?
( ) Yes   (•) No

Figure 5-6. The Summary tab in the Loan Setup dialog box is the fastest way to provide the many answers that the Loan Setup wizard needs.

2. **In the Loan Type section, choose the Borrow Money or Lend Money options, depending on whether you're borrowing money, or someone else is borrowing money from you.**

   These options determine whether the loan is a liability or an asset *for you*. If you choose the Borrow Money option, your loan is a liability, because you have an obligation to repay the balance.

If you choose the Lend Money option, the loan is one of your assets. The money you lend is still your money, plus you'll receive interest from the borrower.

3. **In the Account section, if you're creating a new loan account, turn on New Account and give it a name.**

   Adding "Loan" or "Mortgage" to the account name helps differentiate your liability account from the associated asset account. For example, if your car's asset account is named *02 Forerunner*, name the liability account *02 Forerunner Loan*.

    Tip. The Existing Account option is available *only if* you have a liability account that isn't already linked to a loan. And because of the rarity of that situation, you'll choose the New Account option most of the time.

4. **In the "Have Any Payments Been Made?" section, select either Yes or No. Then click Next.**

   Your answer depends, of course, on whether or not you've made payments on the loan before setting up this Quicken account for it. You'll have a chance to tell the wizard how much you've paid off before you're done (in step 11 on page 196).

5. **On the next screen, in the Loan Information section, in the Opening Date text box, choose the date when you opened the loan, illustrated in Figure 5-7.**

   Quicken automatically fills in the current date, but the chances of that date being correct are slim to none. However, choosing the correct date is key, because the program uses the opening date to calculate accrued interest. (Asking the lender the date that interest begins to accrue is one solution, but you can read the box on page 195 if your lender doesn't call back.)

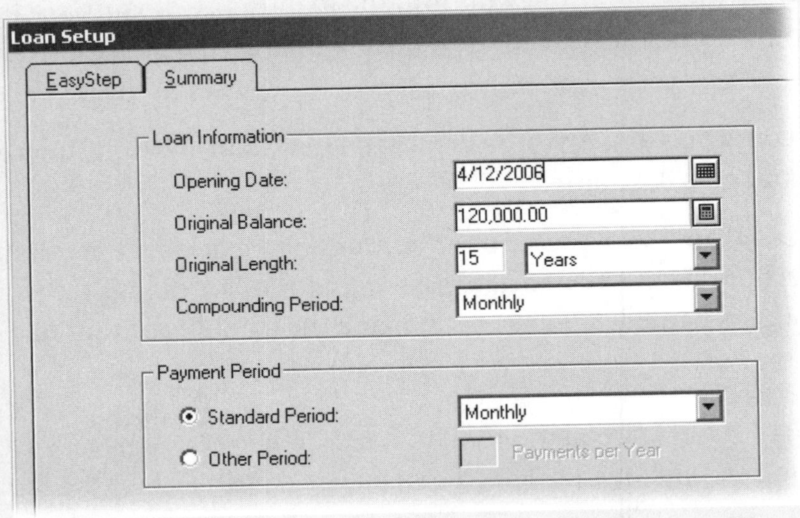

Figure 5-7. In the Opening Date field in the Loan Information box, type or choose the date that appears on your loan or mortgage documents, not the day that you create the loan in Quicken. The program uses this date to calculate how much interest has accrued.

6. **In the Original Balance text box, type the amount that you borrowed when you first opened the loan.**

   If you're creating a loan in Quicken for a real-world loan that you've had for a while, be sure to type the *original* amount you borrowed in this text box. Later, you'll have a chance to tell Quicken the current balance.

7. **In the Original Length text boxes, type the number of time periods and choose the time period duration.**

   Most car loans are set up for 4 years, although some run for 5 years. Mortgages come in many different lengths from 3 years or more for balloon mortgages to 15, 20, and 30 years. Quicken doesn't care if you define the length of the loan in Years, Months, or even Weeks—as long as you specify the correct number of time periods. For example, you know that a 30-year mortgage has an original length of 30 years, but you can tell Quicken that the mortgage length is 360 months as well.

Finding the Loan Opening Date

How do I find the opening date for my loan?

Many mortgages and loans are set up so that your payments pay the interest accrued in the previous month (or whatever your payment period is). You might sign loan papers on December 10, 2005 that show your first payment isn't due until February 1, 2006. Somewhere in between those two dates is the opening date of the loan, but which date is correct?

To keep things simple, most lenders set up loans and mortgages so that the opening date is one payment period prior to your first payment. For example, if you pay monthly and your first payment is February 1, the opening date for the loan is most likely January 1. For a mortgage, you can confirm this date by checking the Uniform Settlement Statement. Line 901 represents the interest you must pay up front and this interest is what accrues between the time you sign the papers and the opening date of the loan. Thus, if line 901 shows interest from December 10 through January 1, you can be sure that January 1 is your loan opening date.

8. **In the Compounding Period text box, choose the period that the financial institution uses to calculate the compounding on the interest you pay.**

   Quicken automatically chooses Monthly, simply because it's the most common compounding period. For other payment schedules, the compounding period is usually the same as the payment period; check with your lender.

9. **In the Payment Period section, choose the Standard Period option and then choose one of the periods in the drop-down menu. Click Next to continue.**

   Quicken's standard payment periods cover most periods that lenders use—from Weekly and Bi-Weekly through semi-Monthly and Monthly, up to Annually and still others in between. If you've borrowed money from your eccentric cousin and have an unusual payment schedule, you can choose the Other Period option and then, in the Payments per Year box, type the number of payments you make in a year.

10. **If the loan includes a balloon payment, enter its characteristics in the Balloon section.**

Balloon loans amortize the loan over a period of time—30 years for a mortgage, for example—but never actually make it that far. Instead, you must pay off the balance in full before then, often after 5 or 7 years.

Quicken selects the No Balloon Payment option automatically. If your loan includes a balloon payment, choose the Amortized Length option and fill in the boxes for the number of periods and the length of the periods. For example, for a balloon loan amortized over 7 years, in the number text box, type 7, and in the period drop-down menu, choose Years.

11. **If you've already made payments on the loan, in the Current Balance section, enter the amount you currently owe on the loan and the date on which that balance applies.**

If you selected No back in step 4 as to whether you had made any payments, the Current Balance section doesn't even appear. That's because the Current Balance is the same as the Original Balance when you first take out a loan.

You can easily find your current balance by looking at your last loan statement. Look for an entry called something like Current Balance or Current Principal Balance. That value should apply as of the date of your most recent payment.

12. **In the Payment section, choose the Payment Amount (P+I) option and then type the amount of your payment and the next due date, as illustrated in Figure 5-8.**

Your loan documents show the payment amount including only principal and interest. For a mortgage, be sure to include only the principal and interest—not other amounts, like escrow payments or private mortgage insurance premiums.

For a new loan, in the "due on" text box, choose the date on which your first payment is due. For a loan on which you've already made payments, choose the date your next payment is due.

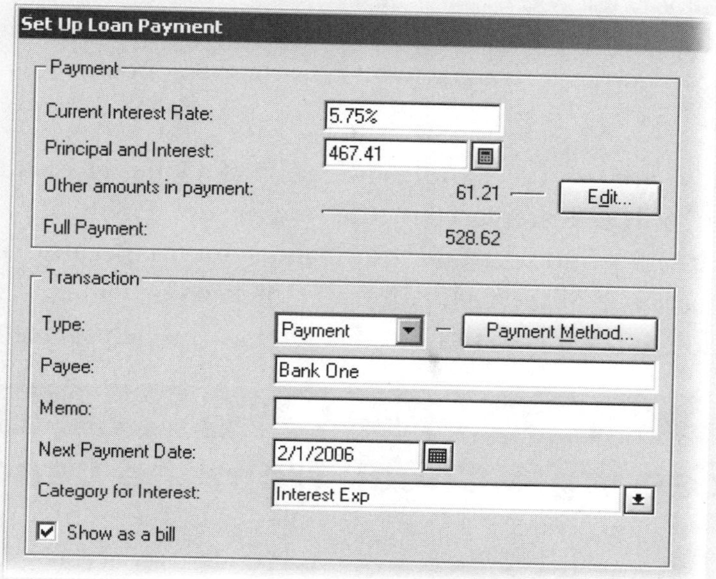

Figure 5-8. Quicken can calculate your payment for you, if you provide the interest rate for your loan. However, your loan documents include the payment that the lender expects, so you're better off entering that value in the Principal and Interest field.

13. **In the Interest Rate text box, type the annual interest rate on your loan document.**

Loan rates are usually advertised as annual rates without compounding, which you'll find in the interest rate section of your loan document. Other documents, like the loan disclosure document, show the annual percentage rate (APR), which represents the effective rate you pay taking into account interest compounding.

Note: If you know the loan interest rate, Quicken can calculate the payment for you. Although the calculation should be accurate if you set up your loan correctly, the payment on your loan document is the one you should go by.

Once you've got the interest rate entered, click Done. The Loan Setup dialog box closes, only to be replaced by the Set Up Loan Payment dialog box, in which you set up and schedule your loan payments. Because scheduled loan payments are one of the high points of Quicken convenience, go on to the next section to learn how to take advantage of this helpful feature.

Receiving a Check from the Lender

When you buy a house, the lender doesn't often write you a check for hundreds of thousands of dollars. When you close on the house, the banks make sure the money all gets where it needs to go. For other smaller loans, the lender may write you a check to deposit in your checking account. You then write your own check to pay for the car or other purchase. Here's how to track this transaction in Quicken:

1. Create the loan as you would normally.

2. Link the loan and the asset account, as described on page 203.

3. In the liability account register for the loan, select the transaction with the words Opening Balance in the Description field. In the Xfer acct field, you see the name of the liability account for the loan, for example, "02 Forerunner Loan."

4. In the Xfer Acct field, choose your checking account. When you do this, Quicken transfers the balance on the loan into your checking account. (In the real world, you must deposit the check you received from the lender into your checking account.)

5. Write a check for your purchase and record it in your Quicken checking account.

Setting Up a Loan Payment

Unless you borrow money from a good friend, chances are there's a hefty late charge awaiting you for a belated loan payment. As soon as you finish creating a loan in Quicken, the program immediately opens the Set Up Loan Payment dialog box. With just a few more steps, you can establish a scheduled transaction for the loan (see page 207). Quicken can remind you to make your loan payment on time or process the payment automatically with a repeating online payment (see Chapter 6). Either way, you can avoid those painful late fees.

Whether you use the Set Up Loan Payment or Edit Loan Payment dialog box, Quicken fills in a few of the Payment section boxes with information from your loan.

- The **Current Interest Rate** text box contains the interest rate you specified for the loan (step 13 on page 197).

- The **Principal and Interest** text box contains the value you provided in the Payment (P+I) text box (step 12 on page 196).

- The **Next Payment** text box contains the payment date you set in the loan (step 12 on page 196).

Compare the values in these three text boxes with the values for your loan. If the numbers don't jibe now, the amortization that Quicken calculates will be off as well.

Before you set up your loan payment, edit the loan to correct the discrepancies. Press Ctrl+H to open the View Loans window. In the View Loans window menu bar, click Choose Loan and select the loan for the payment. When the loan information appears in the View Loans window, click Edit Payment to open the Edit Loan Payment dialog box. (See page 211 for instructions on using this box.)

To complete the loan payment, you must tell Quicken who to pay and which payment method to use. Also, if your payment includes more than principal and interest—property tax or homeowners' insurance escrow, for instance—you add those items here.

Here's how you reap the benefits of a scheduled loan payment in the shortest possible time:

1. **If your loan payment includes more than principal and interest, click the Edit button to the right of the "Other amounts in payment" label.**

   Quicken opens the Split Transaction dialog box, which you first saw in Chapter 4 (page 130). Mortgage payments usually have additional amounts, like escrow payments for property taxes and homeowners' insurance (see the box on page 202), or premiums for private mortgage insurance. For each additional amount in the payment, choose a Category and type the amount. When you've added all the extra amounts, click OK to add the total to the "Other amounts in payment" line, as demonstrated in Figure 5-9.

2. **If you want to print loan payment checks or make payments electronically, in the Transaction section, in the Type drop-down menu, choose Print Check or Online Pmt, respectively.**

   Quicken automatically chooses Payment, which sets your loan payment up as a scheduled transaction. With this transaction type, the program reminds you a few days before your payment is due.

   If you want to check the settings for your payment, click Payment Method. In the Select Payment Method dialog box, you can specify the account to use, whether you want a reminder or an automatic payment, and how many days in advance to process the payment.

   Online Pmt appears in the drop-down menu only if you have a bank account set up for online payments. Online Pmt sets the payment to transmit electronically. If you want your online bill pay service to send the payments without *any* action on your part, click Payment Method and, in the dialog box that opens, select the Repeating Online Payment option.

3. **In the Payee text box, type the name of the lender.**

   If you're printing your loan payment checks, click the Address button to enter the mailing address for the payee.

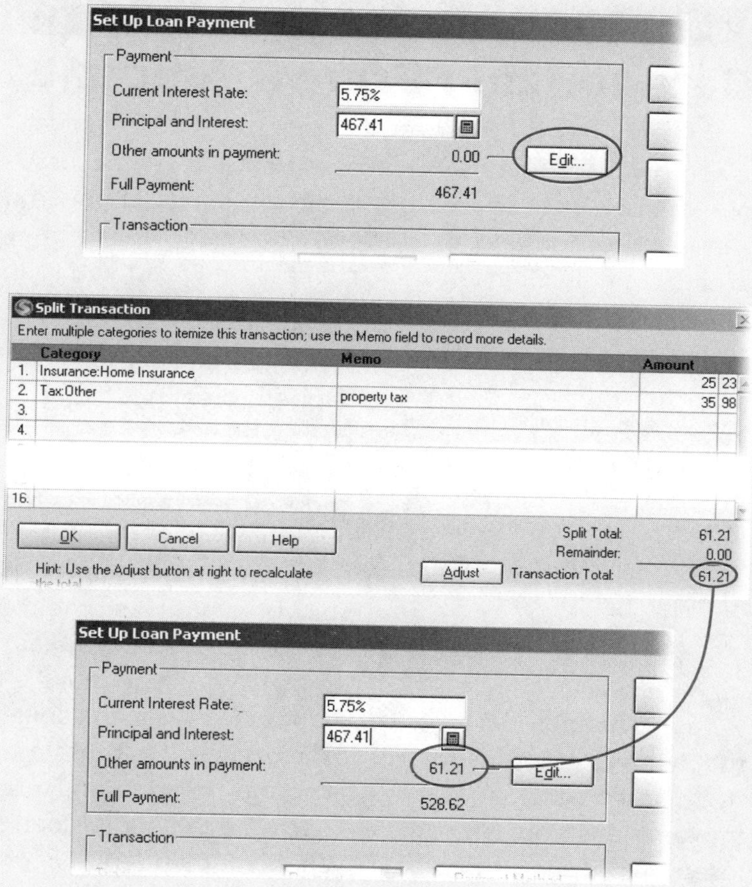

Set Up Loan Payment

Payment

Current Interest Rate: 5.75%

Principal and Interest: 467.41

Other amounts in payment: 0.00 — E_dit...

Full Payment: 467.41

Transaction

Split Transaction

Enter multiple categories to itemize this transaction; use the Memo field to record more details.

	Category	Memo	Amount	
1.	Insurance:Home Insurance		25	23
2.	Tax:Other	property tax	35	98
3.				
4.				
16.				

OK   Cancel   Help

Split Total: 61.21
Remainder: 0.00

Hint: Use the Adjust button at right to recalculate   Adjust   Transaction Total: 61.21

Set Up Loan Payment

Payment

Current Interest Rate: 5.75%

Principal and Interest: 467.41

Other amounts in payment: 61.21 — E_dit...

Full Payment: 528.62

Transaction

Figure 5-9. Top: Quicken fills in the payment amount with values from your loan. Click Edit to open the Split Transaction dialog box.
Middle: In the Split Transaction dialog box, you can enter each separate addition to your loan payment.
Bottom: Quicken adds the total from the Split Transaction dialog box to the loan payment.

Categorizing Escrow Amounts

You can make escrow tracking charmingly simple or expand it into a part-time job. The easiest way to handle escrow is to create a single Quicken category for it (called something catchy like Escrow or Other Property Costs). When you click the "Other amounts in payment" Edit button, enter one split using this category and the total escrow amount in a payment. Quicken won't know how much you pay for different escrow items, but your lender summarizes those expenses for tax reporting at the end of the year.

Another easy way to handle escrow is to calculate the average amounts for each escrow item and create a split for each one. For example, if your escrow payment is based on property taxes of $3,600 a year and an annual home-owners' premium of $900, you can enter one split in your payment of $300 for property taxes and another of $75 for insurance. Your numbers still aren't completely accurate, but you'll have *some* idea of how much you spend on each item. For example, this process may lead you to look for less costly insurance.

If you're a stickler for accuracy (or just happen to enjoy doing things the hard way), you can create an asset account for each type of escrow you pay and choose these accounts for the splits in the payment. (Remember, they're asset accounts because the money is still yours until it's time to pay the insurance, property taxes, or other items.) When you make a loan payment in Quicken, the splits transfer the escrow amounts to your escrow asset accounts. In addition, you'll have to keep an eye on your loan statements. When your lender pays property taxes or insurance premiums, you must follow suit by creating similar payment transactions in your asset accounts.

4. **If Quicken hasn't chosen the correct category for your loan interest, in the Category for Interest drop-down menu, choose the category you want.**

    Quicken automatically chooses its built-in Interest Exp category, which isn't connected to a tax form. For mortgage interest, which is tax deductible, choose Mortgage Int:Bank instead.

5. **Click OK.**

   Quicken adds your loan payment to the Scheduled Transaction List and displays a message box that asks if you want to create an asset account to go along with this loan. For houses and vehicles, you've probably already set up the asset account in Quicken, in which case click No to complete the payment setup. See "Linking an Asset and a Loan" (below) to learn how to connect the loan to the asset it helped you purchase.

   If you need to create the corresponding asset account, click Yes. The program opens the Quicken Account Setup dialog box for an asset account. Follow the steps on page 62 to create the account.

   For loans that pay for things that *aren't* assets, like school loans or debt consolidation loans, click No.

When you're done, you can check out your payment schedule. See the box on page 204.

Linking an Asset and a Loan

Sometimes you want assets linked to loans and sometimes you don't. For example, if you buy a house by taking out a mortgage, linking the asset and the loan means that Quicken can tell you how much equity you have in the house. Or if you're taking out a second mortgage on your house, you may want to link a second loan to the same asset. Whatever the reason, you can easily link an asset and a loan.

 Note: Assets that you own free and clear don't have corresponding loans. Similarly, loans that pay for intangible items don't have corresponding assets. In either case, you don't need to read this section.

Viewing the Payment Schedule and Graph

The View Loans window has three tabs. The Loan Summary tab shows the loan's vital statistics: starting date, amount, payment, interest rate, length, payment frequency, current balance, remaining payments, and—the sign that there's an end in sight—the final payment date. The other two tabs tend to sit lonely and unclicked most of the time, but they come in handy if you're thinking about big loan changes, like refinancing or paying it off early.

If you choose the Payment Schedule tab, you see a full amortization schedule for your loan, like the one shown here: the principal and interest allocation for each payment and the remaining balance after each payment. You need to know how much you pay in principal and interest for tax return preparation. Unless you want the IRS asking a lot of questions, always report the values on the 1098 form from your lender, even if they differ from the ones you see in Quicken.

One reason to consult this schedule is to see whether it makes sense to pay off a loan. As you can see in the figure, amortized loan payments begin as mostly interest and very little principal, but near the end, the payment contains very little interest. At that point, you've already paid most of the price for borrowing the money; you may as well use the lender's money for the life of the loan.

The Payment Graph tab shows a graph of the cumulative principal and interest you pay over the life of the loan. This graph can seem more disheartening than helpful, since it shows you how long it takes to make any obvious dent in what you owe.

Pmt	Date	Principal	Interest	Balance
186	9/1/2021	810.30	152.10	33,146.49
187	10/1/2021	813.93	148.47	32,332.56
188	11/1/2021	817.58	144.82	31,514.98
189	12/1/2021	821.24	141.16	30,693.74
190	1/1/2022	824.92	137.48	29,868.82
191	2/1/2022	828.61	133.79	29,040.21
192	3/1/2022	832.32	130.08	28,207.89
193	4/1/2022	836.05	126.35	27,371.84
194	5/1/2022	839.80	122.60	26,532.04
195	6/1/2022	843.56	118.84	25,688.48

Here are the steps to linking loans to assets:

1. **In the Account Bar, choose the liability account for the loan that you want to link to an asset. In the liability account's register, click the Overview tab.**

   This tab shows basic account attributes, as well as the current status of its balance and equity, as illustrated in the bottom figure in Figure 5-10.

2. **Below the Account Attributes section, click Edit Account Details.**

   The Account Details dialog box opens. Here you can add account details or edit its information, like the asset account to which it's linked.

3. **In the Linked Asset Account drop-down menu, choose the asset account.**

   Quicken lists all the asset accounts in your Quicken data file, as in Figure 5-10.

4. **Click OK.**

   You're done.

You should see the "You successfully created the asset-loan link" in the Account Details dialog box. Check the Linked Asset Account text box to make sure it shows the asset you intended. (If not, go back to step 2 and correct it.)

Making a Loan Payment

If you dutifully performed each step on pages 190–198 when you set up your loan, you should already have a scheduled payment for your loan. With a scheduled payment in place, you can clean house, play cards, or carve voodoo dolls until Quicken reminds you it's time to make a loan payment. Then, you pay your loan just as you would any other scheduled transaction. But every once in a while, you may decide to make an extra payment or pay your mortgage a little early. This section describes how to make loan payments, whether you're making a regularly scheduled payment, paying on a different date than usual, or making an extra payment.

Quicken creates payment transactions that include splits to allocate the payment to the correct amounts of principal, interest, and other payments. Listed next are the program's ground rules.

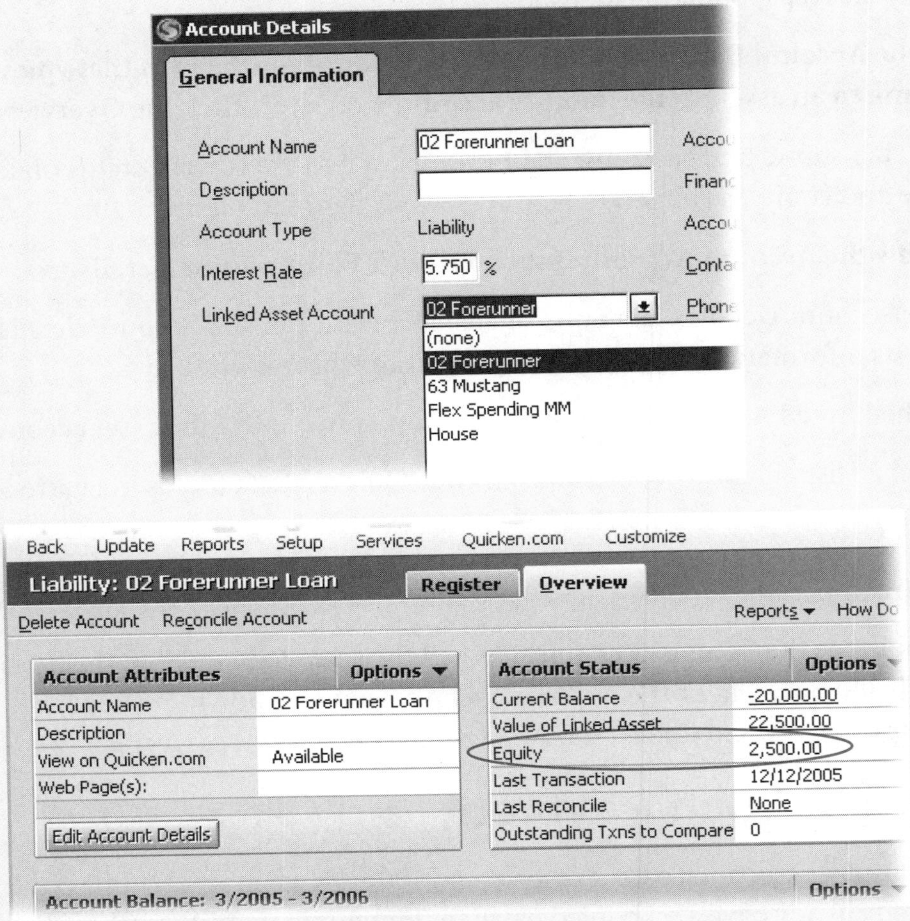

Figure 5-10. Top: In the Linked Asset Account drop-down menu, choose the asset that the loan helped purchase.
Bottom: Once a loan and asset are linked, Quicken calculates the equity in the asset (the current value minus the money owed on it).

▶ Quicken allocates interest to a category for interest expense. (For example, there's a built-in category called Mortgage Int that's associated with IRS Schedule A.)

- Quicken allocates the principal you pay to the loan's liability account. The transfer reduces the balance that you owe on the loan.

- The program allocates other amounts to the categories that you chose when you set up the loan payment.

 Note: Payments don't have any effect on the value for the linked asset account, if one exists. The balance in an asset account indicates the current value of the asset—and making a loan payment doesn't change that.

Making a Regular Payment

If you set up a loan payment as a scheduled transaction, it's hard to miss the reminders that Quicken gives you. In Quicken Home for instance, your loan payment appears right there in the Bills and Scheduled Transaction list. In the Cash Flow Center, your scheduled payments show up in the Cash Flow Alerts list. And, if you view the register for the account that you use to pay your loan, you find the Bills and Scheduled Transactions list at the bottom of the window. The red text and "Overdue!" in the Status column are meant to grab your attention.

To make a payment from the Bills and Scheduled Transaction list, click Enter. The Edit Current Transaction and Enter Into Register dialog box appears. You can click Record Transaction, then write or print the check, and send it off to the lender. (In fact, you can press Ctrl+J anytime to open the Scheduled Transaction List window and enter scheduled transactions—due or not.)

If you use an online bill pay service, you can set up your loan payments in Quicken as repeating online payments. Your bill-paying service takes complete charge of your payments, sending them on schedule until you tell the service to cease and desist. (See the box on page 254 for more advice.)

Paying Ahead of Time

Suppose you have a scheduled payment that you want to make early, perhaps to squeeze an extra mortgage payment into the tax year to increase your deductions. Here are the steps for making a scheduled loan payment on a different date.

Scheduling Downloaded Transactions

If you download transactions from your financial institution (page 233), make sure to enter the scheduled transactions for your loans into your Quicken register *before* you download them. The scheduled transaction includes the correct allocations to principal, interest, and other amounts. When you download, Quicken simply matches the downloaded transaction to your register transaction and accounts for your splits.

If you download a loan payment *without* an existing payment in the register, Quicken creates the transaction in the register. No splits, no link to your loan, no reduction in loan balance. Someone who knows Quicken inside and out can clean this mess up, but you're better off preventing the problem in the first place.

1. **Press Ctrl+J to open the Scheduled Transaction List.**

   You can also choose Tools → Scheduled Transaction List.

2. **In the row for the scheduled transaction, click Enter.**

   The Edit Current Transaction and Enter into Register dialog box appears.

3. **In the Date text box, choose the new date for your payment.**

   You can make the payment earlier or later. If you're postponing a payment, be sure to check the grace period that your lender allows, unless you don't mind handing over your first-born puppy.

4. **Click Record Payment.**

   Quicken adds the payment to the register. Don't forget to write or print the check and mail it to the lender.

Making an Extra Payment

If you decide to make an *extra* loan payment, for instance to use a holiday bonus to pay off additional principal, the View Loans window is the place to go. Here's the drill:

1. **Open the View Loans window by choosing Property & Debt → Loans (or by pressing Ctrl+H).**

   The window title includes the name of the loan that's selected. If the loan you want to pay isn't visible, click Choose Loan in the menu bar and, in the drop-down menu, click the loan you want. Quicken displays the basic values for the loan.

2. **Click Make Payment.**

   The Loan Payment message box appears asking if you want to make a regular or extra payment.

3. **Click Extra.**

   Quicken opens the Make Extra Payment dialog box. Because the payment isn't part of the loan payment schedule, the Amount text box is blank. You must fill in or modify the boxes to fit the payment you're making, as illustrated in Figure 5-11.

4. **In the Date text box, choose the date that you plan to make the payment.**

   Quicken automatically sets the date to today.

5. **If you're paying towards something other than principal, choose it in the Category box.**

   Most of the time, extra payments pay off principal (a noble thing to do because it reduces the length of your loan and the total interest you pay). Quicken automatically sets the Category text box to the liability account for the loan, which transfers the payment amount into the account, thus reducing the outstanding balance.

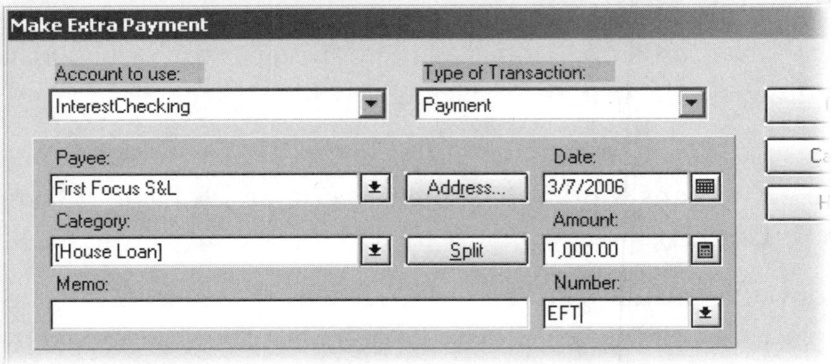

Figure 5-11. For an extra payment, you have to tell Quicken how much you want to pay and when you want to pay it. In the Category text box, the program automatically chooses the liability account so that the payment pays off loan principal. Change the category if you're making an extra payment for escrow or some other purpose.

6. **In the Amount text box, type the payment amount.**

   If you're making an extra payment to reduce your principal, you can choose the payment amount. If your lender is asking for more money to make up for a shortfall in escrow, type that amount.

7. **In the Number drop-down menu, choose how you plan to pay, just like a regular transaction in an account register.**

   Next Check Num, Print Check, Online Pmt, and EFT are the likely choices.

8. **Click OK.**

   Quicken adds the transaction to the register of the account from which you paid.

If you're paying off principal, the payment also acts as a transfer to reduce the balance in the loan liability account.

Editing a Loan

Loan characteristics change from time to time. For example, if you have an adjustable-rate mortgage, the interest rate changes every so often. Each year, your escrow payment increases as property taxes and homeowners' insurance premiums go up. Or you may have made a small error when you initially set up the loan in Quicken. Regardless of the reason, the View Loans window provides the tools you need to make all these changes.

The fastest way to open the View Loans window, shown in Figure 5-12, is by pressing Ctrl+H. If keyboard shortcuts aren't your forte, choose Property & Debt → Loans. Before you begin making changes, in the View Loans menu bar, choose Choose Loan and then, in the drop-down menu, select the loan you want to edit.

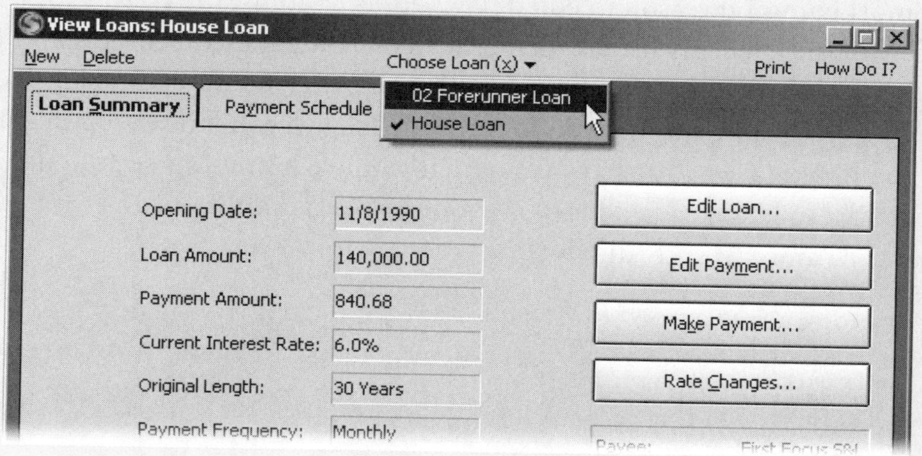

Figure 5-12. Before you make any changes, choose the loan you want to edit. Click the Edit Loan button to change loan details, like an incorrect balance. To change a payment (to increase the escrow amount, for example), click Edit Payment. For adjustable-rate loans, click Rate Changes to adjust the interest rate.

Changing Loan Details

The most common reason to change loan details is to adjust values you initially set up. For example, suppose you chose the No Balloon option when setting up a loan because you didn't know the details of your balloon payment yet, and now you want to fill in the amortized length. Or perhaps you provided the wrong opening date and want to correct that.

In the View Loans window, click Edit Loan. When the dialog box opens, you see the same text boxes and options you ran through when you first set up the loan, as described on page 190. Make the changes or corrections you want and, on the final screen, click Done to save your changes.

Changing Payment Details

The most common reason to edit a payment is to adjust the escrow for a mortgage. Mortgage lenders usually demand an escrow payment for property taxes and homeowners' insurance to ensure that these payments are made. Their money's on the line and they don't want a local government seizing the property due to unpaid taxes. Property taxes and insurance premiums seem to increase constantly, so lenders usually review your escrow account once a year and adjust the escrow amount accordingly.

Note: One reason your payment might drop is when the equity in your home has increased to the point where you no longer need private mortgage insurance.

Changing your payment method is another reason to edit a payment in Quicken. If you set up the payment as a scheduled transaction, say, but want to switch to a repeating *online* payment, use the Edit Loan Payment dialog box.

Regardless of the reason for the change in your payment, in the View Loans window, click Edit Payment to open the Edit Loan Payment dialog box. The steps for changing the values in this dialog box should be familiar—they're identical to adding values in the first place.

Adjusting the Interest Rate

Much as you might want to change the 8.5 percent rate on your 30-year fixed-rate mortgage, you can use the Quicken Rate Changes feature only if you borrowed money with an adjustable-rate loan. When the interest rate changes on one of these loans, the payment changes along with it. (The potential for a smaller payment is one of the charms of an adjustable-rate loan.) With Quicken, you don't have to do any fancy calculator work. You tell the program the new rate, and it automatically calculates your new payment amount.

Here's how you change the interest rate and figure out your new payment:

1. **In the View Loans window, click Rate Changes.**

    Quicken opens the Loan Rate Changes window. As you can see in Figure 5-13, you can create, edit, or delete interest rates. When the interest rate adjusts, add a new rate with the date it becomes effective. Edit a rate if you set the rate or date incorrectly. If you're decades into a loan, you can delete older interest rates to shorten the list.

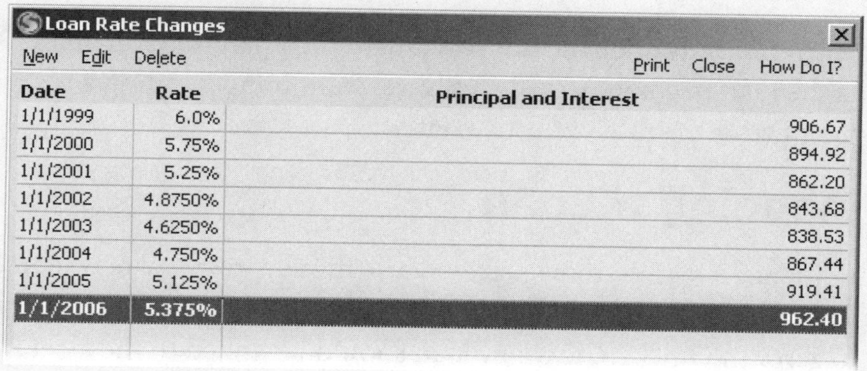

Figure 5-13. In the Loan Rate Changes window, choose New to add the most recent loan interest rate and the date on which it becomes effective. If the list has grown long, you can highlight the applicable row and click Delete to remove older rates that have outgrown their usefulness.

2. **In the Loan Rate Changes menu bar, choose New.**

   The Insert an Interest Rate Change dialog box appears with boxes for the critical values: the effective date of the change, the new interest rate, and the new payment that you'll have to pay.

3. **In the Effective Date box, choose the date on which the new rate becomes effective.**

   Adjustable-rate loans don't change their rates any old time. Some adjust their rates in as little as a month, although loans that adjust once a year are the commonest. The lender will tell you on which day the interest rate takes effect.

4. **In the Interest rate text box, type the new interest rate.**

   The Regular Payment text box is empty until you press Enter or click away from the Interest Rate text box. Quicken calculates the new payment and fills in the box, as you can see in Figure 5-14.

5. **Click OK.**

   Quicken not only adds the interest rate to the Loan Rate Changes list; it also edits the loan payment to reflect the new amount beginning with the first payment after the rate's effective date.

Refinancing a Loan

If you refinance a loan or mortgage, you use money from the new loan to pay off the balance on the old loan along with other fees. The balance on the old loan drops to zero. In Quicken, the new loan should be linked to the asset it's paying for. If the thought of getting all these changes straight makes you sweat, you can relax. This sort of task is nothing more than following the money.

Create the new loan as you would any other. Quicken creates a transaction in the liability account for the opening balance. All you have to do is split this opening balance transaction to account for the items that the new loan covers: paying off the old loan, closing costs, and any accrued interest. Figure 5-15 shows you how.

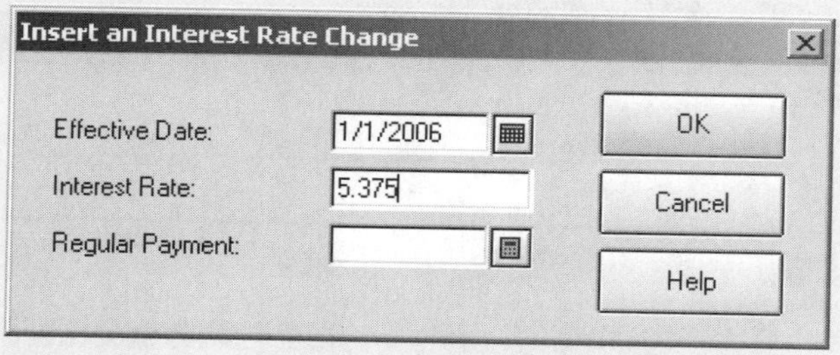

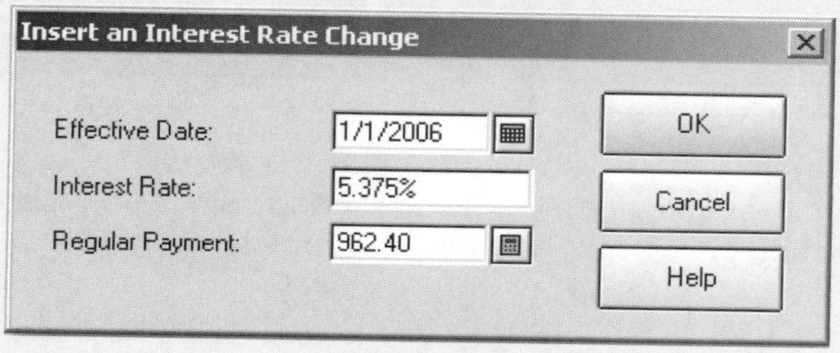

Figure 5-14. Quicken needs only the effective date and the interest rate (top). The program calculates the new payment (bottom).

For example, if you roll the closing costs and payoff interest into the new loan, the split transaction includes three entries, as demonstrated in Figure 5-15:

- **Pay off old loan balance.** To pay off the balance on the old loan, choose the liability account for the old loan in the Category field. In the Amount field, type the balance on the old loan. Quicken reduces the balance on the old loan to zero.

- **Closing costs.** To allocate some of the new loan to pay your closing costs, choose a category like House Cost Basis. (You have to create this category. The category name indicates that you can add the expenses in this category to the original purchase price to increase your cost basis and, thus, decrease the gain, when you sell.) In the Amount field, type the value of the closing fees.

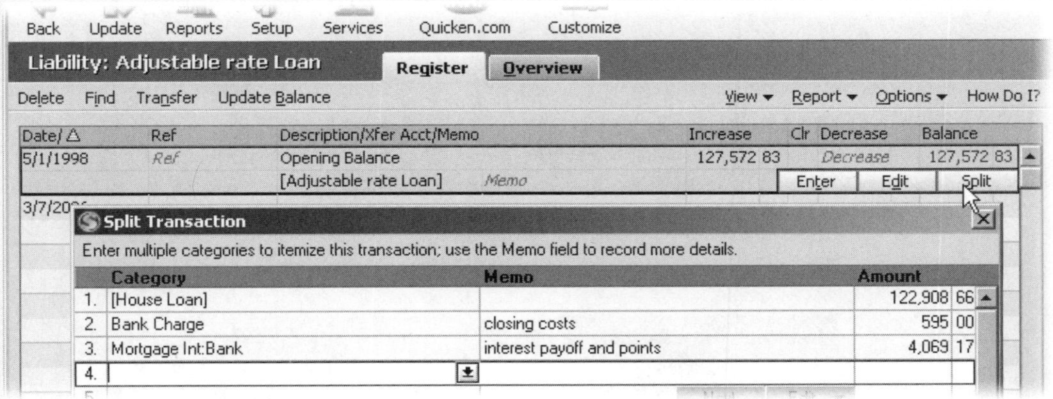

Figure 5-15. Select the Opening Balance transaction for the new loan and click Split. In the Split transaction dialog box, add an entry for each item the new loan pays for.

- ▶ **Pay off interest.** When you close out an old loan, you typically have to pay some interest that accrued after the last payment you made. In the Category field, choose the category you use to track deductible interest expense, like Mortgage Int: Bank.

Click OK to save the splits and then click Enter to save the changes to the Opening Balance transaction.

CHAPTER 6:
ONLINE BANKING

▶ What Quicken Can Do Online

▶ Connecting Quicken to the Internet

▶ Setting Up an Account for Online Services

▶ Updating All Accounts with One Step

▶ Downloading Transactions

▶ Reviewing and Incorporating Downloaded Transactions

▶ Renaming Payees

▶ Setting Up Online Payees

▶ Paying Bills Online

▶ Setting Up Online Transfers

▶ Canceling an Online Payment

Before online banking, your bank balance was like the surprise ending of a film thriller. You had to wait until your bank statement arrived (by snail mail) to discover how much money you had on hand, which checks and deposits had cleared, and whether you were overdrawn. But with Quicken and almost every financial institution offering online banking, you can view those balances and transactions any time, download them into your Quicken data file, and take evasive action to avoid bank fees for bounced checks and low balances.

You can also pay bills online without having to write checks, lick stamps, or drive to the post office. For the ultimate in convenience, you can set up recurring payments so you can go on a long vacation without worrying about missing your mortgage payment.

First, you've got to do some setup. (There had to be a catch.) You need to sign up for your bank's online services, and instruct Quicken how to connect to them. This chapter explains how online services work, and shows you step-by-step how to link Quicken to them, download transactions, and make online payments. You'll also learn how to compare downloaded transactions with ones you recorded yourself (and correct any discrepancies).

 Note: If you prefer paper checks and brick-and-mortar banks, simply skip this chapter. Quicken lets you manage all aspects of your personal finances without ever connecting to the Internet.

What Quicken Can Do Online

Online services boil down to three electronic tasks. Quicken can handle all three, but not all banks do. Bank policies vary widely, so contact yours directly to get all the details. If your bank doesn't offer a certain service—online bill payment, say—you can purchase that option directly from Intuit (see the box on page 219).

- ▶ **Online account access.** Once you set up an account in Quicken for online access—checking, savings, credit card, or investment—you can download transactions that have cleared in that account. If you have *two* accounts at the same financial institution set up for online access (checking and savings, for example), you can electronically transfer funds between accounts.

Paying for Online Services

Whether you pay for online services depends on your financial institution. Some banks offer online account access for free—perhaps because downloading transactions and transferring funds electronically saves them from having to hire staff to handle face-to-face transactions.

However, many banks charge for their online bill payment services, as does Intuit for its Quicken Bill Pay service, and the fees can exceed $10 a month. Before you scoff at a monthly fee for online bill payment, consider how much money you spend on stamps, envelopes, and printed checks, and how much valuable time you spend paying bills each month. For example, paying 15 bills electronically saves $5.55 in stamps alone.

There are two times when it makes sense to use the Quicken Bill Pay service: if your bank doesn't offer online bill payment, or if Quicken Bill Pay costs less than what your bank charges. On the other hand, Quicken online financial services may turn you off with their setup, fees, and occasional downloading glitches. For a different approach to paying bills online, see "Let Payees Come and Get Their Payments" in Online Appendix F.

Quicken online account access works only if your bank supports it. You can find out by checking Quicken's list of participating financial institutions, as discussed on page 64. If you use a financial institution that doesn't support Quicken online account access, you may instead be able to perform online tasks through your bank's Web site without the automatic link to Quicken. (You can learn how to do that on page 229.)

Note: You can download credit card transactions the same way as checking transactions, but to do so you must set up your credit card in Quicken as a liability account and enter individual credit card charges. (Setting up a credit card as a payee and entering only the monthly bill payment won't work.)

- **Online bill payment.** Paying bills with Quicken and your Internet connection takes only a few mouse clicks. Your days of writing checks, stuffing envelopes, digging out stamps, and dropping payments in mailboxes are over. You record a transaction in Quicken, send the instructions to your online bill payment service, and let it do the grunt work.

  But perhaps the most addictive aspect of online bill payment is automatic repeating payments. You can sit back and relax without firing a single neuron over the bills that are due. Quicken takes care of sending online payments on the schedule you set.

- **Shopping for personal finance services.** Quicken includes dozens of links to Web sites that provide personal financial services. If you desire more assistance than Quicken can provide, you can research and comparison shop for loans, insurance, financial institutions, and even financial planners. (See the box on page 219 for more info.)

Note: The links in Quicken take you to the Web sites of Intuit partners, which doesn't mean their services are the best or least expensive. To research all your options, surf the Internet on your own.

Connecting Quicken to the Internet

Chances are you told Quicken about your Internet connection when you installed the program. Online banking aside, Quicken does plenty every time it goes online: It can update your version of the program, show you information about financial services, convey feedback to Intuit, and connect you to support options like the Quicken Forum (see Appendix B).

If Quicken isn't already going online, start by choosing Edit → Preferences → Internet Connection Setup. The first screen of the Internet Connection Setup wizard has three options, which cover all possibilities for Internet access, as shown in Figure 6-1.

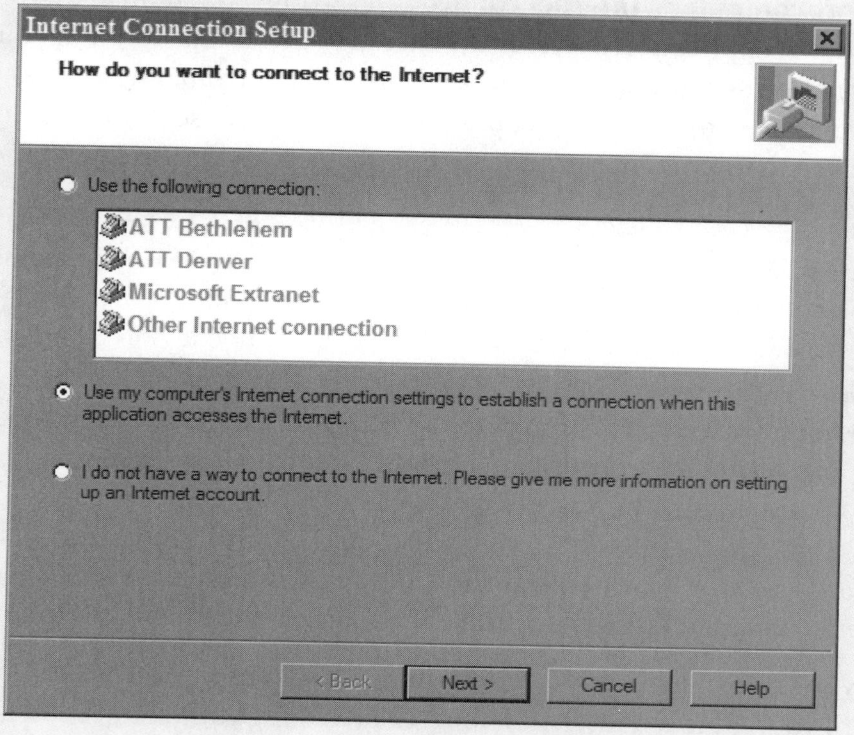

Figure 6-1. When you first set up Quicken to go online, you tell it which connection you want it to use. If you have several ways to connect, you'll see them all listed here. (If you don't have an Internet connection, click Cancel and get your PC online before launching the Internet Connection Setup wizard again.)

▶ **Use the following connection.** The list in the box that accompanies this option displays all of the Internet connections you've set up on your computer. (If you have more than one, and don't see them all listed here, see the box above for further advice.) Select this radio button if you use a dial-up connection: Quicken dials your ISP (or runs your ISP's connection program) when it wants to go online.

You can also select this option to change the Internet connection Quicken uses, or if Quicken is having trouble detecting a connection.

- **Use my computer's Internet connection settings to establish a connection when this application accesses the Internet.** Select this option if you have an Internet connection that's always available, like broadband, wireless, or cable. Despite its lengthy label, this option is the easiest to use. You're telling Quicken to use the Internet connection that's already running whenever it needs to go online.

> **Tip:** Selecting this option is easy *only if* you have a running Internet connection. If Quicken tries to go online only to find no connection, the screen in Figure 6-1 appears, asking you to choose one.

- **I do not have a way to connect to the Internet. Please give me more information on setting up an Internet account.** Unfortunately, choosing this option doesn't offer any meaningful help. If you don't have Internet access, you're not ready for the Internet Connection Setup wizard. Click Cancel, find an Internet Service Provider, and subscribe to its Internet service. When you're online, return to this wizard, and choose one of the other two options.

After you choose your connection option, click Next or Done to complete the setup of your Quicken Internet connection. Testing your connection is as simple as launching one of the helpful hints that takes you to a Web site. For example, choose Help → Ask a Quicken User to see if the program reaches the Quicken Support Forums Web site.

> **Tip:** If Quicken can't connect to the Internet, you first have to determine whether the problem's with the program or your Internet connection. You can easily answer this question by checking for email or opening your Web browser. If those programs can connect, launch the Internet Connection Setup wizard again and check your settings.

Setting Up an Account for Online Services

Connecting the accounts you have at financial institutions to your Quicken accounts is a little more like matchmaking than personal finance. You must first

TROUBLESHOOTING MOMENT

When Connections Don't Appear

The connections you've configured for your computer *outside of* Quicken should appear in the "Use the following connection" box. If they don't, click Cancel to close the Internet Connection Setup wizard. Launch your connection to the Internet as if you were planning to check email. While the connection's running, reopen the Internet Connection Setup wizard, which should now list the connection you're using. Choose the connection, and then click Done.

If Quicken doesn't recognize your connection no matter what you do, don't panic. You can always choose the "Use my computer's Internet connection settings..." option. However, before you perform any Quicken task that requires Internet access, be sure to connect to the Internet outside of the program.

prepare both participants for the relationship, and then introduce them. When you first create an account, as described in Chapter 2, Quicken asks you for the name of the financial institution and whether you want to set up the account for online services. If you took care of setting up your account then, you can skip to "Downloading Transactions" on page 233. If not, then read on.

Before you embark on a mission to connect your account with online services, you must first see if your financial institution works with Quicken's services. For accounts listed in the Quicken Cash Flow Center (including checking, savings, and credit cards), the account Overview tab is the fastest way to do this. In the Account Bar, choose the account and then click the Overview tab. Figure 6-2 shows how you can tell which online services a financial institution offers: you'll see Available (or Not Available) listed for the services your financial institution provides.

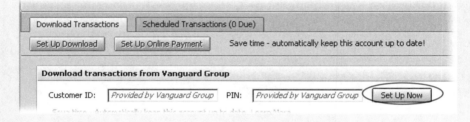

Figure 6-2. Top Left: Next to the names of services like Transaction Download and Online Payment, the word Available appears if it's compatible with Quicken. If the box reads Not Available, you can't use that feature with Quicken.
Top right: Savings accounts don't include an Online Payment through attribute, but you can still pay bills with funds from the credit card account using Quicken's bill payment service.
Bottom: Investment accounts tell you that they handle online services by displaying a Set Up button in the register window.

Your financial institution takes the lead in communicating with Quicken. Financial institutions that use direct connections can do more than those that use Web Connect. As a result, you do less work to link those accounts to Quicken's. Here are the two possibilities:

▶ **Direct connection** is a secure Internet connection that links Quicken directly to your financial institution's computers. With this type of connection and a financial institution that offers the services, you can download your bank statements and transactions directly into your data file, transfer funds between accounts, pay bills online, and email your bank. (You can learn about direct connections on page 234.)

- **Web Connect** uses a secure connection to your bank's Web site to download your statement information, but, unlike a direct connection, the program doesn't automatically load the downloaded information into Quicken. With Web Connect, you must then import the downloaded information into Quicken.

Finding a Participating Institution

Many, but not all, financial institutions support Quicken's online services. If your current bank is behind the times, you can try another institution. Whether you're on the prowl for a new bank or want to apply for online services with your current one, Quicken provides a list of participating financial institutions so you can see—and apply for—the services they offer. As long as you've registered your copy of Quicken, the program updates the list when you go online.

To view the list, choose Online → Participating Financial Institutions. When the Apply for Online Financial Services window appears, you can filter the list for institutions that support different types of online financial services. As shown in Figure 6-3, finding a financial institution is as easy as 1-2-3.

If you're not shopping for a new bank, you can use the Apply for Online Financial Services window to sign up for additional services with the institution you already work with. Here are the services you may find:

- **Any services.** By definition, this link displays financial institutions that support at least one of Quicken's online financial services.

- **401(k) account access.** This link filters the list to show the financial institutions that let you download the transactions for your 401(k) or 403(b) retirement accounts.

Figure 6-3. There are three steps to researching online banking services in Quicken:
1. Click one of the Online Financial Services links to filter the list to show only the financial institutions that provide that service.
2. Click the name of a financial institution to see the details of its online capabilities.
3. If you like what you see, click Apply Now to learn how to get started with their online services.

▶ **Banking account access.** This service lets you download transactions from your bank account into Quicken.

▶ **Bill pay.** Institutions that support this service let you send them bill payment instructions from Quicken (although you usually pay for the privilege).

▶ **Brokerage account access.** This service lets you download transactions from your investment account into Quicken.

▶ **Credit/charge card access.** With this service, you can download your credit card transactions into Quicken.

To find a financial institution that supports all the services you want, click each link and make sure that the company's name reappears each time. If you know which institution you want to use, it's much easier to choose its name in the list and review the information that Quicken displays, as illustrated in Figure 6-3.

 Tip: Before you go through the hassle of relocating accounts, give your current financial institution a call to see if it's planning to offer online services. If you want only online bill payment, you can keep your account where it is and sign up for Quicken's Bill Pay service instead (see the box below).

ALTERNATE REALITY

Using Intuit Online Financial Services

If your bank doesn't offer an online bill payment service or online credit card access, Intuit's happy to earn more of your business. The company offers Quicken Bill Pay and a Quicken Credit Card—although these add-ons aren't free.

In the Apply for Online Financial Services window, click the Quicken Bill Pay link to sign up for Intuit's bill payment service. Click the Quicken Credit Card link to apply for a credit card through Intuit. You can also sign up for these services by choosing Tools →

Quicken Services and then clicking the appropriate link.

Lest you forget, Intuit does its fair share of marketing for these features. Every now and then, a message box pops up asking if you want more information about a personal finance service related to the task you're performing. In addition, in the bottom right corner of the Quicken main window, you'll find a link that rotates between these services, including Quicken Bill Pay or downloading credit card transactions.

Applying for Online Services

The first step in a budding online relationship between Quicken and your bank accounts is applying for online banking services at your financial institution. If you've already started the application ball rolling, you can skip this section. If you haven't, choose Online → Participating Financial Institutions to open the Apply for Online Financial Services window.

Peruse the Financial Institution Directory to find your bank or institution, and then click the link for its name. When the company's details appear in the right pane, simply click the big Apply button to start the process. One of two things happens, depending on whether the financial institution has an online application:

- **No online application.** A window opens thanking you for your interest in online services...and telling you to contact your financial institution. How helpful. In the menu bar, click Home to return to the Apply for Online Financial Services window, which includes the telephone number to call.

- **Online application.** In the Apply for Online Financial Services window, Quicken displays the institution's Web application, as you can see in Figure 6-4. Fill out the application and follow the onscreen instructions.

After you complete the application process, your financial institution will send you confirmation information, a PIN (personal identification number) or password, and so on. Check to make sure your account number and other information is correct. Now you're ready to activate your account for online services, as described next.

Activating Online Services for Your Quicken Account

A week to ten days after you apply for online services, you should have a confirmation letter from your bank with your new customer ID and PIN. To start banking online, all you have to do is activate the corresponding account in Quicken. Here are the steps:

1. **In the Account Bar, select the account you want to activate.**

   The account register opens to either the Register or Overview tab. Either way, you'll see the Set Up Online command in the menu bar.

2. **In the register menu bar, choose Set Up Online.**

   If your financial institution supports direct communication with Quicken, the program opens the Quicken Account Setup dialog box, which immediately asks for your customer ID and PIN, as illustrated in Figure 6-5.

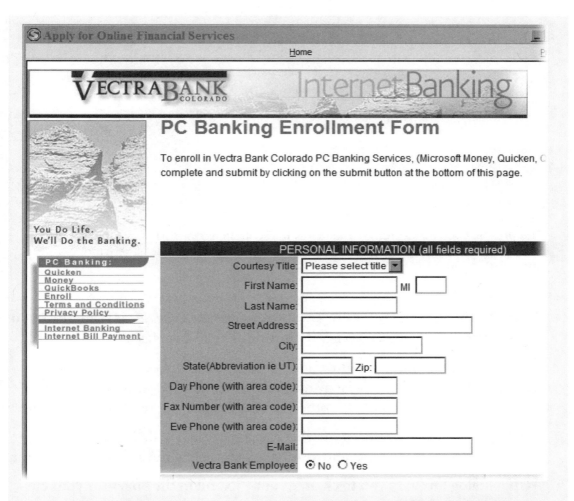

Figure 6-4. Each financial institution has its own way of doing things. Follow the instructions on the Web site to complete its application. You must apply separately to each financial institution whose online services you want to use.

For financial institutions that don't communicate directly, Quicken has Web Connect, which helps you log into the financial institution's Web site to download a transaction file for import to your Quicken data file. If you see a window containing your bank's Web page, skip to "Downloading Statements with Web Connect" on page 235.

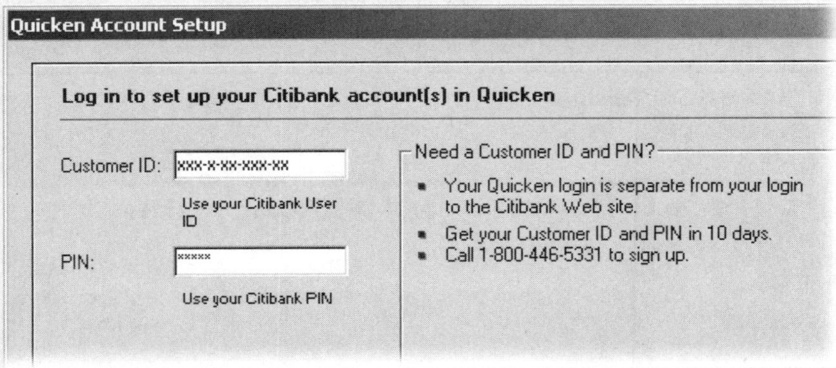

Figure 6-5. Type the customer ID and PIN that your financial institution sent. As with any password, Quicken displays asterisks (*) instead of the actual alphanumeric characters of your PIN.

3. **In the Customer ID and PIN text boxes, type the customer ID and PIN you received from your financial institution. Then click Next.**

   Quicken goes online and downloads information it needs about your accounts from the financial institution. When Quicken and the institution have successfully made each other's acquaintance, you're ready to continue.

   If you *don't* have your customer ID and password, the dialog box tells you how to get them, and even provides the financial institution's phone number.

4. **If a dialog box asks you to change your PIN, fill in the boxes for your current and new PIN.**

   Some financial institutions make you change your PIN immediately.

5. **If a dialog box asks for your account number and bank routing number, type them in the appropriate boxes.**

   For the sake of security, your confirmation letter probably doesn't include the account and routing numbers. Choose Help → Quicken Help. In the Quicken Help window, click the Index tab and type "routing" to display the "What is my bank routing number?" topic. You can also find these numbers on your checks.

6. **If you see a dialog box that asks you to choose the account you're setting up, choose the account in the drop-down menu, and then click Next to continue.**

   You only see this box if you have more than one account set up for online services at the financial institution.

7. **Click Next to complete the setup.**

   Quicken displays a dialog box proclaiming you've succeeded in setting up the account for online services. To download transactions, click Next once more.

To verify that your account's activated, open the register window and click the Overview tab. Next to the service's name, you should see the word "Activated."

Updating All Accounts with One Step

Online financial services are about convenience, so why download transactions and send payment instructions one account at a time? In Quicken, the One Step Update automatically downloads transactions and sends payment instructions for every account you've set up for online services.

It should come as no surprise that this convenience requires some setup. The time you save is well worth the few minutes you need for the setup. To get started, choose Online → One Step Update, which opens the One Step Update dialog box, shown in Figure 6-6.

Although One Step Update can perform all of the following tasks in one session, you can tell it to perform only the tasks you want. For example, you can turn off the Quotes option if you want only your downloaded transactions.

▶ **Quotes.** To download information about your investments, turn on the checkbox for "Download quotes, asset classes, headlines, and alerts." Quicken automatically obtains price quotes, your investments' asset classes, headlines about your investments, and alerts about things like steep price drops. To specify which quotes to download, click the "Select quotes to download" link. See Chapter 9 to learn about working with investments in Quicken.

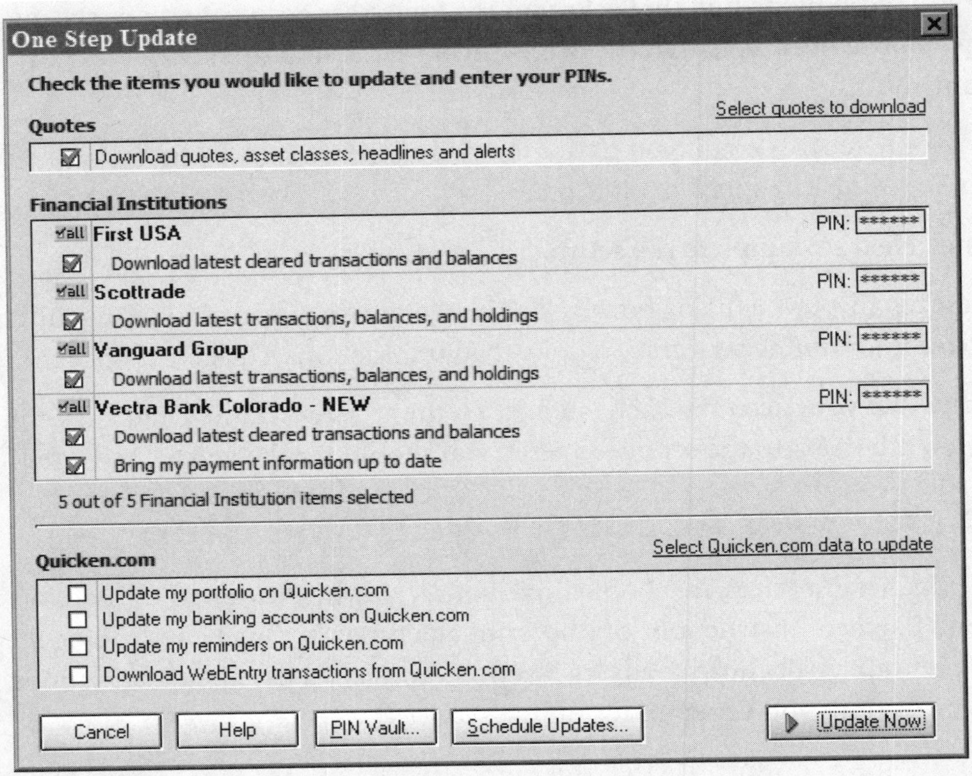

Figure 6-6. With the One Step Update, you can download bank transactions, investment transactions, and investment price quotes. One Step Update can also automatically enter your account PINs or passwords as it is done here.

- ▶ **Financial institutions.** Quicken lists all the financial institutions you've set up for online services. The checkboxes you see for each account depend on the online services you've activated. Accounts that only download transactions have a checkbox for downloading. If you also set up online bill payment, that account has a second checkbox labeled "Bring my payment information up to date."

- ▶ **Quicken.com.** Uploading your financial information to Quicken.com lets you manage your money via the Internet, which comes in handy if you're traveling for business or pleasure. The downside is that your sensitive financial data is stored at Quicken.com. If you think storing your personal information on a Web site is an unnecessary security risk, turn off all checkboxes in this section.

When you're ready to update your accounts, click Update Now. A status dialog box appears, showing you which account it's updating and how far it's progressed. If an emergency arises, click Stop Update. You can run One Step Update later when things have calmed down.

When all of your accounts are up to date, the Online Update Summary window opens. As you can see in Figure 6-7, you can quickly review an account's current balance and whether it has any new transactions. To check the details of downloaded transactions, click Go to Register (for bank accounts) or Go to Account (for investment accounts).

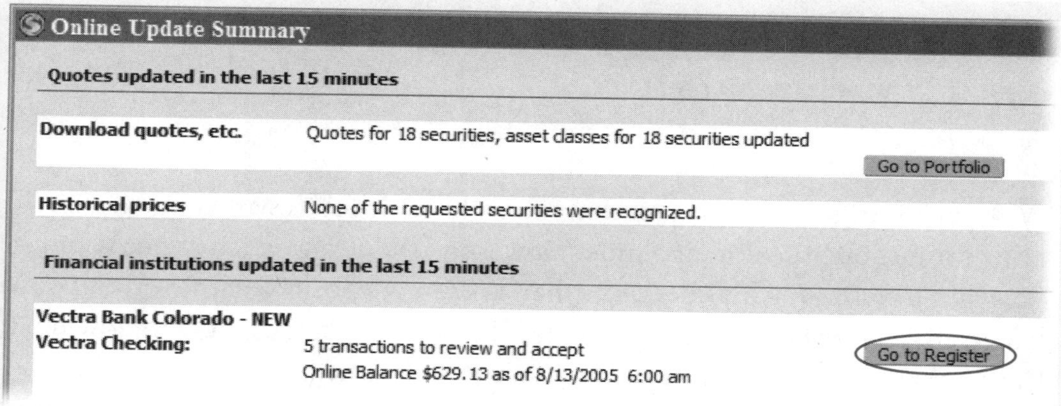

Figure 6-7. If you want to see the transactions that One Step Update downloaded, click the account's Go to Register (or Go To Account for investment accounts) button.

Downloading Transactions

Most financial institutions offer to download transactions in one way or another. With a direct connection, you can download transactions with a single click. Using Web Connect takes a few more steps, but you still get the records from your financial institution long before the statement arrives.

Banking at the Online Center Window

The Online Center window gathers all online tasks in one place. From this one window, you can choose an account; view downloaded transactions, online payments, and emails from your financial institution; send electronic payments; open the Online Payee List window to create or edit your online payees; and open the Scheduled Transaction List window to create or edit scheduled transactions or repeating online payments.

To pay bills online, click the Payments tab, where you can set up your payment. (Instructions are on page 247.) When your bill payments are ready to go, click Update/Send, which both downloads cleared transactions and sends your payment instructions to your financial institution.

With the One Step Update, you don't need to settle for downloading transactions for just one account at a time. However, if you're worried about your cash flow and want to quickly check whether a certain deposit cleared, you can download transactions for only one account. This section explains how to download transactions using direct connections and Web Connect.

Downloading Transactions via a Direct Connection

For financial institutions that support direct connections, you never have to leave Quicken to download your transactions. In the Account Bar, select the account you want to update. The register for the account appears in the top half of the window, and tabs for downloaded and scheduled transactions appear in the bottom half. On the Downloaded Transactions tab, click Download Transactions, as shown in Figure 6-8. The Online Update dialog box opens.

If you use the PIN Vault to store your PINs and passwords, Quicken automatically fills in the PIN text box (with asterisks to hide your actual PIN) and turns on the checkboxes for the online services you've activated. All you have to do is

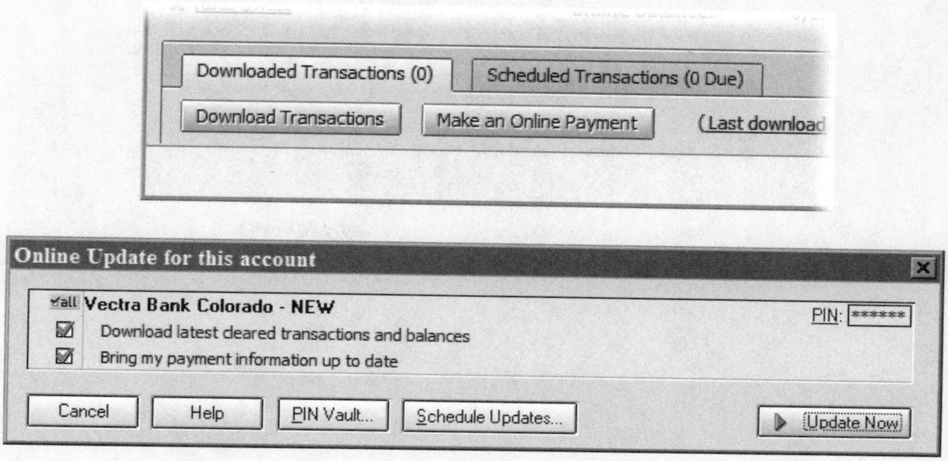

Figure 6-8. Top: Click Download Transactions to get the transactions that cleared at your bank. If you use online bill payment, you can click Make an Online Payment to pay a bill.
Bottom: In the Online Update dialog box, click Update Now to get your transactions.

click Update Now. If you don't use the PIN Vault, type your PIN or password in the PIN box.

A dialog box then displays the status of the communication between Quicken and your financial institution. When the two finish talking, your downloaded transactions appear at the bottom of the register window, as shown in Figure 6-9.

Downloading Statements with Web Connect

The register window doesn't look any different for an account that uses Web Connect. You still see a Downloaded Transactions tab, with a Download Transactions button. The big difference comes when you click that button. Quicken opens a browser window, which in turn displays the Web site for your financial institution.

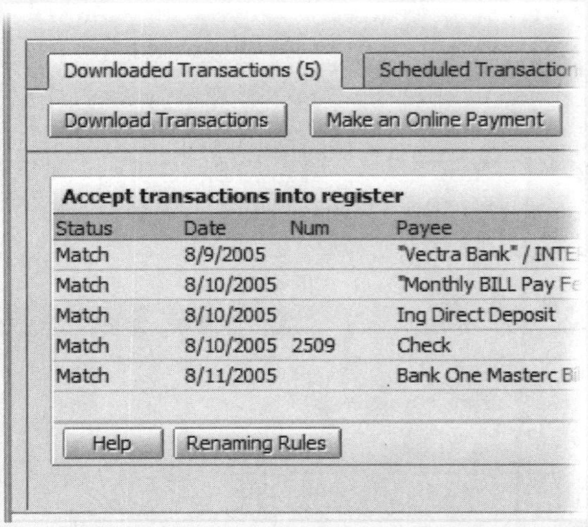

Figure 6-9. Downloaded transactions appear at the bottom of the register window. Depending on your financial institution, you can download transactions from up to 90 days ago. See "Reviewing and Incorporating Downloaded Transactions" on page 237 to learn how to accept downloaded transactions into the register.

Unfortunately, Quicken can't help you find the button or link on this page that downloads transactions. A button or link labeled "Download to Quicken" is a likely candidate, but your financial institution may use a different label or a separate Download page. If you can't find the link, call your bank's customer support for assistance.

Once you find and click the button or link, the browser downloads a file with a *.qfx* extension. The *qfx* stands for "Quicken file transfer," and it indicates a Web Connect transaction file. You may have the option to save or open the file, depending on your bank. To download your transactions, click Open. When the program finishes downloading the file, you can review and accept the downloaded transactions as you would for direct connect downloads, as described in the next section.

Reviewing and Incorporating Downloaded Transactions

If you record transactions in the account register prior to downloading them, you have only to match the downloaded transactions to the ones you entered and then correct any discrepancies. On the other hand, if you don't record transactions in the register—whether due to laziness or a trusting nature—you accept downloaded transactions to create new transactions in the register. You may have to fill in the category or other fields if QuickFill hasn't already done so.

As Figure 6-10 illustrates, the Status column tells you whether Quicken has matched a downloaded transaction to one you entered. Here's what each status value means:

▶ **Match.** Quicken's found a transaction in the register that matches the one it downloaded.

▶ **New.** The register doesn't have a transaction that matches the one Quicken downloaded. Maybe you forgot to record it, or the one you recorded differs from the one the program downloaded.

▶ **Accepted.** You've accepted the transaction either as a match to an existing transaction, or added a new one to the register.

If Quicken matches every transaction and you agree with the program's judgement, your work's almost done. In the bottom right corner of the Downloaded Transactions tab, click Accept All to accept the program's decisions. In the account register in the Clr column, you see a lowercase "c" for every accepted transaction. The "c" indicates that your financial institution has cleared the transaction but you haven't yet reconciled it. (See page 265 for more information on reconciling.) If you'd like to examine the Match and New transactions individually, see the next section.

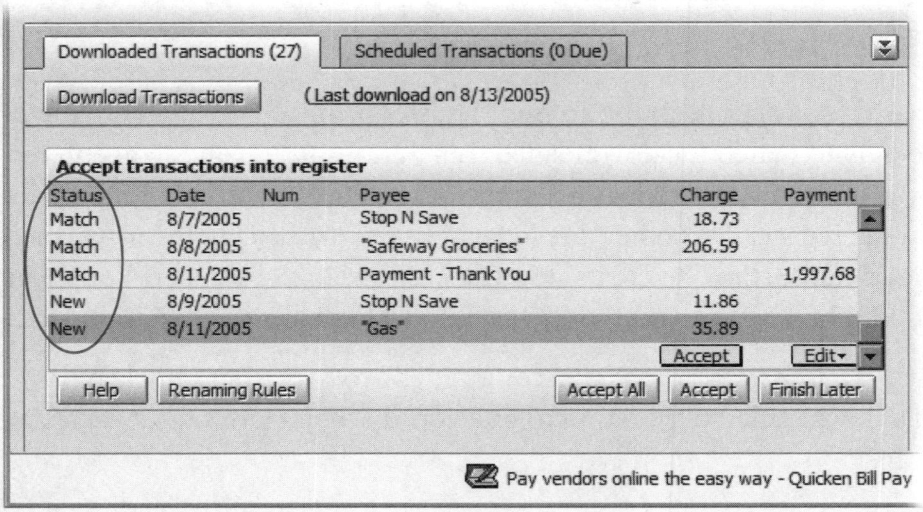

Figure 6-10. A status of Match tells you that Quicken's already matched a down-loaded transaction to one in the register. If the program can't find a matching trans-action, the status is New.

Tip: If you clicked Accept All in haste, you can revert to Quicken's original status assignments by clicking Undo Accept All. With the Match and New statuses back in place, you can accept each transaction individually.

Accepting Transactions

If you forgot to record a few transactions—or you've decided to create transactions by downloading them—Accept All is *not* a good idea. You're likely to accept bank errors (which do happen) or even fraudulent charges (which happen more often than you want to know). If you see even one downloaded transaction with a New status, review each transaction individually and find it on your paper or online statement before accepting it.

In the Downloaded transactions tab, selecting a transaction displays the Accept and Edit buttons immediately below the transaction row. If the transaction is OK, click Accept. If you wish to delete a transaction completely, click Edit, and choose Delete from the drop-down menu (see the box below for more information).

- **Accepting matched transactions.** When you click Accept for a transaction that Quicken matched to one in your register, the program adds a lowercase "c" to the Clr field in the register to indicate that your financial institution cleared the transaction.

- **Accepting new transactions.** If you select a downloaded transaction whose status is "New," Quicken automatically adds a transaction to the register with the information that it knows—the date, the amount, and in many cases the payee. If QuickFill can figure out the category, it fills in that field as well.

In the register, fill in blank fields or correct any values (for instance, replace "Check" in a downloaded transaction with the actual payee name, or change an incorrect category). When the new transaction is complete, click Enter in the register, or click Accept in the Downloaded Transactions tab.

When Quicken Doesn't Match Transactions Correctly

Sometimes Quicken makes the wrong match. For example, you have two ATM withdrawals for $100 in your register, and Quicken chooses the newer one—leaving the older one abandoned and unmatched. To correct these mismatches, select the transaction in the Downloaded Transactions tab, and then click the Edit button that appears beneath the transaction. You have two choices:

- ▶ **Unmatch.** Choose this command if you want Quicken to find another matching transaction, for example, the earlier of your two ATM withdrawals. If the program finds a match, it changes the status to Match. If the new match is correct, click Accept. If it doesn't find a match, the transaction's status changes to New.

- ▶ **Make New.** You can force Quicken to create a new transaction by choosing Make New. The program doesn't look for matching transactions. Instead, it changes the status for the downloaded transaction to New. Click Accept to create a new transaction in your register.

Matching Transactions When Quicken Can't

If you see a downloaded transaction that should match one in the register—but doesn't—chances are a small mistake in the transaction *you* recorded is the culprit. You may have assigned the wrong check number in your Quicken register or typed a 3 instead of an 8. Or you recorded several separate deposits, but your bank consolidated them into one. Whatever the reason, you can manually match a downloaded transaction to one or more transactions in the register.

If a downloaded transaction doesn't match, try scrolling in the account register to the transaction you entered. If your transaction amount doesn't agree with the bank's, adjust the register amount to match the bank's value. When you click Enter and record the updated transaction, Quicken automatically matches it to the downloaded one.

Note: Quicken doesn't match a transaction you recorded if you set its transaction date later than the date it cleared at the bank. For example, if you recorded a transaction with a date of March 6 and the bank cleared it on March 1, change the date in the register, to agree with the bank. Quicken then considers the two transactions a match.

To do your own matching, in the Downloaded Transaction tab, select the transaction, click Edit, and choose Match Manually. The Manually Match Transactions dialog box, shown in Figure 6-11, appears. Turn on the checkbox for each register transaction that you want to match to the selected downloaded transaction. Quicken adds up the amounts for each transaction that you turn on. When the total for the register transactions equals the amount of the downloaded transaction, the Difference value becomes $0.00, indicating a match.

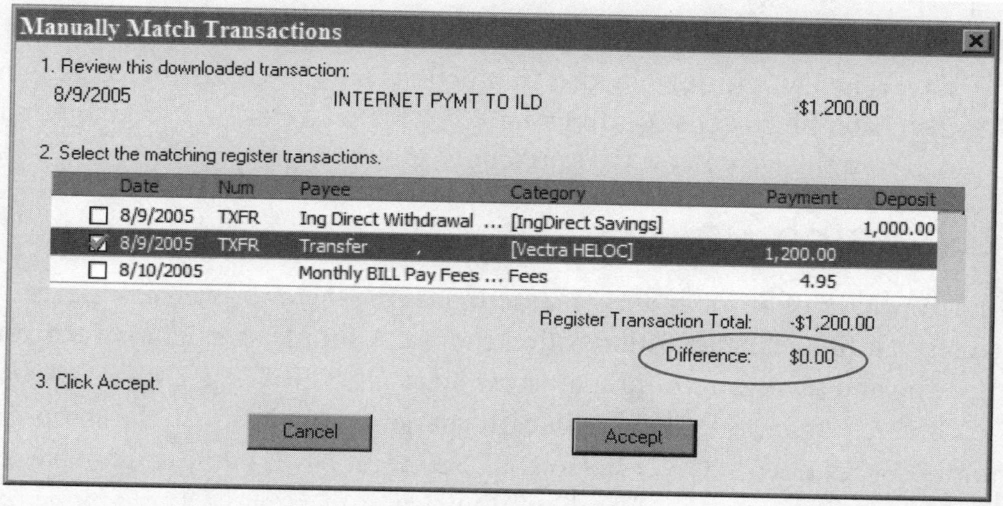

Manually Match Transactions						✕

1. Review this downloaded transaction:

8/9/2005	INTERNET PYMT TO ILD	-$1,200.00

2. Select the matching register transactions.

	Date	Num	Payee	Category	Payment	Deposit
☐	8/9/2005	TXFR	Ing Direct Withdrawal ...	[IngDirect Savings]		1,000.00
☑	8/9/2005	TXFR	Transfer	[Vectra HELOC]	1,200.00	
☐	8/10/2005		Monthly BILL Pay Fees ...	Fees	4.95	

Register Transaction Total: -$1,200.00

Difference: $0.00

3. Click Accept.

[Cancel]   [Accept]

Figure 6-11. When the value of Difference equals $0.00, you have a match between the downloaded amount and the total of the transactions that you selected. Click Accept to record the match.

Note: If you match more than one transaction to the downloaded transaction, Quicken creates Split entries for each matching transaction.

Completing the Incorporation of Downloaded Transactions

Quicken offers several options for finishing your work with downloaded transactions. Here's what each one does and when you might use it:

▶ **Accept All.** If you've reviewed all the downloaded transactions and found no problems, click Accept All. Quicken automatically sets the status for all the downloaded transactions to Accepted.

▶ **Finish Later.** Click this button if you don't have time to finish reviewing and accepting transactions, or if you found a problem that you want to resolve before you finish. Quicken saves the work you've done so far. The transactions await the next time you open the account register.

▶ **Done.** When all the downloaded transactions have a status of Accepted, the Finish Later button changes to Done. Click Done to clear the accepted transactions from the Downloaded Transactions tab.

Renaming Payees

One drawback of downloading transactions is the incomprehensible payee names that financial institutions often choose. A simple transfer between your checking and savings account may show up as "INTERNET PYMT TO TXSA 472GP952." Or a gas-station credit card charge downloads with the station's ID number—"Conoco #00092372918027." You want payee names that make sense, like "Savings Transfer" or "Gasoline." Quicken understands: its *renaming rules* feature lets you replace downloaded payee names with something short, sweet, and meaningful.

Out of the box, Quicken comes with its "Downloaded transactions" preferences set to automatically create renaming rules if you change the payee name for a downloaded transaction. Trouble is, the program doesn't always create *useful* renaming rules.

For example, the last renaming rule in Figure 6-12 is one that Quicken created automatically. If you change a downloaded payee name "LOAF N JUG #9000845453" to "Gas," the program creates a renaming rule that looks for a payee name that is equal to "LOAF N JUG #9000845453" and changes it to "Gas." But if you charge a gas purchase at a different Loaf 'N Jug station, like "LOAF N JUG #1000234901," the renaming rule doesn't catch it. And if you replace this name with "Gas," the program creates a second renaming rule for *that* gas station.

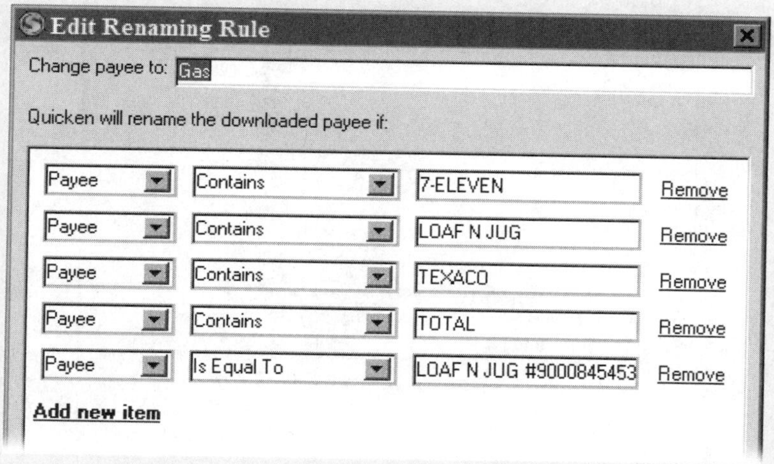

Figure 6-12. Quicken creates renaming rules that check for exact matches with payee names. Editing renaming rules to use a "Contains" or "Starts With" test makes the rules more useful.

Consider creating more flexible renaming rules that catch more of your payees then Quicken's exacting rules. As illustrated by the first four renaming rules in Figure 6-12, you can choose "Starts With" or "Contains." With the "Starts With" test, the downloaded payee must only start with "LOAF N JUG." The "Contains" test looks for the name anywhere in the payee name.

To work on your renaming rules, at the bottom of the Downloaded transactions tab, click Renaming Rules. (You can also choose Online → Renaming Rules.) In the Renaming Rules for Downloaded transactions dialog box, shown in Figure 6-13, you can create, edit, or delete rules.

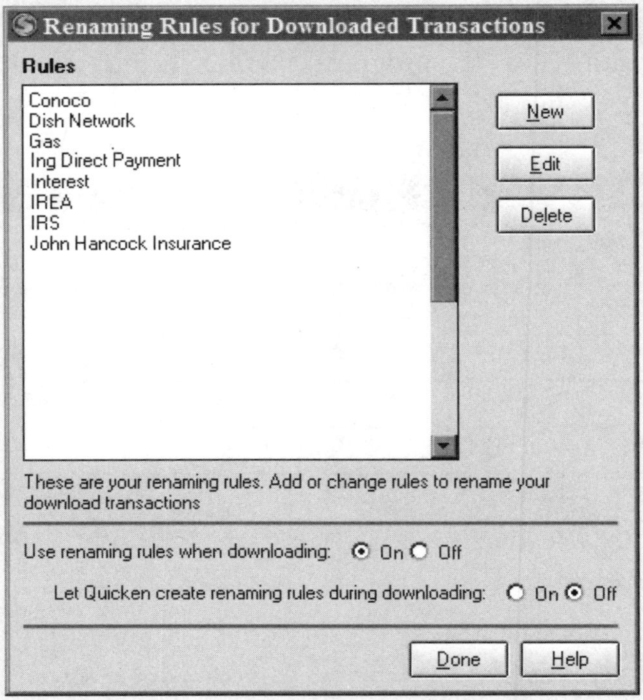

Figure 6-13. To create a renaming rule from scratch, click New. To edit an existing renaming rule, whether one that Quicken created or your own, select the rule and click Edit. To delete a rule you no longer need, for instance for your old mortgage lender, select the rule, and then click Delete.

At the bottom of the Renaming Rules for Downloaded transactions dialog box, you can turn two options on or off:

- **Use renaming rules when downloading.** If you want Quicken to use your renaming rules to replace payee names, select the On option, which almost always makes your register easier to interpret. To keep the payee names as they come from your financial institutions, select Off.

- **Let Quicken create renaming rules during downloading.** You should initially set this option to On, so that Quicken creates renaming rules showing the payee names that you've edited. After the program creates a list of rules, you can quickly run through the list, editing them to make them more effective. Once you have most of the rules you think you'll need, turn this option Off. You can reopen this dialog box any time you realize you need another renaming rule.

Setting Up Online Payees

Before your online bill payment service can send payments, you have to tell it who to pay, where to send the payments, and how the payee will know who the payment's from. In Quicken, Online Payee records include all of this information. Here are the steps to setting up an online payee:

1. **Choose Online → Online Payee List.**

   The Online Payee List window opens, shown in Figure 6-14.

2. **In the window menu bar, choose New.**

   The Set Up Online Payee dialog box opens, as shown in Figure 6-15.

3. **In the Name text box, either type the payee name as it appears on your bill or choose a payee from the drop-down menu.**

   The drop-down menu contains all of the entries in your Memorized Payee List.

4. **Fill in the Street, City, State, and Zip text boxes with the address from your bill.**

   Use the address to which you would send a paper check.

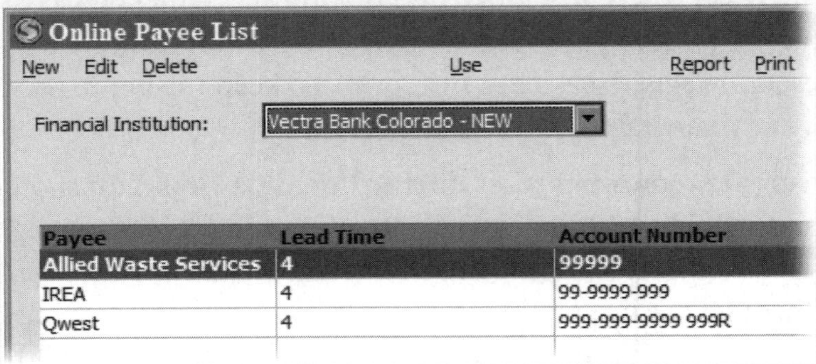

Figure 6-14. In the Online Payee List window, you can create (New), edit, or delete online payees. If you click Use in the menu bar, you can create a new payment to the selected payee.

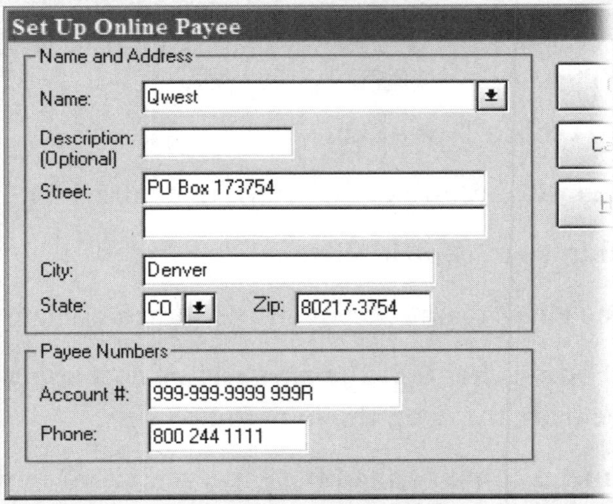

Figure 6-15. In the Name drop-down menu, you can choose a payee from the Memorized Payee List. Fill in the rest of the boxes with the payee's address, telephone number, and your account number.

5. **In the "Account #" text box, type your account number for the payee.**

   If you don't have an account number, you can type some kind of reference, like your last name.

6. **In the Phone text box, type the contact telephone number for the payee.**

   Quicken doesn't use this phone number for automatic dialing, so the number format doesn't matter, but do type the full number with area code. The number's for reference in case a problem arises with the payment.

7. **Click OK.**

   The Confirm Online Payee Information dialog box appears, showing you the values that you entered. Quicken isn't trying to be annoying. If you don't specify the correct address and account number, your payment may not make it to the payee or may be credited to the wrong account.

8. **In the Confirm Online Payee Information dialog box, carefully review the values, and then click Accept.**

   Quicken adds the payee to the list. The lead time shown for each payee is based on the number of days your financial institution sets.

Once you've added an online payee, you can automatically pay its bills, but Quicken won't automatically update the payee information. Be prepared to maintain this information as necessary, as discussed in the box on page 248.

Paying Bills Online

Whether you use the bill paying service that your financial institution offers or you subscribe to Quicken Bill Pay service, you don't have to use special dialog boxes to make electronic payments. Online features are accessible throughout the program.

Editing Online Payees

When a bill comes in, it's always a good idea to scan for changes to the address and account number. If a payee changes the address, you must edit your online payee to match, or your payments may not reach their destination. In the Online Payee List window, select the payee and click Edit in the menu bar.

Account numbers are tougher to change, since you can't change them by editing the online payee. You must delete the existing online payee and create a new one with the new account number.

Setting Up Online Bill Payments

Quicken gives you three ways to create online bill payments. As described below, you can choose one based on how you already prefer to record payments.

- **Cash Flow Center.** In the Account Bar, click Cash Flow Center to display the Cash Flow Center window. At the bottom of the window, the Bills and Scheduled Transactions section lists all the payments to send. By clicking Enter or Edit in the row for a scheduled transaction, you can record or edit that transaction.

- **Account register window.** If you usually record payments in your checking account register, there's no reason to change. In the Num field, choosing Send Online Payment turns a transaction into an online payment.

- **Write Checks.** In the Write Checks dialog box (page 110), turn on the Online Payment checkbox.

- **Online Center.** In the Online Center window (choose Online → Online Center), click the Payments tab. At the top of the Payments tab, shown in Figure 6-16, fill in the text boxes as you would any payment transaction.

Fill in the Delivery date text box with the date that you want the payee to receive the payment. Typically, you'll want to set the Delivery date a few days early, for instance to the date that you'd mail your paper check. If the due date's coming up, you can also choose ASAP to tell your financial institution to process the payment as quickly as it can.

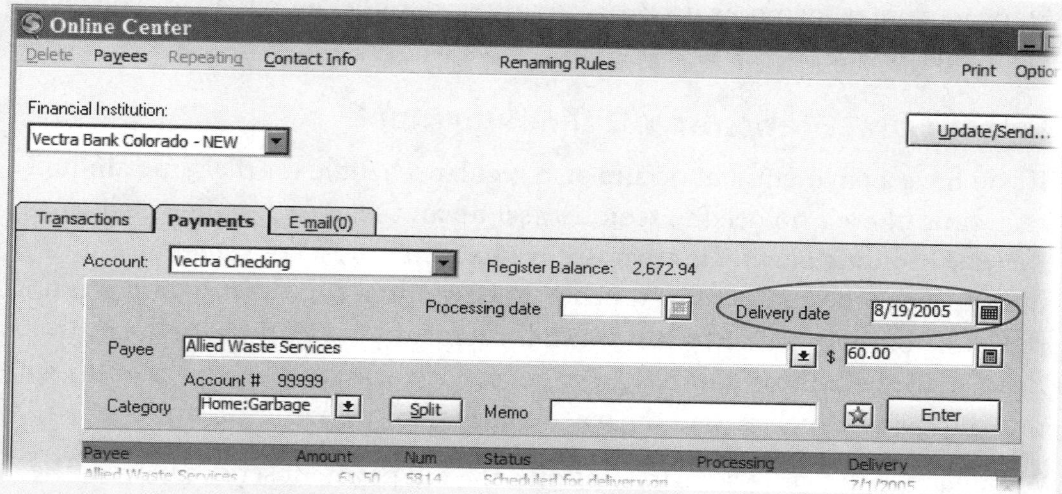

Figure 6-16. Filling in an online payment is almost exactly the same as making a regular payment. The biggest difference is the Delivery date, which should be a few days early to ensure that your payment arrives on time.

Note: You don't have to worry about filling in the Processing date field. In most cases, your bank sets that date based on the Delivery date you specify.

Sending Online Payments

Setting up all the online payments in the world won't help unless you tell Quicken to send the payment instructions to your online bill payment service. If the Online Center window isn't visible, choose Online → Online Center. Click Update/Send. The Online Update window appears, listing your payment instructions (new payments, edited payments, and even cancelled payments). Unless you use the PIN Vault, you have to type your PIN. In the Online Update window, click Update Now to transmit your instructions to your online bill payment service.

After Quicken connects to the Internet and finishes sending your payment instructions, the Online Update Summary window appears (page 233). Click Done to close the window. In the account register, the Num field for your online payments now reads Sent.

Setting Up a Repeating Online Payment

If you have a payment that occurs on a regular schedule for the same amount each time, there's no need to tediously set up and send each online payment. Repeating online payments are possibly Quicken's most convenient feature. You tell Quicken who to pay, how much, and how often, and the program sets up a repeating online payment with your bill payment service. Because the instructions reside with the online bill payment service, you could go for months without launching Quicken, and the payments would still arrive on time.

About a month before a payment is due, the bill payment service records the pending payment using the next scheduled date. The next time you download transactions, Quicken automatically downloads these payments along with your checks, deposits, and transfers. When the delivery date comes around, your payee has its payment with no effort on your part.

Repeating online payments come in two flavors and you set each one up a bit differently. For payments that occur on a regular schedule for the same amount each time, you specify the schedule and the amount for the payment. For loan payments, you set up an online repeating payment and then link it to the loan it pays off.

Setting up repeating online payments

Creating a repeating online payment is almost exactly the same as setting up a scheduled transaction, as described on page 162. You specify the payment and its schedule as usual. Once you've specified the details of the repeating online payment, click OK. Quicken adds the payment to the list of transactions on the Repeating Online tab.

Setting up a repeating online payment for an amortized loan

Making payments on amortized loans is the perfect application for Quicken repeating online payments. The payment amounts are the same each period; the payment schedule is regular; and the onerous late fees are a huge incentive to make sure that your payments arrive on time no matter what. Moreover, although you set up a repeating online payment to handle every payment in the loan's schedule, Quicken automatically calculates the amount of principal and interest you pay each time.

Here are the steps for setting up your amortized loan with a repeating online payment:

1. **Set up your lender as an online payee.**

   Setting up your lender as an online payee is just like setting up any other online payee. The full instructions start on page 245.

2. **Press Ctrl+J to open the Scheduled Transactions List window.**

   You can also choose Tools → Scheduled Transactions List.

3. **In the window menu bar, choose Create New → Scheduled Transaction.**

   Quicken opens the Create Scheduled Transaction dialog box (Figure 6-17).

4. **Set up the transaction as you would a regular repeating online payment.**

   Choose the account you use to make your payments. Choose Online Payment from Quicken for the transaction method. Choose the payee.

5. **In the Category drop-down menu, choose the liability account for your loan.**

   Your accounts appear at the bottom of the Category drop-down menu and are surrounded by square brackets. For example, your liability account may look something like [Mortgage House].

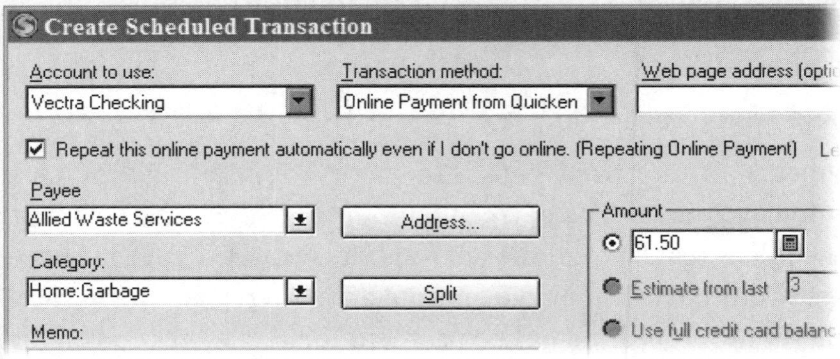

Create Scheduled Transaction

Account to use:
Vectra Checking

Transaction method:
Online Payment from Quicken

Web page address (opti...

☑ Repeat this online payment automatically even if I don't go online. (Repeating Online Payment)   Le

Payee
Allied Waste Services   Address...

Category:
Home:Garbage   Split

Memo:

Amount
⦿ 61.50
◯ Estimate from last 3
◯ Use full credit card balanc

Figure 6-17. Repeating online payments have two settings that differentiate them from scheduled transactions. In the transaction method drop-down menu, choose Online Payment from Quicken. You must turn on the "Repeat this online payment automatically" checkbox.

6. **Click OK to save the repeating online payment.**

   You can specify the amount or the schedule before you click OK, but Quicken obtains this information when you link the repeating online payment to the loan.

7. **Press Ctrl+H to open the View Loans window.**

   You can also choose Property & Debt → Loans.

8. **In the window menu bar, choose Choose Loan and, in the drop-down menu, choose the loan that you want to pay with a repeating online payment.**

   The View Loans window displays the overall information about the loan.

9. **Click Edit Payment.**

   The Edit Loan Payment dialog box appears. For a refresher on editing loans, see page 211.

10. **In the Transaction section, click Payment Method.**

The Select Payment Method dialog box opens, as shown in Figure 6-18.

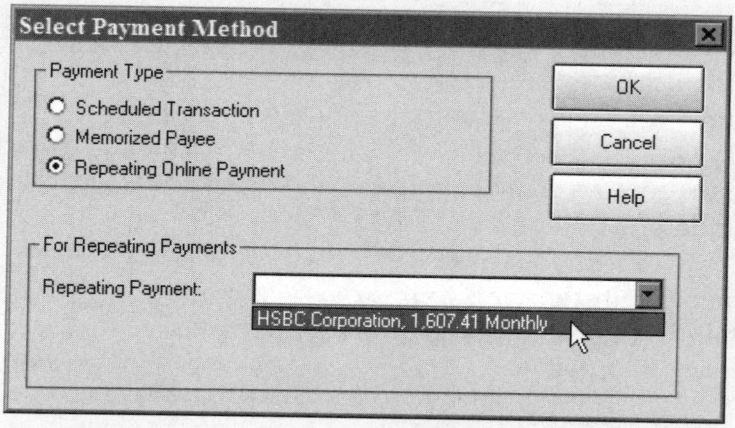

Figure 6-18. When you select the Repeating Online Payment option, Quicken displays the repeating online payments you've set up. Choose the one you created for your loan, and then click OK.

11. **In the Payment Type section, select the Repeating Online Payment option.**

Quicken immediately displays the For Repeating Payments section. If you click the Repeating Payment box, you can choose the repeating online payment you created for your loan from the drop-down menu.

12. **Click OK.**

The Select Payment Method dialog box closes. In the Edit Loan Payment dialog box, the Type field now shows "Repeating Pmt."

13. **Click OK to save the new payment.**

If you ever need to change any parts of this setup, see the box on page 254.

The repeating online payment is ready to go. In the Online Center, remember to click Update/Send to send the new instructions to your online bill payment service.

Editing a Loan's Repeating Online Payment

Repeating online payments are great for loans, but they can also cause some head scratching if you have to alter the payment in any way. For example, suppose your escrow amount changes and you want to update your repeating online payment to reflect your new total. There are several steps and you have to get them in the correct order. Here are the steps in order:

1. Cancel any pending loan payments already with your bill payment service and click Update/Send to send the cancellation instructions.

2. In the View Loans window, edit the loan to change its payment method to a scheduled transaction and set it to be a regular payment instead of an online payment.

3. In the Scheduled Transactions List, delete the repeating online payment for the loan.

4. Create a new repeating online payment for the loan.

5. Edit the loan payment to the new amount and set the Payment Method back to repeating online payment (choosing the repeating online payment you just created).

6. Don't forget to send the new instructions to your bill payment service.

Setting Up Online Transfers

You can set up online fund transfers in Quicken, as long as both accounts are at the same financial institution. Quicken can't transfer funds electronically between different banks. Also, you need to set up both Quicken accounts (checking and investment, say) for the online service.

The register is the easiest place to record an online transfer. Here are the steps:

1. **In the register for the account that holds the money you're going to transfer, create a new transaction.**

   Scroll to the first blank transaction, right-click the register, and then, in the shortcut menu, choose New.

2. **In the Num field, select Oxfr (Online Transfer).**

This option appears only if you have two accounts at the same financial institution that are both set up for online services.

3. **In the Xfer Acct drop-down menu, select the account that'll receive the money you're transferring.**

The source account is the one whose register's open.

4. **In the Payment field, enter the amount that you want to transfer between the accounts.**

If you type the amount in the Deposit field, the transfer brings the money in from the account you set in the Xfer Acct field.

5. **In the register immediately below the transaction, click Enter.**

Quicken completes the transaction in the register, but you're not done yet. Don't forget to open the Online Center (page 234) and click Update/Send to send the transfer instructions to your financial institution.

Canceling an Online Payment

Suppose you sent an online payment for your cable TV subscription, but have decided that your library card is a more cost-effective way to find entertainment. With enough lead time, you can cancel an online payment. Unlike paper checks, which require a stop payment from your bank—at an additional cost—canceling an online payment doesn't cost you a dime.

How much lead time you need depends on your bank, but in general you can cancel any time before the Processing date for the online payment. To find out whether an online payment arrived, or if you want to see if you have time to cancel a payment, click the transaction in the register. Below the Num field, you see a Status link, which you can click to view the payment, including its processing and delivery dates.

Paperwork and Online Banking

The idea of a paperless world may be appealing, but the paper trail is still your best option when something goes wrong. Every now and then, an online payment doesn't reach its destination or goes out with an incorrect amount. A journal for your online transactions can help you sort out the problem with your payee—or prove that you tried to make a payment.

Here's an effective approach that combines a paper trail with Quicken's online features: If you've been using the paper bills and statements you receive to stop drafts around your windows, start filing them (in chronological order) instead. Grab another three-ring binder or hanging folder in your filing cabinet to store paper reports of your online transactions.

If you use One Step Update (page 231) to send online transactions in Quicken, after the update completes, in the One Step Update Summary window, click Summary to view a list of all the transactions you just sent to your bank. Click Print to print a hard copy and store it in the notebook or folder.

You can shred the hard copies of your online transmissions after a year or two. Keeps bills or receipts for seven years, particularly if they're for tax-deductible items. Once they've reached their seventh birthday, shred 'em.

How you cancel a payment depends on the type of online payment. No matter which type of payment you cancel, you must click Update/Send to send the cancellation instructions to your financial institution. Here are the options:

▶ **A single online payment.** To cancel a one-time payment or one instance of a repeating online payment, in the Online Center window, select the payment and then click Cancel Payment. In the confirmation dialog box, click Yes. You'll see Cancel in the Status column.

▶ **A repeating online payment.** To cancel the entire series of a repeating online payment, press Ctrl+J to open the Scheduled Transaction List window. Select the repeating online payment you want to stop, and then, in the window menu bar, choose Delete. In the confirmation dialog box, click Yes.

Note: If the repeating online payment is linked to a loan, you must first break that link. See the box on page 254 for advice on editing loans.

CHAPTER 7:
RECONCILING ACCOUNTS

▶ **Your First Reconciliation**

▶ **Preparing for a Reconciliation**

▶ **Starting to Reconcile**

▶ **Reconciling Transactions**

▶ **Modifying Transactions During Reconciliation**

▶ **Stopping and Restarting a Reconciliation**

▶ **When Your Records Don't Agree with Your Bank's**

Admit it: Your least favorite part of having a checking account is the monthly struggle to get your handwritten register to agree with the bank's balance. No matter how careful you are to record every check, debit card withdrawal, and ATM fee, the numbers never seem to match. Tracking down the error is an exercise in frustration—did the bank make an error? Or do you have to redo your math yet *again*?

Every step of the way, Quicken takes the agony out of reconciliation. First of all, it does the math for you, error-free. If you download transactions from the Web, you may even be able to reconcile with a single click, since your register and the bank's will always agree on which checks have cleared. And if you do transpose numbers or forget to record an ATM withdrawal, Quicken has tools to help you isolate the problem.

With reconciliation being so easy, there's no excuse for *not* doing it. Never again will you bounce a check because you thought you had more funds available. Furthermore, when you reconcile regularly, you're more likely to catch transactions that you didn't make—and catch some con artist using your finances for his fun.

Your First Reconciliation

The first reconciliation for a bank account is always the hardest, because your opening account balance in Quicken rarely equals the opening balance on your bank statement. (These two balances typically match only when you open an account *after* you start using Quicken, when the balances are both zero.) Even if you started out in Quicken by copying the bank's opening balance from a statement, the first reconciliation might uncover stray transactions from earlier periods.

So the first time you reconcile your account, a small discrepancy between your Quicken balance and the bank's doesn't necessarily mean there's an error on either side. You may simply want to dispense with that discrepancy, and then things will be much clearer next month. Fortunately, Quicken can generate a transaction that adjusts your account's opening balance to match the balance on your bank statement, as described in the box on page 265.

Note: After your initial reconciliation, using this shortcut isn't such a good idea. You should investigate any discrepancy you find, since it's likely to be an error or a transaction you forgot to record.

Preparing for a Reconciliation

Part of Quicken's charm is that it doesn't care if you create, edit, or delete transactions right in the middle of reconciliation. But that's not necessarily the easiest way to go about it. If your Quicken register is up to date, you can reconcile your account in mere seconds. If you want to experience that pure, unadulterated pleasure, take a moment *before* you reconcile to make sure that you've entered all the transactions in your account:

▶ **Checks.** Check numbers missing from your check book *and* in Quicken are a big hint that you wrote a paper check and didn't record it in your Quicken data file. Create any missing check transactions.

▶ **Charges.** If you have credit card charges scattered across your desk, gather them up and make sure you've recorded them all in the Quicken credit card account.

▶ **Transfers.** Don't forget to record transfers and ATM withdrawals.

▶ **Deposits.** If you're like most people, you don't forget to deposit checks you receive. Make sure you've recorded those deposits in Quicken as well.

▶ **Online transactions.** For accounts set up to use online banking, download transactions before you reconcile your account. (This step is so useful that Quicken reminds you to do so as soon as you begin reconciliation.)

Tip: If several months have gone by since you last reconciled your account, don't try to make up time by reconciling multiple months at once. You'll just find it harder to spot discrepancies and trace problems to their source. Put your bank statements in chronological order and then walk through the reconciliation process for each statement. With Quicken, each one takes only a few minutes.

Starting to Reconcile

Reconciling an account has two simple, distinct steps. The first is to choose the account you want to reconcile and give Quicken some basic statistics about the account: the ending balance from your bank statement, and any service charges and interest earned during the statement period. This section describes how to kick off account reconciliation.

In the Account Bar, choose the account that you want to reconcile. (You can also press Ctrl+A to open the Account List window, select the account, and choose Go To in the window menu bar.) In the register menu bar, choose Reconcile.

> **Tip:** If the account is set up for online access, you may see a dialog box at this point warning you that your downloaded transactions don't appear up to date. Click Yes to cancel the reconciliation and download transactions. When your account is up to date, choose Reconcile once more.

Depending on whether the account is set up for online access, Quicken opens one of two dialog boxes, both shown in Figure 7-1.

▶ The Statement Summary dialog box (top) appears for accounts that don't use online services. You fill in the text boxes for bank charges and interest with the values from your paper statement.

▶ The Reconcile Online Account dialog box (bottom) opens for accounts set up with online access. You don't have to enter bank charges and interest, because you download those with your other transactions. You can download transactions but still choose to reconcile to your paper statement.

Think twice before you choose the Online Balance option, though. If you turn it on, Quicken reconciles your account to your bank's records every time you download transactions. If you later want to reconcile against a paper statement, you're in for some manual tweaking of transaction reconcile status—a feat that's best left to Quicken experts. (Online balances and paper statement balances rarely match, because your online balance shows the up-to-the-minute status of cleared checks, whereas a paper statement is a snapshot taken at the statement date.)

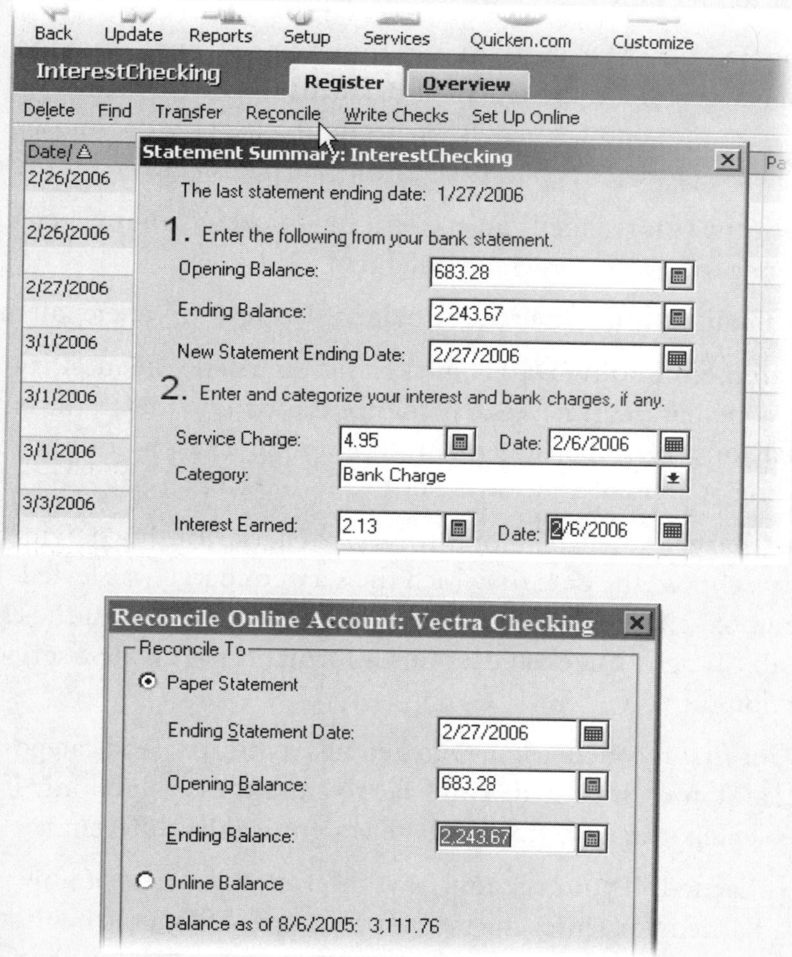

Figure 7-1. Top: Accounts without online access ask for service charges and interest. Bottom: You can reconcile accounts set up to use online access to your paper statement or to the online balance every time you download transactions.

Here's how to fill in the text boxes for reconciliation summary information:

- **Opening Balance.** The program uses the ending balance from the previous reconciliation to fill in the Opening Balance for this reconciliation. If the Opening Balance doesn't match the beginning balance on your bank statement, click Cancel, and go to page 271 to learn how to correct the problem.

  The first time you reconcile an account in Quicken, you must enter the Opening Balance from your previous statement.

- **Ending Balance.** Enter the ending balance from your paper statement.

- **New Statement Ending Date.** Quicken fills in a date one month after the previous reconciliation. If necessary, change this date to match the ending statement date on your paper statement. (For online access accounts, you'll just see the Ending Statement Date, as described in the box on page 265.)

- **Service Charge.** Enter the monthly service charge for this statement. In the Date box, choose the date on which the service charge was levied. In the Account box, choose the account to which you want to post the charge (usually Bank Charge). Quicken uses this information to create a service charge transaction for you.

  After your first reconciliation, Quicken fills in the date and category for service charges and interest earned. You have to enter these values only if you've changed categories or Quicken's date is significantly different.

- **Interest Earned.** If your account pays interest, regardless of how petty, in the Interest Earned box, enter the interest you earned from the bank statement. As you did for service charges, specify the date and the account that you use to track interest you earn.

 Note: If you use online banking, chances are you've already downloaded your service charge and interest transactions. That's why the Reconcile Online Account dialog box doesn't include text boxes for these items.

After you've entered this information, click OK to proceed to the second part of reconciliation, described in the next section.

Automatic Online Reconciliation

No, Quicken doesn't automatically email apologies when you've had a fight with your girlfriend. But the Online Balance option in the Reconcile Online Account dialog box does something almost as useful. When you choose this option, you don't have to fill in the Opening Balance, Ending Balance, or Ending Statement Date boxes. Quicken takes the Opening Balance from the last reconciliation, and it goes online to obtain the current balance as of the most recent banking day.

Turn on the "Auto reconcile after compare to register" checkbox while you're at it. With this addition, you don't have to tell Quicken to reconcile your account. Every time you download transactions, it opens the Statement Summary window for comparing your transactions (see page 262), checks off the cleared transactions, and shows any discrepancies. Whether you write checks by hand, use online bill payment, or have payees pull money from your account, most of the time all you do is click OK, and Quicken reconciles your account up through your most recent downloaded transactions. To learn more about making adjustments to downloaded transactions before reconciling them, see "Reconciling Transactions" below.

Reconciling Transactions

When you click OK in either the Statement Summary or Reconcile Online Accounts dialog boxes, Quicken opens a grand version of the Statement Summary window listing the money that flows out of your account in the Payments and Checks column and money flowing in under the Deposits column. As Figure 7-2 illustrates, your assignment is to mark every transaction that your bank has cleared and, when the Difference value is zero, click Finished to complete the reconciliation.

If you download transactions from your financial institution and match them to the transactions in Quicken, there's not much for you to do besides click Finished. The bank isn't likely to disagree with itself, and you've already cleared

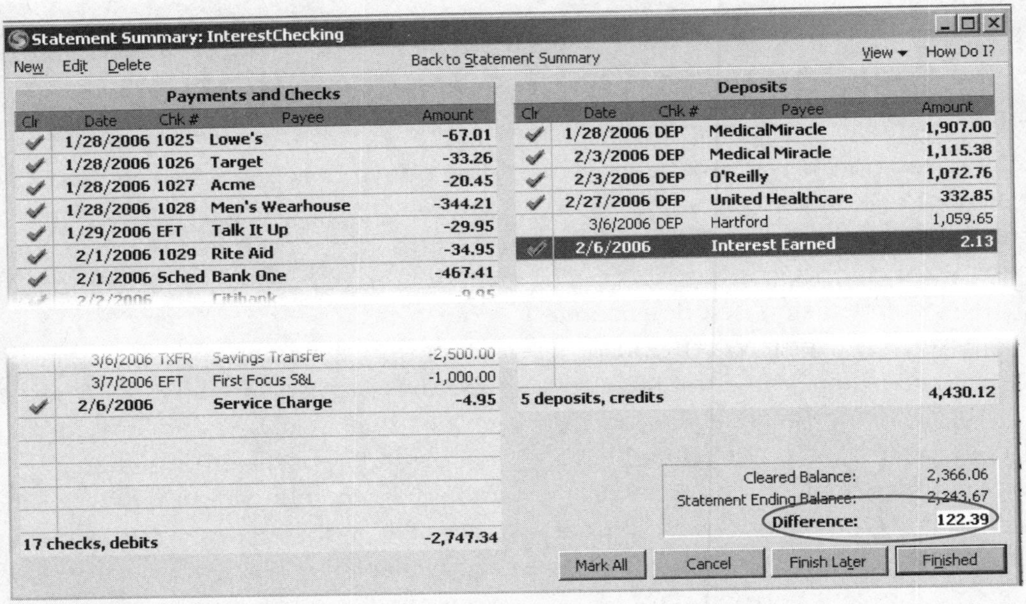

Figure 7-2. Top: To reconcile an account, you mark transactions as cleared in the top half of the Statement Summary dialog box.
Bottom: Quicken calculates how much you've cleared in payments and deposits, which it shows as Cleared Balance in the bottom right corner of the dialog box. The Statement Ending Balance is the amount your bank shows on the statement. Difference is the difference between your cleared balance and the statement ending balance. When Diff equals zero, Quicken and your bank agree. Click Finished and bask in the glory of a perfect reconciliation.

most transactions during your downloads. But if you record transactions in Quicken yourself, you *must* mark the cleared transactions in Quicken to reconcile them to the paper statement.

The Statement Summary window groups payments and charges on the left side with deposits and other credits on the right side. Match each transaction on your statement to a transaction recorded in Quicken, and then add a checkmark in the Clr column to let Quicken know it's cleared. Check it off on the paper statement, too, so you'll know you've done it. If you get to the end and the Difference hasn't yet reached zero, an unchecked transaction in either place is often the culprit. (If you *can't* track down the problem and are desperate to stop searching for that unaccounted-for $1.50, see the box on page 268.)

Clicking in the Clr column toggles the checkmarks on and off. If you download transactions from your bank, Quicken automatically marks them as cleared, so you usually don't have to turn on any transaction checkmarks when you reconcile. What you might have to do, especially if you record transactions manually in the register, is turn *off* the checkmarks for transactions that you recorded in the wrong account, as duplicates, or mismatches. After you turn off a checkmark, in the window menu bar, choose Delete to remove the transaction from the register.

When you click Finished, Quicken displays the Reconciliation Complete dialog box with a hearty congratulation to make you feel good about your accomplishment. The dialog box asks if you want to create a reconciliation report. If you use Quicken only for personal finances and generally breeze through reconciling without problems, click No, the most popular choice by far. On the other hand, for a record of the results of the account reconciliation, whether for the paper trail that accountants and bookkeepers need or to resolve potential problems in the future, click Yes.

 Note: If you reconcile a credit card account, Quicken pops up a Make Credit Card Payment dialog box so you can make a payment on your credit card balance. Better yet, pay it off and eliminate those interest charges and fees.

Even if you reconcile your statements month after month without a hitch, that doesn't necessarily mean your accounts are error-free. For example, you may notice that there are a few transactions from four months ago languishing uncleared. When you review these transactions, you'll probably find a charge you made on a different credit card, a duplicate that you forgot to delete, or some other minor problem. Every so often, the answer is that the check didn't make it to the vendor or your deposit never made it to the bank, so it's worthwhile to occasionally research these old and uncleared transactions.

Adjusting an Account That Won't Reconcile

The first time you reconcile an existing account in Quicken, chances are good that the bank statement and the Quicken account won't match. Moreover, when the Difference value in the Statement Summary window refuses to change to 0.00, reconciling without finding the problem *is* an option. (Before you give up, though, see page 269.)

But if your reconciliation is truly at a standoff, and you see no point in continuing the fight, you can have Quicken add an adjustment to "make" your statement and Quicken records see eye to eye. Simply click Finished in the Statement Summary window. If there was a Difference value other than zero, Quicken automatically opens the Adjust Balance dialog box, shown here. This box tells you what you already know: There's an unresolved difference between the total for the items you cleared in Quicken and the total on your bank statement. If you decide to

give the problem one last look, click Cancel to return to reconciling.

To create an adjustment transaction, fill in the Adjustment Date text box. For example, type the ending date for the statement you're trying to reconcile. Then click Adjust. The program creates an uncategorized transaction to make up the difference.

If you stumble across the source of the discrepancy later, you can edit the transaction. Although the balance adjustment transaction is marked as reconciled, you can change the payee name and the category.

The total of the items you have marked is $1.59 less than the total of the items shown on your bank statement.

You may have Quicken enter a balance adjustment in your register for this amount, or click Cancel to go back to reconciling.

Adjustment Date: 1/27/2006

Adjust   Cancel   Help

Modifying Transactions During Reconciliation

Even if your Quicken register is rife with errors and omissions, getting through reconciliation is surprisingly painless. Quicken immediately updates the

Statement Summary window with changes you make in the account register window, so you can jump to the register window and make your changes. When you return to the Statement Summary window, the changes are there—ready to be marked as cleared.

Here's how you make changes while reconciling:

- **Adding transactions.** If a transaction appears on your bank statement but isn't in Quicken, in the Statement Summary menu bar, choose New. The program jumps to a blank transaction in the account's register window.

> **Tip:** In the Statement Summary window, double-clicking any transaction takes you to that transaction in the register. But once you're in the register, you can record as many forgotten transactions as you want. To get back to the Statement Summary window, underneath the active transaction, click the Return to Reconcile button.

- **Deleting transactions.** If you find a duplicate transaction, select it. In the Statement Summary menu bar, choose Delete. You have to click Yes to confirm your decision before the program deletes the transaction.

- **Editing transactions.** If you notice an error in a transaction, select it and choose Edit in the Statement Summary menu bar. Quicken jumps to the transaction in the account register. Correct the mistake, record the transaction by clicking Enter, and then click Return to Reconcile.

When you work in the register window during reconciliation, you'll see an extra button—Return to Reconcile, as illustrated in Figure 7-3. After you add, edit, and delete the transactions, you can click Return to Reconcile to jump back to the Statement Summary window or, at the bottom of the Quicken main window, click Reconcile.

Stopping and Restarting a Reconciliation

The Statement Summary window includes a Finish Later button for saving your reconciliation work without completing it. But the only time you're likely to click

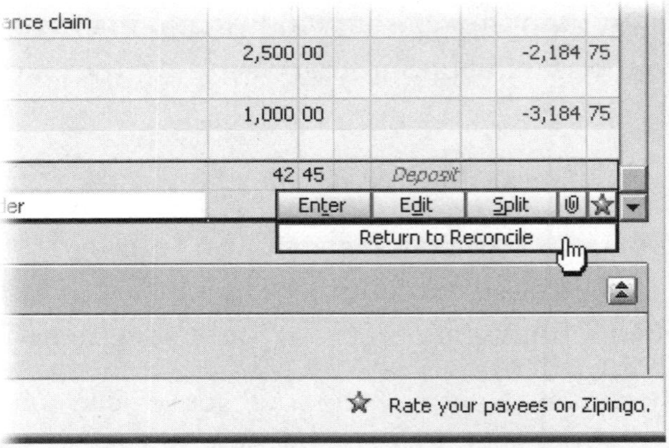

Figure 7-3. You can make changes and corrections to transactions in the register during the reconciliation process. When you're ready, click "Return to Reconcile" (indicated here by the pointing hand).

this button is when you've run into a discrepancy that requires some research. For instance, you're relaxing on Sunday by reconciling your checking account, and notice a questionable bank charge. You can click Finish Later and return to your reconciliation after you've talked to your bank on Monday morning.

In the Statement Summary window, click Finish Later. Quicken closes the window, but it remembers what you've cleared. You'll see a lower-case "c" in the Clr column for each transaction that you've marked, which indicates that the transaction is only tentatively cleared.

When you're armed with fresh information and a strong dose of caffeine, choose Reconcile in the register menu bar. The Statement Summary or Reconcile Online Account dialog box opens, containing the summary values you typed in on your first attempt. If they're still correct, click OK to open the Statement Summary window for another try.

When Your Records Don't Agree with Your Bank's

When you attempt to modify a transaction that you've already reconciled, Quicken would do well to set off flashing lights and sirens warning you of the havoc you're about to wreak. After all, the transaction appeared on your bank statement because it was a done deal, and changing it in Quicken doesn't change it in the real world. Nevertheless, Quicken instead lets you change or delete reconciled transactions with nothing more than a mild message box asking if you're sure you know what you're doing.

But make no mistake: Making changes to reconciled transactions is the quickest way to create mayhem in your accounts. For example, in the register window, deleting a reconciled transaction removes its amount from the Opening Balance when you try to reconcile the account. And *that* means that the Opening Balance won't match the beginning balance on your paper bank statement (which is one reason you might be reading this section).

WORD TO THE WISE

When Your Bank Makes a Mistake

Banks do make mistakes. Digits get transposed, or amounts are flat wrong. When this happens, you can't ignore the difference. In Quicken, you can add an adjustment transaction—as described in the box on page 268—to make up the difference, but be sure to tell your bank about the mistake. It's always a good idea to be polite,

though, in case *you* turn out to be the one at fault.

When you receive your *next* statement, check that the bank made an adjustment to correct its mistake. Delete the adjustment transaction you created and reconcile as you normally would.

Sometimes, subtle errors, missing transactions, or an errant click of an uncleared check can foul your attempts to reconcile an account. Here are some techniques to help bring your records back into balance:

▶ **Look for transactions cleared or uncleared by mistake.** Go through your bank statement again, checking off each transaction you've marked in Quicken. Make sure that every transaction on the bank statement is marked in the Statement Summary window. If you check off each transaction on your paper statement when you mark it in Quicken, simply look for the telltale missing checkmark on your paper statement. Check that no additional transactions are marked. If you want to start over, unmark all of the transactions and begin checking them one by one.

> **Tip:** If the Difference value in the Statement Summary window is positive, you think you have more money than the bank says you do. Chances are you've missed a check you wrote or an ATM withdrawal. If the Difference value is negative, you may have forgotten to record a deposit.

▶ **Look for duplicate transactions.** If you both create transactions in Quicken and download transactions, duplicate transactions are often to blame. Scan the register for multiple transactions with the same date, payee, and amount.

Here's a trick for ferreting out duplicate transactions: Count the number of transactions on your bank statement, and then compare that number to the number of cleared transactions displayed at the bottom of the Statement Summary window (illustrated in Figure 7-2, back on page 266). Unfortunately, this transaction count won't help if you enter transactions in Quicken differently than they appear on your bank statement. For example, if you deposit every payment individually, but your bank shows one deposit for every business day, your transaction counts won't match.

▶ **Look for a transaction equal to the amount of the difference.** This approach helps you find a single transaction that you marked or unmarked by mistake, or a duplicate transaction that you marked as cleared.

▶ **Look for a transaction equal to half the difference.** This technique helps you find transactions that you recorded the wrong way around. For example, if a $500 check becomes a $500 deposit by mistake, your reconciliation will be off by $1,000 ($500 because a check is missing and another $500 because you have an extra deposit).

▶ **Check transactions for transposed numbers.** It's easy to type $95.40 when you meant $94.50. Before you examine every transaction amount for these hard-to-spot errors, divide the Difference value by 9. If the result is a whole number of dollars or cents, such as 5 dollars or 10 cents, chances are you've transposed numbers. For example, say you have a difference of .90, or 90 cents. Dividing by 9 results in .1—that is, 10 cents. If the result is something like 1.52 or .523 (52.3 cents), transposed numbers are not to blame. That this works is one of those facts you must simply accept, like the fact that you can't lick your elbow.

CHAPTER 8: BUDGETING

▶ **Ways to Build Budgets**

▶ **Creating a Budget Automatically**

▶ **Copying the Current Budget**

▶ **Creating a Budget Manually**

▶ **Filling In Budget Values**

▶ **Making a Budget Current**

▶ **Choosing Budget Categories**

▶ **Saving or Restoring a Budget**

▶ **Comparing Your Performance to Your Budget**

If the word "budget" sounds like an unpleasant shackling of your spending creativity, here are four words of advice: *Don't skip this chapter*. A *budget* is nothing more than a plan for spending, saving, and investing the money you make. Whether you do it in Quicken, in another program, or on a piece of paper, a budget gives you a sense of freedom that only comes from having a plan for making ends meet. The only requirement is that your budget works—*for you*. If you can find a way to spend $5,000 a year on shoes and *still* save for retirement, your budget's probably working.

Quicken's budgeting features help you estimate how much money you'll make, and then subtract your estimated expenses. If you're a compulsive shopper, your first crack at a budget may reveal that your expenses outweigh your income. Armed with that knowledge, you can adjust your budget to scale back spending—or take on a second job to help pay for your purchases. On the other hand, if you've been pinching pennies and have money left over each month, a budget helps you come up with a plan for the surplus—like transferring some into savings or investment accounts.

You can create budgets for special purposes, like estimating your annual retirement expenses so you calculate how much you must amass for the swinging retirement lifestyle you envision. Or you can create a budget of mandatory expenses to see how much you need to keep in emergency funds. This chapter explains how to create budgets in Quicken and how to use them to better manage your money.

Ways to Build Budgets

If you're new to Quicken, you won't have any existing financial data to use as a basis for a budget, so you must build a budget from scratch with your best guesses of spending in each category. But with several months of transactions in your data file, you have a record of your actual spending and income, which Quicken can use to build a budget. Moreover, when a budget becomes something you can't live without, you can copy existing budgets to create new ones.

When you choose Planning → Budget and then, in the Budget window, click the Setup tab, you'll see three budget-building methods. Here's what each one does:

▶ **Automatic.** If you have at least several months' worth of data in Quicken, the fastest way to build a budget is using your actual income and expenses. Once Quicken builds a budget from existing transactions, editing the values you want to change is a breeze. The program bases a new budget on the values from the previous calendar year, but you can change the dates that Quicken uses to those for the period that best reflects your income and spending. See "Creating a Budget Automatically" below.

▶ **Manual.** Although this is the most tedious method, it's your only option when you don't have existing data to use. Although you do have to type in all the numbers, you only have to use this approach for your first budget. See "Creating a Budget Manually" on page 283.

▶ **Copy current.** If you've already created a budget in Quicken, you can use it as the basis for next year's budget. Although many of your numbers may change, copying a budget is still faster than starting from scratch. See "Copying the Current Budget" on page 282.

Creating a Budget Automatically

If you have several months of transactions in Quicken, the program can generate a budget based on your actual spending. The closer you are to having twelve months of actual transactions, the more accurately this automatic budget will reflect what you actually make and spend. (Unfortunately, what you earn and spend doesn't necessarily generate a *good* budget, particularly if you can't resist that 75%-off sale on lawn furniture—and you live on the 20th floor.)

So plan to edit the budget Quicken generates. For example, you can rein in your spending in categories you can do without (or do with less in), increase budgeted amounts for categories you expect to go up, or earmark leftover cash for transfer into savings.

What Quicken Budgeting Can and Can't Do

Some folks loathe the idea of tracking their expenditures and cutting off spending if it exceeds their targets. But others go in the other direction and want to control their spending with an iron hand, divvying up their paychecks into buckets of money for different purposes.

Budgeting in Quicken is more laissez-faire than that, but it can still be an effective tool for controlling where your money goes. The idea is to estimate how much you'll earn and spend in different categories—from your salary and earned interest to groceries, utilities, and music. *You* decide how detailed you want to be and how short the periods you estimate will be. Most people work with budgets by month, because they can check their progress more frequently and spot spending problems earlier.

Budgeting, and subsequently measuring your actual spending against your budget, is an exercise in compromise. Your estimated amounts rarely match what you actually spend. Unless the electric utility puts you on a monthly program, your electric bill goes up and down each month; sometimes it's a little more than your budget and sometimes less. These small perturbations are nothing to worry about.

What you're looking for is trends in over- or under-spending. For example, if you budget $50 a month for dining out but find that you're spending $100 or more each month, you must reevaluate your budget. Can you afford twice your allotment for dining out? Or do you want to cut back so you can save more for retirement?

Here are the steps for creating a budget automatically:

1. **Choose Planning → Budget.**

   The Budget window opens to the Summary tab, which either contains all zeroes, if you have no existing budgets, or displays the summary of your current budget.

2. Click the Setup tab.

The Setup tab includes three options for creating a budget and automatically sets the Automatic option, as shown in Figure 8-1.

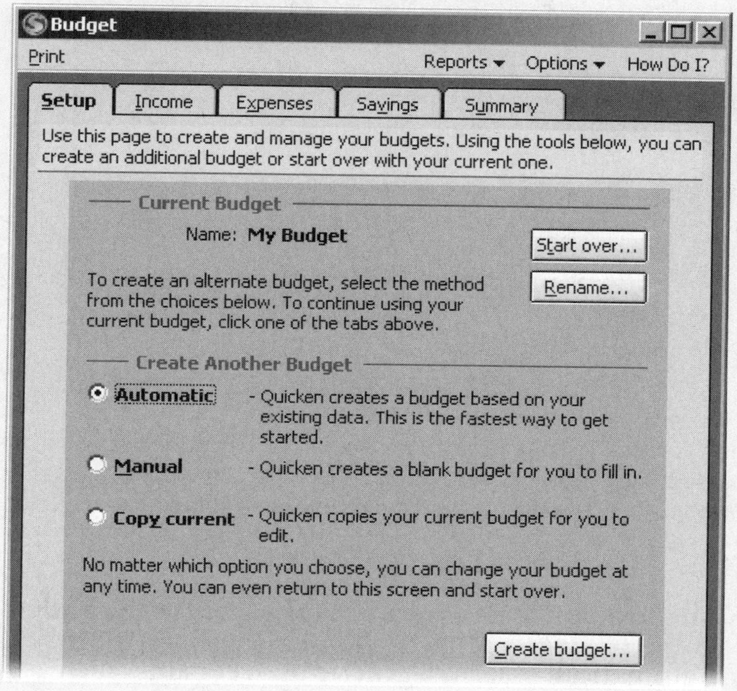

Figure 8-1. You can create a budget from existing data (Automatic), from scratch (Manual), or by copying an existing budget (Copy current). Quicken automatically selects the Automatic option, so you can click "Create budget" without further ado if you have existing transactions.

3. Click "Create budget".

The Create Budget: Automatic dialog box appears with more options for massaging your existing data into a budget, as illustrated in Figure 8-2.

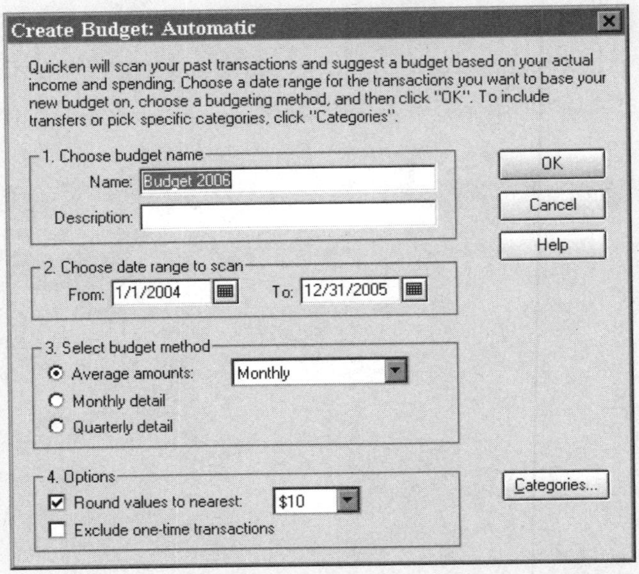

Figure 8-2. The Create Budget: Automatic dialog box includes several options for improving the accuracy of your first pass at a budget. But you should always fine-tune an automatically generated budget to match what you'd like to do in the future.

4. **In the Name text box, type a meaningful name for the budget.**

   Quicken automatically fills in a generic budget name, such as *Budget 2*. For your own benefit, change the name to indicate the purpose of the budget. For example, you can name a budget by calendar year—*Budget 2006*. For a budget with a special purpose, change the name to, say, *Retirement Budget* or *Unemployment Budget*.

5. **In the "Choose date range to scan" section, in the From and To text boxes, type the earliest and latest dates for transactions to include.**

   Ideally, you should choose the most recent twelve months to obtain an accurate picture of annual income and expenditures. If you have less than 12 months of data, fill in the From box with the date of your first transactions in Quicken and fill in the To box with today's date.

6. **In the "Select budget method" section, choose an option to tell Quicken how you want to turn your actual data into budgeted amounts.**

Quicken automatically selects the "Average amounts" option and sets the frequency to Monthly. Using average amounts is the easiest approach and works well for all but the most fastidious budgeters. With this option, the program calculates monthly averages in each category by dividing the total you spent during the date range by the number of months in the range.

Tip: You can use the Average amounts option to generate your budget. When you edit the budget, you can switch individual categories, like Tax Refund or Gas & Electric, to monthly detail to show income and expense that occurs irregularly or changes by season.

Choose the "Monthly detail" option to use your actual monthly values as your budgeted monthly values. For most categories, monthly detail is overkill, but it's a great way to catch all those infrequent expenses, like auto registration, tax refunds, or septic pumping. One way to compromise is to choose "Quarterly detail," which uses the actual quarterly totals as your budgeted quarterly totals.

7. **If you want to round numbers, in the "Round values to nearest" text box, choose the number of dollars to use for rounding.**

Because budgeting is an inexact science, consider choosing $10 for rounding your budget amounts. Quicken will round the value for a category to the nearest $10. If your money is really tight, you can keep the rounding value at $1. On the other hand, the CEO of Intuit might set rounding to $100.

8. **To remove one-time transactions from Quicken's calculation, turn on the "Exclude one-time transactions" checkbox.**

Suppose you received a whopping refund from the IRS in April and bought a motorcycle in May to celebrate *and* spend that windfall. With the "Exclude one-time transactions" checkbox turned off (as Quicken sets it initially), your generated budget will show a large chunk of income in April for your tax refund as well as a large expenditure in an expense category in May.

There are plenty of one-time transactions you may want to include, like annual premiums for property insurance or auto insurance. You're better off leaving the one-time transactions in and removing the ones you don't want when you fine-tune the budget.

 Tip: Quicken automatically selects all of the categories for your budget. If you want to choose specific categories for budgeting, click the Categories button and turn category checkboxes on or off.

9. **Click OK.**

   Quicken displays a message box telling you that it created your new budget, and in the Budget window displays the Income tab. In the message box, click OK. Skip to "Filling In Budget Values" on page 285 to learn how to edit the values in your new budget.

Copying the Current Budget

If next year's budget is almost identical to this year's, copying your current budget and changing a few numbers is the fastest and easiest approach. For that matter, once you have one budget in Quicken, it's almost always easier to copy the current budget.

Here's how you copy the current budget:

1. **Choose Planning → Budgets and in the Budget window, click the Setup tab.**

   Immediately below the Current Budget heading, you'll see the name of the current budget, with other existing budgets listed under Other Budgets.

2. **Make sure the budget you want to copy is the Current Budget.**

   If it isn't, then in the Other Budgets list, select the budget you want to work with and click Open. Click the Setup tab once more.

3. **In the Create Another Budget section, select the "Copy current" option and click "Create budget."**

   The Budget Name dialog box appears so you can give your budget a new name and description.

4. **In the Name text box, type a name for the budget that indicates what you plan to use it for.**

   Quicken's names won't help you pick the right budget. Instead of *Budget 2, Budget 3,* and *Budget 4,* replace Quicken's names with more meaningful ones, like *Budget 2007* or *Budget for a Kept Man.*

    Note: To provide a longer description of the budget, fill in the Description box. For example, you could type a description like "Includes only mandatory categories."

5. **Click OK.**

   The program displays a message box telling you that it successfully created the budget and, in the Budget window, displays the Income tab with the values for the new budget.

Click OK to close the dialog box. You're ready to begin adjusting any of the budget values, as described in "Filling In Budget Values" on page 285.

Creating a Budget Manually

Creating a budget from scratch is far more work than either building one from your data or copying one you've already created. If you don't have existing data or an existing budget, you have to start from scratch. You must add the categories you want to budget, as well as your estimated values for each category. On the bright side, this process forces you to think about how much you expect to spend in each category and where you can show more restraint. Quicken does its best to make the process of manual budget creation as painless as possible.

As you would with any other method for creating a budget, choose Planning →
Budget and, in the Budget window, click the Setup tab. On the Setup tab, select the
Manual option and click "Create budget." The Budget Name dialog box appears.
In the Name and Description text boxes, type a meaningful name and, if you wish,
a more detailed description of the budget. Click OK.

A manual budget in Quicken is truly blank—it doesn't even have categories. A
message box appears that tells you to click the "Choose categories" button, as
demonstrated in Figure 8-3, to select the categories and accounts for which you
want to budget. In this message box, click OK, and you're ready to turn your
blank budgeting slate into a work of art.

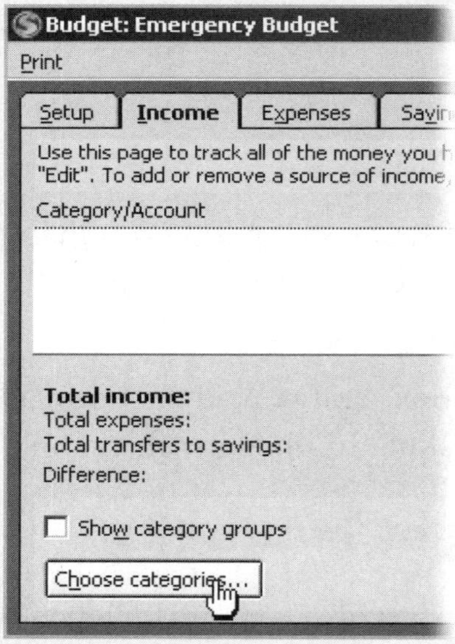

Figure 8-3. When you first create a budget from scratch, it doesn't have any categories. On the Income and Expenses tabs, click "Choose categories" to add categories
to your budget.

In the Choose Categories dialog box, you can select as few or as many categories
as you want. For example, if you're only dipping your baby toe into budgeting,

you can begin by clicking a few individual categories to turn them on. If you're ready to dive in head first, you can click "Mark all" to budget every category. (See page 293 for more detail about selecting categories for your budget.)

With categories in place, you're finally ready to add some budget numbers, which is described in the next section.

(See page 293 for more detail about selecting categories for your budget.)

UP TO SPEED

How the Budget Balances

As budgeting aficionados know, regardless of the numbers in a budget, you'll spend more than the average in some months and, in other months, you'll spend less. If your salary is constant, you'll have money to spare sometimes and resort to raiding the piggy bank the rest of the time.

The key to success, whether you make a budget or not, is to not spend that extra cash on frivolities. Otherwise, you may not have enough to pay the phone bill when expenses peak. Suppose you pay $1200 twice a year for auto insurance. If you don't sock away $200 a month, chances are you won't have the $1200 for the premium when it's due. As you'll learn in this section, you can add budget values to occur in specific months to handle these infrequent but painfully large payments. And you can budget transfers to savings to stockpile the money you need to make those payments.

Filling In Budget Values

Filling in budget numbers in Quicken works the same way, regardless of whether your budget is as blank as your teenager's stare, or full of numbers that happen to be all wrong. Quicken offers several ways to add and adjust numbers, all of which are described in this section.

Before you get started, make sure that the budget you want to edit is current. The name of the budget that you want to edit should appear in the title of the budget window, as shown in Figure 8-4. (To learn how to change the current budget, see page 292.)

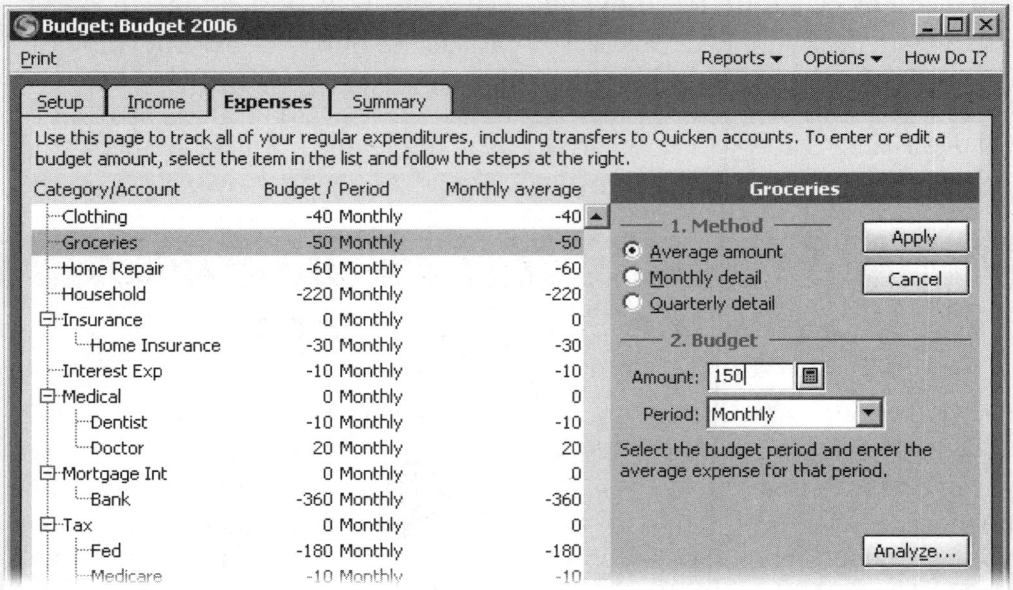

Figure 8-4. The pane on the right side of the Budget window includes options and text boxes for setting the budget values for a category—Groceries, in this case.

In the budget window, you can (and should) change how Quicken displays your categories to get the best overview of your situation. For example, if you want to see all income, expense, and transfer categories on one tab, choose Options → Combined View. To see income categories separate from expenses and transfers, choose Options → Separate View. If you live from paycheck to paycheck, you can choose Options → Income/Expense View to hide the Savings tab altogether.

Average Budget Values

For most categories, average values are the fastest and easiest approach—and they are quite effective for most categories. For example, say your electric bill comes in at $63 this month, $72 the next, and goes over $100 when the outside temperature hits three digits. But overall, the monthly average is about $80. Instead of trying to anticipate the actual monthly figures, you're better off setting the monthly budget value to $80 and let things average themselves out over the course of a year.

Here are the steps for using an average value for a budget category:

1. **In the Category/Account column, click the category you want to edit.**

   When you select a category, on the right side of the Budget window you'll see a pane for setting the budget values for that category, as illustrated in Figure 8-4. Quicken automatically selects the "Average amount" option unless you've previously chosen a different option for the category.

2. **In the Method section, select the "Average amount" option (if it isn't already selected).**

   Depending on the Method option you choose, you'll see different text boxes underneath the Budget heading.

3. **In the Budget section, in the Amount text box, type the average value you want to use. In the Period text box, choose the period to which the average amount applies.**

   Between the amount and a time period, you can create any type of average you want. For a category like Groceries, it's easy enough to type in the amount you spend each month and choose Monthly in the Period drop-down menu.

   But Quicken offers lots of choices for period: daily, weekly, every two weeks, twice a month, monthly, every two months, quarterly, twice a year, and yearly. Regardless of the period you choose, the program calculates the monthly average when you click Apply. For example, if your garbage pickup costs $60 every quarter, you can type an amount of $60 and choose Quarterly. Quicken tells you the monthly average is $20.

   If you don't know what a realistic average might be and have tracked your finances in Quicken for at least a few months, in the bottom right corner of the window, the Analysis section can help. It shows your actual totals for the previous year, month by month, but also calculates an average value using the period you've chosen, as demonstrated in Figure 8-5.

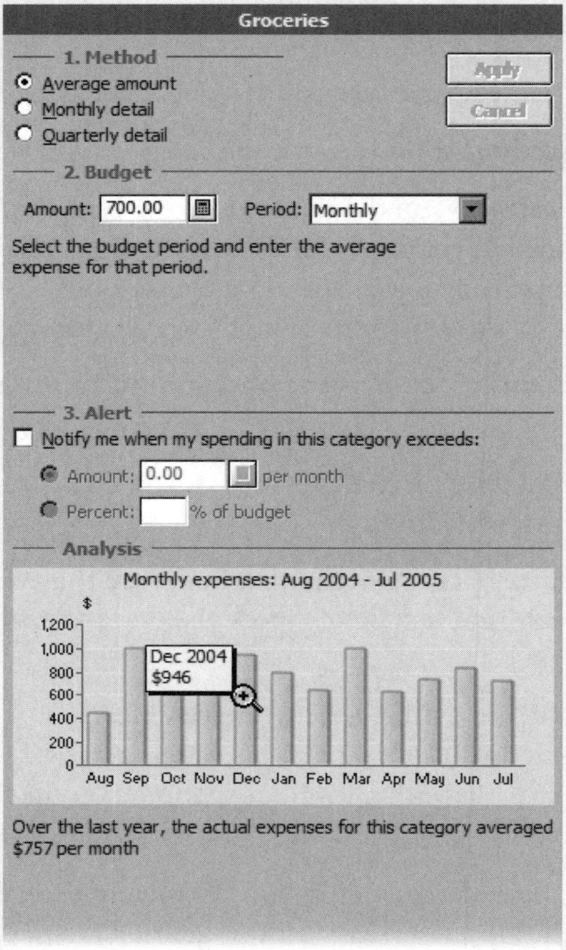

Figure 8-5. The month-by-month analysis in a budget category window helps you decide whether to use an average value or detail. When you choose a period and click Apply, Quicken calculates the average for that period.

Note: If you reduce the size of the Budget window, you must click the Analyze button to see the month-by-month analysis.

4. **Click Apply.**

   Quicken adds the amount and period to the columns on the left side of the Budget window, as shown in Figure 8-6. In the Analysis section, you'll see the average amount for the period you chose. If you want to change your average value, type a new value into the Amount text box and click Apply once more.

At the bottom of the Budget window, you can check whether your budget works. If you'd like Quicken to warn you when you're outspending your budget, you can set up budget alerts, described in the box on page 291. The Income value is how much you earn during a period; Expenses represent how much you spend. If the Difference value is positive, you've got money left over. If the Difference value is negative, you're heading for trouble. You can show these numbers for different lengths of time by choosing a value in the Totals drop-down menu.

Detailed Budget Values

If you want to be more exacting with your budget numbers, you can choose either the "Monthly detail" or "Quarterly detail" option in the Period list (see step 3 on page 287). These options are perfect when you have large payments that always occur in the same month each year, like auto insurance premiums, or amounts that vary from season to season, like those for heating oil. Quicken displays a text box for each month with the "Monthly detail" option (each quarter with the "Quarterly detail" option).

As you can see in Figure 8-7, setting a value requires nothing more than clicking the text box for a period and typing in a value. The Analysis graph is particularly helpful for figuring out when these erratic amounts occur and how much they are. To see the amount you spent, position the pointer over a bar.

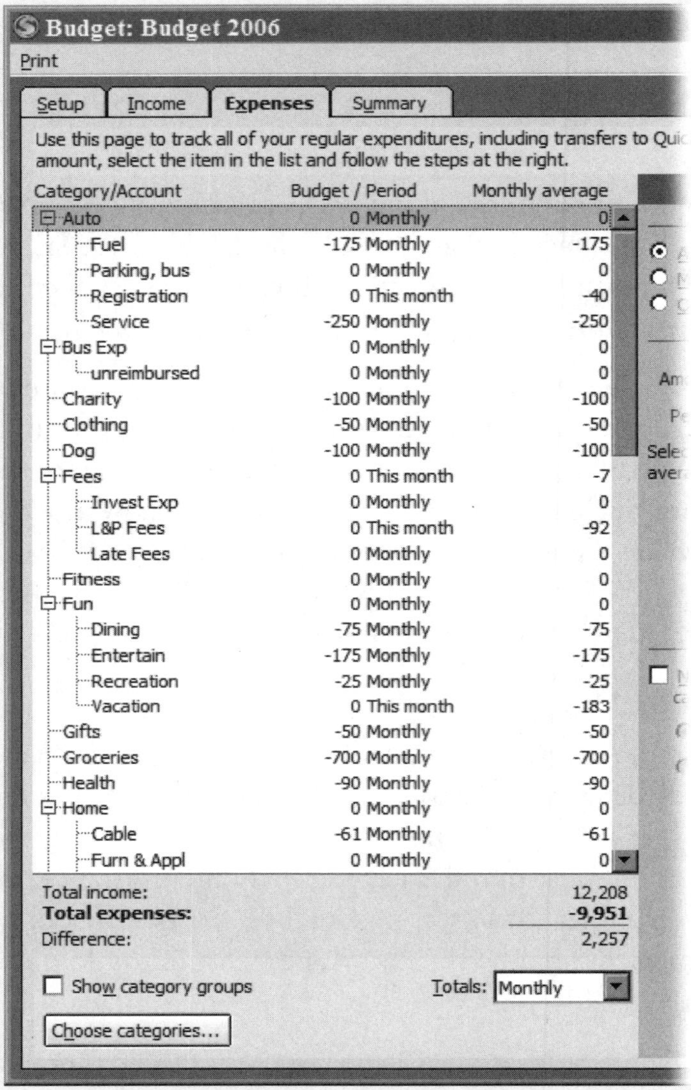

Figure 8-6. For each category in the Budget window, Quicken shows the amount and the period to which that amount applies. The "Monthly average" column displays the monthly average value regardless of how you define your budget numbers. At the bottom of the third column, the values for Income, Expenses, and Difference tell you whether you make more money than you spend or need to tighten your belt some more.

Setting Up Budget Alerts

Quicken can't stay your hand when you're extending it to pass a sales clerk your credit card, but it can remind you that you're spending more than you had planned. When you add budget values, you can also set an alert that pops up if you exceed a specific dollar amount or percentage of your budget value. For subtle reminders, you can tell Quicken to add alerts about overspending to the Alerts you see in the Cash Flow Center. If you need stronger reminders than that, you can set budget alerts to appear in pop-up message boxes.

In the Budget window's Alert section, as shown here, turn on the "Notify me when my spending in this category exceeds" checkbox. For a category that uses average values, you can choose the Percent option to set a percentage of the budget. For example, to

get some early warning, set the Percent text box to *90*. If you want a warning only when you've gone too far, set the value to *110*.

The Amount option lets you specify a dollar amount for the period you use, but this requires regular updating if your budget values change each year.

Groceries

— 1. Method —
- Average amount
- Monthly detail
- Quarterly detail

Apply
Cancel

— 2. Budget —
Amount: 700.00   Period: Monthly

Select the budget period and enter the average expense for that period.

— 3. Alert —
☑ Notify me when my spending in this category exceeds:
- Amount: 0.00   per month
- Percent: 90   % of budget

— Analysis —
Monthly expenses: Aug 2004 - Jul 2005
$

 Tip: If you use an average value for a category and want to switch to the "Monthly detail" option, first change the average value to zero. This changes the value in every period to zero. When you choose the "Monthly detail" option, you can enter budget values only in the months when income or expenses occur without having to remove obsolete numbers in the other months.

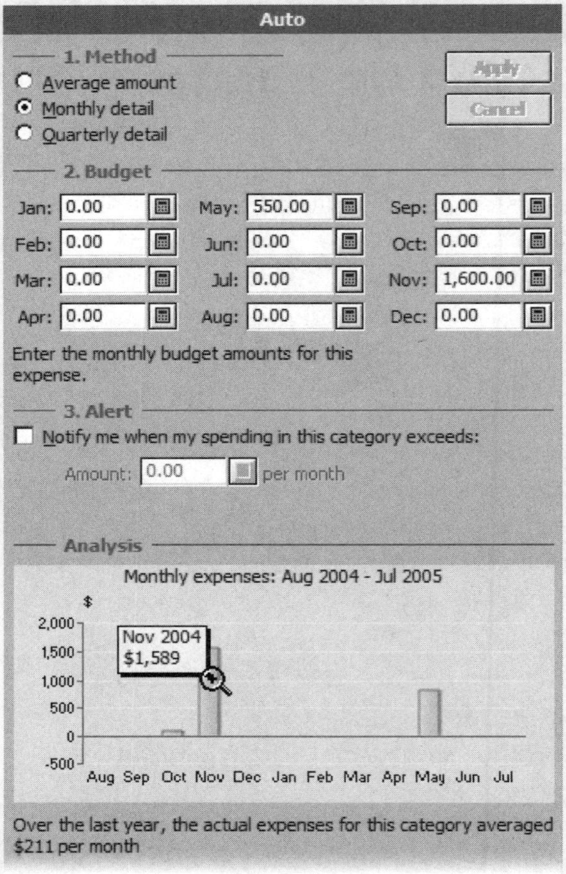

Figure 8-7. Click a text box in the Budget section and type in the budget value for that period (month, in this case). Press Tab to move to the next text box. To see the value of a past period, in the Analysis section, position the pointer over a bar in the lower part of the window.

Making a Budget Current

Although you can build as many different budgets as you want, you can work with only one budget at a time—the *current* budget. Quicken uses the current budget when you choose the "Copy current" option to create a new budget, as you saw on page 282. The program also uses the current budget when you generate reports that compare your budget and actual spending, so it's important to make sure you've got the correct budget set as current.

To change the current budget, choose Planning → Budgets to open the Budget window. Click the Setup tab. In the Other Budgets list, select the budget you want to work with and click Open. Quicken makes the budget you selected the current budget and displays the Income tab containing the current budget's numbers. The program adds the budget name to the window title. For example, the Budgets window title changes to something like Budget: Budget 2006.

Once a budget is current, you can edit any of its values by clicking the appropriate tab: Income, Expenses, or Savings. If you want to use the budget as the basis for a new budget, click the Setup tab and choose the "Copy current" option.

Choosing Budget Categories

In Quicken, budgets don't have to account for every category of income or spending. For example, if you want to create a budget for your retirement spending, you can omit categories for payroll taxes, commuting, and business lunches. Of course, you can add categories for long-term care insurance, greens fees, and Sun City tour maps.

You can change the categories for a budget at any time. As Figure 8-8 shows, the Income, Expenses, and Savings tabs include a button for choosing budget categories.

Adding Income and Expense Categories

If you click "Choose categories" on the Income tab, you'll see only income categories in the Choose Categories dialog box. Clicking "Choose categories" on the Expenses tab fills the Choose Categories dialog box with expense categories only, as you can see in Figure 8-9. And if you click "Choose accounts" on the Savings

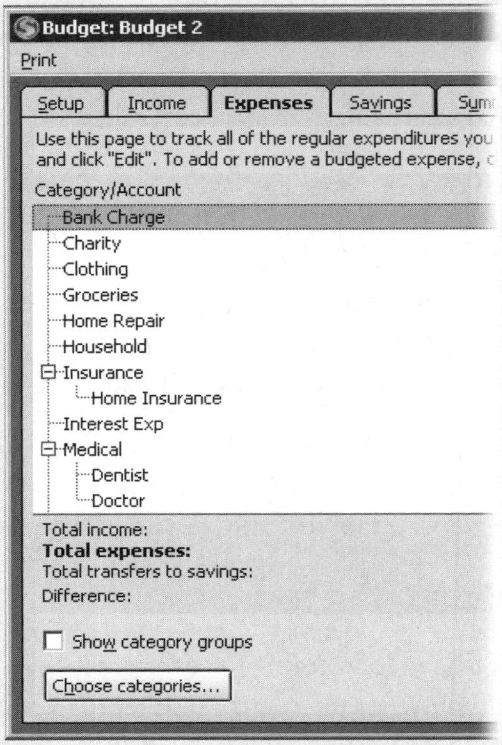

Figure 8-8. On the Income and Expense tabs, click "Choose categories" to select the categories you want to add or remove from the budget. On the Savings tab, you click "Choose accounts" to select the accounts to which you want to transfer savings.

tab, the Choose Accounts dialog box that lists transfers to your bank accounts, asset accounts, and investment accounts appears, as also shown in Figure 8-9.

Here are several ways to choose categories or accounts:

▶ **Mark all.** The fastest way to add categories is to click "Mark all," which adds all the categories in the list (income categories from the Income tab or expense categories from the Expenses tab).

Choose Categories

Expenses

Select the expense categories and accounts that you want to include in your budget.

Category/Account	Type	Description
Dining	Expense	Dining Out
Education	Expense	Education
Entertainment	Expense	Entertainment
Gifts Given	Expense	Gift Expenses
Groceries	Expense	Groceries
Home Repair	Expense	Home Repair & Maint.
Homeowner's Fees	Expense	Homeowner's Fees
Household	Expense	Household Misc. Exp
Housing	Expense	Housing
Insurance	Expense	Insurance
Disability Insurance	Sub	Disability Insurance
Home Insurance		Home Insurance
Life Insurance	Sub	Life Insurance
Interest Exp		Interest Expense
IRA Contrib	Expense	IRA Contribution

OK
Cancel
Help

Mark all
Clear all
Clear 0 amounts

Choose Accounts

Savings

Select the savings accounts that you want to include

Category/Account	Type	Des
TO CD ING 04-12-31 3.5	Bank	
TO CD ING 05-12-31 4.5	Bank	
TO CD ING 06-06-30 4.75	Bank	
TO CD ING 06-12-31 5.0	Bank	
TO CitiSavings	Bank	
TO ING Savings	Bank	
TO InterestChecking	Bank	Mar
TO Marsha's Vacation Club	Bank	
TO 02 Forerunner	Asset	
TO 63 Mustang	Asset	
TO Flex Spending MM	Asset	
TO House	Asset	
TO Jeff's 401K	Invest	
TO Marsha's 401(k)	Invest	
TO Marsha's IRA	Invest	

Figure 8-9. Top: In the Choose Categories dialog box, click "Mark all" to add all of the categories listed to the budget. You can tell Quicken what types of expenses to include in your budget by clicking categories to turn checkmarks on and off. Bottom: In the Choose Accounts dialog box, click transfers to add or remove them from your budget. Click these transfers one at a time to add only the accounts to which you transfer money.

- **Click individual entries.** Clicking an unchecked entry adds it to the budget and displays a green checkmark to indicate its inclusion. Click a checkmarked category to remove it. You can select groups of entries, like the Auto category and all its subcategories, by clicking the first category and then Shift-clicking the last category in the group. You can also Ctrl-click entries to select multiple but not sequential entries.

> **Tip:** Clicking a higher-level category doesn't automatically select all of the subcategories underneath it. You must select the subcategories you want, even if you've already selected their parent category.

- **Clear 0 amounts.** This button is particularly helpful if you've created a budget from your existing data. When you click "Clear 0 amounts," Quicken automatically turns off the categories that didn't have any of your actual transactions assigned to them. If you click this button, it's a good idea to review the list to make sure that you haven't turned off any categories you want to keep. For example, you may not have gone on vacation last year, but you still want to budget for some fun.

- **Clear all.** If you've hopelessly mangled the list of categories and want to start fresh, click "Clear all" to turn off all of the categories shown. You can then click individual categories to turn them back on.

> **Tip:** If you have accounts for certificates of deposit, bonds, and other savings vehicles, you probably don't want to click "Mark all" in the Choose Accounts dialog box. Click the individual accounts that you transfer money to regularly, like your 401(k) or vacation club savings account. The interest that your savings vehicles pay is already covered by an Income category such as Interest Income.

Setting Up Transfers in a Budget

The most effective way to save money is to get it into savings before you realize that you have it, and the same holds true to paying down debt. By budgeting for transfers to savings or to a double-digit credit card, you're halfway to making those transfers a reality. As long as you stick to your budgeted values for income and expenses, you'll have enough money to make the transfers you budget. (If you're not up to the regimentation of regular savings transfers, Quicken provides a feature called a Savings Goal that helps you track how much you've saved, as described in the box on page 299.)

In the Budget window, the Savings tab is the place to say how much you want to transfer between accounts. At the bottom of the Savings tab, click "Choose accounts" to display a dialog box in which you can select the accounts to which you want to transfer money. You should also include accounts that you might transfer money *out* of, such as CDs that mature.

 Tip: If you don't see the Savings tab, in the Budget window menu bar, choose Options → Separate View.

Once you have the accounts added to the Savings tab, shown in Figure 8-10, you can specify transfer values as you would income or expenses. For example, you could add your 401(k) contribution using an average value set to the period that matches your paycheck. On the other hand, if you transfer money to your brokerage account in December when you receive a year-end bonus, you can set up a Monthly detail transfer that occurs only in December.

Saving or Restoring a Budget

When a budget is current, Quicken automatically saves the changes you make to it when you close the Budget window or make a different budget current. If you've worked on your budget for a while and want to make sure that you don't lose your changes to a computer crash or horrible typing accident, in the Budget window menu bar choose Options → Save Budget.

On the other hand, if the dawn of a new day shows your budget to be a total bust, you can choose Options → Restore Budget to replace the current values with the previously saved budget.

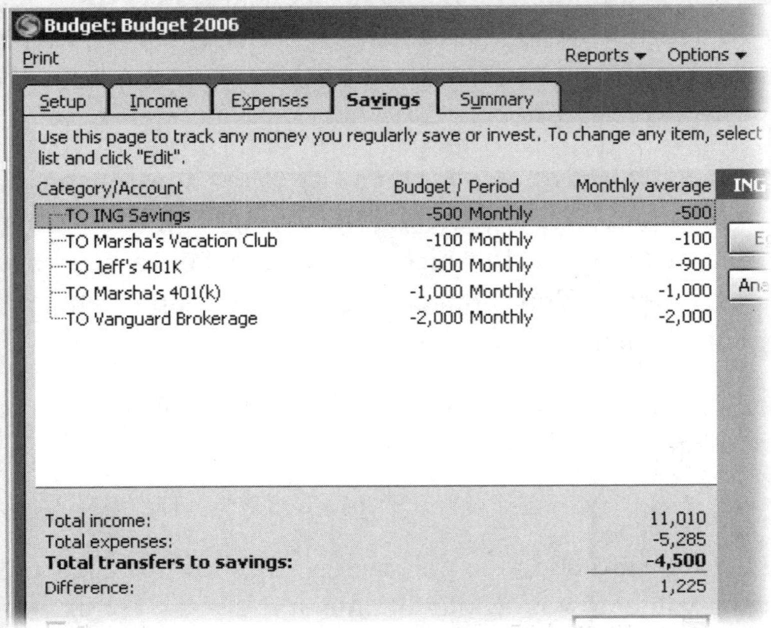

Figure 8-10. The bottom of the budget window shows how much you earn, spend, and transfer to other accounts. If the Difference value is positive, you can decide whether to save more money or reward yourself with some additional spending.

Comparing Your Performance to Your Budget

A personal budget isn't like a corporate or government budget, which stops spending cold when it reaches the budgeted values. Instead, your budget is a target for you to aim for. *You* determine whether you follow the budget or throw discretion to the wind. In Quicken, the Budget window tells you whether your planned budget works, but it doesn't show whether you're sticking to that plan. To see how you're doing compared to your budget, you generate a budget report, which includes how much you budgeted, how much you actually earned or spent, and the difference between the two.

Setting a Goal for Savings

Quicken includes a feature called a *savings goal*, which helps you plan for big-ticket purchases like a car, the down payment on a house, or your liposuction. Choose Planning → Savings Goal to open the Savings Goals window.

You create savings goals by naming the goal, and specifying how much you want to save and when you need the money. Quicken calculates how much you must contribute each month to reach your goal, but it doesn't take into account interest you might earn. If you're planning to save over decades (for example, for retirement), a Quicken savings goal significantly overestimates your monthly savings amount.

But for shorter-term goals, Quicken savings goals help hide the money you've earmarked. You contribute money in an existing bank account to a savings goal. Although the money stays in that bank account, the Account Bar reduces the balance that you see by the money you've contributed to the goal. For example, if you have $5,000 in your savings account and contribute $2,000 of it toward a car down payment, the Account Bar shows a balance of only $3,000.

Quicken includes three ways to compare your budget to actuals, all of which are likely to need some tweaking to display what you want. This section describes your three choices and how to customize them to display the information you need.

▶ **Budget Report.** Regardless of what time period you choose for the report, this tabular report has three columns: actual values, budgeted values, and the difference between the two.

▶ **Monthly Budget Report.** This report shows three columns for each month of the date range you choose: monthly actual, monthly budget, and monthly difference. The last three columns in this report cover the entire time period—in effect, a Budget Report tacked on to the right side of a monthly budget report.

▶ **Budget Graph.** This bar graph provides a high-level view of whether you ran short or had money left over. If a bar is blue and above the horizontal line, you made more than you spent in that month. Red bars below the horizontal line indicate the months when you spent more than you made.

The initial settings for the budget reports show values for the current month, which isn't the best place to start. Here are the steps for altering the Monthly Budget report to show the year to date—and for saving that report so you don't have to customize your report over and over.

1. **To view a budget report, choose Reports → Spending and then choose either Budget or Monthly Budget.**

   The Budget or Monthly Budget window opens and compares your budget for the month to your actual values.

   Note: To view a bar graph of your performance, choose Reports → Graphs and then choose either Budget or Monthly Budget.

2. **In the Date range drop-down menu, choose "Year to date."**

   Quicken displays three columns for each month of the year so far, as illustrated in Figure 8-11.

3. **To save this report, in the report window icon bar, click Save Report.**

   The Save Report dialog box opens. In the "Report name" text box, type a descriptive name for the report like *Monthly Budget Year-to-date*. Quicken automatically sets the "Save in" value to "None (My Saved Reports)."

   Tip: If you like to organize your customized reports, click Create Folder to create a folder for your reports. For example, you may want to keep all year-to-date reports in the same folder. Or you could create one folder for spending reports and a second folder for investing reports.

Monthly Budget - YTD

Date range: [Year to date ▾]

1/1/2006 through 3/20/2006 Using Budget 2006

Category Description	1/1/2006 Actual	- Budget	1/31/2006 Difference	2
OUTFLOWS				
Bank Charge	9.95	10.00	0.05	
Charity	15.00	300.00	285.00	
Clothing	433.21	100.00	-333.21	
Groceries	196.74	600.00	403.26	
Home Repair	100.27	60.00	-40.27	
Household	0.00	220.00	220.00	

Category Description	2/1/2006 Actual	- Budget	2/28/2006 Difference	3
TOTAL Utilities	331.54	245.00	-86.54	
TO ING Savings	500.00	500.00	0.00	
TO Marsha's Vacation Club	75.00	100.00	25.00	
TO Jeff's 401K	400.00	900.00	500.00	
TO Marsha's 401(k)	400.00	1,000.00	600.00	
TO Vanguard Brokerage	0.00	2,000.00	2,000.00	
TOTAL OUTFLOWS	**6,860.07**	**9,760.00**	**2,899.93**	
OVERALL TOTAL	**-2,697.94**	**1,250.00**	**-3,947.94**	

Figure 8-11. Top: If the value in the Difference columns is negative, you've spent more than you budgeted in that category.
Bottom: Before you take corrective action, scroll to the bottom of the report to see if you have a net inflow for the month. For example, the budget forecast is a net inflow of $1,250 for February. However, the actual result is a net outflow of $2,697.94. which shows significantly more spending than planned.

To generate your customized report, choose Reports → My Saved Reports & Graphs and then choose the name of the report.

Budget Course Corrections

Because monthly values tend to vary, comparing the budgeted and actual numbers for a single month is bound to make you a little nervous. Perhaps you hit the grocery store on March 1 and March 31, so it looks like you spent twice as much on groceries as you planned. Here are a few suggestions for how to evaluate your performance and what to do if things go awry.

* The easiest way to stay on top of your budget is to generate a report for the year to date (assuming you have data from January 1 of the current year). By comparing longer periods, you'll smooth out the month-to-month variations. If your income for the year to date is higher than your expenses for the same period, you're OK.

* Check whether actual income is lower than budgeted. If you didn't receive that bonus you counted on or an illness cut into your billable hours, you may want to adjust your budget for the rest of the year to reduce future spending.

* Don't worry about expenses that come in slightly over budget. But if you see a steady trend of overspending, review the transactions in that category to see if there's any way to spend less in the future. (See Chapter 10 to learn how to create transaction reports.)

* If you keep an emergency fund in a readily accessible savings account, you don't have to worry about the occasional month when you spend more than you earn. You can transfer the money you need from savings to checking. Be sure to transfer money *back* from checking to savings in the months that have more income than expenses!

CHAPTER 9:
INVESTMENTS AND
PLANNING

▶ Why Track Investments in Quicken?

▶ Choosing the Right Type of Account

▶ Creating an Investment Account

▶ Setting Up a Security

▶ Recording Investment Transactions

▶ Purchasing a Security

▶ Selling a Security

▶ Recording and Reinvesting Income

▶ Recording a Stock Split

▶ Placeholder Entries

▶ Evaluating Your Portfolio

▶ A Quick Tour of Quicken Planning Tools

Quicken's just as good at tracking investments as it is your checks, charges, and ATM withdrawals. You can keep tabs on investment gains and losses as well as the dividends and interest you earn, which is a huge help come tax time.

But tracking investment transactions also means you can evaluate the performance of your investments. If you hear dogs barking in your portfolio, you can get rid of them and find better places to invest your money. And by reviewing how you've allocated your portfolio among different types of investments, you can tell whether you're putting too many eggs in one nest-egg basket.

This chapter explains when it makes sense to track investments in Quicken—and when it doesn't. You'll learn how to set up your investments, record transactions, and analyze your portfolio. Finally, you'll learn how to use Quicken's planning tools to make the most of your money.

Why Track Investments in Quicken?

Tracking investments in Quicken is quite easy, but it requires a small time commitment. Before you dive into the topics in this chapter, read this section to help decide whether you want—or need—to spend that time.

If you answer "Yes" to any of the following questions, tracking your investments in Quicken makes sense:

▶ **Do you need to report your investment gains and income on your tax return?** One of the big advantages to tracking investments in Quicken is how easily you can gather pertinent investment data for your tax return. At tax time, you can generate Quicken reports for your taxable interest and dividends, as well as gains and losses on sales (short-term, long-term, and the ones in between). If you've ever sold a mutual fund that you've owned and reinvested distributions into for decades, you *know* how painful capital-gain calculations can be. If you track the fund in Quicken, the program instantly spits out the numbers you need.

On the other hand, if all of your investments are in tax-deferred accounts, like IRAs, 401(k)s, and Keoghs, there's no need to track taxable investment income and gains—because there aren't any. (See the box on page 306 for other reasons you may not need Quicken's help with your investments.)

▶ **Do you want to know the returns your investments achieve?** For investments in individual stocks, your return depends completely on when and how much you buy, sell, or reinvest.

If you own nothing but mutual funds, you may not think you need Quicken to calculate your investment returns. After all, mutual funds calculate and report investment returns to their shareholders anyway, as the Securities and Exchange Commission requires. But calculating performance in Quicken offers some benefits over mutual fund company calculations. For example, if you buy a bunch of shares just before a fund's value makes a big jump, your actual return would be *better* than the published figure.

▶ **Do you want to use Quicken to help you make investment decisions?** Investments are a lot like orchids. Even though the stock market is surprisingly hardy, thriving in the financial jungle with only a bit of intervention from the Federal Reserve Board, successfully growing your personal portfolio of investments requires a fair amount of care and feeding. You have to pick investments that match your goals, diversify your investments to reduce risk, and monitor performance to see if corrective actions are in order.

Note: Most of the investment analysis tools that Quicken offers need the details about your investment transactions. For example, the Portfolio Rebalancer can't suggest changes to make if it doesn't know what investments you own.

Choosing the Right Type of Account

Quicken offers four types of investment-specific accounts, but you're not limited to them. Depending on what you invest in, you may find one of the cash- or asset-oriented account types a better fit. You create an investment account just like any other in Quicken, starting from the Quicken Account Setup dialog box shown in Figure 9-1.

When To Skip Quicken Investment Tracking

Quicken's investment tracking features are a huge help if your investments earn capital gains that you have to report to the IRS, or if you have lots of stocks and fund accounts to juggle. If your investment activity is fairly straightforward, though, the extra time spent entering investment data in Quicken may not pay off. Here are some examples:

You invest only in your 401(k). If your investments are limited to your 401(k) or 403(b) account and your account statements are miracles of brevity, the 401(k) Update wizard makes it easy to update your account balance each time you receive a statement. You only need to track these accounts in Quicken, if you want help analyzing and managing the investments purchased with your contributions.

(Note: Because employer-sponsored retirement accounts typically offer limited selections of mutual funds, you can obtain annual performance figures from the account administrator.)

You have only one or two taxable investment accounts. As long as your financial institution sends tax-related statements that are clear and easy to read, you may not need Quicken investment tracking for tax reports.

You track nothing but net worth. To keep track of your net worth in Quicken, you need the value of your assets—including all of your investment accounts, taxable and tax-advantaged alike. But you can keep the value of your account balances up to date *without* tracking every single investment transaction. If you don't care about taxes or performance calculations, you can adjust your account balances manually any time you want to update the value of your net worth.

Quicken has six account types that work for investments. The following describes what each one does:

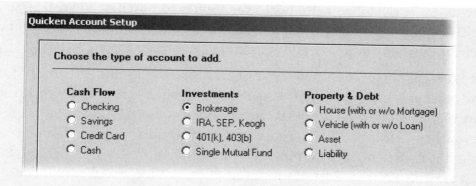

Figure 9-1. If you choose File → New to open the Quicken Account Setup dialog box, you can create any type of investment account, including Asset for real estate and Savings for money market funds and CDs.

▶ **401(k)/403(b).** Named after the sections of the tax code that created them, these are the well-known retirement plans you can sign up for at work. Choosing this account type lets Quicken handle the features of employer-sponsored accounts, including matching contributions that your employer may make, loans you can withdraw, and the tax advantages you receive.

Financial institutions vary in the detail they provide on 401(k) statements. In Quicken, the 401(k), 403(b) account type can track actual shares or dollar values only. (If you don't care about detail, you can use the 401(k) Update wizard to enter summaries from your statements.)

▶ **IRA, SEP, Keogh.** This is the account type to choose for other types of retirement accounts, including IRAs (traditional, Roth, Simplified Employee Pensions, and Education), SIMPLE plans, and Keogh plans.

Note: For an acronym run amok, it doesn't get better than Savings Incentive Match Plans for Employees of Small Employers (SIMPLE). Gets a laugh at bean-counter cocktail parties every time.

▶ **Asset.** If you're tracking real estate purchased as an investment, like land, a house, or an office building, use the Asset or House account type. A House account is perfect if you also borrowed money to purchase the real estate, because Quicken makes it easy to link the asset account to the corresponding loan and liability account, as discussed in Chapter 5.

▶ **Brokerage.** This account type is a catch-all for investments that don't fit any of the other account types. A brokerage account holds one or more securities of any type that Quicken supports (stocks, bonds, mutual funds, real estate investment trusts or REITs, options, and investment cash). Although you might use a Savings account for a single certificate of deposit (CD), you could just as easily keep a ladder of several certificates of deposit from the same bank in one brokerage account.

▶ **Single Mutual Fund.** The name says it all. This type of account only does one thing well: Track a single mutual fund. Choose this type only if you buy a mutual fund directly from the mutual fund company, don't have a cash balance in the account, and hold only one fund in the account.

▶ **Savings.** CDs and money market funds sometimes count as investments. If you set up a separate money market bank account or use CDs for shorter-term cash, Quicken savings accounts are ideal. Simply name the account so that you can tell at a glance it's for a CD or whatever (see page 67 for more account-naming advice). Many brokerage accounts include a linked money market fund for holding cash, and those money market funds can be a part of the Quicken brokerage account you create.

> **Tip:** To move savings accounts from Quicken's Cash Flow Center to the Investing Center, edit the account's details to change the account location (see page 68). This won't change the type of account, only the location.

Creating an Investment Account

In Quicken, setting up an investment account isn't all that different from setting up a banking account. You fill in text boxes, choose options, and click Next until the Quicken Account Setup screen displays the Done button. (See "Creating a Banking Account: Step by Step" on page 62 for all the details.) Investment accounts, though, do include a few additional questions that Quicken doesn't ask for cash flow accounts. This section describes the extra information you'll have to provide.

To create an investment account, start by choosing Investing → Investing Accounts → Add Account (or in the Investing Center window, click Add Account). In the Quicken Account Setup dialog box, you must first provide the financial institution that holds your account—a necessity if you plan to use online services. The program makes it so easy to choose a financial institution (page 64) that you'll fill in this text box in seconds. You also must tell Quicken whether you want to set the account up manually or online.

The next Quicken Account Setup screen displays the different types of investment accounts you can create. After you've chosen the option for the type of investment account and clicked Next, read on to learn how to respond to the rest of Quicken's interrogation.

Note: After you manually create an investment account, you provide other information, like the account number and contact information, only when you edit the account, as described on page 68.

Creating a 401(k) or 403(b) Account

In the Quicken Account Setup dialog box, the "401(k) or 403(b)" option creates an account for your employer-sponsored retirement plan. It's no surprise that you have to answer some questions about your employer and the features that its plan offers. For the eagle-eyed investor, you'll notice that the dialog box title changes to "401(k)/403(b) Setup," as you can see in the bottom figure of Figure 9-2.

Here's the information that's unique to 401(k) and 403(b) accounts:

▶ **Employer Name.** The "Tell us about this account" screen includes the aptly named Employer Name text box, in which you type the name of the employer that provides this retirement account.

- **Current Employer**. As long as the employer for this account still signs your paycheck, leave the Current Employer option selected. If you still have a 401(k) with a previous employer and are just getting around to creating the account in Quicken, choose the Previous Employer option.

- **My Account** or **My Spouse's Account**. This choice can be tricky if you and your spouse take an egalitarian approach to Quicken duties. Who's "me" and who's "my spouse" depends on how you set up your data file and how you file your taxes. Your choices here must match the main taxpayer and spouse on your tax returns—especially if you use your Quicken data to do your returns in Turbo Tax.

  If you don't know which of you is considered the spouse, click Cancel to stop the account creation. Choose Tools → Quicken Guided Setup and, in the Quicken Guided Setup window, click "About You." On the About You screen, the spouse is the person whose name appears in the Spouse's Name boxes. Back in the Quicken Account Setup dialog box, the My Account option is for the person whose name appears in the Your Name boxes. Choose the My Spouse's Account option for the person whom Quicken considers the spouse, as illustrated in Figure 9-2.

- **Does the statement list how many shares of each security you own?** Dig out the last statement that you received from the 401(k) or 403(b) administrator. If the statement tells you how many shares you own of each mutual fund (or other security) choose Yes. Otherwise, choose No.

- **Loans**. 401(k) and 403(b) accounts let you borrow money from yourself, so the next screen in the 401(k)/403(b) Setup dialog box asks if you would like to track loans you've taken against the account. If you haven't borrowed against the account, simply select the No option. (You can add a loan later, if need be, by creating a liability account and linking it to your retirement account.)

  If you have borrowed against the account, select the Yes option. In the "How many?" text box, type the number of loans you've taken. If you indicate that you have loans, when you click Next, the program displays a few additional screens asking questions about each of these loans: a description, the current balance, and the original loan amount.

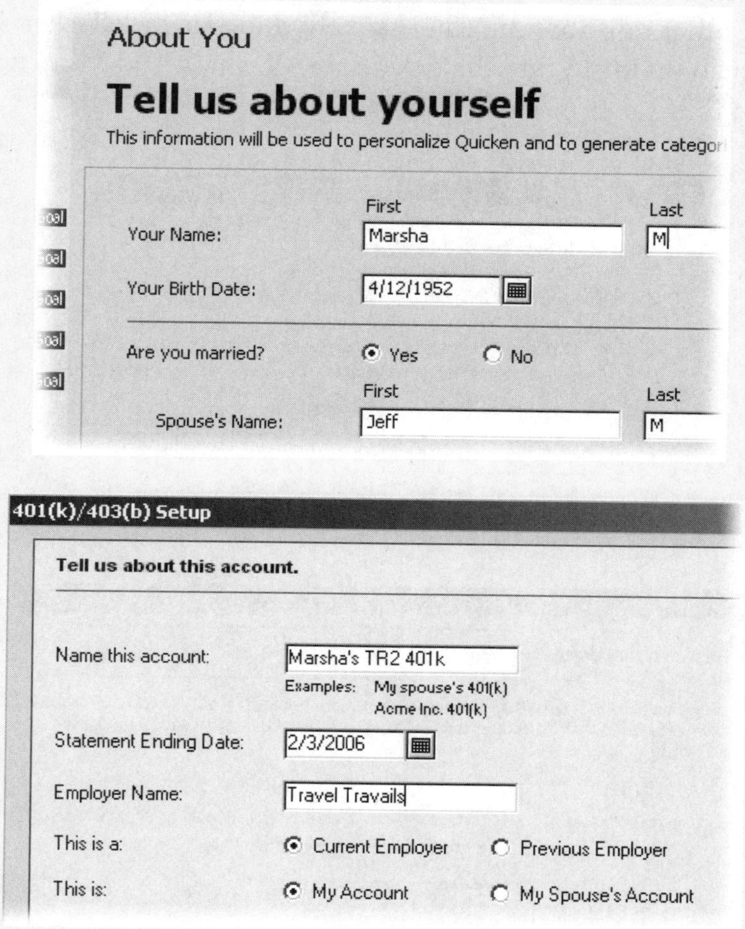

Figure 9-2. Top: Open the Quicken Guided Setup and click About You to see your personal settings.
Bottom: In the Quicken Accounts Setup dialog box, type the employer name, and choose options for Current Employer or Previous Employer, and whose retirement nest egg the account represents.

▶ **Securities.** The next screen, shown in Figure 9-3, asks about the securities that you hold in the account, which you'll see regardless of the type of investment account you create. If you can connect to the Internet, all you have to do is type the ticker symbol for each holding, and Quicken obtains the security name and other information. Alternatively, you can click Ticker Symbol Lookup to go online to find the ticker symbol. Click Add More if you own more than five.

401(k)/403(b) Setup

What securities are in this account?

Enter a ticker symbol for each security in your account.

- If your computer is connected to the Internet, Quicken uses the ticker If you don't know the ticker symbol, click Ticker Symbol Lookup.
- If you are not connected to the Internet, just enter a security name. Y

	Ticker*	Security Name (optional)
1.	fsmkx	Fidelity Diversified International Fund
2.	fdivx	Spartan 500 Index
3.		

401(k)/403(b) Setup

Enter your current holdings information.

This information will be used to set up your initial security holdings. For each security, enter the total number of shares (if known), market value, and select a security type (if the security is not a stock or mutual fund, click Other - you can edit the security later).

Ticker	Security Name	Total Shares	Total Market Value	Stock	Mutual Fund	Other
FSMKX	FIDELITY SPARTAN 5...	103.45	8,442.02	○	⊙	○
FDIVX	FIDELITY DIVERSIFIE...	255.98	7,501.35	○	⊙	○

Figure 9-3. Top: Type the ticker symbol for each security you own in the account. When you click Next (not shown), Quicken goes online to check the ticker symbols and gathers investment information.
Bottom: This is where you fill in your Total Shares and Market Value for each security.

 Tip: If you're ready for a break, you can leave this screen blank and add securities to the account after setup. Quicken pops up a message box asking if you're sure you want to create the account without securities. Click Yes and take that break.

When you click Next, the program goes online and checks the ticker symbols you typed and collects information about your investments, like whether it's a stock, mutual fund, or other type of security. If you tell the program that your statement shows shares, the next screen that appears asks for the shares you own and the total market value. Use the numbers on your last statement.

On the last of the Securities screens, click Next to reach the screen you're waiting for—the Summary screen. It shows the securities you own and the Done button. When you click Done, Quicken adds the account to the ones already listed in the Investing Center and displays the account's Summary tab in the main Quicken window.

 Note: If you haven't set up your paycheck using the Set Up Paycheck feature (see page 168), you'll have a chance to do so while creating your retirement account.

Creating a Brokerage Account

In the Quicken Account Setup dialog box, the Brokerage option creates an investment account that can handle almost anything. The questions you answer are surprisingly simple. You first provide the date of the statement on which you're basing your answers. Here's the other information you must provide for brokerage accounts.

▶ **Cash.** In the Cash text box, type the cash balance in your account.

▶ **Money Market Fund.** For brokerage accounts that come with what's called a sweep fund (for holding cash from sales or interest), in the Money Market Fund text box, type the balance in your sweep fund.

▶ **Securities.** As described in the previous section, you'll see a screen in which you can type the tickers for the securities you own. If you want to add the securities later, leave the boxes blank and click Next.

Creating an IRA Account

In Quicken, an IRA account is simply a brokerage account with tax advantages, so the questions you answer to create one are almost identical to those for a brokerage account, as described in the previous section. Here's the other information you must provide for an IRA account:

▶ **Who owns this IRA?** Choose either the Myself or the My Spouse option depending on whom you've set up as the spouse (page 310).

▶ **What type of IRA is this?** As you probably already know, IRAs come in as many flavors as Starbucks lattes. Choose the type of your IRA from the list shown in Figure 9-4. If you don't know what type of IRA you own, ask your financial institution.

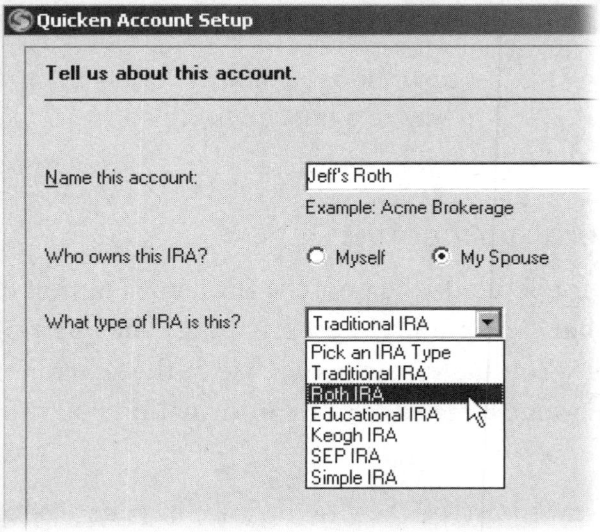

Figure 9-4. Because each type of IRA has its own unique tax advantages, it's important to choose the correct type when you set up the account.

Setting Up a Security

If you typed in ticker symbols when you created your investment account, you may not have to set up a new security for some time. But eventually, your investment advisor will suggest that you buy a new stock, say, or you'll decide to switch mutual funds in your 401(k) account. This chapter explains how to add new securities to the list of ones you already own or watch.

This chapter also introduces a few other lists that you can use to categorize your investments by security type (stocks, bonds, and so on), investing goals (like growth or income), and asset class. Smart investors know there's no such thing as a free lunch on Wall Street. In other words, the investments that offer higher returns almost always come with higher risk. Categorizing your investments in Quicken helps you evaluate whether the risks you take with your investments are paying off—making *you* one of those smart investors.

The Security List

When it comes to working with securities, whether setting one up, editing its characteristics, or reviewing its price history, the Security List window is the place to start. Press Ctrl+Y or choose Investing → Security List, and the window shown in Figure 9-5 appears.

Security	Symbol	Type	Asset Class	Watch
apple	AAPL	Stock	Large Cap Stocks	☑
Dow Jones Industrials	DJI	Market Index	Unclassified	☐
Fidelity Diversified International ...	FSMKX	Mutual Fund	Asset Mixture	☑
GENERAL ELECTRIC CO	GE	Stock	Large Cap Stocks	☑
LOWES COMPANIES INC	LOW	Stock	Large Cap Stocks	☑
NASDAQ Composite	COMPX	Market Index	Unclassified	☐
Russell 2000	IUX	Market Index	Unclassified	☐
S&P 500 Index	INX	Market Index	Unclassified	☑
Spartan 500 Index	FDIVX	Mutual Fund	Asset Mixture	☑

Figure 9-5. In the Security List window, you can add (New), edit, delete, and hide securities. To open the Security Detail View for a security, double-click its name in the list. The last column in the Security List window indicates whether the security is on your Watch list, as discussed in the box on page 316.

Watch Lists and Investing Alerts

You can add a security to Quicken's Watch list by turning on its Watch checkbox in the Security List window. Although the watch list is clearly visible in the Investing Center window, it's not as helpful as you might expect: It shows only price quotes and the change for the day in dollars and as a percentage, which savvy investors know is only a small part of the story. Moreover, you have to *look* at the watch list to see if a price has dropped to your buy price or soared past your "Sell! Sell! Sell!" point.

If you really want to watch a security for events that might trigger you to buy or sell, use an Investing Alert instead. Although you start to set up alerts in Quicken, it's actually Quicken.com that stores and sends them. You can tell Quicken to pop up an alert box on your PC screen, making important investment events hard to ignore.

To set up an alert, choose Tools → Set Up Alerts. In the Alerts Center window, click Investing and then turn on the alerts you want to get, like Price and Volume. Click the "Go to Quicken.com to customize price and volume alerts" link (shown here), to specify the levels that trigger the alerts. For instance, you can tell Quicken.com to notify you when a stock's price drops below $19.50. At Quicken.com, you can even set up an alert that sends a message to your mobile phone, for truly monumental events.

Security Price and Volume.

Price, volume and news alerts allow you to monitor securities.

You can get an alert in Quicken when a security's price rises above (

You can also receive alerts when the price change exceeds a percer percentage greater than average.

You can also receive news and industry buzz such as earnings anno

Go to Quicken.com to customize price and volume alerts.

The Security Detail View

The Security Detail View window is a one-stop-shop for viewing, editing, and updating a security you're tracking in Quicken. As you can see in Figure 9-6, the window includes sections that show security details, a summary of the shares you own (number, market value, cost basis, and so on), a price quote, a price chart, and a transaction history list. To open the Security Detail View window, choose Investing → Security Detail View.

 Note: This window isn't related to a specific account. If you own the same security in more than one account (your husband's and your IRAs, for example), all the transactions for the security from both accounts appear in the Transaction History.

Here are some tasks you can perform from this window:

▶ **Edit the security details.** To change any of the security's details, click Edit Security Details (in the Security Details section, or in the menu bar). See "Editing a Security" on page 322 for the items you might want to change.

▶ **Update security information.** In the window menu bar, choose Update and then choose one of the commands on the drop-down menu to either download information about the security or update the values in its price history.

▶ **Check the value of your holdings.** The Holdings section shows how many shares you own and their market value, cost basis, and the gain or loss by dollars and percentage. The easiest way to see all these values for *all* of your investments is the Portfolio View (see page 342).

▶ **Review transactions.** You can scroll through all the transactions for the security in the Transaction History section. For example, if you're trying to find a transaction because your Quicken records don't match your broker's statement, scan the Shares or Amount column for numbers that match the discrepancy.

▶ **Review price and price history.** The price chart shows a graph of the historical prices for the security, which by itself isn't enough to say buy, sell, or hold. Click More Charting to go online and generate price charts that are more helpful; for instance, to show a chart that compares your mutual fund's price performance to the index that it mirrors.

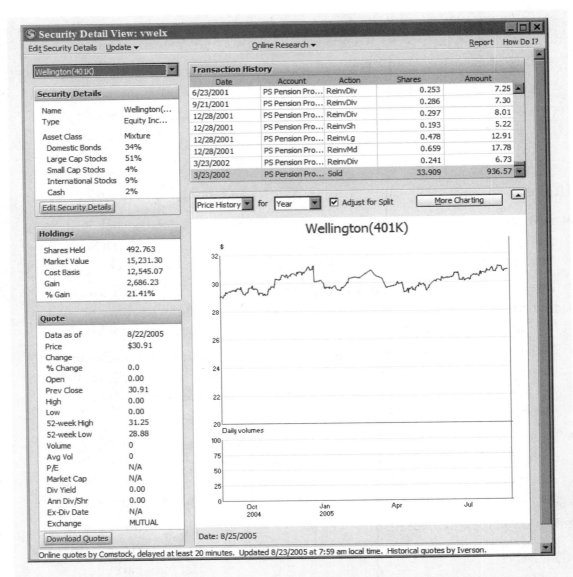

Figure 9-6. The Security Detail View fits everything Quicken knows about an investment you own into one window. You can view details and edit values in the window. And the menu bar includes commands for downloading more data or going online to research the security.

Tip: The Online Research menu button seems ripe with possibilities, but the options on the drop-down menu merely point to pages on Quicken.com, which aren't exactly A-list investment research sites. If you prefer other Web sites, like *money.msn.com*, *finance.yahoo.com*, or *www.investor.reuters.com*, you'll have to use your regular Web browser to reach them.

Adding a Security

You can add securities to your Security List when you create an investment account or as part of recording a purchase transaction (see "Purchasing a Security" on page 329). If you have trouble multitasking, you might prefer to add a security to the Security List *outside* of other tasks. Here are the steps to adding a security:

1. **Press Ctrl+Y or choose Tools → Security List.**

   The Security List window opens, as shown in Figure 9-5. If you're a Quicken veteran, turn on hidden securities so you can easily add items you've owned in the past. In the Security List window menu bar, choose Options → "View hidden securities."

   Tip: Hidden securities have a hand icon to the right of their names. To make a hidden security active once more, select the security and, in the window menu bar, click Hide. The hand icon disappears. Clicking Hide in the window menu bar toggles the setting between hiding and showing securities.

2. **In the Security List window menu bar, choose New.**

   The "Add Security to Quicken" dialog box appears, ready to guide you through several screens of simple questions.

3. **In the first screen, in the Ticker Symbol text box, type the security's ticker symbol and click Next.**

   The first screen asks for the ticker symbol and name, but you can type one or the other and let Quicken fill in the rest. If you type the ticker symbol, Quicken automatically goes online to retrieve the security name when you click Next. Or

type the name in the Name box, and then click Look Up to open a
Quicken.com Web page that finds ticker symbols, as illustrated in Figure 9-7.

To prevent typographical errors, you can select the ticker symbol on the Web
page and press Ctrl+C. Back in Quicken, click the Ticker Symbol text box
and press Ctrl+V to paste the ticker symbol into the text box.

> **Note:** Quicken automatically turns on the "Include this security on my
> watch list" checkbox. (If you're adding a security to your list, you usually
> want to know its current price.) You can remove the security from the
> watch list any time by turning off its checkbox in the Security List window
> (see Figure 9-5). Taking a security off the Watch list after you sell it is a
> good idea, so you don't have to feel your heart sink as its price goes *up*.

After the Quicken One Step Update Status dialog box makes a brief appearance and connects to the Internet to retrieve information about the security,
the final screen in the Add Security to Quicken process appears. As long as
you typed the ticker symbol correctly, the program fills in all the fields for the
security automatically, as demonstrated in Figure 9-8.

If you entered the wrong ticker symbol, you'll see one of two screens:

▶ If the ticker you typed is valid, but incorrect, the last screen of the "Add Security
  to Quicken" won't show the security you wanted to add. Click Back to try again.

▶ If you typed a ticker that doesn't exist, the "No data found for *<ticker>* Company" screen appears. Quicken automatically selects the "Correct ticker symbol and try again" option, so you can retype the ticker symbol and try again. If
  you're sure the symbol is correct, choose the "Add manually" option. You'll
  have to tell Quicken the security type and provide the other information, but
  at least the program won't spin its wheels trying to find a ticker symbol it
  doesn't have in its database.

4. **Once Quicken retrieves the information for the correct security, click
   Done.**

   The program adds the security to the Security List for watching, tracking
   transactions, or both.

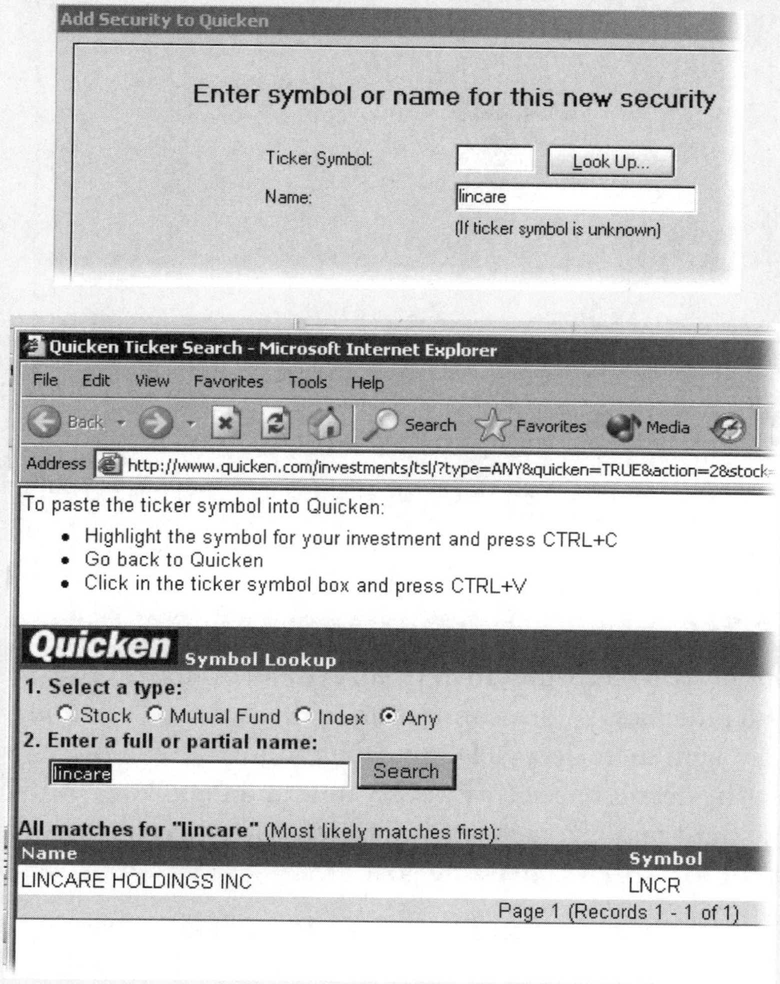

Add Security to Quicken

Enter symbol or name for this new security

Ticker Symbol: [   ] [Look Up...]

Name: [lincare   ]

(If ticker symbol is unknown)

Quicken Ticker Search - Microsoft Internet Explorer

File   Edit   View   Favorites   Tools   Help

◁ Back ▾ ◌ ▾ ✕ ◌ ◌ | 🔍 Search ⭐ Favorites ● Media ◌

Address 🔗 http://www.quicken.com/investments/tsl/?type=ANY&quicken=TRUE&action=2&stock=

To paste the ticker symbol into Quicken:

- Highlight the symbol for your investment and press CTRL+C
- Go back to Quicken
- Click in the ticker symbol box and press CTRL+V

Quicken Symbol Lookup

1. Select a type:
○ Stock ○ Mutual Fund ○ Index ◉ Any

2. Enter a full or partial name:
[lincare   ] [Search]

All matches for "lincare" (Most likely matches first):

Name	Symbol
LINCARE HOLDINGS INC	LNCR

Page 1 (Records 1 - 1 of 1)

Figure 9-7. Top: In the Name box, type part or all of the security name and then click Look Up to open a browser to Quicken.com's ticker search Web page.
Bottom: Quicken automatically fills in the name you typed and displays securities that match that name. The most likely candidates appear at the top of the list.

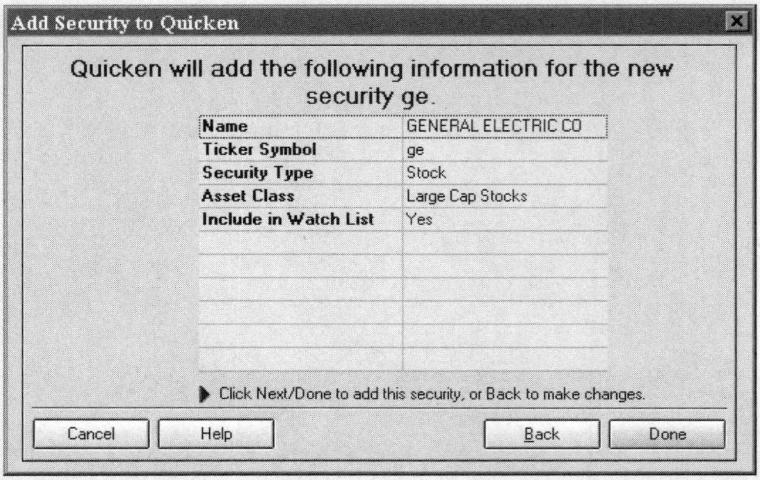

Figure 9-8. Quicken automatically fills in the security information, so your only job is to click Done.

Editing a Security

There's a lot more to securities than ticker symbol, number of shares, and price, as Figure 9-8 indicates. With a connection to the Internet, you don't have to provide Quicken with these details. Despite the program's best efforts, you'll still need to edit the details of a security every now and then. For example, the load on a mutual fund may change after you purchase it, or you may want to assign an investment to a specific investing goal.

To edit these details, in the Security List window (choose Investing → Security List), select the one you want to edit. Then, in the window menu bar, click Edit. The Edit Security Details dialog box appears, as shown in Figure 9-9. You can change any of this information at your discretion.

Usually, you won't need to edit the text boxes at the top of this dialog box, because the name, ticker symbol, and type almost never change. Here are some of the items you might want to change—and why.

▶ **Asset Class.** Quicken uses the values in the Asset Class section to determine the asset allocation of your investments (see page 345). In the Edit Security

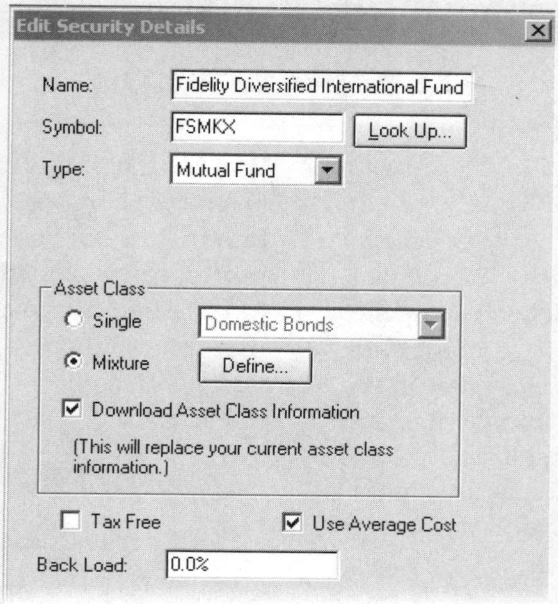

Figure 9-9. In the Edit Security Details window, you can Download Asset Class Information (as indicated in this figure) or edit other values at will.

Details window, the Single option lets you choose one asset class, which is ideal for a stock, bond, REIT, and so on. If the security is a mutual fund, chances are you'll choose the Mixture option and then click Define to specify the percentages in each asset class.

If you're a stickler for accuracy and disagree with the asset class designation that Quicken downloads, turn off the Download Asset Class Information checkbox, and set the asset class to your interpretation. (See the box on page 324 for more advice.)

► **Tax Free.** If the security is exempt from taxes, like some municipal bonds, turn on this checkbox to remove its income and gains from Quicken's reports of taxable events.

Asset Allocation

Smart investors know that asset allocation determines the lion's share of a portfolio's return. So what are these influential asset classes? As you can see in the figure, Quicken (with help from Value Line, an investment data and analysis provider) divvies up the investment universe into Domestic Bonds, Global Bonds, Large Cap Stocks, Small Cap Stocks, International Stocks, Cash, and a catch-all class called "other."

Asset classes each come with a unique combination of risk and return, which is based on decades' worth of historical performance. For example, small cap stocks tend to deliver higher average annual returns, but the risk of a stomach-wrenching nosedive in any given year is higher as well. On the other hand, domestic bonds deliver lower average annual returns but make up for that reduced return with less year-to-year volatility.

Instead of trying to make a big killing by investing everything in the next

Wal-Mart, financial advisors (and savvy investors) consider good asset allocation the foundation of a successful portfolio. By allocating dollars to different asset classes, your portfolio is more likely to grow steadily over the years with smaller drops during down markets.

Asset Class Mixture

Specify the asset class mixture.

Asset Class	Percentage
Domestic Bonds	0%
Global Bonds	0%
Large Cap Stocks	95%
Small Cap Stocks	0%
International Stocks	3%
Cash	0%
Other	2%
Unclassified	0%
Total:	100%
(Must equal 100%)	

Tip: If an investment is exempt from federal tax but not state tax (or vice versa), you can set up categories for each type of interest and dividend. For example, you can create a category called *Interest-StateFree* for interest that's exempt from state tax. When you create a new category (see the next section) and scan the tax line item drop-down menu, you can choose entries like "ScheduleB:Int inc., taxed only by state" or "Schedule B:Int. inc., taxed only by Fed."

▶ **Use Average Cost.** Turn on this checkbox if you want Quicken to use the average cost of your purchases of a security to calculate the cost basis when you sell, which is the easiest way to track shares sold. A *cost basis* is how much you paid, plus any commissions and fees for the purchase, for tax reporting purposes. The program turns this checkbox on automatically when you add a mutual fund.

Tip: The IRS has lots of rules about calculating cost basis, mostly so you can't keep changing the method you use to reduce the taxes you pay. If you want to change the Average Cost setting after you've sold some shares, it's a good idea to ask your accountant or financial advisor.

Categorizing Investments

Besides the Asset Class designation, Quicken includes two lists that you can customize to categorize your investments: security type and investing goal. Although asset classes are one way to categorize investments, you can't change the asset classes that the program uses.

Note: If you're anxious to start tracking your investment purchases and sales, you can skip this section for now and jump to Recording Investment Transactions on page 326. You can add investment categories later.

If you want to develop your own asset class list, you can take over Quicken's Security Type list for the job. This list comes with the usual suspects (Stock, Mutual Fund, Bond, and so on), but you can add, edit, or delete any type on the list. For example, if you invest in REITs and want to track real estate as an asset class, you can add Real Estate as a security type.

Tip: The downside to using the Security Type list for asset allocation is that you'll have pay a visit to the Security Details View window (page 316) to choose the type for each security you add.

The Investing Goal list lets you categorize your investments according to the reason you're investing the money. Although Quicken sets up the Investing Goal List with College Fund, Growth, High Risk, Income, and Low Risk, as you can see in Figure 9-10, you can change the list to match your unique sets of goals. For example, you might change the list to College Fund, Retirement, and Bahamas, if you're investing some money for your kids' education, some for your retirement, and some in high-risk high-return investments to buy a sweet Nassau bungalow. Then, you can generate an Investment Performance report and set the "Subtotal by" field to Investing Goal to see whether the returns for the investments for each goal are what you expect.

To set the Investing Goal as well as a few other fields, in the Edit Security Details dialog box, click Other. The Additional Security Information dialog box appears, as shown at bottom figure in Figure 9-10. These fields are completely optional, but you may fill in the Est. Income text box if you want to track how much income your portfolio generates as a whole. The Broker and Phone fields aren't particularly useful—you probably have that information already stored with your investment account.

Tip: The Comments field can hold notes and reminders about the security. For example, if a mutual fund has a new manager, you might make a note to watch for signs of poorer performance. The problem with the Comments field is that this information is usually out of sight, so it's up to you to remind yourself to check it.

Recording Investment Transactions

If you set up your investment accounts for online services and downloaded transactions (as described in Chapter 6), you'll save yourself hours of data entry

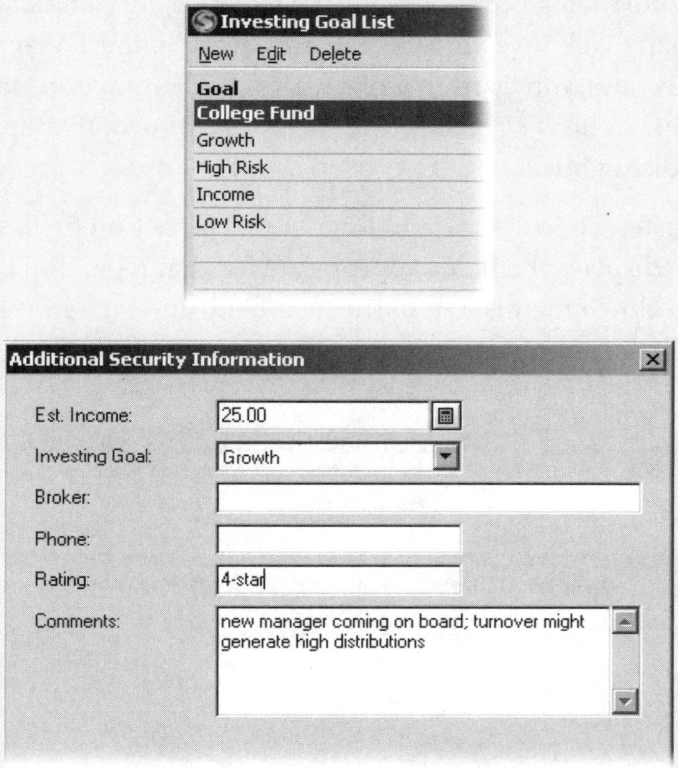

Investing Goal List

New   Edit   Delete

Goal
College Fund
Growth
High Risk
Income
Low Risk

Additional Security Information   [X]

Est. Income: 25.00   [▦]

Investing Goal: Growth   [▼]

Broker: [   ]

Phone: [   ]

Rating: 4-star

Comments: new manager coming on board; turnover might
generate high distributions

Figure 9-10. Top: Set up investing goals to match the goals for which you earmark investments. Then, you can produce reports to analyze performance by your investing goal.
Bottom: In the Additional Security Information dialog box, you can set the Investing Goal for a security. The Est. Income text box is also helpful for tracking potential income.

and head-scratching by letting your financial institution figure out how to record your transactions. If you don't have an Internet connection, or your financial institution doesn't work with Quicken, this section describes how to record the most common transactions.

You can record transactions directly in the account's register or use one of Quicken's helpful dialog boxes. The journey to entering transactions begins with the Account Bar. Click Investing Center, and then, on the Today's Data tab, double-click the account you want to work with. The Transactions tab that appears lets you edit the account's register, and includes a button that opens the Enter Transactions dialog box.

To use the register, choose a transaction type in the Action field, shown in Figure 9-11; Quicken displays the fields appropriate for that type. You can choose values from drop-down menus, tab to the next field, and type in values, just as you do for checking account transactions.

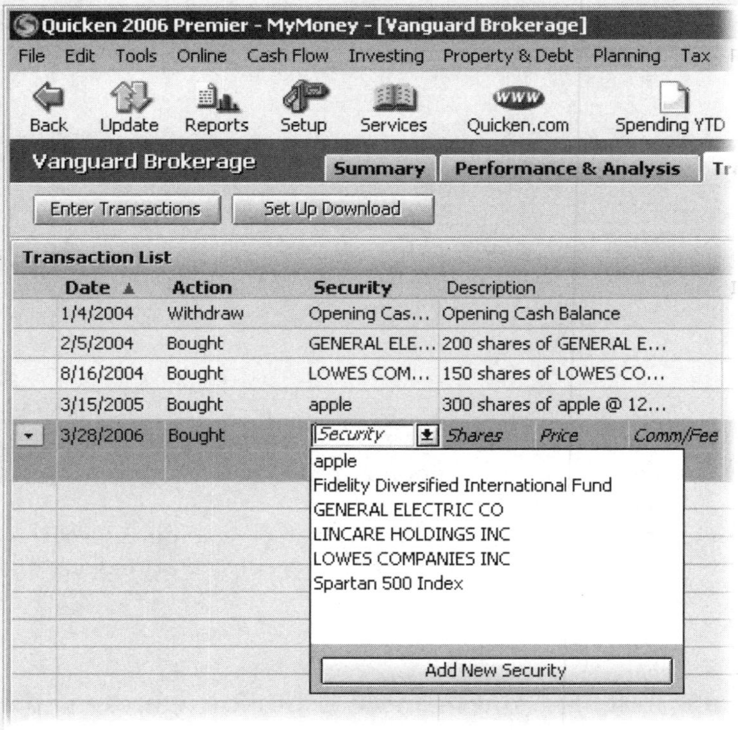

Figure 9-11. In the investment register, you can choose the type of transaction and the security from drop-down menus. The rest of the fields change based on the transaction you're recording.

To have Quicken show you a dialog box, click Enter Transactions at the top of the register. When the box opens, it initially sports a "Buy – Shares Bought" title and displays the fields for a purchase. To record a different type of transaction, choose it in the Enter transaction drop-down menu; the title and fields in the dialog box change accordingly. The following sections show examples of the dialog boxes you'll see for the most common transactions.

Purchasing a Security

When you buy a security, whether it's shares of stock, a bond, or a mutual fund, you use cash in one of your accounts to make the purchase. As you record the purchase, you tell Quicken what you're buying, the number of shares, how much you paid, and the commission. The program calculates the cost of the purchase and transfers the money from the cash account you specify. This section describes the fields you fill in when you purchase a security, which are shown in Figure 9-12.

To open the "Buy – Shares Bought" dialog box, click Enter Transactions. Quicken automatically selects "Buy – Shares Bought" in the Enter transaction drop-down menu. After you record the details of a transaction, click Enter/Done if you have no more transactions to record and want to close the dialog box. If you still have transactions to record, click Enter/New to save the current transaction and start a new one.

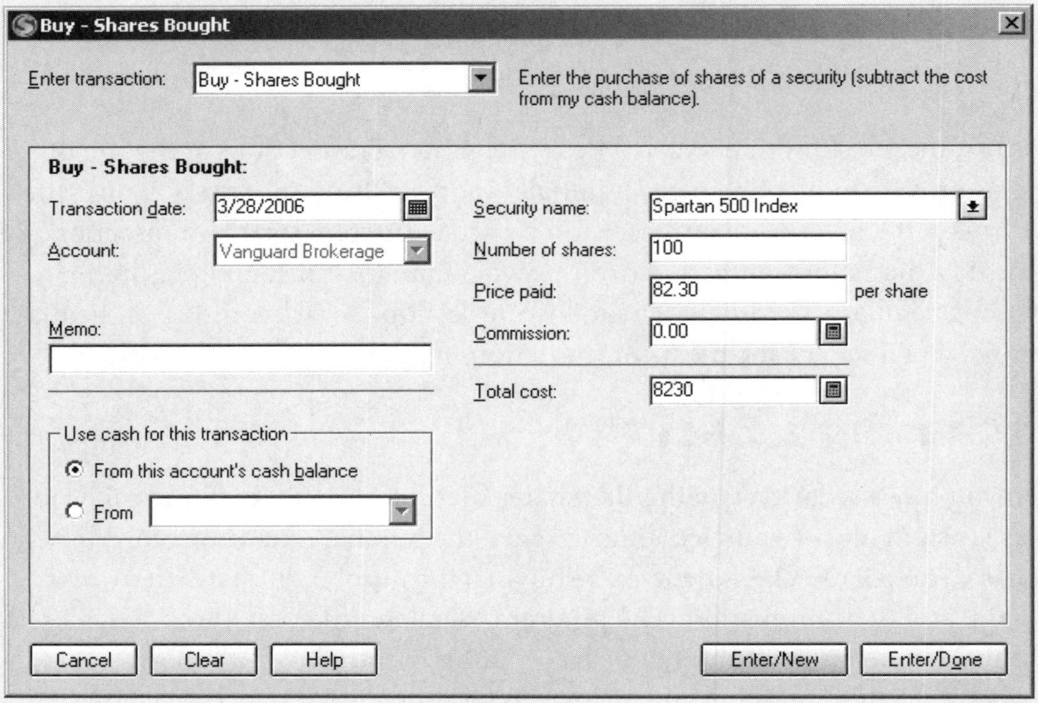

Buy – Shares Bought

Enter transaction:	Buy - Shares Bought ▼	Enter the purchase of shares of a security (subtract the cost from my cash balance).

Buy - Shares Bought:

Transaction date:	3/28/2006 🔲	Security name:	Spartan 500 Index ⬍
Account:	Vanguard Brokerage ▼	Number of shares:	100
		Price paid:	82.30 per share
Memo:		Commission:	0.00 🔲
		Total cost:	8230 🔲

Use cash for this transaction
- ⦿ From this account's cash balance
- ○ From [▼]

Cancel   Clear   Help   Enter/New   Enter/Done

Figure 9-12. Once you choose a transaction type in the Enter transaction drop-down menu, you can tab from field to field to record the details of the transaction.

Here are the fields you fill in when you purchase a security:

▶ **Enter transaction.** Choose "Buy – Shares Bought" to record the purchase of shares of stock, mutual funds, or precious metals. (Bonds have their own Bonds Bought transaction, described in the box on page 333.)

> **Tip:** You can record purchases of precious metals in the "Buy – Shares Bought" dialog box with a few minor translations of the text box labels. In your mind, replace "Number of shares" with number of ounces or number of coins. Then, in the "Price paid" text box, type the price per ounce or per coin.

- **Transaction date.** Quicken automatically fills in today's date. Change the date to the day you made the purchase.

- **Account.** Quicken automatically fills in the account whose register is visible. If you want to record transactions for a different account, close the dialog box; in the Account Bar, click the account; and then, in the account register, click Enter Transactions.

- **Security Name.** The drop-down menu displays all of the securities that you've added to Quicken. If you don't see the security that you've purchased, at the bottom of the drop-down menu, choose Add New Security, which immediately opens the "Add Security to Quicken" dialog box. After you add the security to your Security List, the "Add Security to Quicken" dialog box closes and you're back in the "Buy – Shares Bought" dialog box to complete the transaction.

- **Number of shares.** Type the number of shares you purchased.

- **Price paid.** Type the price per share, not the total amount you paid.

- **Commission.** Type the commission you paid to buy the security.

- **Total cost.** Quicken calculates the total cost based on the number of shares, the price per share, and the commission. If you purchase fractional shares, the total cost that the program calculates is almost always a few cents different from what your financial institution calculates. You can bring the two into agreement by editing the value for either the commission or the price.

The easiest approach is to adjust the value in the Commission text box to make Quicken agree with your financial institution. However, with fractional shares, the discrepancy usually arises because your financial institution calculates the number of shares to a higher degree of accuracy than Quicken. Because you can't match the number of shares, the price is the next best thing. To adjust the price, change the value in the "Total cost" field to match the financial institution's total. When you click another field or Enter/Done, the Recalculate Investment Transaction dialog box appears. Choose the "Price (recommended)" option and click OK. Quicken recalculates the price to make the totals match.

- **Use cash for this transaction.** If the cash for the purchase is in the cash balance for the investment account, select the "From this account's cash balance" option. If you're transferring cash from another account, like a savings account, choose the From option and then choose the account in the drop-down menu.

> **Tip:** Sometimes, you want to add shares to your account without using cash. For example, if you inherited 1000 shares of stock from your grandfather, you don't need any money to buy the shares. After you hand over the stock certificates to your broker, you record this addition using the "Add – Shares Added" transaction type.

Selling a Security

Selling a security is *almost* identical to buying it. In fact, the "Sell – Shares Sold" dialog box contains only two new features over the "Buy – Shares Bought" dialog box, as Figure 9-13 illustrates.

Here are the items in the "Sell – Shares Sold" dialog box that differ from the items you see when you purchase a security:

- **Sell all shares in this account.** If you reinvest dividends, you know that you end up owning fractions of shares. But those thousandths of a share continue to compound and add up to big bucks in the end. Until that time, they simply seem inconvenient. Quicken takes some of the pain away with this checkbox. Turn it on and Quicken automatically fills in the "Number of shares" text box with the number of whole and fractional shares you own in the account.

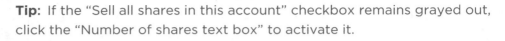

> **Tip:** If the "Sell all shares in this account" checkbox remains grayed out, click the "Number of shares text box" to activate it.

- **Specify Lots.** By choosing specific shares to sell, you can control the capital gains you realize and, thus, the taxes you'll pay on those gains. If you're selling a security in a tax-deferred account, you can ignore this button and simply type the number of shares into the "Number of shares" text box. Likewise, if

A Bit about Bonds

Bonds usually have a face value of $1,000, which means that each bond sells for $1,000 when it's first issued. For example, a $10,000 investment in a new bond issue buys 10 bonds. To record that in Quicken, choose Bonds Bought from the Enter transaction drop-down menu. In the "Number of bonds" text box, type the number of bonds you bought (the face amount you purchased divided by 1000).

Of course, as with any investment, bond prices change. They go up as interest rates go down and vice versa. If interest rates drop after you buy your bonds, the price increases—to $1,008.52 a bond, for example. But price quotes for bonds don't show the dollar amount the way quotes for shares of stock do. Instead, bond quotes are shown as a percentage of face value, which makes for more compact notation—100.852, for example.

Here's the higher math: Divide the current price of the bond (in this case, 1008.52) by the face value (1000) and then multiply by 100 to make it a percentage. The answer is 100.852. If you have trouble following this, ask your 8-year-old daughter. Multiplying by 100 and dividing by 1000 is the same as dividing by 10.

In the Bonds Bought dialog box, the Price text box is followed by the label "(base 100)." Base 100 is simply another name for showing bond prices as a percentage of the face value. So you can type the bond quotes you obtain directly in the Price text box without worrying about the math.

you've set up a security to use the average cost of shares for simplicity (see page 325), this button remains grayed out. Otherwise, to sell specific lots of a security, click the Specify Lots button, and Quicken opens the Specify Lots dialog box shown in Figure 9-14.

The Specify Lots dialog box gives you ultimate control over the shares you sell. You can type numbers in the "Shares to sell" fields to specify exactly which whole and fractional shares you want to sell. However, the buttons in the Auto Select section automatically handle the most popular lot selection tasks for

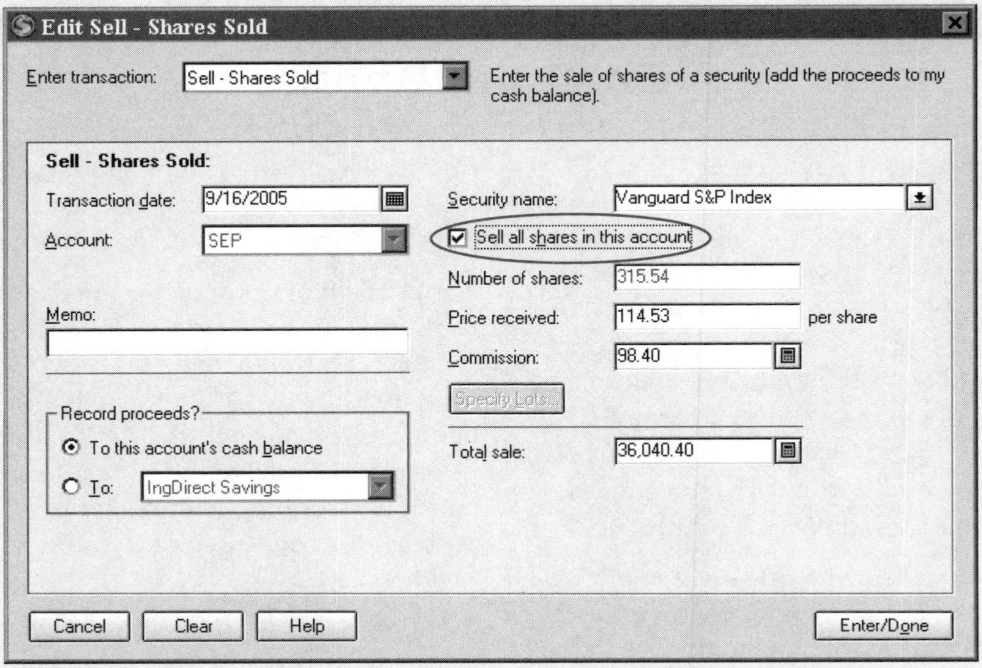

Edit Sell - Shares Sold

Enter transaction: | Sell - Shares Sold ▾ | Enter the sale of shares of a security (add the proceeds to my cash balance).

Sell - Shares Sold:

Transaction date: 9/16/2005 ▦

Account: SEP ▾

Memo:

Security name: Vanguard S&P Index ▾

☑ Sell all shares in this account

Number of shares: 315.54

Price received: 114.53 per share

Commission: 98.40 ▦

Specify Lots...

─ Record proceeds? ─
◉ To this account's cash balance
○ To: IngDirect Savings ▾

Total sale: 36,040.40 ▦

Cancel | Clear | Help | Enter/Done

Figure 9-13. If you turn on the "Sell all shares in this account" checkbox, Quicken fills in the "Number of shares" text box with the number of whole and fractional shares you own. Click Specify Lots (shaded here) to tell Quicken which shares you want to sell.

you. For example, if you click Minimum Gain, Quicken selects the most expensive shares you purchased to minimize your capital gains. Maximum Gain selects the least expensive shares to produce the largest capital gains.

Note: If you don't click Specify Lots and the security isn't set to use the average cost, Quicken sells the oldest shares first, which is the same thing as clicking First Shares In in the Specify Lots dialog box.

In the "Sell – Sold Shares" dialog box, two items have different labels for a sale, but their purpose is the same:

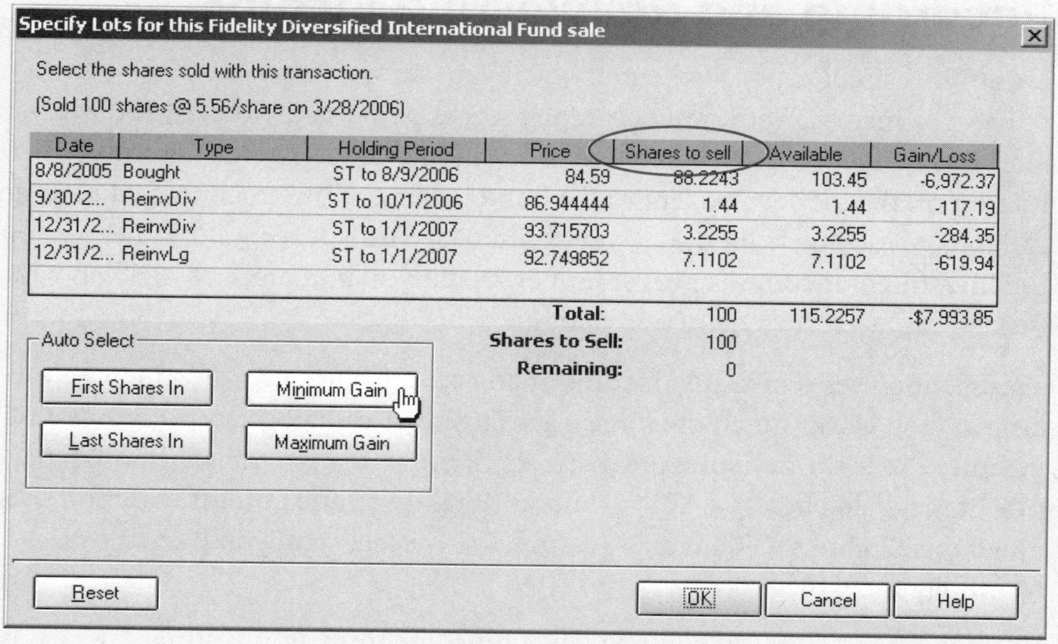

Figure 9-14. If you click one of the Auto Select buttons in the Specify Lots dialog box, Quicken chooses shares to sell. If you want to choose shares, type the values you want to sell into the "Shares to sell" column (circled).

▶ **Price received.** In the "Sell – Shares Sold" dialog box, someone pays you for the security you sell. Instead of "Price paid," as you see in the "Buy – Shares Bought" dialog box, you fill in the "Price received" text box with the share price the buyer paid you.

▶ **Record Proceeds?** This label corresponds to the "Use cash for this transaction" section in the "Buy – Shares Bought" dialog box. Select the "To this account's cash balance" option to deposit the proceeds from the sale into the cash balance of the investment account. To transfer the proceeds to another account, select To and then choose the account in the drop-down menu.

Recording and Reinvesting Income

Lots of investments pay dividends, which you can withdraw as cash to live on or reinvest to increase your nest egg. Many stocks pay cash dividends, and every once in a while you'll get a dividend in additional shares of stock. Bonds pay interest on the money you lent to the bond issuer. And mutual funds distribute all kinds of income from the smorgasbord of securities they hold. Whether you use investment income as pocket money or reinvest it, Quicken's dialog boxes make it easy to record these transactions.

This section uses reinvesting income as an example, but recording income you keep as cash works much the same way. To open the dialog box for reinvesting income, above the investment register, click Enter Transactions. Although the title of the dialog box says "Buy – Shares Bought," in the Enter transaction drop-down menu, choose "Reinvest – Income Reinvested," and you'll see the dialog box in Figure 9-15.

When you receive more than one type of income from an investment, which is almost always the case with mutual funds at the end of the year, using the "Reinvest – Income Reinvested" dialog box is much faster than adding each transaction individually. With your statement in hand, you can type the dollar amount for one type of income in the appropriate Amount field and type the corresponding number of shares in the Shares field.

Recording a Stock Split

A *stock split* is an interesting phenomenon. It changes both the number of shares you own and the price of those shares, so the value of your investment is exactly the same after the split as it was before. For example, a two-for-one stock split gives each investor *twice* the number of shares, each now at *half* the original price. Companies often issue a stock split to keep the per-share price within reach of everyday investors. (As an example of what happens without stock splits, consider Berkshire Hathaway, a company that has grown for years without splitting its stock. At more than $80,000 a share, few investors have the funds to buy even one share.)

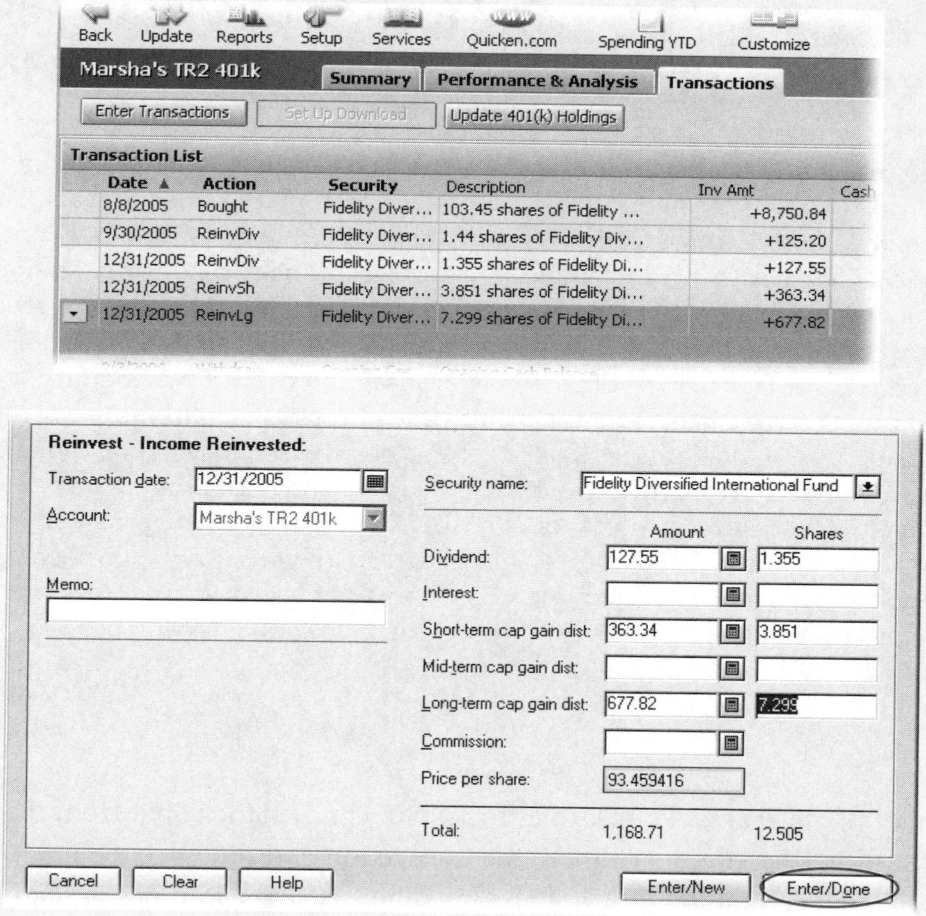

Figure 9-15. Top: As you type in the dollars and number of shares you received in different types of income distributions, Quicken calculates the total dollars and the total number of shares reinvested.
Bottom: Click Enter/Done (circled) in the Income Received dialog box, and Quicken adds separate transactions for each type of income you received.

Although you'd think it would be easier to tell Quicken the ratio of a stock split (like two for one), Quicken makes you enter the number of new shares and the

Recording Income and Stock Dividends

Because the "Reinvest – Income Reinvested" dialog box is meant for income that you immediately reinvest into more shares, it doesn't include a field to specify the account that receives the cash. For income that you retain as cash, in the Enter transaction drop-down menu, choose "Inc – Income (Div, Int, etc.)." The dialog box that appears includes a Transfer account field, which you change to the account that receives the cash. For example, if you keep the cash in the investment account, the Transfer account box should contain the same name as the Account box.

The other type of dividend that you see from time to time is a stock dividend. Instead of paying a dividend in cash, a company pays the shareholders by distributing more shares of stock. For a stock dividend, in the Enter transaction drop-down menu, choose "Div – Stock Dividend (non-cash)." Besides the security name, the only thing you have to provide is the number of new shares you received for each share you own. If you receive .02 shares per share, in the "New shares issued" text box, type *.02*.

number of old shares. To record a stock split, choose Stock Split from the Enter Transaction list. After you choose the transaction date and pick the name of the security that split, in the "New shares" text box, type the number of shares you own *after* the stock split. For example, if a stock splits two for one and you owned 200 shares, you now own 400 shares. In the "Old shares" text box, type the number of shares you owned before the split. The "Price after split" text box is optional—with new and old shares, Quicken can handle the math to figure out the stock price after the split.

Placeholder Entries

Quicken creates *placeholder* entries in your investment accounts, as shown in Figure 9-16, when you add securities to an account without providing all the information about your purchase. For example, if you include securities during account setup, Quicken knows how many shares you own, but not what you paid for them. Quicken also creates placeholder entries if you download investment transactions in which your financial institution says you own shares that don't exist in your Quicken records. Placeholder entries are great for getting you up and running quickly, but eventually you'll need to provide the rest of the information (to obtain accurate tax records when you sell a security, for instance).

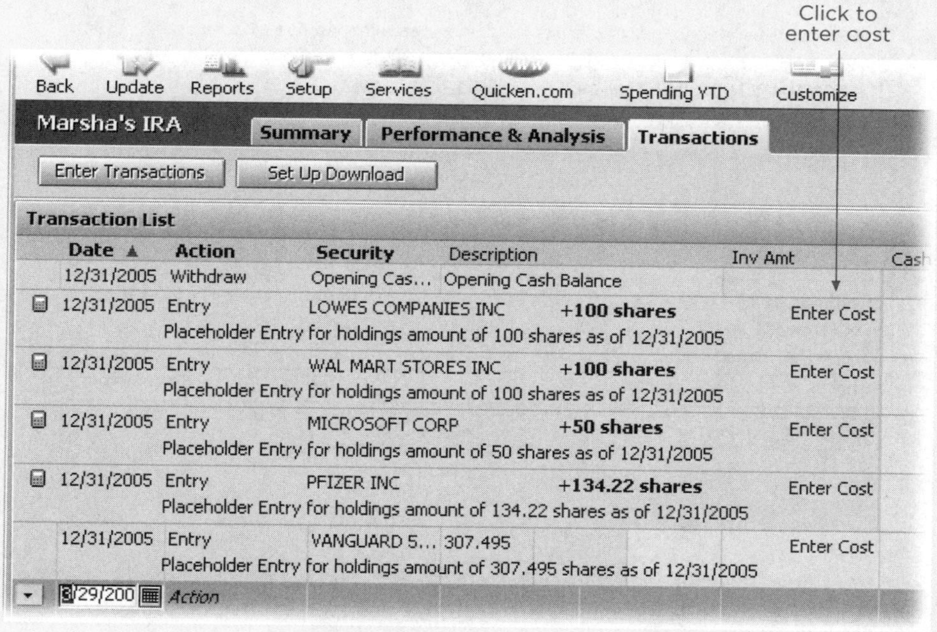

Figure 9-16. Placeholder entries show the security, the date purchased, and the number of shares. Click Enter Cost to fill in the missing information.

To convert a placeholder entry to an actual holding in your investment account, you must provide the purchase cost of the security. To provide the purchase cost, in the investment register, click the placeholder entry's Enter Cost link. The Enter Missing Transactions dialog box opens, as shown in Figure 9-17, which lets you provide the missing cost in two ways: the average cost to purchase all of the shares or by adding the missing purchase transaction. The following sections describe each approach.

Figure 9-17. Click Enter Missing Transaction to fill in the complete details of your purchase. Click Estimate Average Cost to quickly complete the transaction.

Enter Missing Transaction

If you need accurate records for tax reporting, in the Enter Missing Transaction dialog box, click Enter Missing Transaction. Quicken opens the "Buy – Shares Bought" dialog box with the transaction date and security name already filled in.

As described on page 331, you must fill in the "Number of shares," "Price paid," and Commissions text boxes to complete the transaction. For a security that you bought including reinvested dividends, you'll have to calculate the total amount you paid over time to fill in these fields.

> **Note:** If the shares in your account are the result of years of buying additional lots and reinvesting dividends, adding one transaction for all those reinvestments still doesn't provide accurate records for performance reporting. The only way to achieve completely accurate records for both taxes and performance reports is to add buy transactions for your original purchase and each reinvestment.

Estimate Average Cost

Click Estimate Average Cost if you don't have the data you need to provide accurate costs for your purchase. With this approach, your tax reports won't be accurate; nor will performance reports you generate. In the Enter Missing Transaction dialog box for average cost, all you have to provide is either the total amount that you paid for your shares or the average price per share (the total amount you paid divided by the number of shares purchased). When you click OK, Quicken fills in the Inv Amt field with the total amount you paid for the investment. However, the transaction still shows up as a Placeholder entry.

If you stumble across your missing paperwork later, you can fill in all the details of your purchase. In the investment register, double-click the placeholder entry transaction. In the Edit Adjust Share Balance dialog box that opens, click Enter History. This, in turn, opens the Enter Missing Transaction dialog box, shown in Figure 9-17. Click Enter Missing Transaction to fill in the details.

Evaluating Your Portfolio

Between investment reports and views, Quicken provides several ways to evaluate your portfolio. See "A Quick Guide to Quicken Reports" on page 359 to learn about the tabular reports and graphs you can produce and how to use them. This section provides an overview of the investment views and tools that Quicken offers.

The Investing Center is home to a host of investment features and analysis tools. In the Account Bar, click Investing Center. The Today's Data tab shows links you can double-click to open the register for any of your investment accounts. If you set up investment alerts (see the box on page 316), like price and volume for securities, you'll see these at the top of the tab. In addition, you can quickly review account balances, perform online updates, or review the watch list. These tasks are fine for a vague warm and fuzzy feeling, but none of these features help you make investment decisions. Read on to learn how to improve your investment performance.

The Portfolio View

In the Investing Center, click the Portfolio tab to see all the holdings in all your investment accounts, as illustrated in Figure 9-18. Because you can customize the columns that you see in this view, you can find a lot of what you need to know to make investment decisions. For example, if you include the average annual returns for different periods of time, you can see whether investments are delivering the result you expect.

Here are some of the ways you can customize this view:

▸ **Show.** In the Show drop-down menu, you can choose from dozens of views, like Asset Allocation or Tax Implications. Once you display a view, you can customize it further.

▸ **Group by.** You can change how Quicken groups your investments. In the "Group by" drop-down menu, choose from Accounts, Industry, Security, Security Type, Investing Goal, Asset Class, and Sector. For example, if you group securities by account, you can view the returns for individual investments as well as the overall returns for an account. If you want to see how much money you have in each security type, choose Security Type.

▸ **Customize View.** Click Customize View to open the Customize Current View dialog box. You can add, remove, and rearrange any of the columns that Quicken provides and specify the accounts to include and the securities you want to see.

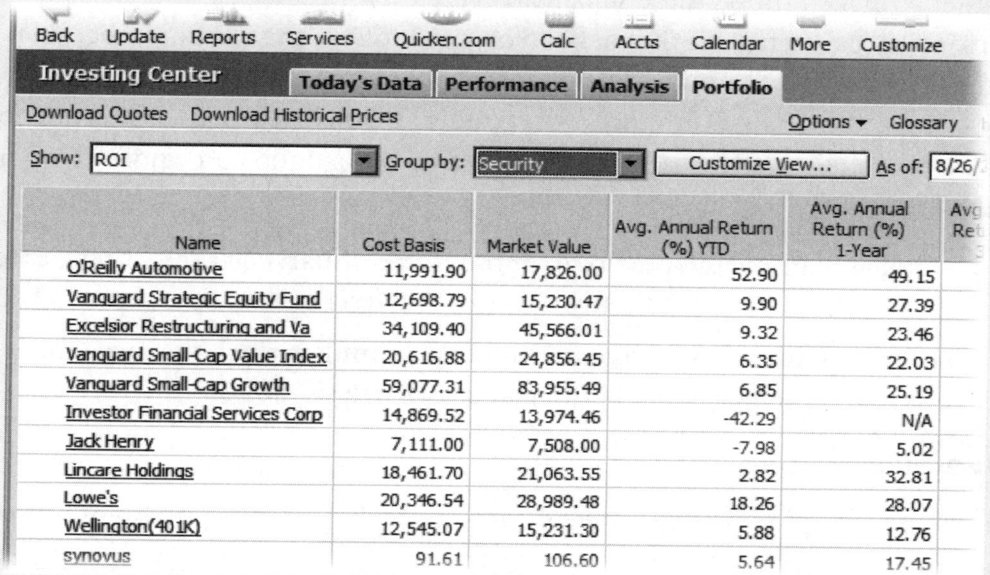

Name	Cost Basis	Market Value	Avg. Annual Return (%) YTD	Avg. Annual Return (%) 1-Year
O'Reilly Automotive	11,991.90	17,826.00	52.90	49.15
Vanguard Strategic Equity Fund	12,698.79	15,230.47	9.90	27.39
Excelsior Restructuring and Va	34,109.40	45,566.01	9.32	23.46
Vanguard Small-Cap Value Index	20,616.88	24,856.45	6.35	22.03
Vanguard Small-Cap Growth	59,077.31	83,955.49	6.85	25.19
Investor Financial Services Corp	14,869.52	13,974.46	-42.29	N/A
Jack Henry	7,111.00	7,508.00	-7.98	5.02
Lincare Holdings	18,461.70	21,063.55	2.82	32.81
Lowe's	20,346.54	28,989.48	18.26	28.07
Wellington(401K)	12,545.07	15,231.30	5.88	12.76
synovus	91.61	106.60	5.64	17.45

Figure 9-18. Click Customize View to select the columns that you want to see. To group your securities in different ways, in the "Group by" drop-down menu, choose a category.

- **As of.** In the "As of" date box, choose a date to see the portfolio values as of that date. For example, if you need to know your account balance for the end of last year, choose December 31.

Tip: You can view your portfolio as of different dates to try to find out when your Quicken records began to disagree with your statements. Type a statement date and compare the share values in Quicken to the statement. If they agree, type the date for the previous statement and repeat until you find the discrepancy.

Performance and Analysis

Like most investors, you'll develop a favorite way of measuring how your investments are doing. You can keep an eye on their average annual returns, for example, or compare their performance to a stock market index. In the Investing

Center, Quicken shows these statistics on the Performance tab. Most of the time, performance depends on the makeup of a portfolio—the allocation between different types of assets, and the quality of its individual investments. In the Investing Center, the Analysis tab shows the results of Quicken's analysis of a portfolio. You can evaluate performance and analyze your portfolio as a whole or by individual accounts:

▶ To look at your overall portfolio, in the Account Bar, click Investing Center and then click either the Performance or Analysis tabs.

▶ To review an individual account, in the Account Bar, click the investment account and then click the Performance & Analysis tab.

Overall portfolio

In the Investing Center, click the Performance tab to see the growth of one or more of your accounts. You can compare your performance to market indexes, as shown in Figure 9-19, to see whether your hard investing work pays off with market-beating returns. To select the accounts you want to evaluate, in the Show Accounts section, choose options like All, Investment, or Retirement.

Individual accounts

The Performance & Analysis tab for individual accounts displays three graphs: Account Value vs. Cost Basis, Asset Allocation, and Allocation by Security. In the Account Value vs. Cost Basis graph, the bars represent your account value each period. The line indicates your cost basis. If the line is below the bars, you've made money with your investments.

You can use the Asset Allocation graph to evaluate whether you're distributing your money in an account appropriately. For example, in a college fund account that you're getting ready to withdraw from, the asset allocation should be predominantly in low-risk investments like bonds or cash.

The Allocation by Security graph is a pie chart of the percentage that each investment holds in the account. If one investment makes up the lion's share of the balance, your account is at risk, should that investment tank.

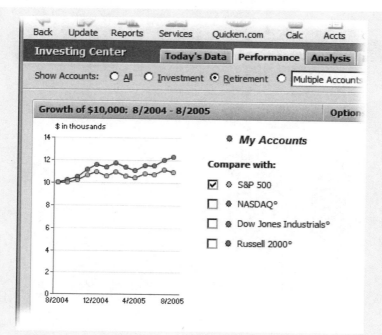

Figure 9-19. To compare your portfolio performance to market indexes, turn on the checkbox for the index that you want. For example, if you invest in small cap stocks, turn on NASDAQ. For large cap stocks, turn on S&P 500.

Evaluating Asset Allocation

The best way to evaluate asset allocation is by clicking Investing Center in the Account Bar and then clicking the Analysis tab. As you can see in Figure 9-20, Quicken shows your asset allocation compared to your target. The legend in the Asset Allocation section lists the percentage of your actual allocation in each class, the percentage you set in your target, and the difference between the two.

If the Difference is negative, you should consider moving money into that asset class. If the Difference is significantly positive, you should consider reducing your investment in that asset class. Of course, these are just guidelines. You must also evaluate other factors, like whether it's a good time to sell a particular stock.

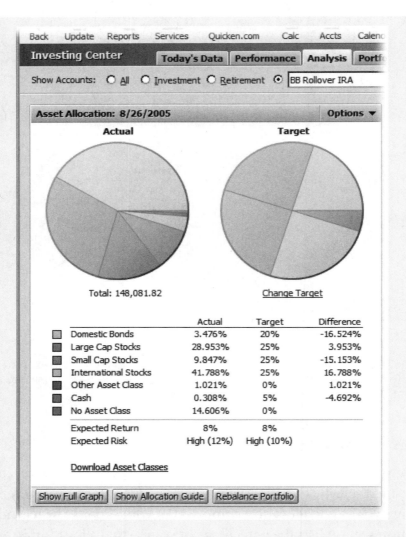

Figure 9-20. If your current asset allocation is significantly different from your target, click Rebalance Portfolio to figure out what changes to make.

If you click Rebalance Portfolio (or choose Investing → Portfolio Rebalancer), the Portfolio Rebalancer tool opens. It tells you how many dollars you need to add or subtract from an asset class to reach your target. If you double-click a pie slice in the Actual Asset Allocation pie chart, you can see the individual investments in that asset class. If you should increase the money in that asset class, these securities are potential candidates to buy. If you should reduce the money in the class, consider selling some of the shares.

ALTERNATE REALITY

Using Portfolio Management Software

If you're a serious investor, Quicken's portfolio features may not satisfy you. For instance, you may want to track the performance of individual investments as well as your overall portfolio. Or you might have more than one portfolio for different financial goals, each with its unique tax requirements.

If you're looking for more powerful portfolio management, Portfolio Record Keeper (PRK), developed by Quant IX Software, Inc. (*www.quantixsoftware.com*) may be the answer. PRK is a standalone program specifically for managing investments. It costs more than Quicken; $139; or $89 for members of the National Association of Investors Corporation (NAIC). However, if it helps you make one portfolio improvement or prevent one tax gaff, the program may pay for itself.

PRK can track an unlimited number of portfolios, yet, at the same time, track the combined values of several portfolios. For example, you can set up a retirement portfolio, a non-retirement.portfolio, and a college fund portfolio, and track them separately to see their individual performance, but also analyze them as a whole.

PRK also handles securities that Quicken can't; in addition to cash, moneymarket funds, all kinds of bonds, common and preferred stocks, and mutual funds, PRK can handle options, dividend reinvestment plans, and even investment club holdings.

The Quick Portfolio Setup feature lets you set up a portfolio with information from your latest brokerage statement or by entering historical transactions. If you already have investment transactions in Quicken, you can export your Quicken data to a .qif file (see "Exporting Quicken Data" in Online Appendix D) to import into PRK.

Capital Gains Estimator

If you want to estimate the effect of a sale on your taxes, choose Investing →
Capital Gains Estimator. This wizard calculates the capital gains tax you'd pay if
you sell a security. It can help you decide what to sell, depending on your goal
(like minimizing taxes).

This tool can also help you identify securities you can sell to offset your gains
with losses. If you don't have any cash to cover a big tax bill, you can also use the
Capital Gains Estimator to calculate the number of shares you have to sell to
obtain the cash you want and the cash you need for taxes.

Portfolio Analyzer

Choose Investing → Portfolio Analyzer to evaluate your portfolio in several
ways. The Portfolio Analyzer wizard displays results and suggestions in the following categories:

▶ **Performance.** The first section shows your average annual returns from the
year to date to the last five-year period. It also shows your five best and five
worst performers.

> **Tip.** Just because an investment is one of your worst performers doesn't
> mean you should sell it. For example, the stock may be in a lull just before
> it shoots up. Similarly, your best performers may be overpriced and candi-
> dates for selling to lock in profits.

▶ **Holdings.** The Holdings section shows pie charts and tables of your holdings.
Use this section to look for securities that make up an overly large percentage
of your portfolio. If that security takes a huge hit, so does your portfolio.

▶ **Asset Allocation.** This view is the same one you see on the Analysis tab for your
overall portfolio, as described in "Evaluating Asset Allocation" on page 345.

- **Risk Profile.** Each asset class has its own combination of expected return and risk (which is measured as how much the return varies from year to year). This section shows asset classes on a bar that ranges from low risk on the left to high risk on the right. Above this bar, you'll see your portfolio, positioned based on its risk.

- **Tax Implications.** This section shows your capital gains and losses for the year, grouped by short-term, mid-term, and long-term.

A Quick Tour of Quicken Planning Tools

Quicken includes several tools to help you plan for the financial events in your life, all of which reside on the Planning menu. Some of these tools are wizards that step you through planning for major goals like retirement. Quicken's financial calculators are self-contained dialog boxes that ask for a few pieces of information and then calculate a result, like the annual contribution you must make to save enough for your child's college education.

Quicken Planning Wizards

Describing the planning wizards in detail is fodder for another book, but the wizards make most of the steps and answers you must provide easy to figure out. This section introduces these tools and what they can help you do.

- **Retirement Planner.** This planner helps you figure out if you're on track to have enough money to make it through retirement. It doesn't leave any stone unturned in the process. You provide information from your age and life expectancy, your estimates of inflation, and investment returns to the assets you own, the contributions you make to retirement accounts, and living expenses you expect you'll need during retirement. As you can see in Figure 9-21, the plan result shows whether your plan is working. And if it isn't, you can try what-if scenarios.

- **College Planner.** As you might expect, the College Planner asks questions about the children going to college, how much you expect college to cost, sources of funding for college, and the savings and investments you have earmarked. In the "Can I afford college?" wizard, the last link is Internet

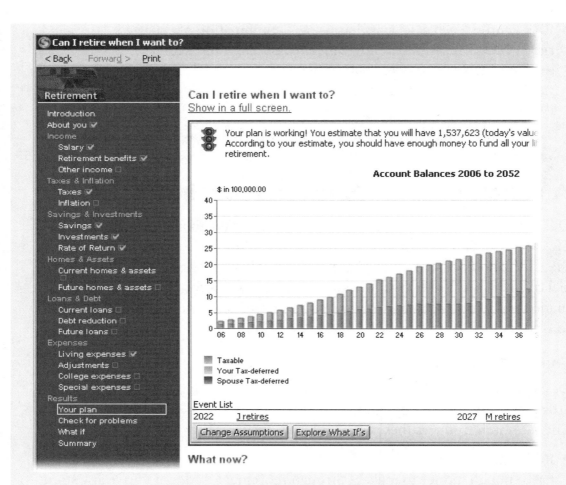

Figure 9-21. Step through the Retirement Planner wizard to tell Quicken about your plans for the future. The program figures out whether you'll have enough to last and lets you tweak values until you have a plan that works.

Resources, which displays links to several valuable Web sites, including sites that help you find financial aid.

▶ **Home Purchase Planner.** When you choose Planning → Home Purchase Planner, the "Can I afford that house?" wizard opens. You can provide information about your income and savings to find out the maximum monthly payment for which you qualify. This wizard can also help you find a house, although chances are you're working with a real estate agent for that.

- **Debt Reduction Planner.** If you're up to your ears in debt, you'll want to work with this planner before any of the others. You can learn which debts to pay off first to minimize the interest you pay (paying off the highest-interest-rate debts first is the most cost-effective). The Debt Reduction wizard actually has multimedia content, so you must insert your Quicken CD into your CD drive to use it.

- **Special Purchase Planner.** For any other major purchase, use the Special Purchase Planner to figure out how to pay for it. In this planner, you provide the cost of the purchase, when you plan to purchase, how you plan to pay, and whether the price might increase between now and the purchase date.

Planning Resources

If you want more help than Quicken provides, choose Planning → Professional Planning Resources. Quicken describes the different types of financial professionals you can use and what they do. You can learn how these professionals are paid and the questions to ask before hiring one. The Professional Planning Resources window includes a "Search online for a CFP Professional (Certified Financial Planner) option," which opens a browser to the Financial Planning Association's Planner Search Web site.

Financial Calculators

If you want to calculate a number without all the extra bells and whistles, choose Planning → Financial Calculators and then choose from Retirement Calculator, College Calculator, Refinance Calculator, Savings Calculator, and Loan Calculator. As you can see in Figure 9-22, you type in values and Quicken calculates results. For example, if you tell the Refinance calculator about your current payment and the new mortgage you're considering, it calculates your new payment and lets you see when the savings would recoup the closing costs.

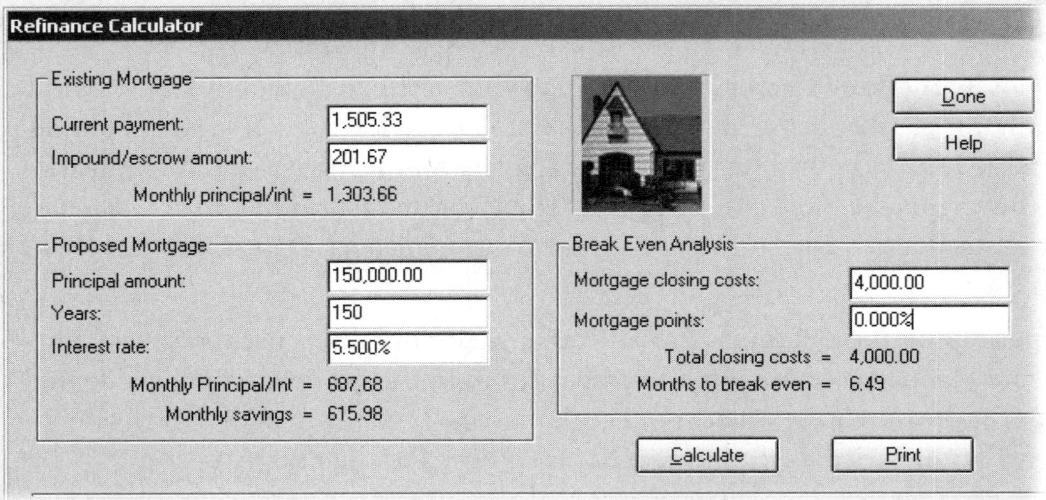

Figure 9-22. Fill in the text boxes in the Refinance Calculator, and Quicken calculates your new payment and how long it takes to break even from the closing costs.

Here's what the financial calculators do:

▶ **Retirement.** This calculator needs some bare-bones information about your retirement. You can calculate the current savings you'd need to succeed, the annual contribution you must make to reach your goal, or the annual income in retirement that your current plan produces.

▶ **College.** With some basic information about college education, you can calculate the annual college costs you can afford, the current savings you'd need to succeed, or how much you must contribute to save the amount you want.

▶ **Savings.** If you're using a savings account to save for a financial goal, you can calculate how much you have to contribute today to reach your goal, the regular contribution you'd have to make, or how much you'll have based on your current balance.

▶ **Loan.** This calculator can figure out the payment you'll owe if you borrow a specific amount or the total amount you can borrow given a specific monthly payment.

CHAPTER 10:
REPORTS AND GRAPHS

- ▶ Running Reports
- ▶ A Quick Guide to Quicken Reports
- ▶ A Review of Report Preferences
- ▶ Printing Reports and Graphs
- ▶ Customizing Reports
- ▶ Saving a Report

Quicken comes with dozens of built-in reports and graphs that show what's up (or down) with your personal finances. The only challenging aspect is figuring out *which* report tells you what you need to know and where you can find it. This chapter demystifies reports and the many ways of generating them.

If you're new to Quicken or financial lingo in general, EasyAnswer reports were made for you, as explained in the box on page 355. These reports tell you what they do in plain English—as in, "Did I meet my budget?" If none of the EasyAnswer reports meets your needs, the Reports & Graphs Center lists all of Quicken's reports. This chapter describes some of the more popular built-in reports, what they're good for, and where you can find them.

If you're a Quicken veteran (or trying to become one), you can take those built-in reports and customize them to your needs: tweak a date range, remove unneeded columns, or add subtotals in different places. You can then launch that report straight from the Reports menu or the Reports & Graphs window. In this chapter, you'll learn how to customize reports to get what you want and then save those reports for future use.

Tip: If none of Quicken's customization tools does what you want, see Appendix B to learn how to export a Quicken report to another program for fancy formatting and other fine-tuning.

Running Reports

Quicken's report categories are broad but distinct, so finding the right report can be as easy as scrolling through the Reports menu to a likely category, and then, on the category submenu, clicking the name of the report you want. But if you'd rather see all built-in and customized reports in one window, the Reports & Graph Center is a better option.

Finding and Customizing Reports

When you choose Reports → Reports & Graphs Center, the Reports & Graphs window opens showing you two clickable lists of reports: Quicken Standard Reports and My Saved Reports. One significant advantage of the Reports &

EasyAnswer Reports

There may be no easy answers in life, but there are some at the bottom of Quicken's Reports menu. EasyAnswer reports help you get started by presenting your options in the form of a question. If you see the question you've been asking yourself, choose it from the menu to start the report. Here are some of the most popular reports in this category:

* **How much did I spend on...?** You choose a category and a period and this report tells you how much you spent.

* **How much did I pay to...?** This report shows what you paid to a specific payee; perfect for finding transactions that you're sure you made, but the payee says otherwise.

* **Am I saving more or less?** This report shows how much money came in and how much went out for two time periods (for instance, this year compared to last year). At the bottom of the report, you saved money during a period if the overall total is positive. And if the value at the bottom of the Amount Difference column is positive, you saved more now than you did in the past.

* **What am I worth?** does the same thing as the Net Worth report (page 368).

* **Did I meet my budget?** produces a Budget report (page 299).

* **What taxable events occurred?** is a Tax Summary report (page 366).

* **How are my investments performing?** is the same as the Investment Performance report (page 363).

* **What are my investments worth?** produces a Portfolio Value report (page 364).

You can also find EasyAnswer reports at the bottom of the Reports & Graphs window.

Graphs window is that you can tweak a report before you run it. For instance, you can change the date range or specify which categories to include. Click a report name, and the Reports & Graphs window expands the report to include the key settings you can change, as shown in Figure 10-1. Click Show Report to see the results. Once a report is visible, you can edit the transactions it contains, as discussed in the box on page 358.

To run a report without any changes, click the report icon (which looks like a piece of paper). If a pie chart icon appears to the left of the report name, you can create the report as a graph. Click the pie chart icon or, if you clicked the report name to expand it, click Show Graph.

That's all there is to generating a report. In the report window, you can then save the report, print it, or click Customize to modify it (see page 373).

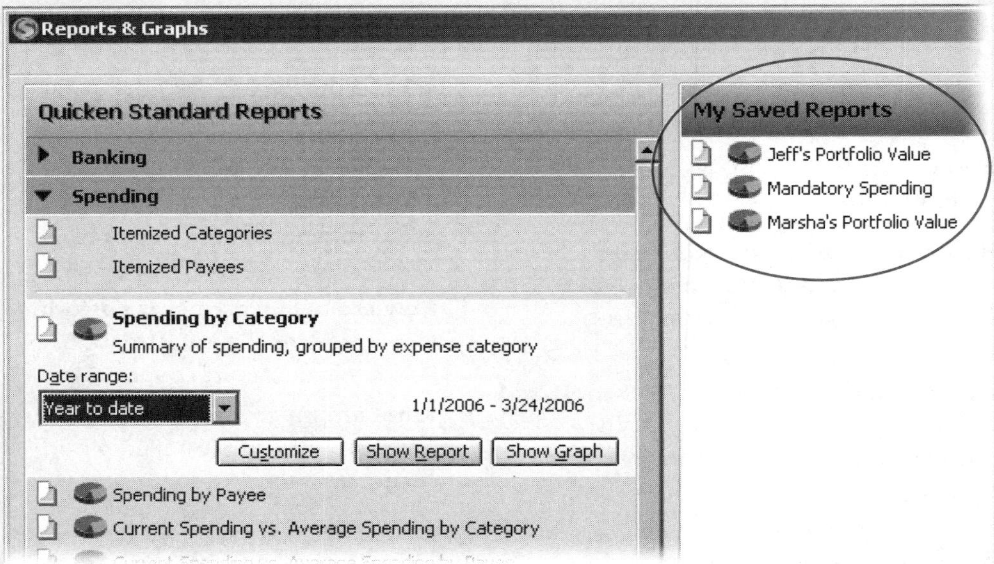

Figure 10-1. Click a report name from My Saved Reports to display settings that you can change before you generate the report.

Tip: Initially, the Reports & Graphs window displays folders that match the categories you see on the Reports menu. To expand a folder, click the triangle to the left of the folder name.

Generating a Report or Graph

In Quicken, almost every report is also available as a graph, and you can transform every graph into a tabular report. In the Reports & Graphs window, click either the report or graph icon to display that format. In a report window, you can click Show Graph or Hide Report to view either or both formats.

 Note: Transactions for hidden accounts don't appear in reports automatically. If you want to generate a report including transactions for a hidden account, first "unhide" the account by turning *off* the Hide In Quicken checkbox. (Press Ctrl+A to open the Account List window and then click the Manage Accounts tab.) Then hide it again after you produce the report.

You can take your pick of how you generate a report or graph. Here are your choices and why you might prefer each:

▶ **Reports menu.** When you know exactly which report you want and don't want to make any changes to it, the fastest method is to choose Reports, scroll to the report category, and, on the submenu that appears, click the report name.

The Reports menu includes several report categories, which display submenus of built-in reports. When you choose Reports → My Saved Reports & Graphs, the reports that you've customized and saved appear on a submenu.

▶ **Reports & Graphs window.** As you can see in Figure 10-1, you can run a report or graph in two ways in this window. Click the report or graph icon to run the report as is, or click the report name to first change settings before generating it.

▶ **Quicken icon bar.** You can add the customized reports that you run more frequently than you brush your teeth to the Quicken icon bar for one-click access, as described in Managing Reports on page 358.

Editing Transactions Within Reports

Every now and then, you generate a report, only to spot a mistake or something suspicious in a transaction, like an incorrect category or an uncleared payment in your checking account that you're sure you paid with a credit card. Quicken provides two convenient ways to edit or inspect transactions.

In Quicken 2006, Intuit has added the ability to edit some transaction fields directly in reports. You can select one or more transactions and add categories and memos that you overlooked. Or you can select a single transaction and correct its payee or category.

In a report, click a single transaction or Shift-click the first and last transactions in a group. Then, in the upper-left corner of the report (above the column headings), click Edit and choose the task you want to perform: Delete transaction(s), Recategorize transaction(s), Rename payee(s), or Edit memo(s).

You can also jump from a transaction in a report to the register in which it resides. Position the mouse pointer over a transaction in a report, and it changes to a magnifying glass. Double-click the transaction to open its corresponding register with the transaction selected.

Managing Reports

At the bottom of the My Saved Reports pane are two additional features for working with your customized reports. In Quicken 2006, you can add reports to the program's icon bar for ready access. In addition to editing and deleting your customized reports, this version of the program lets you categorize your customized reports.

▶ **Manage Toolbar Reports.** If you want to add one of your customized reports to the Quicken icon bar, click Manage Toolbar Reports. In the Manage Toolbar Reports dialog box, turn on the checkboxes for every report you want to launch from the Quicken icon bar, as demonstrated in Figure 10-2.

Figure 10-2. Add a few of your favorite reports to the Quicken icon bar to run them with one click.

▶ **Manage Saved Reports.** To edit, delete, or organize your reports and report folders, click Manage Saved Reports. You can create folders to categorize your customized reports, move reports to different folders, or edit or delete your reports. For example, a Marsha folder could hold reports for her stellar portfolio results. A separate folder for Jeff could show reports for his retirement nest egg. Reports that apply to the entire household can be in a household folder or no folder at all. Figure 10-3 shows the Manage Saved Reports dialog box and the results of putting it to use.

A Quick Guide to Quicken Reports

Most entries on the Reports menu are categories of reports. When you position the mouse pointer over a category, a submenu with report names appears. Read the following sections to learn what each Quicken report category represents—a big help in finding the reports you want—and which reports are most likely to help. If you still don't find the report that you want, you can explore all of the reports in the Reports & Graphs window—or head to page 373 to bone up on customizing reports.

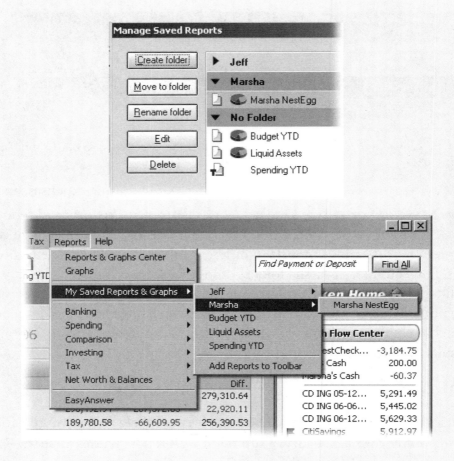

Figure 10-3. Top: Create and rename folders to categorize the reports you save. In the Manage Saved Reports dialog box, you can rename reports, delete obsolete ones, or move reports to a new and improved folder.
Bottom: If you organize your reports with folders, you can quickly find the report you want.

Banking

The Banking report category provides reports that summarize banking activity—deposits, payments, and transfers—in several ways. Here are some helpful reports in this category:

▶ The **Reconciliation** report (see Chapter 7) shows transactions based on whether they've reconciled or haven't yet cleared.

▶ The **Banking Summary** report shows your income, expenses, and transfers between accounts, grouped by category. This is the report to use if you want to see whether your income in a period is enough to cover your expenses, and to see transfers to savings and other accounts.

▶ The **Cash Flow** report is like the Banking Summary report without the transfers between accounts. It tells you whether your income is enough to cover your spending.

▶ The **Transaction** report doesn't set up much formatting, but it includes all transactions in all accounts for the date range you choose. If you want to customize a report to your liking, this report is a good place to start.

Spending

If you're perpetually short on cash or trying to squeeze more savings into your budget, knowing how you spend money is a great place to start. Quicken 2006 has added several new reports to help people discover how they spend money, which is a real plus now that the national savings rate is at an all-time low.

Here are some of the spending reports:

▶ **Itemized Categories** is a lot like the Banking Summary report except that it shows transactions for each category (income, expense, and transfers) for all of your accounts, not just for checking, savings, credit card, and cash.

 Tip: The Itemized Categories report initially shows summaries of top-level categories. To expand a category to see subcategories or transactions, click the + sign to the left of a category or subcategory name. This technique works on other reports that initially show summary values.

- **Spending by Category** shows only transactions for expense categories. If you can't do anything about how much money you make, use this report to focus on finding out where you can cut costs.

- **Current Spending vs. Average Spending by Category** compares how much you spent during one period (like the current month) to your average spending for another period. This report doesn't tell you how you're doing compared to your budget; it only shows whether you're spending more or less during the period than you usually do.

- **Income and Expense by Category** is like the Itemized Categories report without the transfers.

- **Monthly Budget** compares your income, expenses, and transfers to what you planned in your budget. This report is a better gauge of whether you're going to make ends meet than the "Current Spending vs. Average Spending by Category" report.

  When you customize a budget report, the Display tab in the Customize Budget dialog box includes a drop-down menu to select the budget you want to report on.

Comparison

Some of the reports in the Comparison category are repeats from other categories, like the "Current Spending vs. Average Spending by Category" report. And others take reports from other categories and add a comparison to another time period. For example, if you want to plan a future budget, the "Income and Expense Comparison by Category" report in this section shows your income and expenses for one period (such as the last 12 months) compared to your income and expenses for the previous year.

Investing

The Investing category has reports for all sorts of tasks—from tax reporting to planning to gloating over your success. If you have *any* investments, you're bound to use almost every one of these reports at one time or another.

- **Capital Gains.** This report tells you the capital gains you realized on securities you sold and is one thing your accountant asks for at tax time.

- **Investing Activity.** This report summarizes the activity in your investment accounts, including deposits and withdrawals you made; interest, dividends, and gains you received; and the change in market value for the securities you still own. For an overview of what contributed to the change in your portfolio value, this report is it.

- **Investment Asset Allocation.** How you allocate your investments to different asset classes is one way to measure the risk in your portfolio. For example, a portfolio dedicated to small-cap stocks is roller-coaster material, while a portfolio mainly but not entirely in bonds and CDs is steadier (but risk is due to inflation and interest rate changes). The best way to see if your portfolio is diversified is to generate this report as a graph, as shown in Figure 10-4.

> **Tip:** If you double-click one of the slices in the Asset Allocation pie chart, Quicken creates a second graph that shows the allocation of securities within that asset class. If you double-click a slice in this second graph, the program produces a report showing the performance of that security over time.

- **Investment Income.** Whether you need to know how much income you earned from investments for your tax return or you want to see whether your portfolio produces enough income for you to retire, this report shows how much you receive in dividends, interest, and capital gains.

- **Investment Performance.** This report calculates the average annual return your portfolio earned during a period. It uses the balance on the starting date, the present value of the portfolio, and the amount of time you're measuring to calculate this time-based return. For example, as shown in Figure 10-5, running this report for the individual stocks you pick and then running the report again for your index mutual funds can tell you whether you're as good a stock picker as you think you are.

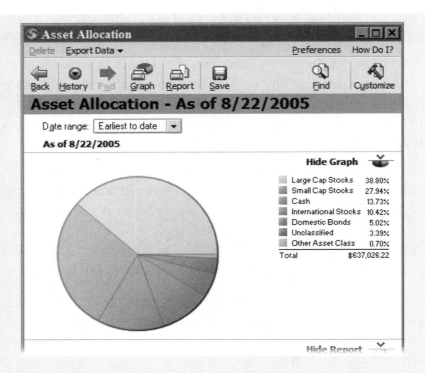

Figure 10-4. The Asset Allocation graph makes it easy to see imbalances between asset classes. In this example, you can see there are a lot of Large Cap Stocks. Maybe the portfolio needs to be rebalanced.

▶ **Investment Transactions.** This report shows all of your investment transactions from dividends to gains to transfers into your investment accounts.

▶ **Portfolio Value and Cost Basis.** If you want to know how much your portfolio is worth compared to how much you contributed, this report's for you. By letting you compare your portfolio's current value to cost basis (page 344), this report tells you how much your investments have earned. (A report that shows *only* portfolio value can be misleading, particularly if you're socking away oodles of money into an investment account but the return is mediocre.)

Stock Performance - Last 12 months

Date range: Last 12 months   Subtotal by: Don't subtotal

8/23/2004 through 8/22/2005

Show Graph

Hide Report

Date	Action	Description	Investments	Avg. Annu...
8/23/2004 - 8/22/2005				
8/23/2004		Beg Mkt Val	64,335.02	
10/1/2004	Cash	0.000		
10/27/2004	Cash	0.000	14,838.50	
10/29/2004	Cash	0.000		
8/9/2005	XOut	Money market		
8/22/2005		End Mkt Val		
TOTAL 8/23/2004 - 8/22/2005			79,173.52	26.35%

Index Performance - Last 12 months

Date range: Last 12 months   Subtotal by: Don't subtotal

8/23/2004 through 8/22/2005

Show Graph

Hide Report

Date	Action	Description	Investments	Avg. Annu...
8/23/2004 - 8/22/2005				
8/23/2004		Beg Mkt Val	106,037.86	
10/5/2004	ContribX		2,250.00	
12/8/2004	ContribX		1,000.13	
2/11/2005	ContribX	Pension BB	1,250.00	
4/13/2005	ContribX	Pension BB	2,750.00	
7/18/2005	ContribX	Pension BB	2,500.00	
8/22/2005		End Mkt Val		
TOTAL 8/23/2004 - 8/22/2005			115,787.99	22.87%

Figure 10-5. Top: This investment performance report shows the average annual performance for a stock portfolio for the last 12 months.
Bottom: By choosing only index fund securities in accounts, this report shows the performance for an index fund portfolio; in this example, there is a little less return than individual stocks, but a lot less work to manage.

Tax

Even if you work with an accountant, the Tax report category is a lifesaver when you want to collect the information that your accountant requests. You can generate reports specific to one tax form or dump all your tax transactions out in one fell swoop, as long as your Quicken categories are linked to tax line items (see the box on page 367).

Tax reports

Although it's the last report in the category, the Tax Summary report is the be-all and end-all of tax reports—it shows all of your tax-related transactions subtotaled by category. If you know how your Quicken categories correspond to lines on tax forms and you've diligently entered all of your tax-related transactions, you can produce this one report and start working on your return.

Tip: To check that you've recorded all monthly and quarterly tax-related transactions, run an itemized category report and make sure you see 12 transactions for monthly payments and four transactions for quarterly payments.

Other reports help you figure out where your tax-related data belongs. Schedule A-Itemized Deductions, Schedule B-Interest and Dividends, and Schedule D-Capital Gains and Losses show only the transactions that apply to that specific tax form. Moreover, the transactions are all neatly subtotaled by the Quicken categories that correspond to the tax lines on those forms.

Exporting tax data to Turbo Tax

If you go it alone preparing your tax returns, chances are you use Turbo Tax, Intuit's program for preparing tax returns. Because one of the big benefits of Turbo Tax is reusing data you've captured in Quicken, you'll be happy to see the "Tax Schedule (for export to Turbo Tax)" report in the Tax category. This report groups and subtotals all of your tax-related transactions by tax form.

Linking Categories to Tax Line Items

Tax reports will be depressingly empty if your Quicken categories aren't linked to tax line items. Fortunately, the program does a lot of this setup for you. When you create a data file, the built-in categories you choose are automatically linked to the correct tax forms and tax line items. Furthermore, when you set up your paycheck with the Paycheck Setup wizard (see page 168), the paycheck deductions you choose are also linked to tax line items.

The only time you need to worry about categories and tax line items is when you create your own categories. If you have categories of your own, you can check to see if they are linked to tax line items correctly. And if they aren't, it's easy to correct that omission—as long as you know the tax form and tax line to use.

Press Ctrl+C or choose Tools → Category List to open the Category List

window. If the list doesn't display Tax and Tax Line Item columns, at the top of the window, turn on the "Display tax information" checkbox.

If you spot a tax-related category whose Tax checkbox isn't turned on, or with a missing Tax Line Item, all is not lost—although the previous year's deductions might be. Select the category, and then right-click it and on the shortcut menu, choose Edit. In the Edit Category dialog box, be sure to turn on the category's "Tax-related" checkbox.

Select the "Standard line item list" option if you're linking the category to a line item on a commonly used tax form. If you're using a more esoteric tax deduction, select the "Extended line item list" option. In the drop-down menu, choose the form and tax line item to which the category corresponds. Click OK and the link is made.

Clearly, printing this report to paper isn't going to help Turbo Tax. To create an electronic file to import into the current year's version of Turbo Tax, in the report window menu bar, choose Export Data → "Report to tax export file."

Net Worth & Balances

If you want to see whether you've mortgaged yourself to the hilt or enjoy seeing numbers that indicate your obscene wealth, the reports in this category tell you that in two different ways.

- **Account Balances.** This report shows the balance in each account you have in Quicken. At the bottom of the report, the program subtracts liabilities from your assets to calculate the Overall Total. This result is also called your net worth (the net of what you own minus how much you've borrowed to own it).

- **Net Worth.** The Net Worth report lists all of your asset accounts first and totals them to show Total Assets (what you own). It then lists your liability accounts and totals the money you owe. But at the very bottom, the Overall Total is the same number you see at the bottom of the Account Balances report.

A Review of Report Preferences

Although Chapter 1 tells all you need to know about Quicken's preferences (page 37), a chapter devoted to reports wouldn't be complete without a brief review of report preferences. Setting the preferences in this section lets you choose how you want *all* of your reports to behave. Choose Edit → Preferences → Quicken Program to open the Quicken Preferences dialog box.

Reports and Graphs Preferences

Here are the preferences you can set for reports and graphs and what you can do with them:

- **Default date range.** By setting this preference, you tell Quicken the date range you want to use for any report that isn't already customized to a specific date range. For example, if you tend to generate reports to review your performance so far this year, choose "Year to date."

- **Default comparison date range.** This preference sets the date range that the program uses automatically when you generate a report that compares two date ranges.

- **Customizing reports and graphs options.** You have two choices for what Quicken does when you customize a report. If you want to keep original reports as they are, regardless of the changes you make in a report, select the "Customizing creates new report or graph" option. If you would rather have Quicken change a report to match your tailoring, choose the "Customizing modifies current report or graph" option.

 Note: If you modify one of Quicken's built-in reports and save it, the program doesn't overwrite the built-in report. It saves your customized report to "My Saved Reports and Graphs" (see page 381).

- **Customize report/graph before creating.** If you can't help making small changes to every report you generate, turn on this checkbox. When you choose a report from the Reports menu, Quicken automatically opens the Customize dialog box.

Reports Only

Tabular reports have a few preferences that determine what you see in the columns and how you interact with the results. Here are the preferences that apply only to tabular reports:

- **Account display.** Quicken automatically selects the Name option to show account names. But if you use abbreviated names and want to see details, choose Description. Or go whole hog and choose Both to display the account name and its description.

- **Category display.** The Name option, which the program chooses automatically, is fine most of the time. The only time you might choose Both is if you want to produce a report of all of your categories along with their descriptions, so you can plan updates to the Category List while lounging in the sun.

- **Use color in report.** Quicken turns on this checkbox automatically, which shows negative numbers vividly in red. You might decide to turn this checkbox off if you have a color printer and don't want to remember to turn off color printing.

- ▶ **QuickZoom to investment forms.** This checkbox is turned on initially, and there's no reason to turn it off. With this preference turned on, you can double-click report items to open the appropriate dialog box for editing that transaction.

- ▶ **Remind me to save reports.** This checkbox is also turned on initially. If you regularly customize reports to save for future use, this preference helps you remember to save those changes. However, if you've saved a host of reports and rarely need a new one, turn this checkbox off to prevent the interruption.

- ▶ **Decimal places for prices and shares.** Out of the box, Quicken sets this preference to 3. If any of your brokerage accounts provide prices and shares to more decimal places, change this setting so you can keep your records synchronized with your financial institution.

Printing Reports and Graphs

In Quicken, you can turn any report or graph you create into either a hard copy or a file. If you save a report as a file, you can use that file to feed other programs for more formatting or calculations.

Printing a Report

Telling Quicken to print a report is easy. In a window containing a report or graph, in the icon bar, click Print Report. In the Print dialog box that opens, Quicken offers printing options that you're probably familiar with from other programs, as shown in Figure 10-6.

Once you've selected the settings you want, click Preview to see if the report is correct before committing it to paper, or click OK to print the report.

Most of the options for printing a report are easy to figure out. The dialog box even includes icons for portrait and landscape orientation, in case you forget which prints "the long way." Here are the options that aren't immediately obvious:

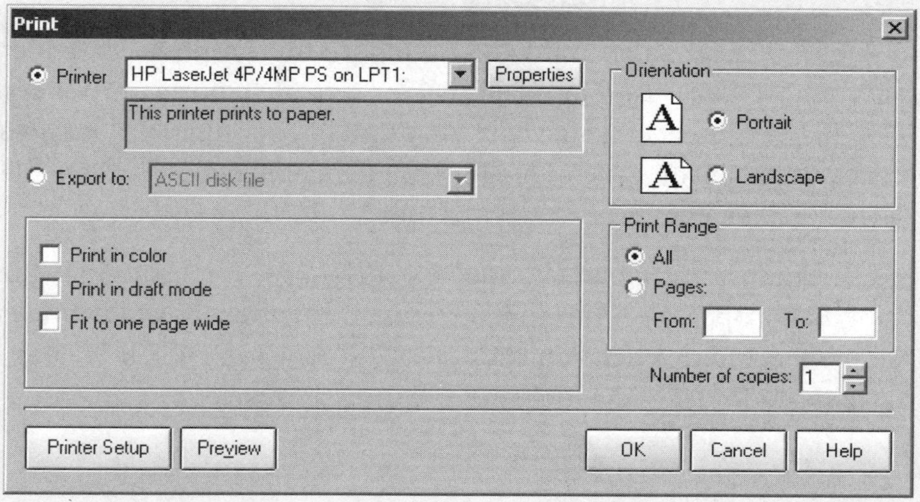

Figure 10-6. Select the Printer option and then, in the Printer drop-down menu, choose the printer to which you want to send the report. You can also choose page orientation, the pages to print, the number of copies, whether to print in color, and a few other options.

▶ **Print in draft mode.** If you're sprinting to the wire to deliver tax information to your accountant, you can turn on this checkbox to print your report using a printer font for faster printing.

▶ **Fit to one page wide.** If a report oozes past the width of a page like your Aunt Hilda on a picnic bench, turn on the "Fit to one page wide" checkbox to girdle the report back to one page width.

If you click Print Graph, the Print dialog box appears, but with more limited options. You can still choose the Printer or "Export to" options, a page orientation, the number of copies, and whether to print in color. If you have a color printer, be sure to turn on the "Print in color" checkbox to make the printed chart easier to read.

Saving a Report as a PDF File

New in Quicken 2006 is the ability to save reports and graphs as PDF files. Although you probably send tab-delimited or text-file reports to your accountant, PDF files are perfect if you want a snapshot of your finances that no one can edit. For example, if you generate reports for loan applications, a PDF file ensures that a bank employee doesn't change a value inadvertently.

In a report window menu bar, choose Export Data → "Report to PDF format." The Print dialog opens, but this time with the Printer text box filled in with Quicken PDF Printer. When you click OK, the "Save to PDF File" dialog box opens. Choose a folder and a filename and then click Save.

Saving a Report to a File

For some reason, Intuit provided two places to transform reports into files. The Print dialog box contains an option to create ASCII text files, tab-delimited files, and comma-delimited files. But you can also create tab-delimited files by choosing Export Data → "Export to Excel compatible format" (see Appendix B). The tab-delimited files that you create in both dialog boxes are identical, so you can generate them with whichever method you prefer.

The easiest way to generate tab-delimited files, which separate each piece of information with a tab character, is from a report window menu bar. You may think that the "Export to Excel compatible format" command applies only to Excel, but many programs can read tab-delimited files. In the "Create Excel compatible file" dialog box, click a folder and a filename, click Open, and your tab-delimited file is ready to import into another program.

The Print dialog box takes a few more clicks, but that's the price you pay for getting to choose any of the three file formats that Quicken handles. In a report window icon bar, click Print Report to open the Print dialog box. Just below the Printer option are the "Export to" option and a drop-down menu of file formats. Here are the choices and when you might want to use them:

- **ASCII disk file.** This format produces a text file that *looks* like the report, but uses space characters to position values in columns and uses different fonts. You can use this format to store an electronic version of your report, but it won't import properly into a spreadsheet or other program.

- **Tab-delimited (Excel compatible) disk file.** Choosing this format produces a file with tab characters separating each value. Although the choice says "Excel compatible," many programs can read files in this format.

- **.PRN (123-compatible) disk file.** Despite this format's convoluted name, it produces a plain old comma-delimited file, which works with 123, Excel, and most other programs. Use this option if you want to import a report to a program that doesn't handle the tab-delimited format that the "Export to Excel compatible format" command produces.

After you choose the type of file and click OK, Quicken opens the Create Disk File dialog box, in which you can specify the filename and where you want to save the file.

Customizing Reports

As you can see in Figure 10-7, the report window provides several ways to customize reports, depending on whether you're looking to nudge a column over, tweak the date range, or perform a major overhaul.

Tip: If you're editing your report to make it fit better on the printed page, consult the box on page 374, too.

You can't edit the way report contents appear right in the report window like, say, a spreadsheet or text document. Instead, you tweak the report's settings in a dialog box, and let Quicken make the changes to the report. Here are your options:

- **Reports & Graphs window.** If you choose Reports → Reports & Graphs Center, you can customize reports *before* you generate them. In the Reports & Graphs window, click the name of a report and then change the settings that appear. Click Show Report to generate the customized report.

Fitting More Report onto Each Page

When a report contains column after column, it's hard to squeeze everything onto a single page of paper. Quicken automatically prints the columns that don't fit on additional pages, but trying to read these multi-page reports leads to paper rustling, grumbling, and ghastly adhesive-tape accidents. Try these approaches for keeping your report to one page width:

* Before you click Print, reduce the width of the report columns. In the report window, drag the double vertical lines between column headings to the right to make a column narrower. Also,

remove any report columns you don't want. (See "Customizing Reports" on page 373 for more info.)

* In the Print dialog box, turn on the "Fit to one page wide" checkbox.

* In the Print dialog box, choose the Landscape option for page orientation. When a report almost fits on an 8 1/2 by 11 sheet of paper, switching to landscape orientation should do the trick.

Before you print, click Print Preview to review your changes before committing them to paper and ink.

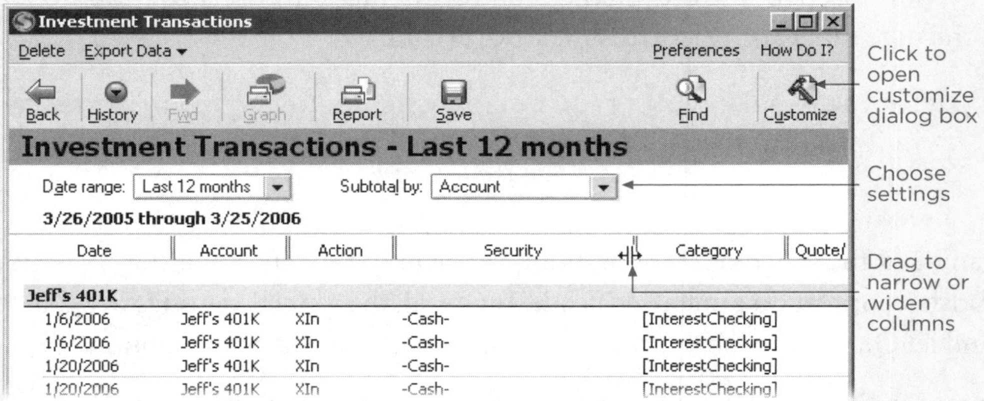

Figure 10-7. In the report window, you can choose date ranges or columns to tweak the report and drag heading separators to resize columns. Click Customize to open a dialog box with even more options (page 373).

- **Customize icon.** At the top of the report window, the icon bar includes the Customize icon, which opens the most powerful of Quicken's customization tools—the Customize dialog box.

- **Report window drop-down lists.** Below the icon bar, you'll see drop-down menus for changing settings, such as the date range or which column to use for subtotaling the report contents.

- **Report headings.** You can drag the double vertical lines between column headings to the left or right to make a column narrower or wider, respectively.

> **Note.** One thing you have almost no control over is the headers and footers of reports. In fact, the only thing you *can* change here is the title of a report. In the Customize dialog box, click the Display tab and, in the Title text box, type the title you want to use. Quicken automatically adds the date range for the report and pages numbers to the report header.

Date Ranges

Different reports call for different date ranges. For example, tax reports often apply to the previous year, whereas a spending report might be for the present year to date. Quicken contains over a dozen preset date ranges that work based on today's date. For example, if it's March 12, 2006, "Year to date" represents January 1 through March 12, 2006, but Last Month covers February 1 through February 28, 2006. And, if none of these date ranges do what you want, "Custom dates" opens a Custom Date dialog box with From and To text boxes for choosing or typing in specific dates.

> **Tip:** Try to avoid *saving* reports using Custom dates. These dates won't change with the passage of time—and eventually you won't care how much you spent on tie-dye T-shirts in 1968.

The pre-set date ranges are numerous, because they mix and match several types of date ranges.

- **Include all dates.** If you're trying to find a payee by searching through old credit card charges, choose "Include all dates." This time period encompasses the first date in your Quicken data file up to and including today.

- **Durations.** Quicken includes three repeating time periods: Monthly, Quarterly, and Yearly. If you choose one of these, the program sets the report to that duration, but also includes an additional drop-down menu to specify which month, quarter, or year you want to see.

- **To Date durations.** You can choose from "Month to date," "Quarterly to date," and "Year to date," which are particularly useful for budget-versus-actual reports. "Earliest to date" does the same thing as "Include all dates." "Custom to date" lets you pick the starting date and the report covers that date to today.

- **Last periods.** Although you can choose periods that range from "Last month" to the Last 12 months, at tax time, "Last year" is a very handy time period to pick. With this date range, you can report on the previous year's data at any time during the present year.

Because date ranges are the most widely revised settings, Quicken gives you several places to set them:

- In the Reports & Graphs window, click a report name to display a date range drop-down menu.

- In a report window, below the report title, you'll see a "Date range" drop-down menu.

- In the Customize dialog box, the "Date range" drop-down menu is in a section of its own at the very top of the dialog box.

Subtotals

In a report window, you can group and subtotal results in several ways, depending on the report. For example, the built-in Investment Performance report comes without any subtotaling; the transactions appear in chronological order. So you may want to add subtotals by account to see the performance return for your accounts separate from your husband's. Or, you can subtotal by security type, investing goal, or asset class to see which kinds of investments are living up to your expectations.

You can change the fields used to subtotal your report in two places:

▶ In the report window underneath the report title, the "Subtotal by" drop-down menu offers several ways to subtotal that makes sense for the report.

▶ In the Customize dialog box, click the Display tab. In the Headings section, look for the "Subtotal by" drop-down menu.

Figure 10-8 shows an example of how subtotaling can convey the information you need.

Adding and Removing Columns in Reports

Each built-in report comes with a set of columns, all of which are initially displayed. In some reports, you can't change the columns at all, but in others, you can choose which of the columns to hide or show.

As you can see in Figure 10-9, checkmarks show the columns that are visible. Clicking a turned-on checkbox turns off a column. Clicking an empty box turns the column on. To return the report to the columns that Quicken displayed originally, click Reset Columns.

Customizing Other Report Content

As you can see in Figure 10-10, the Customize dialog box includes several tabs, which change depending on the type of report you're working on. Each tab contains all sorts of tailoring tools, many of which can remain as they are through years of successful Quicken use.

Here are some of the tabs that appear and some of the changes you can make on each:

▶ **Accounts.** You can choose the accounts to include in a report to produce more surgical reports; for example, to examine your retirement accounts separate from your spouse's. You can turn accounts on and off by clicking them one at a time or by clicking Mark All or Clear All. Quicken initially hides accounts that you marked as Hidden in the Account List (see page 69). If you want information from bank accounts you've closed (and subsequently hidden in Quicken), turn on the "Show (hidden accounts)" checkbox.

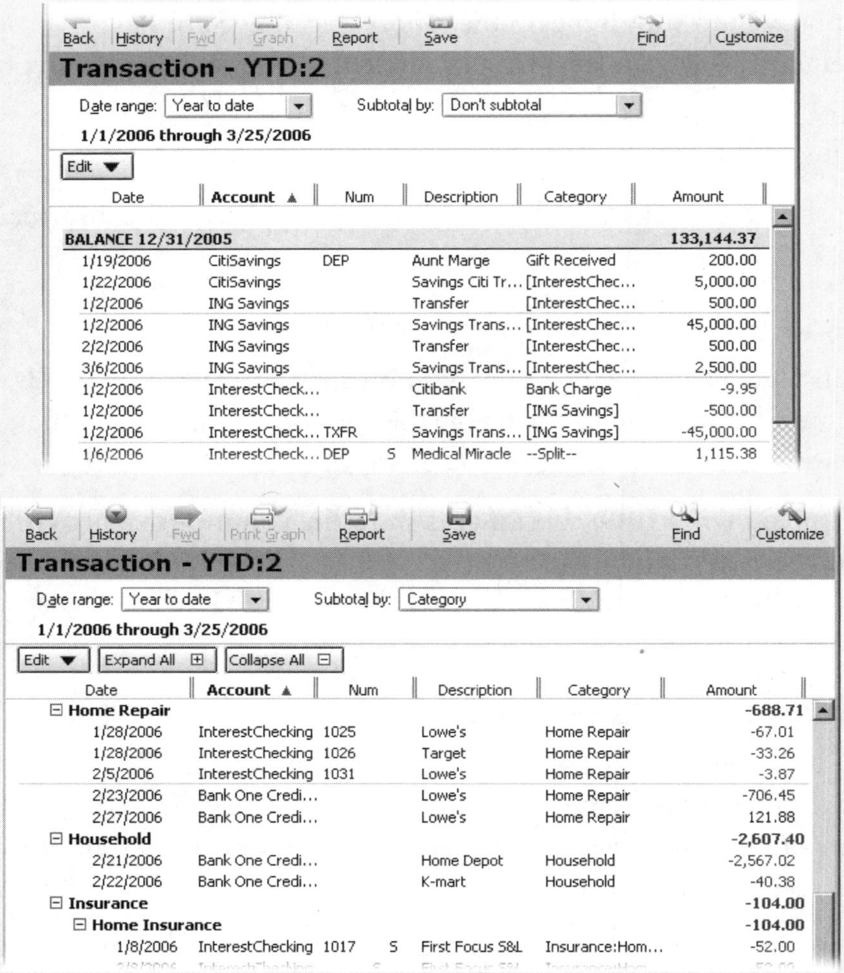

Figure 10-8. Top: Without subtotaling, Quicken displays report results in chronological order.
Bottom: By subtotaling results (by subcategory in this case), you can see how much you spent in different categories, or how much you earned from different investments.

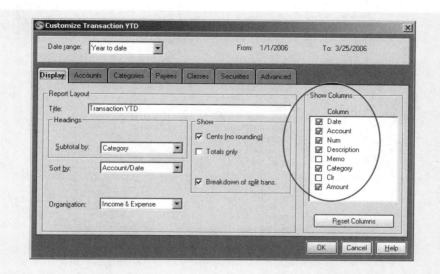

Figure 10-9. In some reports, you can turn columns on or off by clicking their check-boxes. If you can't modify the columns in a report, the Show Columns section is conspicuous by its absence.

▶ **Categories.** You can choose individual categories, turn all categories on or off, or search for a specific category. You can also add additional criteria to look for transactions assigned to a specific payee, or that have categories and memos that contain the text that you specify.

▶ **Advanced.** The Advanced tab is, well, advanced, but some of the settings can come in handy more than you'd expect. For example, if you want to look for transactions that have obstinately remained uncleared, you can turn off the "Newly cleared" and Reconciled checkboxes and keep the "Not cleared" checkbox turned on. To change any report to a tax-related report, turn on the "Tax-related transactions only" checkbox.

Tip: The "Include unrealized gains" checkbox is good for what-if games. Suppose you want to see how your taxes would be affected if you sold different stocks in your taxable investment account. Turning on this checkbox would show the capital gains you'd have if you sold stocks at their current prices.

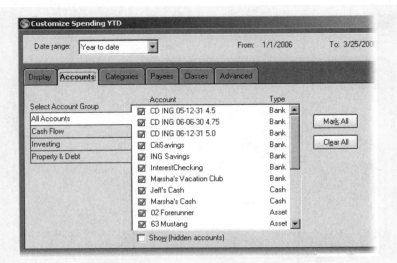

Figure 10-10. Top: Choosing accounts to include is a common change to reports. You can turn individual accounts on and off, or turn all accounts on and off at once. Bottom: Choosing categories is a great way to pinpoint trouble spots in your spending or find specific transactions.

Sorting Reports

Some Quicken reports come sorted, but the sort order isn't immediately obvious. If a report is sortable, in the report window menu bar, you'll see the Sort command. Click Sort and a menu of sort options appears with a checkmark to the left of the current sort order. Choose the sort order you want, and Quicken applies it to the report immediately. (You can also click Customize. The "Sort by" drop-down menu is on the Display tab in the Customize dialog box.)

Sort orders for reports are similar to the sort orders you can apply to an account register. For example, the "Sort by" drop-down menu includes Account/Date, Date/Account, Account/Check#, Amount, Payee, and Category.

 Note: In the Customize dialog box on the Display tab, you can turn off the Cents checkbox to see amounts rounded to whole dollars.

Saving a Report

Once you've customized a report, there's no sense in repeating the same steps every time you need to run the same report. That'd be silly. By saving your customized reports, you can run them again and again by choosing Reports → My Saved Reports & Graphs, and then choosing the report name.

A saved report memorizes all your settings—things like date range, accounts, categories, sort order, and so on—but not the data itself. For example, if you save a report whose date range is set to Monthly, the report initially shows the results for June when you run the report in June, but shows results for December when you run the report in December.

Saving a report is so easy, there's no reason ever again to recreate a customized report.

1. **Review the report to make sure that it contains the information and formatting you want. Then, in the report window icon bar, click Save.**

   Quicken opens the Save Report dialog box.

Tip: If you notice later that you missed a setting, you can make that change and save the report again. If you use the same name for the saved report, Quicken asks you to confirm that you want to replace the existing saved report.

2. **In the Report name box, type a name that indicates what the report does, like *Marsha's Portfolio Performance*.**

   If you intend to add the saved report to the Quicken icon bar (see page 357), make the report name brief but as meaningful as possible.

Tip: Position your favorite reports at the top of the customized reports list by putting a letter "A" at the beginning of their names.

3. **If you want to save the report to a certain folder, in the "Save in" drop-down menu, choose the folder you want.**

   If you don't save the report to a folder, the report appears below the folders on the My Saved Reports & Graphs submenu. (Saving customized reports and graphs to folders is new in Quicken 2006.)

4. **Click OK.**

   Quicken saves the report.

APPENDIX A: KEYBOARD SHORTCUTS

▶ Task Shortcuts

▶ Working with Transactions

▶ Dates

▶ Moving Around in Quicken Windows

You can perform almost any task in Quicken simply by clicking something—the Icon Bar, a toolbar, a shortcut menu, a menu-bar menu, or an onscreen button. But the seconds you spend mousing around from click to click insidiously eat away at your productivity.

If you spend even a few minutes a day with Quicken, keyboard shortcuts are your friend. They take you right where you want to go in a fraction of a second. This appendix lists Quicken's most useful keyboard shortcuts. Each section starts with the best ones to commit to memory.

For a complete list of Quicken's keyboard shortcuts, search the Help file (press F1 to open Help) for "keys" or "Quick keys." (Quicken Help doesn't have an index entry called "keyboard shortcuts.")

Task Shortcuts

These keyboard shortcuts open the windows and dialog boxes for the tasks you perform most often.

TASK	KEYBOARD SHORTCUT
Open a file.	Ctrl+O
Back up a file.	Ctrl+B
Open the Quicken Help window to the topic for the current window or dialog box.	F1
Open the Account List window.	Ctrl+A
Open the Category List window.	Ctrl+C if "Quicken standard mapping" is turned on in Preferences; Shift+Ctrl+C if "Windows mapping" is turned on
Open the Memorized Payee List window.	Ctrl+T
Open the Scheduled Transaction List window.	Ctrl+J

TASK	KEYBOARD SHORTCUT
Open the Write Checks dialog box to a new check.	Ctrl+W
Open the Calendar window.	Ctrl+K
Open the Portfolio View window.	Ctrl+U
Open the Security List window.	Ctrl+Y
Print the current transaction or report.	Ctrl+P
Open the Quicken Home window.	Alt+Home

Working with Transactions

Whether you're creating, editing, saving, or deleting transactions, keyboard shortcuts make your work move faster.

TASK	KEYBOARD SHORTCUT
Record the current transaction.	Ctrl+Enter; or Enter, if the Tab key is set to move from field to field in Preferences
Select an item in a list, such as a category in a transaction drop-down menu.	First letter of item
Memorize a transaction to the Memorized Payee List.	Ctrl+M
Find a transaction.	Ctrl+F
Go to a new transaction in the current register.	Ctrl+N or Ctrl+End
For a transfer between two accounts, go to the corresponding transaction in the other account.	Ctrl+X (if "Quicken standard mapping" is turned on)
Void a transaction.	Ctrl+V (if "Quicken standard mapping" is turned on)
Insert a transaction in the current register.	Ctrl+I
Delete the current transaction.	Ctrl+D

Although some of these keyboard shortcuts are old friends, they all help you edit portions of a transaction more quickly.

TASK	KEYBOARD SHORTCUT
Recall a name and fill in the field (QuickFill).	Type the first few letters of the name, and then press Tab
Scroll in the QuickFill list.	Ctrl+up arrow or Ctrl+down arrow
Increment a check or other transaction number by one.	+ (Plus key)
Decrease a check or other transaction number by one.	- (Minus key)
Open the Split Transaction window.	Ctrl+S
Cut a field in a register.	Shift+Del
Copy a field in a transaction.	Ctrl+Ins
Paste a copied field in a transaction.	Shift+Ins
Delete the character to the right of the insertion point.	Del
Delete the character to the left of the insertion point.	Backspace

Dates

When choosing the date for a transaction, you don't have to type the date or click the calendar. Here are some handy keyboard shortcuts for moving to the date you want. When a date field is active, press these keys to change the date.

TASK	KEYBOARD SHORTCUT
Move to the next day.	+ (Plus key)
Move to the previous day.	- (Minus key)
Change the date back to today.	T
Display the Date calendar.	Alt+down arrow
Choose the first day of the month.	M

TASK	KEYBOARD SHORTCUT
Choose the last day of the month.	H
Choose the first day of the year.	Y
Choose the last day of the year.	R

 Tip: For shortcuts that move to the beginning or end of a time period, such as M, pressing the key additional times moves further forward or backward in time. For example, if pressing M once moves to June 1, pressing M two more times moves to April 1.

Moving Around in Quicken Windows

These shortcuts apply to windows and dialog boxes.

TASK	KEYBOARD SHORTCUT
Move down one row (that is, to the next transaction in a register or report).	Down arrow
Move up one row in a register or a report.	Up arrow
Move to the first transaction in a register, or the first row in a report.	Ctrl+Home
Move to the last transaction in a register or a report.	Ctrl+End
Move to the next field.	Tab or Enter, depending on your preference setting
Move to the previous field.	Shift+Tab
Move to first field in a transaction.	Home twice
Move to last field in a transaction.	End twice
Move to the beginning of the current field.	Home
Move to the end of the current field.	End
Move down one screen in a scrolling window.	Page Down

TASK	KEYBOARD SHORTCUT
Move up one screen in a scrolling window.	Page Up
Choose the transaction dated the previous month in a register window.	Ctrl+Page Up
Choose the transaction dated the next month in a register window.	Ctrl+Page Down

APPENDIX B:
QUICKEN HELP

▶ Quicken Help

▶ Task-Specific Quicken Help

▶ Quicken Product and Customer Support

▶ The Quicken Forums

▶ Other Quicken Resources

Between planning your financial moves and recording them in Quicken, you're bound to need some help along the way. Unfortunately, finding answers to your questions isn't always easy. Quicken's online help is renowned for telling you what you already know, while remaining mysteriously silent on what you don't.

Quicken Help, which you access within the program, is best when you're looking for step-by-step procedures. It falls short, though, when you're trying to learn what Quicken can do and how to apply it to your present financial quandary. The Quicken online forums, accessed via the Internet, are a better source of answers to gnarly problems like how to allocate a refinanced loan to pay off an old mortgage and a plethora of closing costs. As you'll see in this appendix, there are many ways of finding help—one of which is sure to suit your style.

 Tip: A Google search can glean solutions to Quicken problems from a wide variety of Web sites.

Quicken Help

If you tend to flit from topic to topic as you work, Quicken Help keeps quick answers at your fingertips. Choose Help → Quicken Help. On the left side of the Quicken Help window are three tabs, each of which offers a different way of finding information. Each method has its pros and cons:

▶ **Index.** The Index tab is ideal when you're looking for help on a series of topics. You can scan the index just like one in a book. On the Index tab, as you type a keyword, the index jumps to the closest matching index entry, as demonstrated in Figure B-1. When you see the keyword you want, double-click it to view corresponding help topics. If more than one help topic applies to your keyword, Quicken displays a dialog box in which you can choose the specific topic you want.

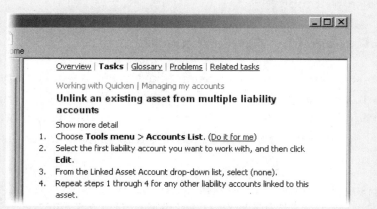

Figure B-1. Top: Double-click an index entry to find related help topics.
Bottom: Most help topics contain step-by-step procedures, but some provide brief
descriptions of what you can do with Quicken features. Underneath the topic title,
click the "Show more detail" link to read about optional or less-frequented features.

Tip: At the bottom of each help topic, you can see the Quicken editions to which it applies. Before you get too excited about a feature, check whether your version of the program includes it.

- **Search.** The Search tab lets you type in more than one keyword. When you type in your keywords and click List Topics, Quicken looks for the topics in Help that contain all of the keywords you provided. Typing more keywords limits the topics you see (with luck) to the ones that answer your question.

- **Contents.** If you crave instruction on a broad topic, the Contents tab is the fastest way to see what's available. You can drill down through main topics (like Investing), to specific tasks (like "Set up or edit a watch list").

Tip: As you navigate from one help topic to another, you can click Back in the Quicken Help icon bar to display previous topics, or click Print to print the current topic.

Task-Specific Quicken Help

When you're in the middle of a task and have no idea what an option or button does, crawling through help topics is way too much trouble. There's no reason to ignore options that you don't understand or click buttons without quite knowing what they do. Here are a couple of ways to find help topics directly related to what you're doing:

- **F1.** Pressing F1 opens Quicken Help to the topic most relevant to the task at hand. For example, if the Write Checks window is active, pressing F1 displays the "Write a check" topic. Pressing F1 while you're staring at the Category List displays the "Working with categories" topic, which includes some background as well as links to how-tos for category-related tasks.

  Some topics do help, but others aren't worth the click to view them. For example, one help topic for payee addresses warns you to limit the number of lines to five if you want the address to print properly. Pretty good advice. But the help instructions for updating addresses give "obvious" a whole new meaning: "Update the address and any other necessary information...".

Hiding the %$^&*# Help Window

Besides telling you what you already know, the Quicken Help window has another annoying quirk. It won't yield the floor (or screen, in this case) when you click the main Quicken window. For example, clicking a register selects a transaction, but the Quicken Help window resolutely sits on top, blocking your view (and ability to turn on checkboxes or otherwise complete your task).

If you want to read the Help instructions *and* perform the steps of a task at the same time, an enormous monitor is the ideal solution. If you aren't so fortunate, here are some other options:

* **Hide.** In the Quicken Help window icon bar, click Hide, which reduces the width of the window by hiding the pane with the Contents, Index, and Search tabs. All you see is the pane with the Help text. When you want to find another topic, click Show in the icon bar to display the three tabs again.

* **Minimize.** In the top right corner of the Quicken Help window, click the Minimize button, which hides the window (and the instructions). When you're ready to read about the next step, click the Quicken Help button (the one with a yellow question mark) in the Start menu bar to restore the window to view.

* **Resize panes and windows.** Make the Help window smaller by dragging the border between the search pane and the text pane. Drag the right side of the Help window to make it narrower. Quicken wraps the contents in both panes to fit the new slimmer profile.

▶ **Help button.** The Help button that lurks at the bottom of most dialog boxes also opens Quicken Help to a topic specifically about the features in the dialog box, as Figure B-2 illustrates.

▶ **How Do I?** At the right of each Quicken window's menu bar, you find the How Do I? command. Click it to open a Quicken Help window filled with links to how-to topics for that window, as shown in Figure B-3.

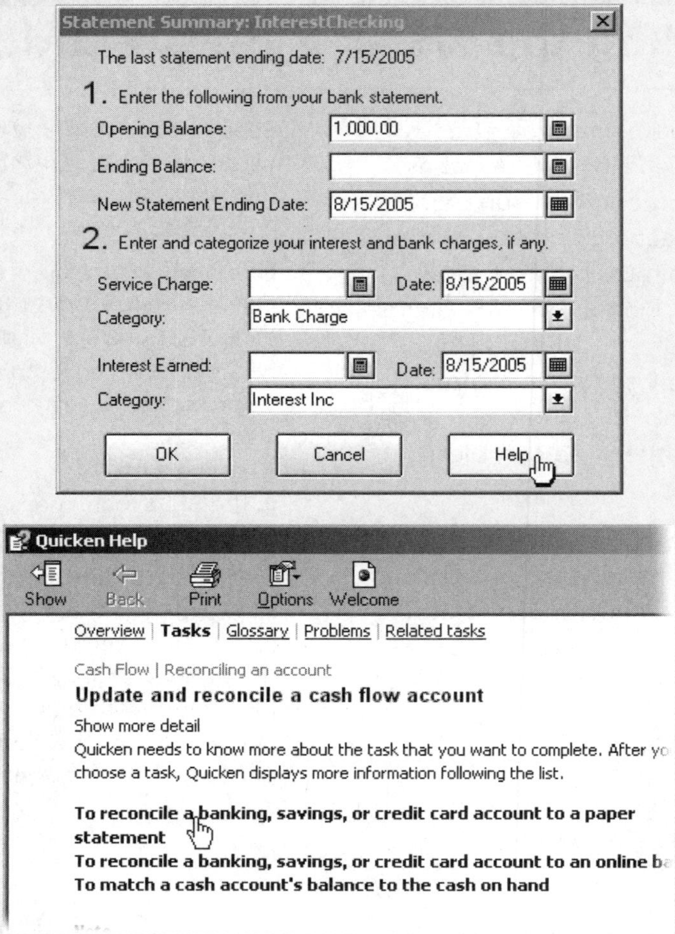

Figure B-2. Top: If a dialog box contains a Help button, click it to learn how to put the dialog box to use.

Bottom: The help topic you see relates to the task that the dialog box performs, but it also may contain subtopics. If a hand pointer appears when you point to a subtopic, click to read more instructions.

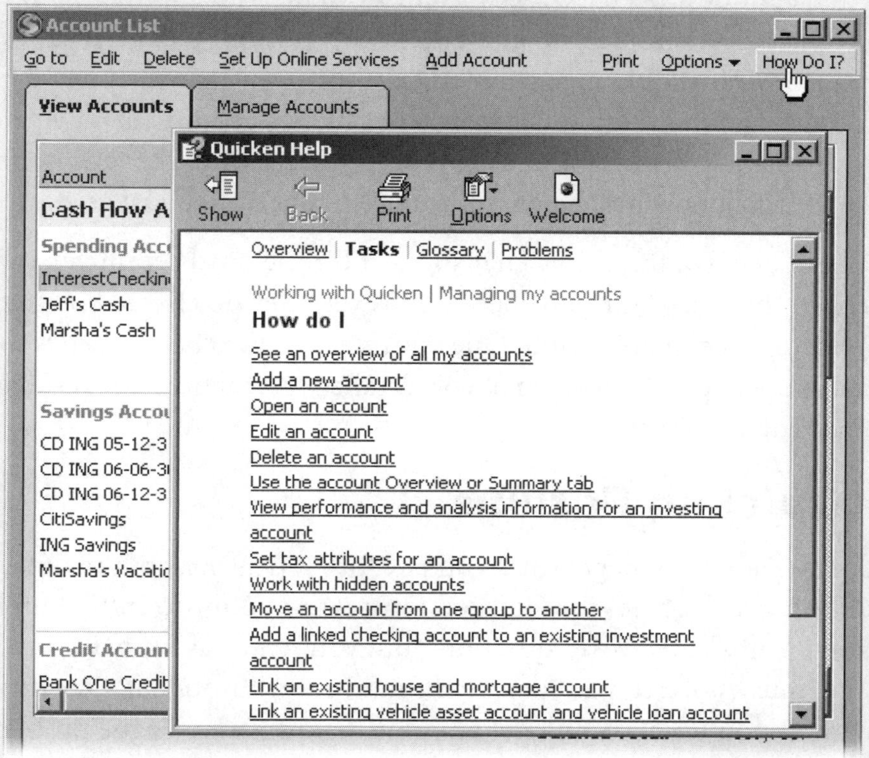

Figure B-3. Choosing How Do I? in a window menu bar lets you choose from a number of related help topics.

Quicken Product and Customer Support

If you're desperate enough to pay for assistance, choose Help → "Product and Customer Support" to open a window with links to all manner of assistance—both free and for-fee. As well as same the Help files you've seen (and given up on) in Quicken, there are links to a variety of online resources, support pages, and phone numbers. You can click the Quicken Technical Support Home Page link to access the Quicken knowledge base. Or click the "Contact Intuit and Others" link to find the phone number for fee-based technical support.

Quicken telephone and chat support hooks you up with a human—sometimes for a price. However, there's no guarantee that an Intuit technical support person can solve your problem, particularly if it involves financial finesse in addition to Quicken handholding. Support fees can be steep, which adds unneeded stress to an already stressful situation. Before you resort to the telephone or chat, see "The Quicken Forums" below for free help that's often just as effective.

Intuit doesn't charge for online chat support for the most recent version of Quicken (in this case, Quicken 2006). However, they do charge for chat support if you're using an earlier version. One advantage to the chat service is that the technical support person will email you detailed instructions for resolving your problem if you ask for them.

The Quicken Forums

Although the adage "You get what you pay for" is true *most* of the time, don't be mislead by the lack of fees for Quicken forums. Not only do Intuit employees prowl the forums and answer questions, but you're just as likely to get an answer from someone who's felt your pain and found a way through it. One downside to the forums is you usually don't get an immediate answer. Vague problem descriptions and rambling questions may not get a response at all. (See the box on page 397 for advice.)

To use the forums, you must register. When you do, be sure to choose the option to get an email message when someone replies to your question. Otherwise, you'll have to keep going online to check for responses.

To visit the forums, choose Help → Ask a Quicken User, which takes you to the forum for your specific edition of the software. In your browser, type *www.quickenforums.com* and then choose the forum for your software (Quicken Personal Finance Software for Windows, for example).

A forum includes several top-level topics, although an inordinate number of topics fall under "Registers, reconciling, accounts, and other core features." "Investments in Quicken" is another topic that appears to generate mass confusion, with more than 600 discussions and almost 3000 individual posts.

Forum Etiquette

The Quicken Forums are an exercise in diplomacy. They're not the place for wild rants about how awful the software is...at least, not if you want Intuit folks to go the extra mile to help you.

Furthermore, you can converse better with the experts on the forum if you've read Quicken's online help and tried a couple things on your own first. To maximize your chances of getting a solution, be succinct and specific when you describe your problem. For example, include:

* What you're trying to accomplish
* The steps you took
* What Quicken did or didn't do
* What you want in the way of help

The more detail you provide, the better someone can understand your problem and come up with a solution.

To post a question (or an answer), you must log into the forums. If you haven't registered, click the Register link and choose a name and password.

You can navigate the forums by scanning the highest-level topics. If a discussion topic sounds similar to your problem, click it to read the posts. Many discussion titles are woefully nebulous, so it's often faster to click Search and then type a few words, like "account reconcile error." When it's done searching, the page shows you a list of posts that contain the words you're looking for. You can search a specific topic or all topics, or limit posts to a date range. You can even look for posts from a specific member, if there's one whose answers tend to make sense to you.

Other Quicken Resources

The Help menu contains a few other entries that you may find useful. Choose Help and then choose one of the following:

▶ **Learn About Setting Up Quicken.** Choosing this menu entry opens Quicken Help to a topic that can get you started in any of the financial areas of Quicken: cash flow, investment, property and debt, taxes, or business.

- **Learn About Downloading Transactions.** Downloading transactions can be a real timesaver…until the process breaks down. Although transaction downloads are often simple, choose this entry if keeping your Quicken accounts and bank accounts in sync has suddenly become a chore.

- **User Manuals.** Choose this entry to access the manuals that Intuit provides for the software. Although these manuals address the basics (like *Getting Started with Quicken*, which tells you how to set up the program), you can view them with Adobe Acrobat Reader or print them to read at the beach.

INDEX

Numerics

H

hard disk crashes, 96
help (see Quicken Help)
hiding closed accounts, 69
Home Purchase planner, 350
house accounts, 183

I

income and expense categories, 5
income category, 72
Index tab, 390
Intuit Online Financial Services, 227
investment accounts, 60, 304–326
  401(k)s and 403(b)s, 307
    creating accounts, 309
  asset accounts used as, 307
  bonds, 333
  brokerage accounts, 308
  choosing, 305
  creating, 308–314
    brokerage accounts, 313
    IRA accounts, 313
  IRA, SEP, and Keogh accounts, 307
  placeholder entries, 338
    estimating average costs, 341
    missing transactions, entering, 340
  portfolio evaluation, 341–349
  recording and reinvesting income, 336
  recording income and stock dividends, 338
  reports, 362
  savings accounts, 308
  securities, purchasing, 329–332
  securities, selling, 332–335
  setting up, 314–326
  single mutual fund accounts, 308
  stock splits, recording, 336
  transactions, recording, 326
investment tracking, 304
  when not to, 306
investment transactions
  entry in investment register, 8
  preferences, setting, 45
IRA accounts, 307
  creating, 313

K

Keogh accounts, 307
keyboard mappings, 40–42
keyboard shortcuts, 12, 384–388
  dates, commands for working with, 386
  print command, 385
  Quicken Home window, opening, 385
  Security List, opening, 385
  selecting items in a list, 385
  task commands, 384
  window navigation commands, 387

L

launching Quicken, 16
liabilities, 5, 181
liability accounts, 61, 183–190
  creating, 189
  estimating value, 188

COLOPHON

Mary Brady was the production editor for *Quicken 2006 for Starters: The Missing Manual*. Carol Marti was the proofreader. Reba Libby and Claire Cloutier provided quality control. John Bickelhaupt wrote the index.

Nicole Skillern created the series cover design. Linda Palo produced the cover layout. Marcia Friedman designed the hand lettering on the cover.

Tom Ingalls designed the interior layout. Keith Fahlgren converted the text and prepared it for layout. Robert Romano, Jessamyn Read, and Lesley Borash produced the illustrations.

Better than e-books

Buy *Quicken 2006 for Starters: The Missing Manual* and access the digital edition FREE on Safari for 45 days.

Go to www.oreilly.com/go/safarienabled
and type in coupon code 6AI8-85AH-KM1C-KAGQ-82CD

Search
thousands of
top tech books

Download
whole chapters

Cut and Paste
code examples

Find
answers fast

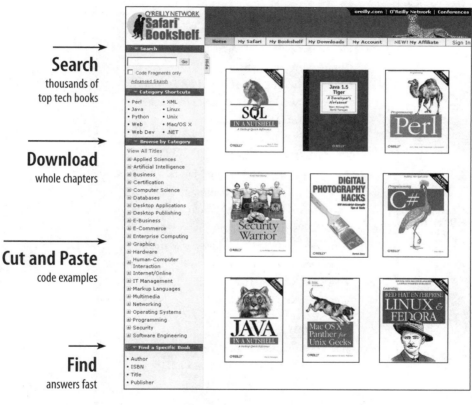

Search Safari! The premier electronic reference
library for programmers and IT professionals.

Related Titles from O'Reilly

Missing Manuals

Access 2003 for Starters: The Missing Manual

AppleWorks 6: The Missing Manual

Creating Web Sites: The Missing Manual

Dreamweaver MX 2004: The Missing Manual

eBay: The Missing Manual

Excel: The Missing Manual

Excel for Starters: The Missing Manual

FileMaker Pro: The Missing Manual

FrontPage 2003: The Missing Manual

GarageBand: The Missing Manual

Google: The Missing Manual, *2nd Edition*

Home Networking: The Missing Manual

iLife '05: The Missing Manual

iMovie HD & iDVD 5: The Missing Manual

iPhoto 5: The Missing Manual

iPod & iTunes: The Missing Manual, *3rd Edition*

iWork '05: The Missing Manual

Mac OS X: The Missing Manual, *Tiger Edition*

Office 2004 for Macintosh: The Missing Manual

Windows 2000 Pro: The Missing Manual

Windows XP for Starters: The Missing Manual,

Windows XP Pro: The Missing Manual, *2nd Edition*

Windows XP Home Edition: The Missing Manual, *2nd Edition*

Pogue Press

Mac OS X Panther Power Hound

Switching to the Mac, *Tiger Edition*

Windows XP Power Hound

O'REILLY®

Our books are available at most retail and online bookstores.

To order direct: 1-800-998-9938 • *order@oreilly.com* • *www.oreilly.com*

Online editions of most O'Reilly titles are available by subscription at *safari.oreilly.com*

Keep in touch with O'Reilly

Download examples from our books

To find example files from a book, go to: *www.oreilly.com/catalog* select the book, and follow the "Examples" link.

Register your O'Reilly books

Register your book at *register.oreilly.com* Why register your books? Once you've registered your O'Reilly books you can:

- Win O'Reilly books, T-shirts or discount coupons in our monthly drawing.
- Get special offers available only to registered O'Reilly customers.
- Get catalogs announcing new books (US and UK only).
- Get email notification of new editions of the O'Reilly books you own.

Join our email lists

Sign up to get topic-specific email announcements of new books and conferences, special offers, and O'Reilly Network technology newsletters at:

elists.oreilly.com

It's easy to customize your free elists subscription so you'll get exactly the O'Reilly news you want.

Get the latest news, tips, and tools

www.oreilly.com

- "Top 100 Sites on the Web"—PC Magazine
- CIO Magazine's Web Business 50 Awards

Our web site contains a library of comprehensive product information (including book excerpts and tables of contents), downloadable software, background articles, interviews with technology leaders, links to relevant sites, book cover art, and more.

Work for O'Reilly

Check out our web site for current employment opportunities:

jobs.oreilly.com

Contact us

O'Reilly Media, Inc.
1005 Gravenstein Hwy North
Sebastopol, CA 95472 USA
Tel: 707-827-7000 or 800-998-9938
      (6am to 5pm PST)
Fax: 707-829-0104

Contact us by email

For answers to problems regarding your order or our products:
order@oreilly.com

To request a copy of our latest catalog:
catalog@oreilly.com

For book content technical questions or corrections: **booktech@oreilly.com**

For educational, library, government, and corporate sales: **corporate@oreilly.com**

To submit new book proposals to our editors and product managers:
proposals@oreilly.com

For information about our international distributors or translation queries:
international@oreilly.com

For information about academic use of O'Reilly books:
adoption@oreilly.com
or visit:
academic.oreilly.com

For a list of our distributors outside of North America check out:
international.oreilly.com/distributors.html

Order a book online

www.oreilly.com/order_new

O'REILLY®